Easy Meat:
Inside Britain's Grooming Gang Scandal

Photo by Linsenhejhej (Wikipedia Commons)

Easy Meat:

Inside Britain's Grooming Gang Scandal

Peter McLoughlin

Published by New English Review Press
a subsidiary of World Encounter Institute
PO Box 158397
Nashville, Tennessee 37215
&
27 Old Gloucester Street
London, England, WC1N 3AX

Cover Art & Design by Kendra Mallock

ISBN: 978-1-943003-06-8

First Edition

NEW ENGLISH REVIEW PRESS
newenglishreview.org

[T]here is a specific problem which involves Pakistani heritage men... who target vulnerable young white girls. We need to get the Pakistani community to think much more clearly about why this is going on and to be more open about the problems that are leading to a number of Pakistani heritage men thinking it is OK to target white girls in this way.... These young men are in a western society, in any event, they act like any other young men, they're fizzing and popping with testosterone, they want some outlet for that, but Pakistani heritage girls are off-limits and they are expected to marry a Pakistani girl from Pakistan, typically. So they then seek other avenues and they see these young women, white girls who are vulnerable, some of them in care... who they think are easy meat.
—Jack Straw, Member of Parliament (1979-2015), Jan. 2011

Narrated Aisha:
I used to play with the dolls in the presence of the Prophet, and my girl friends also used to play with me. When Allah's Messenger used to enter (my dwelling place) they used to hide themselves, but the Prophet would call them to join and play with me. (The playing with the dolls and similar images is forbidden, but it was allowed for `Aisha at that time, as she was a little girl, not yet reached the age of puberty.)
—Sahih al-Bukhari Book 78, Hadith 157
http://sunnah.com/bukhari/78/157

Narrated Hisham's father:
Khadija died three years before the Prophet departed to Medina. He stayed there for two years or so and then he married `Aisha when she was a girl of six years of age, and he consumed that marriage when she was nine years old.
Sahih al-Bukhari Book 63, Hadith 122
http://sunnah.com/bukhari/63/122

Contents

9 - Victorian Values 288

Conclusion   296

Foreword

THIS IS A shocking book. It is written with care, but the facts seem hard to believe. Be prepared, because there is something to feel angry about on most pages: how much of this crime there is; how long it has gone on; its blatancy; and the lengths power has gone to to cover it up. But worst of all, the victims' helplessness and pain.

That anger will spread as knowledge of this crime spreads. Looking away won't work any more. But the more you look at this crime, the worse you realise it is. And this stops people looking at it.

It is hard to think of a crime more apt to cause public rage than the rape of native girls by immigrant gangs. Rape's long use as a weapon shows the fear and anger it causes.

And this is the basis of our plea to the powers that be to stamp out this crime by any lawful means. We ask them to think of the threat to their grip on power.

Vigilante gangs disable society. Their violence is a short cut from Queen's peace to all against all. It tears at the fabric of law. If that violence can be used on child rapists then thieves and cheats will be next.

The threat of vigilante justice

Let me tell a story about how power can spin out of the system's hands. It is violent, but violence is what happens when hate meets civil chaos. I have tried to play down the facts to assuage the sensitive.

A group of ex soldiers, with weapons and intelligence training, are bored with their new lives. They are tired of the pubs which keep them in touch with each other and with what gave a sense of pride and purpose. Their patriotism is weak in the face of serious crime.

They formed a dim view of Islamic ways on their tours of Iraq and Afghanistan. And its growth in Britain is now a serious gripe, fuelled by beer and boredom. Gripes turn to rage at the child rape gangs. And rage turns to boasts about how fast they could deal with them.

One of them talks about how many Muslims are guilty of grooming crimes relative to the number of Muslims in the land. He's been looking at the news reports and seen that pretty much the lot of them have Muslim names. Despite being only 5% of the population. They work out that Muslims look to be 170 times likelier to do this than non-Muslims.[1]

One of them points out that it's worse than that. There's not one case where the girl was a Muslim and the men were non-Muslims: 'They're raping our kids. We're not raping their kids.'

They say they could put a stop to it once and for all. They mean, if they were given the chance, like.

Mad at each new crop of bearded thugs staring from the front pages, their talk gets more sober. Weeks later, reports of useless police work turn sober talk to planning. Tipped off about a bed-and-breakfast joint where this crime happens, planning turns to sober acts.

But they don't plan a reprisal raid, as one or two Sikh groups seem to have done. For them, prevention is better than cure.

One of them gets a tip-off from a jaded child protection worker. They watch the premises, see when the 13 year old girl is led into the house. And at what times the clients come in. Then one night they lie in wait.

They force their way in. A terrible massacre follows. They shoot

---

1 Some of the calculations get lost in the bar room hubbub, but they are as follows: Muslims make up around 90% of offenders from the lists of convictions, where guilt and innocence had been tested in a courtroom. But Muslims make up 5% of the population. Their calculations were:

- The likelihood of individual Muslims to commit this offence is: $90 \div 5\% = 1{,}800$
- The likelihood of individual non-Muslims to commit this offence is: $10 \div 95\% = 10.53$
- So the likelihood of individual Muslims to commit this offence, compared to individual non Muslims, is: $1{,}800 \div 10.53 = 170.94$

In other words, a Muslim man is 170 times more likely than a non-Muslim man to commit this crime. There is mathematical squabbling, and swearing about whether the figure can really be so steep. But that is the figure settled on.

dead all the men in the room, at point blank range.

They are caught, held, and charged. They plead not guilty.

The dreadful scene proves the killings. CCTV puts them at the scene. So they admit the facts but claim the defence of prevention of a crime. The prosecution must rebut this defence beyond reasonable doubt, and argue that the men's acts were not reasonable because too much force was used.

The Defendants cite American laws that allows 'deadly force' against burglars, even if the owner is not at risk. The same laws have been touted for this country, with public support. They state that most people think the gang rape of children is worse than burglary. They refer to the BBC report, 'No charge for Texas dad who killed daughter's rapist' story, and the comments beneath.[2]

The prosecution say the killers could have told the authorities. But the killers point out that the authorities already knew. They got their tip off from a Council worker. And nothing had been done about it.

The judge is rightly worried by the men's defence. But she must let it go to the jury. She guides them properly. Can killing be reasonable when police and the Councils are paid to stop child rape?

The jury retire but can't reach a verdict. Later, news reports say half the jurors saw no wrong in killing child rape gangs.

A retrial is held, and, unusually, a second retrial. But still no verdict. So the judge tells the foreman to acquit.

The celebrations outside the court have more to do with football chants than analysis of the dovetail joint between law and civil society.

News of the acquittal spreads fast. Other gangs learn that it is OK to kill child rapists, especially those Muslim ones.

In some parts, these vigilante gangs are soon the people to go to with crimes and disputes. They even open their own brothels. And some of those are a bit casual about age limits. The liberal press spot this irony. But the police are slow to come down for fear of spoiling a calm stalemate.

We don't paint this foul scene to gloat, but to warn. It is not so far fetched as we hope. Once conflict breaks out, it hides every sin. The ruthless know this. And a lack of law, the need for safety, enables them to pull in those around them.

So authorities need to stamp out this grooming crime fast and hard. It is not enough just to condemn it. They must suppress it. If not then we—who are now called firebrands—will try to preach restraint

2 20 June 2013 http://www.bbc.co.uk/news/world-us-canada-18522383

and be brushed aside with: '*They rape our children.*'

— Gavin Boby
Law And Freedom Foundation
January 2016

Preface

WHEN WE began writing this book in 2013, we were astounded by the refusal of the establishment even to acknowledge the problem of these grooming gangs. Between 1988 and 2011, there was barely one media report per year in Britain concerning their existence. It seemed to us that the principal reasons why these gangs were getting away with their 25-year reign of terror was because a) the gangs were not white whilst most of the victims were, and b) unlike the victims, the gangs were well organised and were also part of a highly-motivated community which would not only help them evade capture, but certain members would actually seek to block any investigation into the activities of the gangs. One way we sought to break through the political correctness surrounding this issue was by highlighting the history of the phenomenon and how (non-white) Sikhs had been the first victims and were still largely unacknowledged victims. In doing so, we wanted to refute the idea that it was 'racist' to address this phenomenon and to expose the fact that nearly every institution which should have been helping the victims was either turning a blind-eye or was actively involved in a cover-up.

As we finish this book, we are aware how much the media have turned on the official narrative peddled by authorities at both the national and local level. When we publicised the statistic of at least 10,000 victims in an earlier online version, we were mocked; but now senior police officers and Members of Parliament are indicating that the number of victims may be between scores of thousands and even as many as one million. No one is laughing now.

The British Prime Minister has apparently spoken of imprisonment for those child-care professionals who turn a blind-eye to the activities of the grooming gangs, and has compared the threat posed by these gangs to the threat from terrorism. However, considering that these remarks by David Cameron were made in the run-up to a General Election, it may turn out that these are empty words from the current Prime Minister. After all, in 2006, Cameron was quoted as saying that 'Muslim extremists are like Nazis', but in the following decade, we saw no sign that he had taken any significant steps to prevent the growth of this 'Nazism'.

Despite the attempt to provide references for as much as possible in this study, this is not a book written by academics in criminology, sociology, history or cultural studies. We are sure that if such professionals had turned their attention to the subject at hand, they would have produced a superior artefact.

Without the generous funding of Alex Felix this work would not have seen the light of day. Thanks to Shimonn, Paul and Kay for proof-reading the entire book several times.

As new convictions occur, we will update the tables found at http://www.pmclauth.com. As the scandal unfolds additional material and any errata will also appear on the website.

— January 2016

Introduction

Many girls are terrified and with reason ... a girl had her tongue nailed to the table when she threatened to tell.
            – former government advisor, *Daily Mail*, 2008

THE SEXUAL abuse of children takes different social forms: from sporadic child abductions, to organised child pornography rings, to abuse by parents or care-home staff. All of it is awful, and none of it should be ignored. The phenomenon of gangs of men who loiter around schoolgirls, luring them into a life of addiction and prostitution is a distinct category of child sexual abuse, but a category that the authorities in Britain have deliberately ignored for 25 years. They ignored it, despite it being clearly put on the national agenda as long ago as 2003, and being known as a local phenomenon in heavily islamized towns as long ago as the late 1980s. If these groups of men had been white non-Muslims, then action would have been taken decades ago to eradicate the problem as soon as it was identified. The fear of 'stranger danger' is instituted in UK schools, where strangers are not allowed to enter and wander around the premises. But for decades, gangs of men could hang around school gates with impunity.[1] What principally protected these men was the colour of their skin.

There are some specific features and events which should have

---

1 See the photos in *Appendix 4: Leeds School Warning* and *Appendix 5: Sheffield School Warning*.

made it obvious to the authorities and the media that a new social phenomenon was occurring in Britain. What should have been of interest to the authorities?

· gangs of Muslim men hanging around school gates in cars
· schoolgirls contacting police and social services and telling them that they had been abused
· parents contacting police and social services with their fears and accumulated evidence
· extended families of Muslim men being associated with this child abuse
· schoolgirls being abducted or going missing for days on end
· stories of men luring girls with gifts, then turning them into addicts
· families having to abandon their daughters to stop the daughter luring other relatives into the clutches of the gangs
· connections between the grooming gangs and drug dealers

What should have been of interest to the media and academics?

· Muslims who generally have little to do with non-Muslims being involved in sexual relationships with underage non-Muslim girls
· gang violence between Sikhs and Muslims over claims about grooming
· Sikhs creating organisations to teach their girls what the gangs were doing
· reports that devout Muslim organisations were instructing Muslim men to deceive and subjugate non-Muslim women
· refusal of the Muslim community to condemn these crimes and their failure to inform police
· international parallels between this phenomenon in Britain and its occurrence in the Netherlands

Between 1988 and 2003, evidence of all of these things must have been known to many police officers, social workers, academics and journalists. Yet we will show that, with very few exceptions, these incidents were not publicised in the national media, nor by the campaigns of child-care charities, nor by official reports, nor in academic books. On the rare occasion when the phenomenon would be discussed in more than the briefest detail, political activists and the authorities would come together to stop the public from knowing more: political correctness would be used to make sure that people did not speak about this phenomenon, enabling the perpetrators free rein to sexually abuse schoolgirls for decades. Yes, decades. We know that in an age where parents are not allowed to smack their children, this sounds unbelievable: for decades thousands of professionals who pride themselves on supposedly protecting our society turned a blind-eye to the organized seduction and rape of schoolgirls.

Finally, by 2011 the conspiracy of silence was broken: once the barrier was breached, the news media in Britain spent several years providing shocking stories to the public. In September 2012, *The Times* newspaper carried an extensive overview of what had been going on. It stated that 'for more than a decade organised groups of men were able to groom, pimp and traffic girls across the country with virtual impunity.'[2] *The Times* went on to quote a welfare expert describing this as '*the biggest child protection scandal of our time*.'[3] We will show that even the coverage in *The Times* has understated the scale of the problem: it is arguably the biggest child-protection scandal in Britain in the last 100 years, and the political ramifications of this scandal are at least as great as The Profumo Affair.[4]

By the start of 2015, a senior police officer was talking in terms of 'tens of thousands' of current victims of the grooming gangs,[5] and a Member of Parliament (for an area which was regarded as highlighting the problem) was stating there could be as many as 1 million victims nationally (in suggesting this extraordinary victim-count we can only assume that she was referring to the total number of current and past victims). Remember: these are schoolgirls being systematically targeted for sexual abuse, and the perpetrators are principally getting away with it because of the colour of their skin and minority religious status. Al-

---

2 Andrew Norfolk, 'Police Files Reveal Vast Child Protection Scandal', *The Times*, 24 Sep 2012 http://www.thetimes.co.uk/tto/news/uk/crime/ar ticle3547661.ece.

3 *Ibid.* (emphasis added)

4 http://en.wikipedia.org/wiki/Profumo_affair.

5 'Police chief warns of more Rotherham-style abuse cases', *BBC News*, 16 Oct 2014, http://www.bbc.co.uk/news/uk-29639374. This statement did not receive much attention, other than this minor article on the BBC website. It is hard to credit that such a significant claim as this would not be given a higher profile by journalists and politicians.

most every part of the establishment has had some hand in the cover-up of this horrific reign of criminality. By the end of 2014, the Association of Chief Police Officers (ACPO) stated that the number of victims of the grooming gangs is 'tens of thousands' each year. If the ACPO claim is even remotely credible, then there could easily be 100,000 victims over the past 20 years,[6] with only 177 of the perpetrators ever being convicted. We cannot imagine another serious crime where the ratio of victims to convicts is so low.

How could a phenomenon of this size have been concealed for so many decades? It does not look like the concealment took the form of an actual conspiracy, and with very rare exceptions it is hard to find evidence that people were instructed not to refer to the distinctive features of this phenomenon (namely, the disparity in ethnicity between the perpetrators and the victims). Thus, it is hard to believe that the relevant individuals were purposefully concealing the problem. Rather, the cover-up of this problem is a manifestation of the sinister power of political correctness. Professional people felt so restrained by what political correctness allows to be expressed that they felt incapable of drawing attention to the distinctive features of this phenomenon, fearful of the cost to their career, livelihood, professional reputation and even social standing. Moreover, this was a vicious circle: because so few would speak the truth, their own inaction and silence served to increase the fear of transgressing political correctness among their co-workers and among those people in related professions. The cover-up required no conspiracy. The cover-up worked more through omission than through commission. In some instances staff were explicitly told not to draw attention to disparity in ethnicity; in most cases it seems it was not even necessary to give explicit instruction to social workers and police officers. The fear of being accused of 'racism' meant that for decades there was scarcely any official recognition of the grooming gang phenomenon. That the victims were mostly white schoolgirls whilst their abusers were almost entirely Muslims with darker skin, meant the gangs could operate with impunity.

Once prosecutions and convictions began to rise in the years following 2009, the population of Britain became increasingly outraged by what they learned of the grooming gang phenomenon, but they know only a fraction of the scandal.[7] In England, this epidemic of child-rape

---

6 See Chapter 4 for a more detailed explanation of how the total number of victims could be 100,000 or even higher.

7 We made a decision that this study would attempt to avoid sensational detail,

by grooming gangs has been going on since at least 1988; moreover, the victims have not only been white schoolgirls, but also Asian Sikh girls: most people have no idea that the phenomenon can be documented as beginning so long ago, nor that the victims are more likely chosen on ideological motivation rather than racial motivation. Despite more than a decade of disinformation by child-care professionals, academics, and political activists, even the earliest claims (1988 to 2003)[8] were that the gangs were overwhelmingly Muslim.[9] The reports of this massive over-representation of Muslim men in this crime spree has been borne out by the prosecutions of the last three to four years,[10] but it is clear that this discrepancy in ethnicity must have been known long ago and should have been made public. Because the predators were Muslims, the agencies who are responsible for child-protection have almost entirely failed in their job to protect vulnerable children. From a fear of

---

and would provide the minimum amount of detail required to indicate the horrors involved. Mostly this study confines itself to exposing where organisations have failed, who must have known what and when; to evidence-gathering and statistical extrapolation; and forays into areas of theology and cultural analysis where others will not tread.

8 See section 3.6 *1988 Sikh/Muslim violence*, and section 3.8 *2003 Bradford/Keighley* of Chapter 3. In 2003, Muslims were less than 3% of the UK population, yet already reports of these gangs stated the gangs were 'overwhelmingly Asian'.Anna Hall, 'Hunt For Britain's Sex Gangs, C4' Broadcast 2 May, 2013 http://www.b roadcastnow.co.uk/in-depth/hunt-for-britains-sex-gangs-c4/5054504.article. We will see below whether or not it was reasonable for all the principle figures involved in this 2003 controversy to have stated that the gangs were 'Asian' rather than 'Muslim'.

9 CROP (Coalition for the Removal of Pimping) is the only charity to work exclusively with the schoolgirl victims of pimping and their families. CROP was set-up in 2002.

> [T]he families had suffered mainly at the hands of Pakistani men. "The vast majority are white families and the perpetrators are Pakistani Asians," the organisation's chair of trustees, Hilary Willmer, was quoted as saying. Sources inside Crop placed the percentage as high as 80 per cent, although Kurdish, Romanian and Albanian gangs were also involved.

Paul Vallely, 'Child Sex Grooming: the Asian Question', *The Independent*, 10 May 2012 http://www.independent.co.uk/news/uk/crime/child-sex-grooming-the-Asian-question-7729068.html. Thus, an organisation which has worked exclusively in this area for over a decade says that 80% of the perpetrators are Pakistanis. What the journalist does not make clear in the above article, is that Kurdistan, Romania and Albania are areas which have been Islamised for centuries. Albania is 60% Muslim, and Kurds do not have their own country, but are spread out over many Muslim countries, and the vast majority of Kurds are Muslim. See also http://en.wikipedia.org/wiki/Islam_in_Romania.

10 See *Appendix 1: Grooming Gang Convictions*, and notice almost all of those convicted have Muslim names (non-Muslim names in the list of convictions have been rendered in bold).

being called 'racist', police forces across the country have buried the evidence.[11] National agencies busied themselves with cybercrime, bullying in schools, and the trafficking of children into Britain—almost anything to avoid attending to this very serious sexual and violent abuse going on across England.

Even documents which supposedly address the problem have gone out of their way to avoid discussing why some 'ethnic groups' are massively over-represented as perpetrators, whilst the schoolgirl victims are overwhelmingly of a different ethnic group. Yet the professionals never deemed it important to declare this, and even denied the pattern existed. Until 2012, the media in Britain did not once discuss the similarities between Muslim grooming gangs here and Muslim grooming gangs in the Netherlands (even though English-language media in the Netherlands were reporting on these gangs as early as 2001).[12] Throughout the last twenty years, no ordinary member of the British public had any reason to associate the town of Rotherham in South Yorkshire with systematic, organised child abuse.[13] Despite government agencies in Rotherham knowing about (and privately discussing) the Muslim grooming gangs from 1996, a 2010 document by Rotherham Safeguarding Children Board stated that, 'great care will be taken in drafting . . . this report to ensure that its findings embrace Rotherham's qualities of diversity. It is imperative that suggestions of a wider cultural phenomenon are avoided.'[14]

---

11 Following an inquiry in 2013 into the events in Rochdale, the socialist MP for the town said that the police had been actively ignoring reports by the victims. 'The biggest issue to come out of this report is that Greater Manchester Police (GMP) were effectively discriminating against poor, white, working-class girls, so that's not about a failure to spot abuse, that is about actively ignoring abuse that was going on when it was brought to their attention', 'Rochdale grooming: "Shocking" failure over sex abuse' *BBC News*, 20 Dec 2013, http://www.bbc.co.uk/news/uk-england-mancheste r-25450512.

12 Carin Tiggeloven, 'Child Prostitution in the Netherlands', *Radio Netherlands*, 18 Dec 2001 http://web.archive.org/web/20080627112924/http://www.radionetherlands.nl/currentaffairs/region/netherlands/netherlands011218.html

13 A search of national news databases, going back to 1985, did not turn up any relevant results until the year 2010.

14 From the 2010 report, quoted in Andrew Norfolk, 'Police Files Reveal Vast Child Protection Scandal', *The Times*, 24 Sep 2012 http://www.thetimes.co.uk/tto/news/uk/crime/article3547661.ece. This quotation encapsulates the problem: despite all the evidence that different parts of Rotherham's "diverse" community had conflicting cultural values, leading to serious harm for the vulnerable parties in this conflict (the schoolgirls), political correctness and the doctrine of multiculturalism meant that the professionals whose job it was to help the vulnerable were consciously commanding that these diverse cultural values could not be discussed. Multiculturalism came about

The 2012 analysis in *The Times* focused on Rotherham, where 200 'restricted-access documents' showed that, in that one borough alone, 'police and child protection agencies have held extensive knowledge of this crime model for ten years, yet have never publicly acknowledged its existence.'[15] Back in 1996, Rotherham Council conducted an investigation into the organized grooming activities of gangs. The report identified that most of the perpetrators were Pakistani Muslim men (Kurdish Muslims and Kosovan Muslims were also identified as perpetrators).[16] The Times article states that in 2002, Rotherham Council produced a report which identified 3 brothers from one Pakistani Muslim family as being linked to the sexual exploitation of 54 girls from the area. The Muslim men in this case seem typical of many of the men involved in this crime. And we believe that the behaviour of Rotherham council is typical of the behaviour of many, perhaps most, councils in areas with any significant Muslim population. In recent years, the government seems to have decided to treat that borough as if the problem there was somehow unique.[17]

Many people who are not involved in a professional capacity with child-care might think that this grooming phenomenon came about because the child-protection agencies were under-staffed. However, the website of the National Society for the Protection of Children (NSPCC) refers to a 'National Working Group ... [which] links over 1000 practitioners who are working on the issues of child sexual exploitation (CSE) and trafficking in the UK.'[18] Considering there are so many paid professionals working on trafficking and the sexual exploitation of children, we should be asking very serious questions about how and why these grooming gangs have been allowed to operate with impunity for the better part of 25 years. That same page from the NSPCC website lists the research available in this field, and by 2013 it was a pitifully small list of documents, considering the decades of evidence of the gangs' existence, the thousands of victims, and the surge in historical prosecutions since

in order to deny that there is any significance to cultures having different values and to conceal that there will be conflict when these incompatible values come together. Political correctness is the means by which such denial is enforced.

15 Andrew Norfolk, 'Police Files Reveal Vast Child Protection Scandal', *The Times*, 24 Sep 2012 http://www.thetimes.co.uk/tto/news/uk/crime/ar ticle3547661.ece.

16 *Ibid.*

17 See Chapter 4 *Rotherham: Designated Scapegoat.*

18 NSPCC 'Research on child sexual exploitation', Jul 2013, http://www.nspcc.org. uk/Inform/resourcesforprofessionals/sexualabuse/sexual_exploitation_research_wda85130.html.

2010.[19]

The book you are reading is an attempt to fill in the gaps left by researchers in accounting for this phenomenon. We will demonstrate the scale of the problem, how the appropriate government agencies have done almost nothing to expose the network of criminality and exploitation, how Islamic theology and history can explain the rise of this phenomenon, and how political activists have obfuscated the problem through the misuse of the narrative of 'racism'. Acts of omission and active concealment occurred to prevent the public from realising that multiculturalism is a fundamentally incoherent doctrine, a doctrine cobbled together to conceal the serious conflicts which have arisen when peoples from vastly different cultures, with different values, are forced to live together. Over the past few years the victims of the grooming gangs, or their parents, have started to publish their own stories.[20] We dwell as little as possible on the gruesome details of what happened to the victims. Instead we try to show the complicity and denial of the agencies and authorities. We see this book as an historical record, an attempt to form a view of what was known and what was being ignored—articulating all this before more and more of the evidence disappears. This book surveys the available information, and attempts to expose patterns which are not obvious at first sight.

We believe that our analysis will show that there are indeed *prima facie* reasons for considering Islamic doctrine to be at the root of this problem, both in Britain and in the Netherlands. We are not making any claim that our brief examination of Islamic doctrine and Muslim culture is the last word on these matters. We are prepared to be the first to look into this, something which none of the experts have dared consider. Sometimes we will refer to discussions by Muslims who are not experts on Islam. Some critics will argue that the opinion of such people should not count. However, we are interested to show how Muslims are interpreting their own religion and culture, and are not necessarily interested in the casuistry of some Sheikh. But we will cite statements from Muslim experts to show what they say to Muslim audiences. We will show that there are good reasons to believe that the values found in Islamic doctrine pervade Muslim communities, in Britain and elsewhere.

Given the way in which this debate has been framed, we can-

---

19 See Appendix 2: Grooming Gang Chronology.

20 See Emma Jackson, *The End of My World: The Shocking True Story of a Young Girl Forced to Become a Sex Slave*, Ebury Press, 2010. See also Kris Hollington, *Unthinkable: The Shocking Scandal of Britain's Trafficked Children*, Simon & Schuster, 2013.

not help but make much reference to 'race' and to distinctions such as 'white', 'black', 'Asian', etc. Let us state clearly from the outset: it is our opinion that the modern concept of race is so unclear as to be vitually meaningless, yet nevertheless is used principally as a cudgel by the Left-wing racism industry. Futhermore, that same industry sees profit in conflating race with religion. For example, Barack Obama is considered to be 'America's first black president', yet there's no reason to believe that Obama is any more black than he is white. There has even been recent controversy as to whether some of America's 'black' activists (e.g. Rachel Dolezal) have any natural physical characteristic in common with someone born in Africa 500 years ago which would distinguish such activists from all the other 'white' people. The concept of 'transracial' has even been put forward for someone who thinks he is a black person born into a white person's body! In the United Kingdom, Jews and Sikhs are legally considered to be 'racial groups',[21] even though people can join one of these religions and become a Jew or a Sikh, and thus can 'change race'. Attempts have been made through legislation to classify Muslims as a race, even when Islam is one of the most proselytising religions on the planet, and in countries like the UK, Muslims boast[22] of how many of the indigenous white population are converting to Islam (and would thus presumably be changing from 'white' to 'non-white'). A Black man born in Britain is said to be British, but the discourse of race does not permit a white man born in Africa to be African.

It should go without saying that most Muslims in Britain are not involved with the grooming gangs. There may even be Muslim communities where there are no grooming gangs operating.[23] However, the

---

21 http://www.parliament.the-stationery-office.co.uk/pa/ld200203/ldselect/ldrelof/95/95w22.htm

22 http://faith-matters.org/2011/01/06/islam-converts-mainly-women/

23 However, there is strong evidence to show that the problem now extends across England. Vicky Smith, 'Child sex slave gangs in EVERY city in Britain: Police chief's warning after Oxford grooming horror', *The Mirror*, 15 May 2013, http://www.mirror.co.uk/news/uk-news/child-sex-s lave-gangs-every-1891898; Justin Penrose & Vicky Smith, 'Police probe at least 54 more evil child sex grooming gangs', *The Daily Mirror*, 19 May 2013, http://www.mirror.co.uk/news/uk-news/police-probe-least-54-more-1896991. It is notable in the preceding report that the police forces of West and East Midlands did not report any ongoing investigations; yet a Muslim women's organisation has recently presented claims that there are huge problems with 'Asian' grooming gangs in the Midlands and says: 'community leaders, schools and families need to stop dismissing the sickening attacks or covering them up.' See Neil Elkes, 'Shocking report claims young Asian girls are being groomed for rape in Birmingham', *Birmingham Mail*, 20 Feb 2014, http://www.birminghammail.co.uk/news/midlands-news/

massive over-representation of Muslim men among those convicted for these kinds of crime seems to indicate that being male and being Muslim are the most significant characteristics when it comes to identifying the motivation of these gangs and their customers. Where the gangs are operating, it is clear that there are significant numbers of Muslims who are either actively protecting the gangs' activities, or who know what the men in their community are doing and are silent about it.[24] Every decade, the Muslim population of Britain almost doubles in size, so there is every reason to believe that without some major changes in our society, the activities of these gangs will grow and grow.[25] We hope that the information contained in this book will help inform the public and

shocking-report-claims-young-asian-6728673. Despite London having a population of 8 million, and a very large Muslim community, our table of convictions (*Appendix 1: Grooming Gang Convictions*), might lead one to believe that the grooming gangs are operating mostly in the north of England. However it looks as though the police and social services in London might have been ignoring a huge problem: a recent report claims that police in London were notified of 500 victims in just 6 months, with 10% of the cases being described as 'very serious'. See Justin Davenport, 'Detectives investigating 50 "very serious" child grooming sex cases in London', *London Evening Standard*, 3 Feb 2014, http://www.standard.co.uk/news/crime/detectives-investigating-50-very-serious-child-grooming-sex-cases-i n-london-9103637.html.

24 At the conclusion of a trial in the north-east of England in 2014, the judge stated that the behaviour of the gang revealed a 'profoundly worrying attitude about the offending'. Joe Willis, 'Three Middlesbrough men jailed for grooming under-age girls for sex', 13 Feb 2014, *The Northern Echo*, http://www.thenorthernecho.co.uk/news/11009663.Three_Middlesbrough_men_jailed_for_grooming_underage_girls_for_sex/. After all the publicity surrounding convictions of gangs in Oxford, Rotherham and Rochdale in recent years, it seems as though the gangs are not stopping their activities. Moreover, the above news report states:

> The court heard that the girls [the victims] had been taunted and insulted by friends and family of the defendants since coming forward, including being bombarded by obscene messages, called sluts and accused of being racist.

This shows that the Muslim community continues to see the non-Muslim victims as the problem, not the Muslim perpetrators. This is a distinctive feature of the grooming gang phenomenon throughout its history. In all other forms of sexual abuse involving children, communities blame the abusers not the children.

25 Some 30 miles north of Middlesbrough, police have arrested another 30 men for grooming activities. 'Northumbria Police want to speak to 80 female victims or witnesses to sexual exploitation in Newcastle', 7 Feb 2014, http://www.chroniclelive.co.uk/news/north-east-news/northumbria-p olice-want-speak-80-6684173. By Spring 2015, this large operation against grooming gangs in Newcastle saw the police make many arrests, but only a subset of those arrested were charged. Of the 22 men charged by police, almost all have Muslim names. See http://www.northumbria.police.uk/release-details.asp?id=103354

professionals about the true scope of this problem.

Referring to the phenomenon as 'grooming' does not begin to capture the seriousness of the problem. We think it is important to emphasize that from the very beginning, many have described the problem as taking schoolgirls as 'sex slaves'. Those who have described the phenomenon in these terms include the victims, their families, some chid-care professionals, and journalists.[26] Jack Straw, a former Home Secretary under a socialist government, and the Member of Parliament for a heavily-islamised town throughout his career, characterised the relationship between the grooming gangs and their victims in even darker terms: he was widely-quoted as saying that the perpetrators viewed their victims as 'easy meat', which carries the implication that the gangs did not even see the schoolgirls as human.[27] When we started gathering material in 2013, we could not have predicted that within 18 months devout Islamic jihadi groups in Iraq, Syria and Nigeria would be openly taking schoolgirls as sex-slaves. Below we will examine reasons why this phenomenon resonates with the history of slave-taking in Islam (see Chapter 7, section 7.7 *Sharia Law: Legality of Slavery*). However, for the sake of using the same euphemistic terminology widely-used in discussions of this phenomenon, we will refer to it as 'grooming', whilst attempting not to ignore the aspect of enslavement.

---

26 From the earliest reports of the activities of these Muslim gangs in the late 1980s, and throughout the following three decades, the phenomenon was seen as schoolgirls being taken as 'sex slaves'. 'Sikh girls "used as sex slaves"', *The Independent*, 24 Jun 1989. 'Children as young as 11 are enslaved in a squalid life of prostitution in Bradford...' said one local newspaper in the 1990s: 'Scandal of child-sex on Bradford streets', *Telegraph & Argus*, 14 Jul 1998, http://www.thetelegraphandargus.co.uk/archive/1998/07/14/8075434.Scandal_of_child_sex_on_Bradford_streets/. Kathryn Knight, 'Is political correctness stopping police ending the misery of the teenage sex slaves?'. *Daily Mail*, 27 Mar 2008, http://www.dailymail.co.uk/femail/article546809/Is-political-correctness-stopping-police-ending-misery-teenage-sex-slaves.html. Emma Jackson, *The End of My World: The Shocking True Story of a Young Girl Forced to Become a Sex Slave*, Ebury Press, 2010. Vicky Smith, 'Child sex slave gangs in EVERY city in Britain: Police chief's warning after Oxford grooming horror', *The Mirror*, 15 May 2013, http://www.mirror.co.uk/news/uk-news/child-sex-slave-gangs-every-1891898. Sue Reid, 'How I was branded racist for exposing the truth: SUE REID reveals how she was accused of "making it up" after warning of young girls being traded as sex slaves in provincial towns', 05 Feb 2015, *The Daily Mail*, http://www.dailymail.co.uk/news/article-2940327/How-branded-racist-exposing-truth-SUE-REID-reveals-accused-making-warning-young-girls-traded-sex-slaves-provincial-towns.html.

27 'Jack Straw: Some White Girls are "Easy Meat"', *BBC News*, 8 Jan 2011, http://www.bbc.co.uk/news/uk-england-derbyshire-12141603

ONE

The Grooming Gang Phenomenon

One [schoolgirl] was still so frightened of her attacker that she initially refused to give evidence for fear he would hurt her again. She had been raped and prostituted at 11 by a man who bought her little gifts and showed her the first affection she had known.

– Daily Express, 2013

ONE OF THE defining features of this crime is the ethnic/cultural homogeneity of the gang members, and the refusal of other members of their community to speak out about them or to condemn their behaviour. The gangs are often made up of brothers and members of their extended family, who take part in the grooming and/or rape of the schoolgirls.[1] In both Britain and the Netherlands, the gangs appear to be overwhelmingly men who are Muslim. Through the doctrine of multiculturalism, enforced via political correctness, the gangs in Britain

---

1 A glance down the list of convictions, comparing the surname and the towns in *Appendix 1: Grooming Gang Convictions* reveals that many of those convicted in a particular town are almost certainly family relatives. This social inter-relationship only very rarely occurs in other cases where adults are grooming children for sex. In those cases, usually the adults are either unrelated or are working alone (for fear of exposure or criticism from their friends or relatives). The grooming gang phenomenon thus shows distinctive new characteristics.

were basically operating with impunity between 1988 and 2009.[2] There is evidence to suggest that the gang members either saw nothing wrong with what they were doing, or considered themselves to be above UK law.

Typically the gangs target schoolgirls, aged between 11 and 16.

> The gangs want virgins and girls who are free of sexual diseases. Most of the men buying sex with the girls have Muslim wives and they don't want to risk infection. The younger you look, the more saleable you are.[3]

The schoolgirls they target are overwhelmingly non-Muslim, while the gangs are overwhelmingly Muslim. The girls are often lured into the clutches of the gang using a young Muslim man who befriends/seduces the girl.

> The grooming and abuse was said to be systematic, tactical and repetitive. The defendants had family or friendship links. Younger boys were the girls' initial point of contact...[4]

None of this is accidental; here we are not talking about cross-cultural romantic relationships. This is not about misunderstood lovers, Abdul and Juliet. What is so unusual about this disparity in ethnicity, is that Muslims in Britain generally have little or no interaction with the indigenous population.[5]

The schoolgirl will be given money and presents, flattered by compliments and by being taken into a world of adults. She will be introduced

---

2 See the dearth of convictions before 2009 *Appendix 2: Grooming Gang Chronology.*

3 Julie Bindel, 'Girls, Gangs and Grooming: The Truth', *Standpoint Magazine*, Dec 2010 http://www.standpointmag.co.uk/node/3576/full

4 Andrew Norfolk, 'Police Files Reveal Vast Child Protection Scandal', *The Times*, 24 Sep 2012 http://www.thetimes.co.uk/tto/news/uk/crime/ar ticle3547661.ece

5 'Asians "behind most racial violence"', *BBC News*, 09 Feb 2001, http://news.bbc. co.uk/1/hi/uk/1160552.stm; 'Is Britain becoming more segregated?', *BBC News*, 26 Sep 2005, http://news.bbc.co.uk/1/hi/talking_point/4259764.stm; 'Bishop warns of no-go zones for non-Muslims', *The Telegraph*, 06 Jan 2008, http://www.telegraph.co.uk/news/ uknews/1574694/Bishop-warns-of-no-go-zones-for-non-Muslims.html; 'Why the survey of British Muslim attitudes is so profoundly disconcerting', *The Independent*, 25 Feb 2015, http://www.independent.co.uk/voices/comment/why-the-survey-of-british-muslim-attitudes-is-so-profoundly-disconcerting-10070358.html; 'Senior civil servant to head-up integration review', *Asian Image*, 20 Jul 2015, http://www.asianimage.co.uk/news/13464998.Senior_civil_servant_to_head_up_integration_review/

to drugs and alcohol. And once she is manipulated into considering the initial, alluring youth as her 'boyfriend', she will be persuaded/coerced into having sex with his relatives/friends. From there it is a downward spiral of rape and prostitution, often with the schoolgirl suffering severe mental and physical pain, even torture.[6] If the girl tries to escape, the gang will punish her with various forms of physical and mental abuse, threats and intimidation, and even brutal violence. 'The pimps even use pregnancy as a form of punishment... girls who were made pregnant by customers and then forced to have backstreet abortions.'[7] The gangs are clearly not just doing this for sexual pleasure. They are criminal gangs, making money from the schoolgirls they pimp out. If a schoolgirl gets out of their clutches, they stand to lose large amounts of money, so they go to extreme lengths to ensure the schoolgirls are compliant and available. The victims keep acceding to the gang's demands, because they are threatened with their home being bombed, or their mother being gang-raped.[8] The child-care professionals and Left-wing activists turned a blind-eye to schoolgirls enduring threats and violence and rape, conditions more typical of a country at war.

The Muslim grooming gangs are systematic and well-organised in their behaviour, and the collusion of the community is extensive: 'Taxi drivers, shop owners and security guards who work in the shopping arcades where the girls are recruited are also involved.'[9] The gang members exploit the opportunities in our society where schoolgirls are least protected, such as girls who are going home from school, or who are in some form of local authority care (often in towns some distance from their biological family).[10] Some of the socialist politicians whose

---

6 See Julie Bindel, 'Mothers of Prevention', *The Sunday Times*, 2007 http://www.thesundaytimes.co.uk/sto/news/uk_news/article72310.ece; Andrew Norfolk, 'Police Files Reveal Vast Child Protection Scandal', *op. cit.*

7 CROP (Coalition for the Removal of Pimping) spokesman quoted in Julie Bindel, 'Mothers of Prevention', *The Sunday Times*, 2007 http://www.thesundaytimes.co.uk/sto/news/uk_news/article72310.ece

8 http://www.youtube.com/watch?v=RFIfcTqBsZc&t=184

9 Julie Bindel, *op cit*. See also 'Taxi driver in Rochdale sex grooming gang case "plied girl with vodka" court told', *Manchester Evening News*, 20 Mar 2012, http://www.manchestereveningnews.co.uk/news/greater-manchester-news/taxi-driver-in-rochdale-sex-grooming-684881; James Tozer, 'Police "hid" abuse of 60 girls by Asian takeaway workers linked to murder of 14-year-old', *The Daily Mail*, 7 Apr 2011, http://www.dailymail.co.uk/news/article-1374443/Poli ce-hid-abuse-60-girls-Asian-takeaway-workers-linked-Charlene-Downes-murder.html

10 In September 2013, a Government Minister produced a report which criticised social services departments in councils for

constituencies were among the first places for this phenomenon to be observed, claimed the perpetrators were 'like any other young men, they're fizzing and popping with testosterone' (Jack Straw),[11] or that the perpetrators didn't want an arranged marriage (Ann Cryer).[12] However, some Muslims (who spoke on the condition of anonymity) painted a very different picture.

> The men explain that some of the grooming was initiated on the instructions of older relatives. Other young men were seeking kudos. Some clients were paying customers - perhaps £10 for sex with a 14-year-old white girl. Others were being repaid a favour.[13]

It is hard to know if it was wishful thinking, naïvety or political correctness that led politicians to make out that this was more like Romeo and Juliet than the white slave trade. If one calculates the average age of those convicted of grooming offences, the average is 28 years, old enough to have daughters the same age as the schoolgirls they have groomed.[14] Looking at the characteristics of those convicted, it is clear the vast majority of these Muslim men were probably married or in relationships; they were far from being adolescents who were unsure of what was right and what was wrong. If they were already married (even

---

the 'indefensible' practice of 'decanting' problem children to far-flung homes, away from friends and family, and routinely located in some of the country's worst crime hot spots.... the majority of children's homes are situated in neighbourhoods blighted by crime. Three out of 10 are located in the worst crime hot spots in the country. It also reveals the locations of the 1,718 children's homes in England, showing how they are heavily concentrated in just two areas: the North West and the West Midlands, both of which have been at the centre of grooming scandals.
John Bingham, 'Gove: "Absurd" secrecy left care children at mercy of paedophiles', *The Telegraph*, 12 Sep 2013, http://www.telegraph.co.uk/news/politics/10305488/Gove-Absurd-secrecy-left-care-children-at-mercy-of-paedophiles.html.

11 David Batty, 'White girls seen as "easy meat" by Pakistani rapists, says Jack Straw', *The Guardian*, 8 Jan 2011, http://www.theguardian.com/world/2011/jan/08/jack-straw-white-girls-easy-meat

12 Channel 4 'Asian Rape Allegations', *Channel 4 News*, 27 Aug 2003, (from archive. org) http://web.archive.org/web/20100620042427/http://www.channel4.com/news/articles/society/law_order/Asian+rape+allegations/256893

13 Andrew Norfolk, '"Some of these men have children the same age"', *The Times*, 5 Jan 2011. Other reports have claimed that the pimps can make hundreds of pounds a day for a girl.

14 See *Appendix 1: Grooming Gang Convictions*.

if it was an arranged marriage), possibly with daughters the same age as those they were victimizing and corrupting, they would be justifiably angry if they discovered that strangers were plying their own daughters with alcohol and drugs in order to rape them. But the victims were not Muslims and therefore were apparently seen as fair game. What is harder to understand is how the community from which these non-Muslim victims came could turn a blind eye to the suffering of its children.

If the victims of these grooming gangs are not already estranged from their parents when the Muslim gang first ensnare them, the gang will use techniques to drive a wedge between the girl and her parents, *e.g.* by exploiting teenage rebellion and encouraging the girl to believe her family are trying to control/constrain her. If the parents find out what is going on and try to intervene, the gang can alienate the schoolgirl from her parents by accusing the parents of being racists: 'The pimps are adept at trading on teenage rebellion and use similar methods... of convincing the girls all white people are racist.'[15]

If none of this works, and the parents' intervention looks like it will threaten the gang's activities, then the parents too may be subject to blackmail, intimidation or violence: 'the family was even forced to leave their home leading to her daughter receiving a phone call in which she was threatened with having her face cut off, and members of her family having their throat slit and being decapitated.'[16] Often the gangs threaten to set fire to the family's home.[17] It really strains credibility that the police and the media could ignore such threats and persecution for decades. Similar stories of threats to families can be found in reports of the Dutch equivalent of the grooming gangs.

Some of the people we have spoken to have lost relatives to the gangs, and these family members have told us, that to avoid relatives of the schoolgirl from being ensnared, some families have had to cut off all contact between the groomed schoolgirl and the extended family, to prevent the gangs' tentacles reaching further into their family. This experience of secondary ensnaring is recognised by others:

---

15 Julie Bindel, 'Mothers of Prevention', *op. cit.*

16 Arthur Martin, 'Faces of True Evil: Judge Jails Depraved Sex Gang for 95 Years After they Committed Grotesque Abuse on Girls as Young as 11', *The Daily Mail*, 27 Jun 2013 http://www.dailymail.co.uk/news/article-2349784/Sadistic-paedophile-sex-gang-brothers-given-lengthy-prison-s entences-exploiting-underage-girls.html

17 The gangs are undoubtedly threatening to set the house ablaze with the family inside. Andrew Norfolk, '"Some of these men have children the same age"', *The Times*, 5 Jan 2011.

Jean was soon to find out just how indoctrinated her daughter had become when she discovered Sally's photographs and profile were posted on a website. She was posing with the flag of Pakistan. There were 97 names of Asian men posted on it who had made contact with her. She was asking for Asian men to "date." She said she hated white people. There were other girls' photographs on the site, one of whom Sally had recruited, as were other girls who were being pimped.[18]

In these situations families feel guilt because they failed to prevent their daughter being ensnared. But those feelings of guilt are increased by them having to leave their daughter in the clutches of the gang in order to protect female siblings and cousins of their daughter. If they do not do this, their problems will be magnified, as the gangs will use one groomed girl to ensnare other girls.[19] Almost without exception the Muslim community would close ranks and protect the gangs, but the schoolgirls and their families were abandoned to their fate. It is hard to explain how the two different communities could react so differently to this phenomenon. We have no doubt, had the tables been turned, and gangs of non-Muslim men were raping Muslim schoolgirls, the towns of England would be ablaze with destruction.

A girl who is considered to be the property of one of the gangs can face extraordinary violence if she should try to leave or to tell the police what is being done to her. Sara Swann, who has worked extensively with the victims, has told of a girl who had her tongue nailed to the table when she told a grooming gang that she would go to the police.[20] Another girl was threatened with having her face blown off with a gun, whilst another girl was pinned down and a kettle of boiling water held over her face.[21]

If, by some extraordinary circumstance, a schoolgirl manages to get away from the gang before she has outlived her usefulness to them, if she manages to get the police and the court system to initiate a pros-

---

18 Julie Bindel, *op. cit.*

19 'Woman lured girls to be raped by three men', *BBC News*, 2 Aug 2011 http://www.bbc.co.uk/news/uk-england-lancashire-14381083

20 Kathryn Knight, 'Is political correctness stopping police ending the misery of the teenage sex slaves?', *Daily Mail*, 27 Mar 2008, http://www.dailymail.co.uk/femail/article-546809/Is-political-correctness-stopping-police-ending-misery-teenage-sex-slaves.html. See also http://www.youtube.com/watch?v=RFIfcTqBsZc&t=1806

21 http://www.youtube.com/watch?v=RFIfcTqBsZc&t=1845

ecution, the intimidation of the gang will intensify as the perpetrators face the prospect of conviction and exposure.

> The court heard how a 16-year-old girl was bombarded with 350 text messages and phone calls and given money in an attempt to stop her giving evidence. She was coerced into travelling to Bradford where she was told to write a letter to say she had made up allegations that she had been abducted and sexually abused when she was 12...[22]

Because these gangs are well-organised and have systematically manipulated the behaviour and mind of their schoolgirl victims, and since they are prepared to use violence and intimidation to interfere with the legal process, the chances of getting a conviction are very slim. But that should never have been a reason for the authorities to choose to ignore the problem. These threats and violence should make it clear that the those who have been convicted are almost certainly the tip of the iceberg. As we will disclose, legal measures have existed in the UK since the late 1980s which could and should have been used by the courts to protect the victims. Again we find it hard to comprehend how the authorities could fail, over and over again, to avail themselves of the existing legal measures to deal with this phenomenon.

A recent parliamentary report into these criminal gangs (Home Affairs Select Committee, June 2013) said:

> There is no guidance specific to localised grooming or child sexual exploitation cases. Many of the issues which are hallmarks of localised grooming—victims returning to their attackers, the length of time it takes victims to report the crime, previous interaction with the police and social services, the use of drugs and alcohol by perpetrators to strip their victims of their inhibitions, which lead to inconsistent recollections of events — are what led the Crown Prosecution Service to deem witnesses unreliable in the Rochdale case when it was first presented for prosecution. As such, it may be necessary for the Crown Court Bench Book to include directions relating to these sorts of cases to ensure that juries are made

---

22 'Grooming victim got 350 phone threats from Brierfield men', *Lancashire Telegraph*, 19 Jul 2013, http://www.lancashiretelegraph.co.uk/news/10560927.Grooming_victim_got_350_phone_threats_from_Brierfield_men/

aware the witnesses "unreliability" is often behaviour which may be, directly or indirectly, a result of their being groomed and sexually exploited.[23]

It is time the authorities finally recognised the extent and seriousness of this problem, and applied the existing legal measures to ensure convictions and to protect the victims. If necessary make changes to judicial procedure or even changes to the criminal law. The scandal is that it should have taken 25 years to even reach the stage we are at. More and more schoolgirls fall prey to the gangs, because police and social workers believe they cannot secure convictions. Historically the judiciary have proven to be the fundamental problem when it came to ridding our country of this scourge. They should have applied the existing laws and court procedures such that the child's interests were put before those of the adult, such that there could have been no possibility to claim that a child incapable of giving consent was consenting, such that the victim got to give her testimony by video without being cross-questioned for days on end by a series of aggressive barristers, with the victim just feet away from the gang who had groomed and raped her.

That Parliamentary report on grooming gangs recognised that 'Asians' are hugely over-represented in these gangs:

> with this specific model of offending, there is a widespread perception that the majority of perpetrators are of Asian, British Asian or Muslim origin. This would certainly seem to be the case from the major grooming prosecutions which have gone to court so far...[24]

It appears Parliament thinks that if there were more information about the number of those perpetrating this crime, then *perhaps* "Asians" would not be so over-represented in the statistics. However, the Parliamentary investigation began at the end of 2012 and finished in June 2013, and throughout 2013 more convictions took place, with no sign that the phenomenon is any different than that accepted by Parliament. Indeed, what is notable about the names of those convicted is not that they are just "Asian" names, but most of those convicted have Islamic

---

23 Home Affairs Select Committee Report 'Child Sexual Exploitation and the Response to Localised Grooming' 10 Jun 2013 http://www.publica tions.parliament.uk/pa/cm201314/cmselect/cmhaff/68/68i.pdf p. 43.

24 *Ibid.*, p. 52.

names (the name "Mohammed" is, by a very long way, the single most common name among the men convicted of these types of crime; see *Appendix 1: Grooming Gang Convictions*).

1.1 Defining the Problem

When the Child Exploitation and Online Protection agency (CEOP) finally came to publicly offer expert guidance on the subject of the grooming gangs, they defined the problem of "localised grooming" thus:

> a form of sexual exploitation, previously referred to as "on street grooming" in the media, where children have been groomed and sexually exploited by an offender, having initially met in a location outside their home, usually in a public place (such as a park, cinema, on the street or at a friend's house). Offenders often act in concert, establishing a relationship with a child or children before sexually exploiting them. Some victims of "street grooming" may believe that the offender is in fact an older "boyfriend", introducing peers to the offender group who may also be sexually exploited.[25]

This is the barest possible definition of the problem, and is only useful to distinguish between this type of grooming and online grooming of children via websites, or grooming where the perpetrator is a family member (or known to the child on the basis of a fiduciary relationship *e.g.* a teacher, football coach, social worker etc.) There are many more aspects to the problem, which also make 'localised grooming' a new and distinctive phenomenon.

The specific phenomenon of localised grooming requires the offender to inhabit a culture or milieu where it is acceptable to broach to friends, colleagues and relatives the possibility of raping under-age girls.

> The groomers were men in their early twenties. Their customers were older relatives, friends or contacts. They travelled to the girls' home town to have sex with them or had their victims delivered by car to Pakistani communities in

---

25 CEOP, 'Out of Mind, Out of Sight - Breaking Down the Barriers to Understanding Child Sexual Exploitation', Jun 2011, http://ceop.police.uk/Publications/, p..5.

northern England and the Midlands.[26]

A man who can't take part in the sexual abuse of children for fear of disapproval or fear of being reported to the police, must seek like-minded people anonymously, typically online. In Britain, this kind of crime mostly involves white men, because 80% to 90% of the men in Britain are white: race or ethnicity tells us nothing about this crime or who is more likely to be involved. With the grooming gangs, the prevalence of one ethnicity is so out of proportion with their numbers in Britain, that ethnicity becomes highly significant. This reality behind 'localised' grooming means that cultural factors are all-important (only a racist would think that race is a determining factor). Far from being swept under the carpet, such cultural factors need to be addressed first and foremost when dealing with this crime. The fact that an Islamic background dominates the profiles of 'localised groomers', whilst online groomers are predominantly white males, indicates that Muslim culture finds this crime to be far more acceptable than do other ethnicities in Britain.

No mention is made in the CEOP definition of the inverse relationship between the ethnicity of the perpetrator and that of the victim. No mention is made of the way in which the Muslim community closes ranks, supporting the perpetrators rather than the victims. No mention is made of the pimping of the victims by the gang. No mention is made of the violence and threats made against the child and even her family. Whilst the report is entitled 'Out of Mind, Out of Sight', this sexual exploitation was out in the open for all to see; it was just that fear of being accused of 'racism' prevented people from acting on what they could see going on. Disentangling the concepts of 'race' and 'religion' is central to dealing with this problem. Our report will address specific components of Islam and Muslim culture which explain why it is that these crimes have Muslim men so overwhelmingly represented amongst the perpetrators.

Greater Manchester Police (GMP) claim that part of the difficulty in identifying 'localised grooming' is because:

> it is not a crime per se. It is made up of a number of other offences. The challenge is joining together those links and

---

26 Andrew Norfolk, "'Some of these men have children the same age; they are bad apples"; Sexual grooming; The grooming of white girls by gangs of Pakistani heritage is an issue that few in the community will address', *The Times*, 5 Jan 2011.

identifying it as child sexual exploitation [CSE].[27]

It is for this reason that the definition of the problem should not just be defined in the most general way, but should include as many pertinent and specific features as possible, in order to overcome the problem in identifying when it is going on. Thus, when reporting to the Home Affairs Select Committee on 'localised grooming', GMP estimated that in the previous 2 years alone, they had more than 30 prosecutions which fit the category of CSE, but 'they were unable to record how many of the number of rape and other sexual offences cases prosecuted were related to child sexual exploitation.'[28] That is, many convictions for other sex and drug-related crimes have not been identified conclusively as part of the activities of a grooming gang, but if more information was acquired, the police think that many of these 'isolated' incidents would actually be part of a pattern of grooming activity. So, sustained surveillance and the systematic collation of information is important not just for successful convictions, but also in establishing that these crimes are actually being committed in the first place. However, the dependence of the police on information-gathering and deduction would be of far less importance, if the Muslim community had been prepared to report their brethren to the police, and had they been willing to testify in court about what they knew was going on. Moreover, if from 1995 schoolgirls in towns with significant Muslim populations had been forewarned about what the grooming gangs were doing and how these gangs operate, the victims themselves might have been able to alert the police to grooming activities, long before the victims had been seduced and entrapped. In the absence of specific laws, the absence of help from Muslim communities, and the absence of knowledge on the part of the schoolgirls which would enable them to realise they were being groomed, the police must rely on expensive and complicated information-gathering and analysis. Even when a victim testified, it was claimed that juries would not believe the victim and that the case would fail.

Appendix I is a list of convictions (since 1997)[29] which meet the criteria used by Andrew Norfolk in his 2011 study, which clearly identified the 'pattern of exploitation.'[30] Whilst 177 individuals are listed in

27 Home Affairs Select Committee Report, *op cit.*, p. 33.

28 *Ibid.*

29 *Appendix 1: Grooming Gang Convictions.*

30 Andrew Norfolk, 'The 17 cases identified by *The Times* which showed a pattern of exploitation', *The Times*, 5 Jan 2011, http://www.thetimes.co.uk/tto/news/uk/crime/

our table (around 90% having Muslim names), we must conclude they are just the tip of the iceberg.[31] As the comments from Greater Manchester Police make clear, there are other convictions for rape and other sexual offences which will not meet the strict criteria for inclusion in that table, but which are very likely signs of the activities of grooming gangs. Thus, there was a conviction in Manchester which we exclude from our list because there was only one man involved in the abduction and one schoolgirl victim, but there were many other men involved in the rape/pimping of that schoolgirl; from the many men involved in that schoolgirl's ordeal, only that one perpetrator was prosecuted (the other perpetrators were never caught, because the convicted man refused to identify them).[32] Thus, we exclude that conviction from our table of grooming gang convictions. There may be scores of such convictions which do not meet our strict criteria for inclusion as examples of this grooming phenomenon.

---

article2863078.ece. This article also appears in some on-line news databases under the title, 'Organised gangs, vulnerable girls: a pattern of exploitation unfolds; Sexual grooming': 'The Times identified 17 cases in which men groomed girls they met on the street. Most of the offenders were of Pakistani origin and most of the victims were white.'

31 Moreover, in order to focus on the specific problem of organised gangs perpetrating grooming, we have excluded from this analysis the cases of individual Muslim men who have been convicted of grooming schoolgirls. See 'Exeter businessman admits grooming and meeting schoolgirl at hotel', *Express & Echo*, 15 April 2014, http://www. exeterexpressandecho.co.uk/Exeter-businessman-admits-grooming-meeting/story-20960321-d etail/story.html, and 'Taxi driver Mohammed Ashraf admits raping girl, 14, in Edinburgh', *BBC News*, 22 April 2014, http://www.bbc.co.uk/news/uk-scotland-edinburgh-east-fife-27114762, and 'Man said God would punish him for raping girl of 14, court told', *Telegraph & Argus*, 24 April 2014, http://www.thetelegraphandargus. co.uk/news/11167653.Man_said_God_would_punish_him_for_raping_girl_of_14 court_told/. Some of these stories seem to be considered so unimportant that they do not get reported by news websites, *e.g.* 'Man jailed for grooming and sexually assaulting girls', *Rochdale Online*, 01 April 2014, http://www.rochdaleonline.co.uk/ news-features/2/news-headlines/86323/man-jailed-for-g rooming-and-sexually-assaulting-girls. It may well be that some or all of these men were connected to larger gangs, but that in the specific instances where they were caught, there was insufficient evidence for others to be prosecuted. These four cases are all convictions from one month in 2014, ranging from Bradford and Rochdale, to Exeter and Edinburgh.

32 'Pervert sentenced after raping 12-year-old', *Manchester Evening News*, 13 Sep 2007 http://www.manchestereveningnews.co.uk/news/local-n ews/pervert-sentenced-after-raping-12-year-old-1003364

1.2 Tip of the Iceberg

Even when a case can be considered as being within the parame-
ters of our class of convictions for 'localised grooming', there are many
other men who are caught up in these prosecutions, but who are not
found guilty. Thus, in his retrospective survey of convictions, Andrew
Norfolk provides some details about court cases which show that those
convicted are but a small section of other men who are implicated along
with the convicts.[33]

year	arrested	charged	convicted
1997	23	5	3
2005		10	2
2007	20	3	2
2009		7	4
2010		8	5

We can infer from this that for every man convicted there are
probably between 2 to 10 other men who were directly implicated, but
for whom there was insufficient evidence to secure a conviction. If this
is true, it means that with this crime there are very many perpetrators
getting away with it. It is not just that there are convictions for sexual
crimes (or drug-crimes) which may also be connected to a grooming
gang: even when a grooming gang is identified and a case can be built
up against some of the gang-members, many of those arrested are never
charged, many of those charged are never convicted and many more
escape being arrested or charged. There is a strong incentive for the gang
to use violence or intimidation to stop their victims from testifying or
from even identifying other gang members. Even members of the Muslim community who played no part in a gangs' grooming/pimping activities have gone out of their way to protect the gang members.[34]

---

33 Andrew Norfolk, 'Revealed: conspiracy of silence on UK sex gangs', *The Times*, 5
Jan 2011 http://www.thetimes.co.uk/tto/news/uk/crime/article2863058.ece

34 A trial in Burnley, Lancashire concluded in April 2013, with a Muslim man named
Mohammed Imran Amjad being jailed for the sexual abuse of a child. However,
months later a Muslim woman receptionist who worked for the local government
in that town was 'jailed for attempting to derail' the trial of him and other men for
grooming. Five other men in that trial were cleared of rape, sexual assault and child
abduction at Burnley Crown Court in April 2013: 'she accessed a confidential database
60 times over 15 days to find details of the witness and her family.' 'Lancashire Council
receptionist jailed after attempting to derail grooming trial', *BBC News*, 30 August
2013, http://www.bbc.co.uk/news/uk-england-lancashire-23907268. This demonstrates

This difficulty in securing convictions serves as a negative feed-back-loop to police and social services, who think it is not worth identifying that a crime is taking place, when the chance of stopping it or achieving justice is so slight (and the likelihood of being accused of 'racism' is so high). Part of the problem in securing convictions is that the accused get away with claiming that the schoolgirls were consenting, rather than groomed and exploited. This means that quite often a case collapses with none of the accused being found guilty. In 2010, police in Rotherham managed a successful prosecution of a gang, but two subsequent cases in that town failed.[35] In a separate part of the country, another large-scale prosecution failed in July 2013.[36] In between, another trial at Stafford Crown Court collapsed in September 2011. When the risk of a prosecution failing because of witness/victim intimidation from criminals is so high, what the police need is public support, not false accusations of 'racism.'

1.3 Invisible Victims

One of the popular misconceptions is that the victims are all from children's homes or are under the guardianship of social services. However, it seems that the majority of the victims are not in state control, with only 14% being 'in care.'[37] In many discussions of this grooming phenomenon, people have been all too happy to blame the victim for her abuse and to blame the victim for coming from a dysfunctional family. But in such cases, the child should not be blamed if she does come from a dysfunctional family: the child does not choose to be born into an unstable environment. Moreover, in some cases, the child had even been put into care by her family, because she was already in the clutches of the grooming gangs. With no assistance from the police or social workers, parents sometimes would try and put their children 'in

---

the way in which the Muslim community helps not only to cover up this crime during the months and years in which the schoolgirl is being raped, but they also actively work to destroy the case once a prosecution is initiated.

35 Andrew Norfolk, 'Police Files Reveal Vast Child Protection Scandal', *The Times*, 24 Sep 2012 http://www.thetimes.co.uk/tto/news/uk/crime/ar ticle3547661.ece

36 'Ribbon trial: Jury discharged - no verdict on three men', *Bucks Free Press*, 24 Jul 2013 http://www.bucksfreepress.co.uk/news/10568337.R ibbon_trial_Jury_discharged_no_verdict_on_three_men/

37 Julie Bindel, 'Mothers of Prevention', *op. cit.*, Whilst only 14% of the victims are living in children's homes, this still shows that gangs are more successful at luring such schoolgirls, as not 14% of all children are in children's homes.

care' with the council, in a vain hope that in this way their daughters would be protected and beyond the reach of the gangs.[38] It is grotesque for anyone to then turn round and accuse the family of being dysfunctional because they put their child into state protection, once the family recognised their inability to protect their child from violent, organised gangs who operated with legal immunity because teachers, social workers and police were permitting the gangs to work undisturbed.

Even if the girls were mostly under the guardianship of the state, that should have been all the more reason for the social workers to intervene. Such children have often been not only taken away from their biological family, but were also often relocated to towns a long way from any relatives. These towns often have a high Muslim population. It could hardly have been designed to be more dangerous for these schoolgirls: predatory men, social workers who are politically correct, girls who may be headstrong, wayward or abused, far away from anyone with real concern for the girls' well-being. It is a recipe for disaster.

Wherever there is the opportunity for the gangs to intervene beyond the watchful eye of parents/carers, they will use that opportunity. There is much evidence that the gangs station themselves outside schools and takeaways, and inside shopping malls. They will repeatedly importune schoolgirls walking between home and school, not taking 'No' for an answer. Many parents will have no idea that their daughter is being subjected to the wiles and lure of the determined and organised gangs. And if the politically-correct brainwashing has been successful, a schoolgirl may even consider herself 'racist' for refusing the advances of these Muslim men.

By the time you are reading this, it might be hard to grasp how deep and how enduring was the silence around these grooming gangs and their victims. But in 2012 Andrew Norfolk, a principal journalist for *The Times*, stated 'when we first started to investigate this 2 years ago, no-one [from the child-care professions] would speak to us.'[39] A journalist of long-standing, with an impeccable record, working for one of

---

38 'I wanted the three of them [my daughters] to be put into child protection but they wouldn't do it. I must have called in to social services eight or nine times and phoned them lots of times.' Nigel Bunyan, 'Rochdale Grooming Trial: Police Knew about Sex Abuse in 2002 but Failed to Act', *The Telegraph*, 9 May 2012 http://www.telegraph. co.uk/news/uknews/crime/9254982/Rochdale-grooming-trial-police-knew-about-sex-abuse-i n-2002-but-failed-to-act.html

39 Andrew Norfolk, 'Reality of Sexual Grooming Gangs in the UK - interview of Andrew Norfolk and Sikh Awareness Society', http://www.youtube.com/watch?feature=player_detailpage&v=WbUIfvYbjRc&t=1180

the most respected newspapers in the world, could not get professionals in 21st century Britain to speak to him about a phenomenon that is probably the worst child-care scandal in the country in 40 years! It is a situation which defies belief. These were public servants, who would not talk about child-rape and prostitution, which they knew had been going on for years. They were not the rapists. They were not being paid by the criminals. But political correctness and multiculturalism had left them too scared to speak about these horrific crimes. No wonder these grooming gangs felt untouchable. The conflicts and confusions caused by multiculturalism left the staff unsure of their moral and professional values; the tyranny of political correctness meant they did not dare articulate or even acknowledge what they were seeing and hearing.

When he testified before parliament, Andrew Norfolk said that after the publication of his 2011 analysis of the pattern of exploitation (which demonstrated that Muslim men were hugely over-represented as the perpetrators), suddenly Norfolk:

> was contacted by so many people who had refused to speak to me before. When you have a Director of Children's Services ringing and saying, "My staff are jumping for joy in the office today because finally somebody has said what we have not felt able to say," and ... very senior police officers saying exactly the same.[40]

Those who are responsible for instilling such fear into public officials should be held accountable. As we will show below, between 1988 and 2011 there was barely one news report per year on the phenomenon of these Muslim gangs, and their systematic grooming and pimping of schoolgirls: a testimony to the power of political correctness.

In a later analysis, Andrew Norfolk reported on the hundreds of unpublished reports on Muslim grooming gangs in Rotherham by police and social services. For example, in 2002 a Home Office-funded research project showed that 56 schoolgirls had sexual links to 3 Pakistani brothers. This had all the hallmarks of 'localised grooming.' Police and social services discussed this case for years without ever identifying that the men were Muslims; they never acknowledged publicly what was going on and, according to Andrew Norfolk, they never did anything to stop it.[41] They were 'terrorised' by political correctness and multi-

---

40 Home Affairs Select Committee Report, *op. cit.*, p. 56.

41 Andrew Norfolk interview, *op. cit.*

culturalism. And when people refuse to acknowledge reality because of political correctness, their actions serve to enforce and strengthen this mechanism of control. Speaking the truth becomes heresy.

The refusal of social workers, police, journalists and academics to attend to this subject from 1988 to 2011 ensured that the victims remained invisible, and ensured that the gangs could extend their reach across the entire country. We will show, that by 1996, it was not only in South Yorkshire but also in West Yorkshire where police, social services and child-care professionals knew what were the characteristics of this crime. We cannot calculate the harm done by refusing to publicly identify this problem by the mid 1990s.

1.4 National Dimensions

Whilst police forces in the North-West of England are considered the most expert in dealing with this type of criminal activity, the problem is now nationwide. The grooming problem appears to have started with Muslim gangs grooming Sikh girls in Birmingham in the 1980s, but by the the start of the 21st century it appears to have extended to include all the major towns of Lancashire and Yorkshire. And given recent convictions in Oxford, London, Ipswich and the north-east of England, it looks like the gangs are working in most of the country (see *Appendix 12: Map of Grooming Gang Convictions*). An absence of gang members being convicted in an area does not mean they do not operate in that area: the gangs are known to traffic the girls from their home town across the country (to Bristol, Manchester, Birmingham, Bradford and Dover), offering the schoolgirls up for sexual services to a network of customers.[42] And there are areas of the country with large Muslim populations but relatively few prosecutions (for example, London and the West Midlands). There are indications that this lack of prosecutions is not necessarily because there are no grooming gangs those areas. The near total absence of prosecutions in areas like West Midlands and the East Midlands is almost certainly because of policy decisions made by local government, police forces and state prosecutors.

Recently, one newspaper took the initiative of asking all the police forces in England and Wales whether or not they had current investigations into specific grooming gangs.[43] Whilst 1 in 3 forces did not

---

42 Andrew Norfolk, 'Police Files Reveal Vast Child Protection Scandal', *The Times*, 24 Sep 2012, http://www.thetimes.co.uk/tto/news/uk/crime/ article3547661.ece

43 Justin Penrose & Vicky Smith, 'Police probe at least 54 more evil child sex grooming

respond, from those organisations who did respond, it transpired that in early 2013 there were at least 54 on-going investigations into different grooming gangs in various parts of the country. Some of these investigations concerned grooming gangs in Devon, Kent and Suffolk, counties far away both geographically and demographically from the towns of Lancashire and Yorkshire, the type of towns which people might imagine would be the scene of these crimes. Often we have heard reports of related events which strongly indicate that gangs are operating in an area, even when we have been unable to locate even a single failed prosecution of a grooming gang in that area.[44]

1.5 International Dimensions

The problem of Muslim grooming gangs is not confined to Britain: it also exists in the Netherlands. In the Netherlands, their existence has been publicly acknowledged by their national media since at least 2001. A report by *Radio Netherlands* said:

> Another large group (also 5,000) are "ordinary" Dutch schoolgirls, aged 13 or 14 from a "regular home environment" who are lured into prostitution by so-called "lover-boys"... handsome-looking [male] adolescents who appear to have made it in life. They're well-dressed, drive expensive cars and lavish presents on these young and susceptible girls, who will quickly fall in love with them. "Of course, they'll have sex and after a while the girl will be forced to have sex with one of his friends, which will open the way for prostitution."[45]

It took the British media until 2011 to truly acknowledge what the Dutch were discussing from 2001.[46] 'Last year, 242 lover boy crimes were inves-

---

gangs', *The Daily Mirror*, 19 May 2013 http://www.mir ror.co.uk/news/uk-news/police-probe-least-54-more-1896991

44 'Teenager groomed to sell drugs', *The Bolton News*, 10 Mar 2011, http://www.the-boltonnews.co.uk/news/8900946.Teenager_groomed_to_sell_drugs/

45 Carin Tiggeloven, 'Child Prostitution in the Netherlands', *Radio Netherlands*, 18 Dec 2001 http://web.archive.org/web/20080627112924/http://www.radionetherlands.nl/currentaffairs/region/netherlands/netherlands011218.html

46 See also Frank Bovenkerk et. al, '"Loverboys" of modern pooierschap in Amsterdam', Willem Pompe Instituut voor Strafrechtswetenschappen, Utrecht, 2004 http://www.prostitutie.nl/fileadmin/nl/6._Studie/6.3_Documenten/6.3g_Mensenhandel/pdf/

tigated by police, half of them involving the forced prostitution of girls under 18. Campaigner Anita de Wit says this is a fraction — "one per cent" — of the true number.[47] This is yet more evidence that a decade has been lost in pursuing these criminals, because those speaking out about these abusive gangs were accused of 'racism'. The Dutch were admitting to a huge problem, and working out ways to tackle it, a decade before the authorities in Britain would even publicly admit the problem existed. Yet there is good evidence to indicate that charities and police authorities in the UK were aware of the similarities with Holland, going so far as to use the euphemistic phrase coined by the Dutch ('Lover Boys') in publications in the UK.

The story from Holland is almost identical to the problem here. In Holland young girls are seduced by a 'boyfriend', then prostituted far and wide (Holland, Belgium, France). The victims were ignored by the police: 'Victims who have the courage to report the crime are often not taken seriously and are sent away.'[48] As in Britain, even if the gangs got to court, they get away with it because of a lack of evidence, or because the victim withdraws her testimony.[49] The 'Loverboys' also exhibit shocking levels of cruelty towards the schoolgirls they have ensnared.[50] One bru-

---

onderzoeksrapport-loverboysinamsterda m.pdf; Linda Terpstra and Anke van Dijke en Marion van San, 'Loverboys, een publieke zaak, Tien portretten', Amsterdam, SWP, 2004; Linda Terpstra and Anke van Dijke *Loverboys: Feiten en cijfers. Een quick scan,* Amsterdam, SWP, 2005.

47 Sue Reid, 'A Feminist Revolution that Cruelly Backfired', *The Daily Mail,* 23 Nov 2012 http://www.dailymail.co.uk/news/article-2237170/Why-Amsterdams-legal-brothels-lesson-Britain-telling-truth-sex-gangs-race.html

48 Loretta van der Horst,'Victims of "loverboys" not taken seriously by Dutch police', *Radio Netherlands Worldwide,* 16 Jun 2009, http://www.r nw.nl/english/article/victims-%E2%80%9Cloverboys%E2%80%9D-not-taken-seriously-dutch-police

> In May 2009, Dutch writer and victim of a loverboy Maria Mosterd claimed 74,000 euros in compensation from the Thorbecke school, her former high school in Zwolle, in the north west of the Netherlands. Ms Mosterd says that the school failed to provide a safe learning environment and ignored her frequent absences. She describes how at the age of twelve she was captured by a loverboy and the subsequent struggle to cut herself loose from him.

49 Ibrahim Wijbenga, 'Lover Boys', *Al Jazeera,* 15 May 2012, http://www.aljazeera.com/programmes/witness/2012/05/201251115345899123.html. Interestingly, Wijbenga says 'In the Netherlands, many "Lover Boys" - and some of their victims - are of Moroccan origin. It was this connection to the country of my own roots that inspired me to gather more information on them and their practices.' Other reports we have read state that the number of Moroccan victims is less than five in total.

50 'In July 2007, a Moroccan loverboy named Abdessamad was sentenced to 12 years

tal gang of Muslim brothers tattooed their names onto the women they 'owned'. The pair 'were found guilty of leading an international human smuggling gang, thought to be responsible for forcing more than 100 women into prostitution in the Netherlands, Germany and Belgium.'[51]

It is estimated that in the Netherlands, at least 40% of the 'Loverboys' are Moroccan, with most of the others being from the Dutch Antilles and the Dominican Republic.[52] Because the police are hesitant to pursue the criminals, often families end up moving across Holland to live in a different city, just to get their child away from the gang.

Muslim grooming gangs are thus operating at a national level in two neighbouring countries.[53] But until 2011, our media were not discussing this similarity between Britain and Holland at all.

> In a chilling parallel to the scandal sweeping Britain's towns
> and cities, where a multitude of girls have been lured into sex-
> for-sale rings run by gangs, the Dutch pimps search out girls
> at school gates and in cafes, posing as "boyfriends" promis-
> ing romance, fast car rides and restaurant meals. The men ply
> their victims with vodka and drugs. They tell them lies: that

---

in prison. He frequently tortured and raped his victim, a Dutch teen-age girl. One of the cruel things he did to this defenseless girl was causing small knife injuries and then pouring vinegar and chlorine into the wound. When she became pregnant he subjected her to forced abortion. She was not his only victim. Abdessamad was not in Holland during the trial, so he was sentenced in absentia. He is probably in Morocco now.' Emerson Vermaat, 'Crime and Terrorism: The Role of Moroccan Immigrants In Holland, Belgium and Spain', *Militant Islam Monitor*, 25 Sep 2008, http://www.militantislammonitor.org/article/id/3640

51 'Convicted human trafficker vanishes', *Dutch News*, 16 Sep 2009, http://www.dutchnews.nl/news/archives/2009/09/convicted_human_trafficker_van.php

52 Emerson Vermaat, 'Crime and Terrorism: The Role of Moroccan Immigrants In Holland, Belgium and Spain', *Militant Islam Monitor*, 25 Sep 2008, http://www.militantislammonitor.org/article/id/3640. However, another analysis, on an Arabic website, says that the majority of the perpetrators are "Dutch-Moroccan." Ibrahim Wijbenga, 'Lover Boys', *Al Jazeera*, 15 May 2012, http://www.aljazeera.com/programmes/witness/2012/05/201251115345899123.html. Wijbenga also notes that Turks are to be found among the men being prosecuted for these kinds of crimes. Muslims (mostly Moroccans and Turks) are thought to be 5% of the population of Holland. http://en.wikipedia.org/wiki/Islam_in_the_Netherlands#D emographic_situation

53 It also appears that the phenomenon may exist in Germany too. Dialika Krahe, 'Schoolgirls Controlled by Loverboys: Math Class in the Morning, Turning Tricks at Lunchtime' *Der Spiegel*, 9 Jul 2010, http://www.spiegel.de/international/europe/schoolgirls-controlled-by-loverboys-m ath-class-in-the-morning-turning-tricks-at-lunchtime-a-705104.html

they love them and their families don't care for them. Then, the trap set, they rape them with other gang members, often taking photos of the attack to blackmail the girl into submission. Befuddled, frightened, and too ashamed to tell parents or teachers, the girls are cynically isolated from their old lives and swept into prostitution.[54]

The typical behaviour of the Muslim grooming gangs (targeting non-Muslim girls, getting them addicted to drugs and/or alcohol, then pimping them out) has also been seen among Muslims in the United States.[55] Since there are few Muslim enclaves in the United States, we should expect such activity to be far less prevalent there than in Britain or the Netherlands.

1.6 Counting the Victims

Having established that the cases which end in convictions are just the vaguest indication of the true scale of the problem, let us try to assess the number of victims in Britain affected by these gangs. One thing is clear to us: the grooming gangs have been active for (at least) 25 years in England; yet at most, the experts and the media are now talking about this being a problem that has existed for no more than 10 years. Thus, when we use numbers here, they are derived from statements/estimates made by these experts working with the assumption that the gangs have been operating for 10 years. We contend that the true duration of this phenomenon is more than twice what the media and experts will admit.

Andrew Norfolk disclosed that there are hundreds of internal reports by police/social services into these grooming gangs, and most of these reports have never been made public. Norfolk cites a 2010 report by the police intelligence bureau 'warning that thousands of such crimes were committed in the county [of South Yorkshire] each year.'[56] Thus, we have one expert report asserting that, in just one county of England, there are thousands of these crimes each year. Rather than publish these

---

54 Sue Reid, *op cit.*

55 'Sioux Falls Man Convicted in Sex Trafficking Case', FBI, 06 Dec 2013, http://www.fbi.gov/minneapolis/press-releases/2013/sioux-falls-man-convicted-in-sex-trafficking-case

56 Andrew Norfolk, 'Police Files Reveal Vast Child Protection Scandal', *The Times*, 24 Sep 2012 http://www.thetimes.co.uk/tto/news/uk/crime/ article3547661.ece. Without having access to these reports, we will assume that the 'thousands of crimes' relates to hundreds of girls, being raped multiple times in just one year.

reports and bring the subject into the public domain, the police and local council chose to keep parents in the dark, leaving schoolgirls unprotected and parents unaware of the risks and threats their daughters faced. Schoolgirls were leaving the security of their family to get an education, but if the girls were getting any education about the dangers of these grooming gangs lurking outside school and on the streets, that education was not coming from the schools or the authorities. Rather than have the families or the wider community know what was going on, the schoolgirls were left to fend for themselves.

The Coalition for the Removal of Pimping (CROP) is the only charity which has focused on working with the victims of localised grooming and their families.[57] The estimate by CROP is that there are 10,000 children who are the victims of sexual exploitation across the country.[58] Many of the schoolgirls are victims of the grooming gangs for more than 1 year. Taking the shortest period in which this phenomenon of grooming gangs has existed (a window of 10 years), it would be reasonable to say that, on the most conservative estimate, CROP are referring to 1000 new girls being groomed by these gangs each year in that 10 year period. Another report that would seem to indicate the feasibility of such estimates states that 'Police found 2,409 children and young people had been confirmed as victims of sexual exploitation in gangs or groups between August 2010 and October 2011.'[59] Further investigation may lead us to conclude that CROP meant that at any one time, there were 10,000 schoolgirls who were currently in the clutches of the gangs. In the first edition of *Easy Meat*, we thought that the idea that CROP could mean that there were 10,000 victims each year was too shocking to be credible. But within 12 months of our book being first published, senior police officers stated their belief that there were 'tens of thousands' of victims each year in the UK.[60]

---

57 CROP is now known as PACE, Parents Against Child Sexual Exploitation.

58 Paul Vallely, 'Child Sex Grooming: the Asian Question', *The Independent*, 10 May 2012 http://www.independent.co.uk/news/uk/crime/child-s ex-grooming-the-Asian-question-7729068.html

59 David Barrett 'Thousands of Child Sex Abuse Victims, says Minister', *The Telegraph*, 21 May 2013, http://www.telegraph.co.uk/news/uknew s/crime/10071898/Thousands-of-child-sex-abuse-victims-says-minister.html. This statistic was based on a belated analysis by The Children's Commissioner, whose report confused matters by conflating the phenomenon of localised grooming with that of black gang culture. Thus, The Children's Commissioner statistic may not just include those schoolgirls who are the victims of the grooming gangs.

60 'Police chief warns of more Rotherham-style abuse cases', *BBC News*, 16 Oct 2014,

Assuming that each year there are more than 10,000 new victims each year, how many prosecutions are there each year? According to the parliamentary report into localised grooming, 'In 2012, Lancashire police had had 100 successful prosecutions relating to child sexual exploitation whereas South Yorkshire had had none.'[61] But it needs to be borne in mind that this figure of 100 convictions by one police force alone should not lead us to have any confidence that even the best force in the country has got this problem under control.[62] Those 100 convictions could relate to girls who were being exploited years before the trial; and in the year of the trial perhaps the gangs across the country acquired 1000 new victims. Moreover, the term 'Child Sexual Exploitation' is generally being used to conceal the grooming gang phenomenon within wider sexual abuse. Thus, estimating the scale of this problem is exceedingly difficult. By the start of 2015, the socialist MP for Rotherham, which in the last couple of years has been the epicentre of the grooming scandal, was quoted claiming that there could be as many as 1 million victims nationally in recent decades.[63]

1.7 Realising the Damage

Having referred to the numerical scale of the problem, we need to turn our attention to understanding the scale of the problem when it comes to the actual physical, mental or social suffering of the victims and their families.

Following the standard operating procedure of the grooming gangs, 11 to 15 year old schoolgirls are deliberately addicted to alcohol and serious drugs as both "rewards" and as means of control by the gangs.[64] The most obvious physical damage to the schoolgirls is that they suffer physical trauma from rape and multiple sexual infections.[65] Some

---

http://www.bbc.co.uk/news/uk-29639374

61 Home Affairs Select Committee Report, *op. cit.*, p 34.

62 A BBC documentary from 2008 tracked the actions of Lancashire Police's dedicated unit, a unit which amounted to one-and-a-half officers, who bemoaned the need for hugely-improved intelligence resources. See section 3.14 *2008 BBC Panorama: Teenage Sex For Sale.*

63 Lucy Thornton, 'Child sex abuse gangs could have assaulted ONE MILLION youngsters in the UK', 05 Feb 2015, *Daily Mirror*, http://www.mirror.co.uk/news/uk-news/child-sex-abuse-gangs-could-5114029

64 'Teenager groomed to sell drugs', *The Bolton News*, 10 Mar 2011, http://www.theboltonnews.co.uk/news/8900946.Teenager_groomed_to_sell_drugs/

65 One 13 year old victim, when examined by a nurse, was thought to have been

of them get pregnant, and undergo backstreet abortions (sometimes it seems that pregnancy and abortion is used by the gangs as a form of punishment).[66] Some of the girls have been branded by their 'owners'.[67] In some cases, what the girls have gone through has been described as 'torture'.[68] In short, the schoolgirls suffered a catalogue of physical abuse: 'had been scratched, choked, beaten, branded, gang raped, burnt, and sexually assaulted with knives and a baseball bat.'[69] It goes without saying, that schoolgirls could not undergo all these violent and sexual abuses, living in fear of reprisals, without these girls suffering immense psychological damage: one psychiatrist said 'more than two-thirds had depression and post-traumatic stress disorder.'[70]

When parliament finally looked into this problem in late 2012, their report summarised the manifold ways in which the victims are damaged mentally and emotionally:

The nature of child sexual exploitation can have a catastrophic effect on the victim with evidence showing that victims have been diagnosed with borderline personality disorder and emerging psychosis as a result of their experiences... Victims often suffer with feelings of trauma, betrayal and stigmatisation. They may also blame themselves. The court process itself can often compound this trauma with victims feeling as though they can make a choice between seeking therapy and perusing [sic] justice.[71]

raped more than 50 times. Andrew Norfolk, 'Revealed: conspiracy of silence on UK sex gangs', *The Times*, 5 Jan 2011, http://www.thetimes.co.uk/tto/news/uk/crime/article2863058.ece

66 'Oxford exploitation trial: Girl had "back-room abortion"', *BBC*, 17 Jan 2013, http://www.bbc.co.uk/news/uk-england-oxfordshire-21059681

67 Allison Pearson, 'Oxford grooming gang: We will regret ignoring Asian thugs who target white girls', 15 May 2013, http://www.telegraph.co.uk/news/uknews/crime/10060570/Oxford-grooming-gang-We-will-regret-ignoring-Asian-thugs-who-target-white-girls.html

68 Sandra Laville 'Oxford gang found guilty of grooming and sexually exploiting girls', *The Guardian*, 14 May 2013, http://www.theguardian.com/uk/2013/may/14/oxford-gang-guilty-grooming-girls

69 Ben Wilkinson, 'Grooming gang face sentencing hearing', *Oxford Mail*, 26 Jun 2013, http://www.oxfordmail.co.uk/bullfinch/10507248.Grooming_gang_face_sentencing_hearing/

70 'Grooming: a Life Sentence', *BBC File on Four*, Jun 2013, http://news.bbc.co.uk/1/shared/bsp/hi/pdfs/11_06_13_fo4_grooming.pdf, p. 7.

71 Home Affairs Select Committee Report, *op. cit.*, p. 36.

The damage to the schoolgirls is also of great significance when it comes to the judicial process. These victims have already been so confused and abused by the gangs, it can be hard for the schoolgirls to grasp that they are the victims, that they have been consciously and systematically exploited. The gangs have had control over them for so long, and have often managed to destroy each girl's relationship with her carers, such that, even in adult life, these girls can often not even be considered as independent adults. Then the judicial process can be used by the gangs to affect the outcome of the trials, either by threatening the girls in the lead up to the trials, or by intimidating them within the court room. During one recent trial, one of the victims attempted suicide following her first day of testimony.[72] In another case, a girl received 350 phone threats from the brother of a man on trial for grooming her, in his attempt to stop her testifying against the accused.[73]

We must also consider something even more gruesome: it is entirely possible that some girls who have 'gone missing' have in fact been murdered by the gangs, with the possibility that their bodies will never be found. The grounds for considering that the gangs could take their threats this far are based on the cases of Charlene Downes, Paige Chivers, Fiona Ivison and Laura Wilson. Laura was groomed, and when she got pregnant by an older Asian man, he stabbed her and threw her body in a canal.[74] When it wasn't social workers ignoring or concealing such evidence, it was the police turning a blind eye. Paige Chivers was groomed, and went missing in 2007. Four years before Paige Chivers went missing, Charlene Downes also went missing. Both were among 60 girls who were identified in a police report as being groomed in Blackpool by 'Asian men'.[75] Fiona Ivison was killed by a 'customer' at the age

72 Martin Robertson 'Girl, 17, tried to kill herself after first day in witness box during trial of ten men accused of grooming her for sex at 11', *The Daily Mail*, 6 Aug 2013, http://www.dailymail.co.uk/news/article-2385239/Teenager-17-accused-gang-men-grooming-sex-11-tried-kill-day-wit ness-box.html

73 'Grooming victim got 350 phone threats from Brierfield men', *Lancashire Telegraph*, 19 Jul 2013, http://www.lancashiretelegraph.co.uk/news/10560927.Grooming_victim_got_350_phone_threats_from_Brierfield_men/

74 Daniel Miller, 'Social workers hid fact they knew teenage mother was at risk from sex grooming gangs SIX YEARS before she was brutally murdered', *The Daily Mail*, 7 Jun 2012, http://www.dailymail.co.uk/news/article-2155823/Social-workers-hid-fact-knew-teenage-mother-risk-sex-grooming-gangs-SIX-YEARS-brutally-murdered.html

75 James Tozer, 'Police "hid" abuse of 60 girls by Asian takeaway workers linked to murder of 14-year-old', *The Daily Mail*, 7 Apr 2011, http://www.dailymail.co.uk/news/

of 17, having been groomed by a gang when she was 14.[76]

As more information is coming into the public domain with each trial, the authorities seem to be giving more seriousness to the threats and violence of these gangs. In a case that is scheduled to come to trial soon, ten men from Coventry are being held on remand and the alleged victims/witnesses are living under 'safeguarding arrangements... being supported by specially-trained police officers from the public protection unit.'[77] Whether or not the arrangements offer enough security to ensure the trial proceeds to its conclusion is another matter entirely.

Whilst the victims have suffered tremendous damage, their families too have often suffered alongside them. The threats made to the victims are extended to their family as well: 'he threatened to firebomb my home and rape my own mother if I tried to escape.'[78] The families may well have been powerless to stop the gangs, and their attempts to get police and social services involved fell on deaf ears. Yet, some try and rescue their child, endure threats of violence, try to put their family back together, and then they face the claim that somehow it was the schoolgirl and/or her parents who were to blame for this abuse taking place. It is hardly surprising that given the failure by the state and the media to take these gangs seriously in the first place, many parents developed racist or phobic attitudes to anyone Asian.[79] Some of the parents have spoken of homicidal feelings instead of feelings of powerlessness. Parents have suffered in frustration as they were ignored by the police and social services; maybe they had to abandon a child to stop her dragging her sisters or cousins into the gangs' clutches; some put their children 'into care', often in the vain hope that this would protect their child when the family could not. Out of frustration and anger, ordinary law-abiding

---

article-1374443/Police-hid-abuse-60-girls-Asian-takeaway-workers-linked-Charlene-Downes-murder.html

76 Julie Bindel, 'Mothers of Prevention', *op. cit.*

77 Les Reid, 'Ten charged with trafficking teen girls in Coventry "sex gang" probe', *Coventry Telegraph*, 2 Aug 2013, http://www.coventrytelegraph.net/news/coventry-news/ten-charged-coventry-sex-gang-5429952

78 Julie Bindel, 'Girls, Gangs and Grooming: The Truth', *op.cit.* (See also Rachel Halliwell: 'My daughter came home drunk so I grounded her, unaware paedos had threatened to kill her. Evil was always going to win', *The Sun*, 5 Feb 2013, http://www.thesun.co.uk/sol/homepage/woman/real_life/4779384/PARENTS-speak-out-against-paedo-gang.html).

79 Daniel Trilling, 'How the Rochdale grooming case exposed British prejudice', *New Statesman*, 15 Aug 2012, http://www.newstatesman.com/2012/08/how-rochdale-grooming-case-exposed-british-prejudice

citizens felt like they wanted to kill the gang members.

We now have some sense of the scale of the problem (although no doubt these words must only skim the surface of the deep suffering of the schoolgirls and their families). As we will see next, in Britain this grooming phenomenon appeared to start with Muslims grooming Asian (Sikh) victims in the West Midlands in the 1980s. But it has spread to engulf most of the cities and large towns of England, and now the victims are overwhelmingly white. Every convicted man probably correlates with 2 to 10 other men who have not been convicted yet who were implicated with the same systematic abuse for which any single gang member was convicted. And even the experts agree that there are *at least* 1000 new victims each year. The damage to the schoolgirls and to their families is immense. The damage to communities is immeasurable. And as indicated by the photographs in *Appendix 4: Leeds School Warning* and *Appendix 5: Sheffield School Warning*, there is no end in sight to this problem.

TWO

Sikh Victims of Grooming Gangs

[T]his issue is about the Muslim community.
– Sikh Media Monitoring, *Daily Mail*, 2011

"A FACTOR that may reinforce the perception of localised grooming being carried out by Asian men against white girls could be the under-reporting of offences against children from ethnic minorities."[1] The refusal of the police, child protection services and the media to acknowledge that Muslim gangs have been grooming Sikh girls is a significant part of the phenomenon. By ignoring this factor, those who protect the grooming gangs have been able to project the image that such Muslim gangs were a fantasy of white racists.

From the earliest evidence in the 1980s, it seemed that Muslim gangs were targeting Sikh girls in the Midlands. The Muslim gangs could have singled out Sikh girls due to the long-standing resistance of Sikhism to Islamic domination. Or it could have been more contingent: Sikh girls were nearby and it would be easier for the Pakistani Muslims to minimise suspicion by pretending they were Sikhs, luring Sikh girls more easily than white girls with this deception. Whatever the root

---

1 Home Affairs Select Committee Report 'Child Sexual Exploitation and the Response to Localised Grooming', 10 Jun 2013, http://www.publications.parliament.uk/pa/cm201314/cmselect/cmhaff/68/68i.pdf p. 55.

cause, the available historical evidence currently points to Sikh girls being the first victims of the Muslim grooming gangs in Britain.

There is no indication whatsoever that the authorities or the media took these crimes seriously at the time, resulting in Sikhs taking the law into their own hands. As time has gone on, and the Muslim population of Britain has increased and spread across the country, the gangs appear to have turned their attention to young girls from the indigenous population. Considering the expert estimates of the number of victims, and the increase in prosecutions since 2010, the lack of prosecutions between 1988 and 2010 is appalling. The signal that police, social services and the media sent to these gangs was: carry on with what you are doing, we are not going to stop you, we are not going to expose your crimes.

A Sikh media group says that Britain cannot defeat the Muslim grooming gangs 'unless the politically correct lobby stop putting up a smokescreen to hide the fact that this issue is about the Muslim community.'[2] Other Sikh organisations have claimed that Muslim men were going to great lengths in order to seduce and/or convert Sikh girls (the Muslim men would pretend to have a Sikh name, wear jewellery that indicated the wearer was a Sikh).[3] Sikh websites have claimed that, as far back as 1992, Muslim men were given specific instructions from Islamic fundamentalist organisations (groups which seek to re-establish the Islamic state, the Caliphate). We have been not been able to refute or verify these allegations. The idea that a devout religious organisation would encourage such behaviour goes against the grain of our usual associations conderning religious fundamentalism and sexual morality.[4]

2 Rebecca Camber & James Tozer, 'Teenager who Lured Girls into House to be Raped by Asian Gang is Jailed for Seven Years', *The Daily Mail*, 3 Sep 2011, http://www.dailymail.co.uk/news/article-2033022/Teenager-lured-girls-house-gang-raped-Asian-gang-jailed-seven-years.html

3 http://www.whyichoseSikhism.com/?p=know&s=10secrets

4 Andrew Norfolk thinks that the idea that pro-Caliphate groups were encouraging this is 'nonsense', https://www.youtube.com/watch?v=RZCQ9ZWfCuQ#t=503. We're not aware of any proof by Norfolk that the documents discussed in section 3.7 *2001 Derby and 'Real Caliphate'* and section 3.11 *2005 Luton and "Real Caliphate"* are fake, or the claims by Sikh organisations that pro-Caliphate organisations were doing this as early as 1990 are false. Norfolk has mentioned "sharia law" as an explanation for why these grooming gangs were targeting young girls, but appears to have no explanation for why the Muslim community have done nothing about these gangs in the past 25 years. We wonder how he would account for the failure of 75% of mosques to read out a sermon condemning the grooming gangs? Reading out a sermon condemning the rape of schoolgirls seems to be a very small step for religious organisations to take, yet

What can be objectively verified, is that these claims were to be found on Sikh websites as long ago as 2004 (and possibly much earlier).[5] Thus, in 2004, at the height of the controversy concerning the Muslim grooming gangs in Bradford, there were good reasons for the media, the multiculturalists and the child-care professionals to have known about the claims being made by Sikhs. Any group who claims to believe in multiculturalism should have been paying attention to what the Sikh victims were saying about gangs of Muslims in Britain preying on Sikh schoolgirls.

Serious attention needs to be paid to the decades-long abuse of Sikh girls by Muslim gangs: Sikh girls were still being abused by Muslim gangs as late as 2013. From the earliest years, Sikhs took many steps to try to warn society about this, from creating pressure groups to risking imprisonment. When the police and other institutions would do nothing to stop the grooming gangs, other non-Muslim communities never responded as the Sikhs did, physically attacking grooming gangs. When white non-Muslims spoke of the overwhelmingly Muslim grooming gangs, they were accused of 'racism', and thus marginalised and ignored. Some of this must come down to greater solidarity within the Sikh community, and with them having their own organisations (such as the Sikh Awareness Society) dedicated to warning Sikh schoolgirls and their parents. But also the narrative of racism could not be used to sow doubt among Sikhs, the way the Left used it to marginalise any white person who spoke about the grooming gangs. Whilst CROP existed locally in Leeds before going national, it is likely to be much harder for CROP to reach every teenage girl in Britain than for Sikhs to use networks within their much smaller community to raise awareness of the problem. As we

despite all the bad publicity around the Islamic association with the grooming gangs, the vast majority of mosques did not take part. There are 1500 to 2000 mosques in Britain, and only 500 read the sermon. http://news.bbc.co.uk/1/hi/magazine/7118503. stm. Other mosques "shunned" the sermon: Ben Wilkinson, 'National sermon on child grooming shunned as a stunt by many Muslims in Oxford', *Oxford Mail*, 29 Jun 2013, http://www.oxfordmail.co.uk/news/10516465.National_sermon_on_child_groom-ing_shunned_as_a_stunt_by_many_Muslims_in_Oxford/

5 Independent historical archives of websites show that this page could be found on that Sikh site on 3 Aug 2004, preceeding the groundbreaking *Channel 4* programme was being attacked by the Left as 'racist'. That is, Sikhs were warning that they had evidence that devout Muslim groups in Britain were organising systematic grooming campaigns against non-Muslim girls, both white and Asian. http://web.archive.org/web/20040803070716/http://www.whyichoseSikhism.com/?p=know&s=10secrets The document may well have existed before that, but the internet archive may not have taken copies before 2004.

will show later, there is every indication that our national agencies have shamefully failed when it comes to developing an awareness campaign directed at schoolgirls. But if the media and the Left had not spent so much time ignoring the Sikh victims and vilifying the white victims, both CROP and the Sikh Awareness Society (SAS) would presumably be much better financed and have far greater reach.

Even in January 2013, when a group of 40 Sikh men attacked a Muslim restaurant in Leicester (because they thought it was the workplace and home of one of the Muslim men who had groomed and raped a Sikh schoolgirl), the police did not disclose that the men who attacked the restaurant were Sikhs.[6] A few days after the attack, the local newspaper reported that the city police commander had stated that the attack was 'sparked by misinformation regarding the rape of a teenage Sikh girl.' The police commander went on to say there was 'a rumour that a Sikh girl has been raped and Leicestershire Police has done nothing despite being in possession of video evidence of that rape. This is not true.'[7] Yet within weeks of the attack on this restaurant, five men in that city were being prosecuted for 22 charges of sexual exploitation of a girl. In reports on the trial, the ethnicity of the victim was not specified, and a banning order had been issued to prevent the names of the men from being published (even though all of the men were adults, and were not apparently awaiting trial for other offences, which might have been an excuse for withholding their details). The police and/or the Crown Prosecution Service (the CPS is the state prosecutor who makes decisions about which cases to bring to trial and how they will be handled) had gone to great lengths to conceal any details about the men, requiring the local newspaper to get the judge to disclose these facts.[8] In reporting

---

6 The police stated they had CCTV imagery, but would not release it; they stated they wanted witnesses to come forward, but would not describe the attackers or the victims of the attack. Peter Warzynski, 'Diners flee as mob of 40 men attack Moghul Durbar restaurant in Leicester', *Leicester Mercury*, 16 Jan 2013, http://www.thisisleicestershire. co.uk/Diners-flee-mob-40-men-attack-Moghul-Durbar/story-17863811-detail/story. html

7 Peter Warzynski, 'Peace talks held after rampage at Moghul Durbar restaurant', 17 Jan 2013, *Leicester Mercury*, http://www.thisisleicestershire.co.uk/Peace-talks-held-rampage-Moghul-Durbar-restaurant/story-17880361-detail/story.html

8 'At their two previous court appearances, an order was imposed banning publication of their names, addresses and dates of birth. The Mercury, however, has successfully challenged this order, which was removed yesterday by District Judge John Temperley.' 'Child Exploitation Case – Five in Court', *Leicester Mercury*, 9 Feb 2013, http://www. thisisleicestershire.co.uk/Child-exploitation-case-ndash-court/story-18100272-detail/ story.html

on the case at the beginning of February, we were told that one of the men, Wajid Usman, was 'of no fixed abode', yet in subsequent court appearances, it was stated that some of the sexual abuse had occurred in a flat above the Moghul Durbar restaurant, where Wajid Usman had been living.[9] That a Sikh girl was being raped and prostituted by some Muslim men associated with the Moghul Durbar restaurant might not have been 100% accurate, but it was far from being 'misinformation' and 'rumour'. The full truth was possibly worse.[10]

The convicted men were Muslim, the girl was Sikh, and some of the abuse had indeed taken place at the restaurant the Sikhs had attacked.[11] Furthermore, if the police did know about the sexual exploitation of this Sikh girl before the restaurant was attacked, no evidence has come to light to suggest they were taking any action to stop the gang's activities. The predatory Muslim men were only prosecuted once the Sikhs had drawn attention to these crimes by taking the law into their own hands. As one Sikh organisation stated about this case in Leicester in 2013: 'it appears that racially motivated grooming of girls by groups of Pakistani Muslim men stems from 1990s onwards and is being underplayed by the Police, media and politicians fearing political correctness.'[12] Another significant feature of this case is that the victim 'told police that boys at college had paid her for sex before she met the men',[13] which suggests she may already have been the victim of Muslim grooming activities before she met these men who were eventually convicted. Thus, the grooming of this Sikh girl could have been far more extensive than the eventual conviction indicates.

In September 2013, *BBC's Inside Out* programme focussed on the

9 Suzy Gibson, 'Men "exploited vulnerable teenager", court told', *Leicester Mercury*, 30 Jul 2013, http://www.leicestermercury.co.uk/Men-exploited-vulnerable-teenager-court-told/story-19583988-detail/story.html

10 'Leicester child prostitution trial: Six men jailed', *BBC News*, 30 Aug 2013, http://www.bbc.co.uk/news/uk-england-23896937

11 Whether or not all the Muslim men were in fact connected with that restaurant has never been disclosed.

12 'Underage Sexual Grooming: Five Arrested in UK', *Sikh24*, Jan 19 2013, http://www.Sikh24.com/2013/01/underage-sexual-grooming-five-arrested-in-uk/

13 'Leicester child prostitution trial: Six men jailed', *BBC News*, 30 Aug 2013, http://www.bbc.co.uk/news/uk-england-23896937. There are many times since 1988 when Sikhs have attempted to stop Muslims grooming Sikh girls in schools and colleges for sex. See section 3.1 *1988 Sikh/Muslim violence*, section 3.6 *1998 Sikh Awareness Society Starts*, section 3.7 *2001 Derby and 'Real Caliphate'*.

forgotten Sikh schoolgirl victims of the grooming gangs.[14] Whilst the *BBC* should be commended for finally making this programme, they made no mention of the history of predation by Muslim grooming gangs on Sikh girls from 1988 onwards. Significantly, when the *BBC* news website reported on the television programme about the Sikh victims of grooming gangs, not once did the website report mention the claim made in the programme by Sikhs: that the perpetrators are overwhelmingly Muslim.[15] The *BBC News* report implies that it was Sikh men who were grooming Sikh girls! So, as one part of the *BBC* is giving coverage to Sikh activity to stop gangs of Muslims grooming Sikh schoolgirls, another arm of the *BBC* is trying to conceal what the programme was actually about. Twenty-five years after the first news reports of Muslim gangs grooming Sikh girls appeared in the British news media, our national broadcaster ignores the specifics of the problem, and gives no indication of just how long this abuse this has been going on. The full scale of how this grooming phenomenon has affected Sikhs in Britain probably merits a book of its own. Since 1998 Sikhs have had their own organisation dedicated to this problem, and so we have no doubt they have enough material for a detailed account, which would shed new light on the phenomenon. We can only bring attention to some of the aspects concerning Sikhs in Britain.

14 http://www.youtube.com/watch?v=7hXTM7ehvtk

15 Zack Adesina, 'Sexual grooming victims: Is there Sikh code of silence?', *BBC News*, 2 Sep 2013, http://www.bbc.co.uk/news/uk-23921570

THREE

Chronology: Cover-up to Collapse

It has taken nearly two decades for the truth to emerge, but only now are we discovering the chilling extent of the abuse, and the level of cover-up.

– whistleblower, *Daily Mail*, 2015

IN 2011 a wave of reports swept across the news media, indicating that they had finally woken up to the phenomenon of the Muslim grooming gangs. This was followed in 2012 by the Home Affairs Select Committee undertaking an investigation into this scandal (with the Committee's report finally being published in June 2013). However, it was not always so, and between 2004 and 2011, there was only one journalist who stuck with this story. We are going to examine what was allowed to be said in the national debate at various points since the earliest manifestations of this problem. In the very limited debate on these grooming gangs in Britain, the self-censorship of the media can be directly traced back to the early part of the 21st century. Until the last few years, it has been very rare indeed for the news media to report that these crimes were going on at all. And even now when the media are discussing the grooming gangs, it is exceptional for a reporter to mention that the phenomenon goes back into the last century.[1] For

---

1 One rare exception to this is a report on *Russia Today* in May 2013, where Sean

the sake of posterity, and so that the necessary corrective action can be taken in Britain, we will document the evidence that shows that the phenomenon was identifiable by 1988 at the latest. The media, politicians, Muslim organisations, and child-care professionals marginalised and ignored the problem for the following 20 years. In 2014, in the wake of a report into what had been suppressed in the town of Rotherham, some MPs started to admit their colleagues had known what was going on but didn't take action:

> MP Barry Sheerman, who chaired the Commons Children, Schools and Families Committee [...] said MPs were aware vulnerable children were being sexual exploited "up and down the country". He said: "We knew about that, we didn't do enough about it. Members of this house, many of us, knew what was going on."[2]

Until there is a Public Inquiry and MPs are questioned about what they knew, it is hard to know exactly what Mr. Sheerman means. However, in this chapter, we will explore the information that was publicly available from 1988 to 2011. This will give us some indication concerning what MPs should have known.

In the deluge of news reports of arrests, of convictions and of catalogues of failures by police and local authorities, the following important point should be borne in mind: as late as December 2010, the feminist author Julie Bindel was a lone voice stressing that there was an urgent need to acknowledge these Muslim grooming gangs exist, and that white liberals were still in denial.

> These gangs will be allowed to operate with impunity if we deny their existence in some sort of twisted attempt to be anti-racist and culturally sensitive. Some people, including many white liberals, are loath to admit what it is going on.[3]

Thomas says that the crimes of the grooming gangs go back to 'the early 1990s, if not before'. https://www.youtube.com/watch?v=RZCQ9ZWfCuQ#t=81. In this report, Andrew Norfolk of *The Times* says that the metropolitan elite in London chose to ignore this problem for 20 years. https://www.youtube.com/watch?v=RZCQ9ZWfCuQ#t=517

2 'Rotherham child abuse scandal: New victims come forward', 02 Sep 2014, http://www.bbc.co.uk/news/uk-england-south-yorkshire-29036742.

3 Julie Bindel, 'Girls, Gangs and Grooming: The Truth', *Standpoint Magazine*, Dec 2010, http://www.standpointmag.co.uk/node/3576/full

In 2007 Bindel was writing for *The Times* about the grooming gangs, but by 2010 writing about this phenomenon was so taboo that Bindel's follow-up piece appeared not in *The Times*, nor *The Guardian*, nor *The Independent*, but in a very minor publication called *Standpoint* (a conservative magazine, prioritising freedom of speech). It is a credit to a radical feminist like Bindel that she stood by the story rather than worrying about what was good for her career. That she should be writing this in such a minor publication at the end of 2010 shows the determination to ignore it by the politically-correct elite in the media. Andrew Norfolk's pivotal article appeared in *The Times* in January 2011, and marks the point at which the establishment started to talk about the phenomenon in a more open manner. Considering the media exposure given to the grooming gang phenomenon since 2011, it is hard to realise that prior to 2011 brave souls like Julie Bindel were lone voices.

Our society has a veritable army of salaried staff who are responsible for the welfare and protection of children: social workers, teachers, medical staff, police forces, charities and sociologists. Yet this grooming phenomenon has been covered up for decades. Whilst Andrew Norfolk referred to it as 'a conspiracy of silence', this cover-up did not require an explicit conspiracy: the power of political correctness was sufficient to ensure that, almost without exception, those who were witnessing the problem would look the other way and remain silent. Professionals, who were admired by all and sundry for having jobs which meant they looked after some of the most vulnerable members of our society, were either so ideologically committed to multiculturalism or so fearful of financial and social ruin because of political correctness, they violated the most basic principles of their profession. In most cases there was no need to actively conspire to conceal what was happening: provided all their colleagues and the related professions were kept silent by political correctness; omitting either to speak or to act was enough to ensure the grooming gangs could operate unimpeded.

By 2013 CROP/PACE noted: 'Suddenly, professionals are waking up to the nature of grooming under-age children, and how they are prepared for a life of sexual assault, rape and the enforced selling of sexual services to adult males.'[4] To most members of the public who have any knowledge of this crisis, they think it goes back to 2003, when it was first broached explicitly in the national media, at which time the subject

---

4 PACE, 'The grooming of children for sexual exploitation is largely misunderstood', 21 Jan 2013, http://www.paceuk.info/the-grooming-of-children-for-sexual-exploitation-is-largely-misunderstood/

was suddenly controversial and then suddenly silenced. However, our investigations show that the problem goes back at least to 1988. Indeed, there are even statements from some retired policemen who say that there were cases in the 1970s of Muslims in Britain grooming young non-Muslim girls.[5]

3.1 1988 Sikh/Muslim violence

The earliest manifestation of the Muslim grooming gangs, which we can establish with an objective reference, is in 1988. That year, in Wolverhampton, there were violent confrontations between Muslims and Sikhs. Sikh men formed into gangs to protect young Sikh girls from being groomed by gangs of Muslim men.

The main Sikh gang was called Shere Punjab. Some of the Sikh gang members received criminal convictions because of their attacks on Muslim gangs. In 1988 *Look East*, the BBC current affairs programme concentrating on Asian issues, included a segment on the 'gang-warfare' in Birmingham between Sikh gangs and Muslim gangs.[6] Here is a list of some of the incidents of violence in 1988 between Muslims and Sikhs cited in that *BBC* programme:

- Feb 19, disorder in Handsworth, Sikh versus Muslim
- May 21, 3 Muslims attacked in Soho Rd. by Sikhs
- May 27, Sikh youth stabbed following fight at daytime disco in Hurst St.
- May 30, violent disorder outside the Milestone pub
- May 30, incident on Ladypool Rd. Sparkbrook, 1 Muslim received wounds
- Jun 2, Sikh charged for possession of pump-action shotgun
- Jun 2, 24 arrested following fight between Muslims and Sikhs

It seems clear that the violence was not short-lived, and that it was rapidly escalating. The violence came to an end in the summer of 1988, when the police arrested and charged Sikhs and Muslims.

According to a Muslim youth worker in the programme, it all start-

---

5 Jaya Narain 'Police chief: "We couldn't speak out on Asian sex gangs for fear of appearing institutionally racist"', *The Daily Mail*, 12 Jan 2011 http://www.dailymail.co.uk/news/article-1346291/Police-chief-We-speak-Asian-sex-gangs-appearing-racist.html

6 *BBC Look East*, 1988 http://www.youtube.com/watch?v=MJoWIHlPmp8

ed when the Sikh gang 'handed leaflets out saying that Muslim youths are coming round our schools... they are abducting our girls... and they are raping them an putting them into prostitution.'[7] The description in this written warning to the Sikh community (and maybe to the Muslim community) about the behaviour of the Muslim grooming gangs is consistent with the phenomenon as it extended its reach across the whole country over the following decades. At this point in time, it was almost certainly true that most people in Britain knew nothing about either Islam or Sikhism, and could probably not even distinguish between Muslims and Sikhs. Nevertheless, these allegations and the escalating violence, should have been of interest to journalists, social workers and academics.

The Sikh gang Shere Punjab said they gave the police the names and car registration details of those Muslims involved in grooming non-Muslim girls.[8] Police claimed they would sort out the problem, if Shere Punjab "stepped out of the way." Chief Superintendent David Love is interviewed in the programme and denies that they were ever given any of this information, and denies that they ever received any information about the girls being abducted. After 25 years, it may be impossible to establish the truth about these claims. However, the story from these Sikhs seems credible, since 20 years later police forces in other parts of the country were also refusing to act on information supplied by the family of grooming victims, including photographic evidence and car registration numbers.[9]

3.2 1989 Sikhs convicted

Following the violence cited in the *BBC* programme from 1988, there was a report in *The Independent* newspaper in June 1989: 13 Sikh men were on trial for vigilantism, (we presume this was a prosecution carried over from the previous year). Note how the headline of this 1989 report (quoted below) describes the Sikh girls being 'used as sex slaves' by the Muslim gangs, and in the body of the story the Sikhs describe how the Muslim gangs use these Indian girls for 'sex and prostitution'. Here is an extract from that article:

---

7 *Ibid.*

8 http://www.youtube.com/watch?feature=player_detailpage&v=MJoWIHlP-mp8&t=301

9 Julie Bindel, "Mothers of Prevention", *The Sunday Times*, 2007 http://www.thesundaytimes.co.uk/sto/news/uk_news/article72310.ece

Sikh girls 'used as sex slaves'

GANGS OF Muslim men toured daytime discotheques kid-napping Sikh girls to use as sex slaves, a court was told yes-terday.

The jury at the trial of 13 Sikh men at Birmingham Crown Court heard claims that one gang forced girls into prostitu-tion and blackmailed their parents.

The Sikhs were said to be members of the Shere Punjab, a vigilante gang, who were arrested - armed with sticks and bottles - while on their way to confront the rival Muslim gang, the Aston Panthers, in Handsworth, Birmingham, last June.

Gurmek Singh Chahal, 20, told the court [the Muslim gang] the Panthers used Indian girls for sex and prostitution...[10]

We can find no record that Muslim grooming gangs were ever the target of arrests and prosecutions at this time, and none of the expert reports describe any prosecutions before the early to mid-1990s. We can find no evidence that the authorities did anything to stop the Muslim grooming gangs, but came down heavily on the Sikh men when they tried to in-tervene in the absence of any state intervention. Three of the Sikh men in this case received criminal convictions for trying to stop the Muslim grooming gangs. One would expect the police to have prosecuted mem-bers of the Muslim gangs too (after all, 24 men were arrested in the sum-mer of 1988). However, there is no sign that the police, the media or the child-care professionals took any notice of the Sikhs' allegations of 'sex slavery'. There is every reason to believe that in these circumstances, the Muslim grooming gangs continued, and if anything were emboldened by the success of their operations.

3.3 1991 "The earliest case..."

Between 1989 and 2003, there was virtually no national media attention concerning these Muslim grooming gangs.[11] However, in an

---

10 'Sikh girls "used as sex slaves"', *The Independent*, 24 Jun 1989.

11 The only exception was an apparently context-less story from 2001: *The Telegraph*

interview with the Sikh Awareness Society, Andrew Norfolk does indicate that grooming activities were known about in Bradford in 1991: the gang were taking girls from a children's home, prostituting them, then returning them to the children's home at night.[12] There were no criminal convictions arising from these events in 1991, but it seems clear from this story that the child-care professionals knew what was going on (whether they notified the police is another matter, and there is no indication that the media reported on this case). Norfolk says: 'These were Pakistani men doing it - that was never made public at the time.'[13] The disparity in ethnicity between the gangs and their victims, and the concealment of this by the authorities, was to remain a constant theme for the next twenty years.

Norfolk points out that in 1995, a few years after this 'earliest case', Bradford was the first city in Britain where a project was set up to help the victims of the grooming gangs. When this interview with Norfolk took place in 2012, he points out how strange it is that Bradford had not had a single prosecution of a grooming gang despite the city having a bigger problem with grooming gang activity than probably anywhere else in the country.[14] A grooming gang in Bradford was convicted later in 2012; more than twenty years after cases were first being discussed by child-care professionals in that city.[15]

---

carried a report on Muslims in Derby attacking 'Asians' in a school, over claims that Muslims had been instructed to groom Sikh schoolgirls. See section 3.7 *2001 Derby and 'Real Caliphate'*.

12 Andrew Norfolk, 'the first one that fits the pattern I'm studying is 1991', 'Reality of Sexual Grooming Gangs in the UK - interview of Andrew Norfolk and Sikh Awareness Society', http://www.youtube.com/watch?v=WbUIfvYbjRc&t=1325

13 http://www.youtube.com/watch?feature=player_detailpage&v=WbUIfvYb-jRc#t=1366

14 Andrew Norfolk interview with Sikh Awareness Society, *op. cit.* Convictions did occur in nearby Keighley and Skipton in 2005 and 2009, respectively. Though the heavily Islamised town of Bradford had surprisingly few prosecutions, despite Norfolk saying grooming was known be going on there at least as early as 1991.

15 There is much evidence of other 'lone' Muslim male paedophiles who were raping under-age girls. Here is one case, where a Pakistani was able to flee the country half way through his trial for child-rape. 'All-ports alert as East Bowling child rapist could try to flee country', *Telegraph and Argus*, 15 Oct 2010, http://www.thetelegraphandar-gus.co.uk/news/local/localbrad/8454127.Hunt_for_man 58_.../ It is entirely possible that this man was also connected to grooming gangs or was aware of them getting away with their activities.

3.4 1995 Bradford: *Streets and Lanes*

In 2011, when reports on the Muslim grooming gangs could no longer be kept out of the media, the children's charity *Barnardo's* published a report entitled 'Puppet on a String: the Urgent Need to Cut Children Free From Sexual Exploitation.'[16] The report states:

> [A]t *Barnardo's*, we know from our 16 years' experience op-
> erating specialist services in the UK that it is far more wide-
> spread than is generally recognised. And we are finding that
> the victims are becoming younger and the exploitation more
> sophisticated, involving organised networks that move chil-
> dren from place to place to be abused... There is a shocking
> lack of awareness that stretches from the front-line of prac-
> tice to the corridors of government... Urgent action is re-
> quired to address this, which is why *Barnardo's* is publishing
> this report and launching a campaign calling for reform.[17]

The report goes on to say that the *Streets and Lanes* project has existed in Bradford since 1995.[18] From their reference in 2011 to 16 years of experience in this area of child sexual exploitation, it seems clear that *Barnardo's* is alluding to this project.

Barnardo's created this *Streets and Lanes* project in Bradford with £677,000 funding from 'statutory agencies.'[19] This would have been a very significant amount of money in 1995. The local media in Brad-ford reported that the purpose of this project was 'to help teenage girls, usually run-aways, picked up at Bradford Interchange by unscrupulous men and groomed for prostitution.'[20] Notice there is no mention of any disparity in ethnicity between the perpetrators and the victims. This disparity is one of the most significant features of this grooming gang phenomenon, and there is no reason to doubt that this well-funded *Bar-*

---

16 'Puppet on a String: the Urgent Need to Cut Children Free From Sexual Exploita-tion', 2011, http://www.barnardos.org.uk/ctf_puppetonastring_report_final.pdf

17 *Ibid.*, p. 1.

18 *Ibid.*, p. 2.

19 Sara Swann, 'Helping girls involved in "prostitution": a Barnardos Experiment', pg. 277 of *Home Truths About Child Sexual Abuse: Policy and Practice*, Catherine Itzen (ed.), Routledge, London, 2000.

20 Jim Greenhalf, 'How do we Make the Streets Safer?', *Telegraph & Argus*, 1 Jun 2010, http://www.thetelegraphandargus.co.uk/news/news_behind/8194620.How_do_we_make_the_streets_safer_/

nardo's project was dealing with grooming gangs principally constituted by Muslim men. But one will search in vain to find any mainstream child-protection organisation refer to this disparity. When reading something which makes no reference to such a significant detail, most people would assume that both the perpetrators and the victims were white, non-Muslims as are most people in Britain.

According to *Barnardo's* this project was aimed at educating 5 to 13 year old children:

> Girls and young women who already know the experience of being exploited have space to talk alone, in groups, in safety at the drop-ins and outside the building in other safe spaces... They can be immediately screened for sexual health services... in this young woman friendly environment.[21]

Sara Swann, who was the director of the *Streets and Lanes* project, points out that the victim of this sexual exploitation is normally ensnared by a 'boyfriend' (aged 18 to 25, but even as old as mid-40s) who showers her with gifts, collecting her in his car outside the school on an almost daily basis. He proceeds to make her dependent on him, perhaps changing her name, but proceeding to destroy her connections with other people. He ends up furthering his control of her, often by humiliation, threats and fear, all the while pretending that this is a loving relationship. The final stage is that he has total control when she becomes a 'willing victim': she will end up having sex for him, without even seeing any of the money herself. She will even lure others into the clutches of her controller and his network.[22] In a report from the local newspaper in 1998, *Barnardo's* staff talk about the *Streets and Lanes* project, and it looks remarkably like the Muslim grooming gang phenomenon.[23] We can find

---

21 'Case Study: *Barnardo's Street and Lanes* Multi-agency Service', 2004, http://www.doh.gov.uk/children/nsfcasestudies.nsf/5084709fa3844f c680256f-2c00339f59/28bdb53249f6fa2380256f6a003f240a?OpenDocument. This document has now disappeared from the internet.

22 Sara Swann, 'Helping girls involved in "prostitution": a Barnardos Experiment', pp. 278-282 of *Home Truths About Child Sexual Abuse: Policy and Practice, op. cit.* It is clear that, by the year 2000, Swann is describing something indistinguishable from the phenomenon which came to be known as "localised grooming", which CEOP claim was not identified until 2011.

23 'Scandal of child-sex on Bradford streets', *Telegraph & Argus*, 14 Jul 1998, http://www.thetelegraphandargus.co.uk/archive/1998/07/14/ 8075434.Scandal_of_child_sex_on_Bradford_streets/

no evidence from the mid 1990s where either Swann or *Barnardo's* refer publicly to the ethnicity of the men who groomed these schoolgirls in this, the first project dealing with the victims of the grooming gangs in Britain, a project located in the borough with the greatest concentration of Muslims in Britain.[24] Nevertheless, subsequent remarks by others who worked with *Barnardo's*, state that the men involved were 'overwhelmingly' Asian.[25]

3.5 1996 Rotherham

By the mid 1990s there was undeniable evidence available to police and child-care professionals that the grooming gangs were operating on a large scale. In a 2012 report, Andrew Norfolk had access to huge numbers of unpublished reports by police and social services, dating from 1996 onwards.

Norfolk says that in Rotherham in 1996:

[A] social services investigation uncovered concerns that girls were being coerced into "child prostitution" by a small group of men who regularly collected them from residential care homes. Two years later, 70 girls from the town were said to be involved. The findings led to a one-year, Home Office-funded research project on the "detection, investigation and prosecution of offenders involved in sexual exploitation in Rotherham."[26]

Children as young as 11 are enslaved in a squalid life of prostitution in Bradford - and the law is failing to protect them, a shocking report reveals today...Of 100 under-18-year-olds in touch with project workers last year, the average age was 14 and the youngest was 11. And this is just the tip of the iceberg, workers say. Teenagers are being exploited by older pimps who lock them up like animals in bedsits and deny them access to food or a toilet... Most of the youngsters are too scared to fight back against their violent pimps... *Barnardo's* is demanding a change in the law so that men who seek sex with children are prosecuted for the serious crime of unlawful sex...And they are warning parents to be aware of the risk to their children - as a third of the youngsters seen by the scheme are still living at home with their unwitting mums and dads.

24 'UK Muslim Demographics', *The Telegraph*, 4 Feb 2011, http://www.telegraph. co.uk/news/wikileaks-files/london-wikileaks/8304838/UK-Muslim-DEMOGRAPH-ICS-C-RE8-02527.html

25 Anna Hall, 'Hunt For Britain's Sex Gangs, C4', *Broadcast*, 2 May 2013, http://www. broadcastnow.co.uk/in-depth/hunt-for-britains-sex-gangs-c4/5054504.article

26 Andrew Norfolk, 'Police Files Reveal Vast Child Protection Scandal', *The Times*, 24

The Home Office report was apparently completed in 2001, but was never published. Muslim-operated taxi firms and takeaway food shops were a significant part of the grooming/pimping operation.[27] The pimps were collecting girls from 'outside schools, bus and train stations, [state-controlled] residential homes and homeless projects.'[28] Numerous multi-agency forums and meetings were held. Nothing significant came of this report, and it never received the media attention which it deserved.

In 1997 Risky Business, an out-reach project was set up in Rotherham (the sinister events around the treatment of this group only received public attention at the end of 2014).[29] So, around the same time that *Barnardo's* was setting up a project in Bradford, a similar project was being set up in Rotherham. The problem with grooming gangs were thus manifest in both towns by the early 1990s, sufficient to warrant setting up out-reach programs which the victims could contact. Yet the local populations of these towns were not made aware of what was going on in their towns. Moreover, that such sinister events should be happening simultaneously in towns in two different counties never became a national story. It took almost another decade for the concept of the grooming gangs to break into the national news agenda; and no sooner had the issue surfaced nationally, than a huge cover-up meant sure it did not surface again in the national news agenda until 2011.

Norfolk says that even while the Home Office report was being written, 'the headmaster of a Rotherham secondary school sent a letter to parents warning that some of his pupils were being used by adults for sex.'[30] So, police, social services, and schools knew about the grooming

Sep 2012, http://www.thetimes.co.uk/tto/news/uk/crime/article3547661.ece

27 As we see in later cases in other parts of the country, this is a common theme.

28 Andrew Norfolk, 'Police Files Reveal Vast Child Protection Scandal', *op. cit.*

29 See p. 7 of Alexis Jay, 'Independent Inquiry into Child Sexual Exploitation in Rotherham 1997 - 2013', http://www.rotherham.gov.uk/downloads/file/1407/independent_inquiry_cse_in_rotherham. Jay goes on to say (p. 31) that:

> Child sexual exploitation became the focus of attention in Rotherham in the late 1990s, when the Risky Business project was established. Several experienced workers told us that they had come across examples of child sexual exploitation from the early–mid 1990s onward, and there was awareness at that time that looked after children in local residential units were at risk of being targeted.

30 Andrew Norfolk, 'Police Files Reveal Vast Child Protection Scandal', *op. cit.* Even today when there is some media and political attention being paid to these grooming gangs, schools are sending home notices to parents, warning them that gangs of 'Asian

gangs' activities in the West Midlands, West Yorkshire and South York-shire, but still there was no national media or political attention being paid to what was going on. How were the innocent victims supposed to protect themselves from being ensnared by the well-rehearsed and sophisticated techniques of organised adults, when almost no-one was prepared to tell these schoolgirls or their parents how the gangs operat-ed? An extraordinary and sinister threat had appeared on the streets of England, but no strategic attempt was made to warn parents or school-girls in general.

3.6 1998 Sikh Awareness Society starts

One community did try to warn schoolgirls and parents about the threat posed by the grooming gangs: the Sikh community. In 1998 the Sikh Awareness Society was set up to educate Sikhs about the continu-ing activities of the Muslim grooming gangs. Clearly, the problem with the grooming gangs in the West Midlands had not gone away. Here is what the SAS website said in 2007[31]:

> The Sikh Awareness Society (SAS) was established in 1998 amongst growing concerns of the "grooming" of our youth.

> In Britain today Sikh youth are still actively targeted on the basis of their religion and history. This historically linked hate-crime causes much emotional distress to the families in-volved with the majority of these cases ending up in abuse...

> The SAS originally operated as a discreet, confidential ser-vice, providing counselling and support to the West Mid-lands Sikh community.

> Due to an increasing number of calls from distressed Sikh families; in April 2006 we decided to expand our services and go nationwide...

---

men' are sitting in cars outside the school gates. Sometimes the schools doing this are sending home letters to parents whose children are 11 years old or younger (see *Ap-pendix 4: Leeds School Warning* and *Appendix 5: Sheffield School Warning* below).

31 'About Sikh Awareness Society' This is from the Internet Archive copy of the SAS website of 2007. The earliest archived copy of the SAS website we can find is from that year. http://web.archive.org/web/20070707161016/http://www.sasorg.co.uk/about.html

We initially started out in "problem areas" i.e. towns/cities where we knew of serious hate-crime in the past.

We quickly came to realise it is a national problem and far more deep-rooted.

It is interesting to note that SAS started in the West Midlands, the area where Muslim grooming gangs were operating in 1988. What is also of note, is that by 2006, SAS were recognising that these gangs were operating at a national level (something that the rest of the country is only now realising). From other reports by SAS, it is clear that the Muslim grooming gangs were targeting girls as young as 12.[32]

It is to the shame of journalists, feminists, socialists and multiculturalists that from the late 1990s they did not amplify the message of Sikh Awareness Society. We have reason to believe that the children's charities and other agencies were aware of the extent and nature of the problem by the time that SAS was set up, but chose to remain publicly silent because of the discrepancy between the ethnicity of the perpetrators and the ethnicity of the victims.[33] If the media had picked up on the work of SAS in the late 1990s, then the entire debate on the grooming gangs would never have blamed 'Asians' in general. It would have been clear to all that the problem was fundamentally religious rather than racial.

---

32 http://www.youtube.com/watch?v=PRtWcyo-xj8

33 The director of a *Channel 4* television programme about the grooming gangs in Bradford later stated:

> In October 1996... I met Sara Swann, who ran Bradford's Barnardo's Streets and Lanes project. Barnardo's was interested in making a film to warn teenagers and educate parents ... the girls were white and living in multi-cultural Bradford and the perpetrators were Asian... everybody wanted to pretend it wasn't happening. All anyone seemed concerned about was the risk of a race riot if we mentioned it.

Anna Hall 'Hunt For Britain's Sex Gangs, C4' *Broadcast* 2 May 2013, http://www.broadcastnow.co.uk/in-depth/hunt-for-britains-sex-gangs-c4/5054504.article

Since child-care professionals were privately informing journalists like Anna Hall of this problem, we cannot believe that they were not discussing it with other journalists, government agencies, academics, political activists, etc. See section 5.9 *Barnardo's* and section 3.13 *2008 My Dangerous Loverboy*.

3.7 2001 Derby and 'Real Caliphate'

Sikhs were also involved when violence erupted at a school in Derby in 2001. This violence occurred because of the existence of a document where devout Muslim fundamentalists appeared to be encouraging young Muslims to seduce Sikh and Hindu girls into Islam.[34] Thus, according to a report in *The Telegraph* at the time:

> A Muslim group calling itself Real Khilafa [sic] has been trying to whip up trouble by distributing a letter encouraging young Muslims to take out Sikh girls to get them drunk and convert them to Islam. The letter has incensed the considerable Sikh community and the police have been present at meetings called by community leaders.[35]

The letter claims that the Koran authorises Muslims to use violence or deceit in order to convert or subjugate 'kafirs'.[36] The idea that devout, pro-Caliphate Muslims could be systematically trying to seduce non-Muslim girls must have seemed incredible back in 2001. Yet by 2014, the news media was running many stories about the pro-Caliphate jihadis of Iraq, Syria and Nigeria using the Koran to justify themselves taking women and schoolgirls as sex-slaves. In this light, such documents from 2001 take on an ominous significance.

3.8 2003 Bradford/Keighley

After all these supposedly unrelated, local reports indicating grooming activity in Wolverhampton, Rotherham and Derby, the prob-

---

34 *Appendix 6: 'Real Khilafah - Letter to Moslem Youth'* contains a facsimile copy of what is claimed to be the letter distributed by a devout Muslim organisation, encouraging Muslim men to deceive and seduce non-Muslim girls. We have found a transcript of this letter from a Pakistani internet forum from 2 Nov 2001, which does at least establish that the copy we have included in the Appendices was known about in 2001: http://groups.yahoo.com/group/PakistanForum/message/24491. The copy of the letter found on that Pakistani forum is dated '13 April 2001.' The letter is also mentioned on a Sikh website in 2001: http://fateh.sikhnet.com//sikhnet/discussion.nsf/By+Topic/9a6a5f28a8d544ff87256af8006e9709?Open.

35 Nick Britten, 'Children Injured in School Rampage', *The Telegraph*, 17 Oct 2001, http://www.telegraph.co.uk/news/uknews/1359683/Children-injured-in-school-rampage.html

36 In Islam 'kafir' is an abusive Arabic term for Sikhs, Christians, Hindus, Buddhists etc.

lem in Bradford finally appeared on the national news agenda. How the phenomenon of the grooming gangs was treated in the coverage of Bradford at this time was eventually to shape the reporting of the problem for almost 10 years.

On 22 August 2003, *Channel 4 News* announced that they had 'uncovered details of an 18 month police and social services investigation into allegations that young men are targeting under-age girls for sex, drugs and prostitution in the West Yorkshire town of Keighley.'[37] In that story, the Labour MP for Keighley at the time, Ann Cryer is quoted as saying 'I believe there is a very strong cultural reason, it's nothing to do with the religion lets [sic] make it quite clear, its [sic] to do with the Asian culture, which wants these young men to marry these very young girls from their village...'[38] Cryer said that it is because they do not want arranged marriages with 'very young girls from their village' in Pakistan that Muslim men 'look for very young girls through this organised sex ring that we are seeing in Keighley.' She does not explain what part of 'Asian culture' would lead the parents to want their sons to marry 'very young girls' from Pakistan, nor why this should lead to 'organised' rings of men who seek to exploit 'very young' non-Muslim girls near Bradford, and get them addicted to drugs and alcohol and then turn them into prostitutes. Ann Cryer's explanation left it up to the population of Britain to assume that Hindu, Sikh and Buddhist men were also doing this, as these activities were supposedly part of 'Asian culture'[39] rather than men from one specific religious group.

A few days after that story appeared, the local newspaper reported that Ann Cryer:

> called on members of the town's Asian community to work together against alleged criminal activity involving some young men in the area. Police and social services have launched an inquiry after parents reported concerns about the welfare of their daughters in the town.[40]

---

37 'Asian Rape Allegations', *Channel 4 News*, 27 Aug 2003, (from archive.org) http://web.archive.org/web/20100620042427/http://www.channel 4.com/news/articles/society/law_order/Asian+rape+allegations/256893

38 *Ibid.*

39 *Ibid.*

40 'MP's appeal after abuse allegations', *Telegraph & Argus*, 26 Aug 2003, http://www.thetelegraphandargus.co.uk/archive/2003/08/26/ 8010529.MP_s_appeal_after_abuse_allegations/

Ann Cryer is reported as saying 'My hope is that this adverse publicity will embarrass these young men into more appropriate behaviour.' A decade later, and after thousands and thousands of ruined lives, we know that this was a vain hope.

Even though no Muslims are named in this news report, it is interesting how much care is taken not to offend the community which was protecting the grooming gangs. Note how the above quotation from the local newspaper 'alleges' that these crimes have taken place, and how the parents 'concerns' are merely 'reported'. The article went on to say: 'It is claimed more than 30 white girls, some said to be as young as 11 or 12, have been raped, abused and prostituted by Asian men in their late teens and twenties over the last 18 months.'[41] These are incredibly serious crimes, yet the local newspaper talks about it as if the claims came from nowhere, and have no substance, possibly casual calumny. Yet only a few days earlier, *Channel 4* had said that they had details of an investigation by police and social services that had lasted almost 2 years! Would the police and social services spend so much time investigating this, if there was no evidence for it? In a town which had seen extraordinary 'race riots' by Muslims 2 years earlier, would *Channel 4* have risked reporting on the grooming gangs if the evidence looked dubious or insubstantial? And if this investigation into such serious criminality had been going on for 18 months in Bradford, shouldn't the local newspaper and the local Member of Parliament have known something about it before the story was broken by a national television company? In hindsight, given the then recent riots by Muslims, it seems that *Channel 4* showed great courage in exposing the grooming gangs in Bradford in 2003.

Once the media and politicians had turned their attention to these grooming gangs in 2012, the public learned some more about the events in Bradford around 2003. While the Parliamentary investigation was underway in 2012, Cryer is quoted as having said that in 2003 'she was approached by about six mothers who said their daughters were being groomed for sex by Pakistani men.'[42] In that later report it says that back in 2003, 'Ann Cryer had tried to intercede with the community by asking a councillor to speak to Muslim elders, but the Muslim elders had said it was not their affair.' But the above quotations from contemporaneous reports of what Cryer actually said in 2003 show that in claiming that it was to do with 'Asian culture' rather than religion, she had led

41 *Ibid.*

42 'Muslim gang "white rape" claim prompts row', *BBC News*, 13 Nov 2012, http://news.bbc.co.uk/1/hi/uk_politics/2102470.stm

the public to believe the problems were nothing to do with Islam. Since Islam comes from Arabia rather than Asia, and since Asia has many religions and cultures other than those of Muslims, the public was led to believe that what was happening in Bradford involved criminal grooming gangs from many different religions. But Cryer was talking to Muslim leaders in order to get the grooming gangs to stop; there was apparently no need for her to talk to Hindu or Sikh leaders to get their youths to stop grooming young white girls. Thus, even at the time, Cryer should have been able to perceive the difference between Muslim culture and Asian culture.

We are aware of no evidence showing that Ann Cryer spoke out about the activities of the grooming gangs before August 22 2003, when *Channel 4 News* disclosed the existence of the 18-month investigation into the grooming gangs by Bradford Council and West Yorkshire Police. Surely as the MP in that region she should have known about such a major investigation into the activities of the grooming gangs? Perhaps she had known about this investigation, but had chosen to remain silent, as the previous year she came under criticism from Left-wing Muslims for 'damaging race relations' when she stated that, 'Asian gangs' in her constituency were out of control.[43] Reflecting on these events now, it seems likely that the 'Asian' gangs who were out of control were probably also connected to the grooming activities (although any explicit connection may not have been known to Ann Cryer at the time).

3.9 2004 *Edge of the City*

Throughout 2003, *Channel 4* had been making a documentary in the *Dispatches* series which dealt with the Muslim grooming gangs in the Bradford area. The item that appeared on *Channel 4 News* in the above section probably came about because of the research that had gone into this *Dispatches* documentary. But in 2004 the entire documentary was withdrawn from broadcast, simply because part of the documentary reiterated the claim that Muslims were grooming white children for sex.[44] Pressure was brought to bear on *Channel 4* by the West Yorkshire Police and by Left-wing and black activist groups.

---

43 "Asian Gangs" out of Control', *BBC News*, 6 Jul 2002, http://news.bbc.co.uk/1/hi/uk_politics/2102470.stm

44 The documentary has gone down in history as having 'been banned' and just after it was withdrawn from the schedule, even Muslim barristers were heard in interviews talking about it having 'been banned'.

Anna Hall, who made the documentary for *Channel 4* was living in Leeds at that time and had received information by the director of *Barnardo's Streets and Lanes* project, which we have seen was a project which *Barnardo's* had been running in Bradford since 1995.[45] The full documentary about Bradford social services focused on a range of work done by the Council, and just a quarter of the documentary was about the grooming gangs. However, before the documentary could be shown in May 2004, *Channel 4* conceded to censorship at the instigation of Colin Cramphorn, the Chief Constable of West Yorkshire Police. According to Anna Hall, 'it was three weeks before local elections and he feared riots.'[46] It was only 3 weeks before elections for local councillors and it was only 3 years after Muslims had rioted in 'race riots' in Bradford and Oldham, so the threat of them rioting again was very potent: 'The fires that burned across Lancashire and Yorkshire through the summer of 2001 signalled the rage of young Pakistanis and Bangladeshis of the

---

45 See: Anna Hall, 'Hunt For Britain's Sex Gangs, C4' *op. cit.*

    In October 1996... I met Sara Swann, who ran Bradford's *Barnardo's Streets and Lanes* project. *Barnardo's* was interested in making a film to warn teenagers and educate parents about a pattern of child sexual exploitation that Sara had been following for a year... men were targeting girls aged 11 and up, giving them phones, taking them out and showering them with attention and affection. After they had sex, the men would introduce their friends to the girls, who would be asked to sleep with the new group of men.

    Police seemed powerless to stop it because the girls thought these men were their boyfriends. However controlled and degraded they felt, they were also very frightened. The explosive thing: the girls were white and living in multi-cultural Bradford and the perpetrators were Asian...

    I tried to get a film off the ground at *Channel 4*, but other commitments left it on the back burner... What was unbelievable was that men were gang-raping young girls and everybody wanted to pretend it wasn't happening. All anyone seemed concerned about was the risk of a race riot if we mentioned it.

    After nearly two years, I made a 90- minute doc, *Edge Of The City*. We dared to describe the Bradford perpetrators as 'overwhelmingly Asian.' The film was scheduled to go out in May 2004, three weeks before the local elections in Bradford, where 10 BNP candidates were standing three years after Asian 'youths' were indicted in a 'race riot'.

    After the council viewed it, West Yorkshire's chief constable asked for the film to be postponed amid fears of more riots. All hell broke loose. The BNP got hold of the story and used the film as propaganda. Police and social services said nothing. Several small voices in the Asian press said that if the story were true, it shouldn't be swept under the carpet....

46 Maggie Brown, 'The Woman on a Mission to Expose Sexual Abuse', *The Guardian*, 21 May 2013, http://www.theguardian.com/lifeandstyle/ 2013/may/21/woman-expose-sexual-abuse-telford

second and third generation...'[47]

If ever there was an issue that cried out for local parliamentarians to address,[48] and to use their powers to hold the police and child-care services to account, it is surely over the issue of the rape and prostitution of schoolgirls. Instead of allowing for the democratic process to hold people to account, a national broadcaster crumpled to pressure from someone who should himself have been facing investigation for the failure of his organisation. The charge of 'racism' and the threat of violence from Muslims over the revelations concerning the grooming gangs (who had already been operating in Bradford for 15 years before this documentary was made) led *Channel 4* to censor itself. *Channel 4's* self-censorship when faced with allegations of racism and potential 'race riots' inaugurated years of media concealment concerning this grooming gang phenomenon. In their wildest dreams, most criminals could not envisage an alliance of sociologists, politicians, police officers and religious fundamentalists helping to cover up the gangs' criminality.

Leading up to eventual broadcast of *Edge of the City* once the elections were over, pressure groups again attempted to get the documentary permanently banned, with a letter-writing campaign to the Labour government ministers.[49] Three months after it was originally scheduled to be broadcast, the *Edge of the City* documentary was finally shown, albeit in an abnormally late night slot for such a documentary. Even so, it was watched by almost 2 million people. But as the director of the documentary recently noted, it brought about no change.[50] It is possible that if *Channel 4* had aired the programme in May 2004, then candidates may have been elected to the local council who would have campaigned on this issue and if elected, those representatives would then have had a democratic mandate to try to stop this abuse. It seems clear that, as a matter of law as well as common sense, the possibility of a violent reaction to a lawful inquiry into so serious a matter should not have been considered a good reason to withdraw or postpone the documentary.

Around the time of the broadcast in August 2004, West Yorkshire

---

47 Arun Kundnani, 'From Oldham to Bradford: the Violence of the Violated', 1 Oct 2001, http://www.irr.org.uk/news/from-oldham-to-bradford-the-violence-of-the-violated/

48 At this point, as far as most of the people of Britain were concerned, this problem was entirely local to Bradford.

49 'Campaign to Stop Race Documentary', *BBC News*, 17 Aug 2004, http://news.bbc.co.uk/1/hi/entertainment/3572776.stm

50 Maggie Brown "The Woman on a Mission to Expose Sexual Abuse", *op. cit.*

Police and Bradford Council said they:

> had spent the past two years investigating the allegations, but found "no evidence of systematic exploitation"...it is important to note that some of this programme was filmed nearly two years ago and things have moved on since.[51]

These easy denials in 2004 have been reversed. In Bradford, in the first 6 months of 2013 alone, 'the tally of suspected predators now stood at 90 arrests'.[52]

3.10 2005 *Radio 5* programme

On 18 December 2005, *BBC Radio 5 Live* also broadcast a programme about the grooming gangs. The programme apparently covered material that was consistent with the *Channel 4* documentary. When the Left-wing Asian activist Sunny Hundal commented on this *Radio 5* programme, he said that this programme did not simply repeat the claims from the *Edge of the City* documentary.

> The report looked at the way in which "these children are 'groomed' into believing that these 'pimps' are in fact their boyfriends." It also asks why "so many of the men implicated in these crimes are British Pakistanis"...It covered the same area (and slightly more) as the *C4* doc [sic].[53]

But Hundal also pointed out that by 2005 West Yorkshire Police had, 'without explanation', now shut down the special unit they had set up to investigate these type of crimes.[54]

We can clearly see the detrimental effect of the campaign by the racism groups and the Left to stop the Muslim grooming gangs becoming an electoral issue in Bradford in 2004. Once the *Channel 4* documentary was withdrawn and stigmatized as 'racist', the local council and the police force jointly denied there was a problem. They claimed that

---

51 "Campaign to Stop Race Documentary", *BBC News, op. cit.*

52 "'We'll tackle the sexual predators'", *Telegraph & Argus*, 11 May 2013, http://www.thetelegraphandargus.co.uk/news/10413534. We ll_tackle_the_sexual_predators/

53 'The Case of Pakistani Men "Grooming" Young White Girls - Part 2', *Asians In Media*, 19 Sep 2005, http://www.Asiansinmedia.org/news/article.php/radio/1109

54 *Ibid.*

the information in that documentary was two years old, suggesting that the problem had been resolved, when there is every reason to believe it was getting worse.[55] Then, when the hue and cry had died down, the police quietly closed the unit which was investigating these crimes! This provides a very good explanation as to why, despite the controversy in 2003 and 2004, there were no convictions in Bradford between 2005 and 2013. If the police had not closed down this special unit, who knows how many perpetrators they would have found in the subsequent years, who knows how many hundreds of schoolgirls could have been saved from a life of sex slavery.

Hundal described the situation as 'political correctness gone mad.' Hundal went on to point out that even the 'useless' local community leaders say the police are 'too politically correct and unwilling to disturb racial and religious sensibilities.'[56]

> What it [the Radio 5 programme] should have said was - "A year after C4 uncovered abuse by Pakistani men of young white girls, nothing seems to have changed. The abuse is carrying on, the police is [sic] powerless and has done little, and neither have the so-called community leaders." That would brought [sic] focus to why the police is [sic] failing the local community in tackling these youths.[57]

It might appear to the reader that the socialist Sunny Hundal was an exception, someone with the clarity and courage to point out that there should be some sociological or ideological investigation as to why so many of the men who were involved in grooming these schoolgirls were Muslims. *Au contraire*: Sunny Hundal insists in this piece that it is irrele-

---

55 In the middle of 2013, 45 men in West Yorkshire were arrested, with all the indications being that many of these men were 'Asian.' Suzannah Hills, 'UK's biggest child sex gang uncovered as 45 men are arrested over abuse of girls as young as 13', *Daily Mail*, 18 Aug 2013, http://www.dailymail.co.uk/news/article-2396486/UKs-biggest-child-sex-gang-uncovered-45-men-arrested-abuse-girls-young-13.html. Subsequently 15 Muslim men in Keighley (ages ranging between 17 to 62 years of age) were charged with various offences, including rape of a child. http://m.thetelegraphandargus.co.uk/news/13770142.Fifteen_defendants_appear_in_court_today_accused_of_child_sex_offences/ The charges pertain to offences between 2011 and 2012.

As *Appendix 1* shows, in 2015 another 9 men were convicted of grooming offences in Leeds. There's no indication that the men responsible for the grooming offences in that area between 1991 and 2004 have been identified and punished.

56 'The Case of Pakistani Men "Grooming" Young White Girls - Part 2', *op. cit.*

57 *Ibid.*

vant that the grooming gangs were almost entirely Muslims. He inveighs against political correctness gone mad, yet will not consider that there might be some connection between Muslim culture and this unusual form of criminality: 'I was frequently asked if this was a widespread problem, implying whether Muslim (or Asian) men picked on young white girls for cultural reasons. That is of course rubbish, and these are simply criminals...'[58]

3.11 2005 Luton and 'Real Caliphate'

Whilst journalists and commentators refused to talk about the religion of the grooming gangs, in 2005 Clive Gresswell wrote an article in a Luton newspaper, apparently quoting from a letter which it was alleged a devout Islamic organisation was distributing to Muslim men, encouraging them to seduce non-Muslim women, using intoxication as part of the process.[59] After the controversy in Bradford in 2003 and 2004, this story should have resonated loudly across the country. But it was never picked up by the national media. As we have seen above, Sikhs were embroiled in violence in Derby in 2001, following claims that Real Khilafah there had been instructing Muslims to groom non-Muslim girls.[60] In the light of these many incidents where Sikhs were warning about the grooming gangs, it is astonishing that in 2005 the national media should ignore claims that Islamic organisations in England were allegedly running campaigns to encourage such grooming activities.

It defies belief that the national media and 'anti-racist' activists could ignore these events in Luton, when just one year earlier they denounced the 'racism' of those who pointed out that it was 'Asians' grooming white schoolgirls in Bradford and Keighley. Here were reports indicating as clearly as possible that race was not the issue: here was evidence that Muslims were being given religious-ideological justification for sexually seducing non-Muslim girls, as part of a supremacist Islamic project. But from 2004 onwards, where Muslim grooming activities were concerned, the vast majority of journalists, child-care profes-

---

58 *Ibid.*

59 See *Appendix 6: Real Khilafah - Letter to Moslem Youth* for a facsimile copy of the letter from Real Khilafah, and *Appendix 7: Luton Article on Real Khilafah* for a facsimile copy of the article by Clive Gresswell.

60 We have found no evidence to suggest the organisation reported in this 2005 incident in Luton is a different organisation to that mentioned in the incidents in Derby in 2001.

sionals and political activists seem to have adopted a policy of 'see no evil, hear no evil'. The pressure groups had succeeded in their attempt to ensure that no-one would dare speak out about these gangs prostituting vulnerable schoolgirls.

By this time, more Sikh organisations were also making the astonishing claim, that as far back as the early 1990s, other fundamentalist Islamic groups were advocating that Muslim men in Britain should deceive non-Muslims girls and seduce them into Islam.[61] The Sikh websites claimed that these devout Islamic organisations were telling Muslim men to target vulnerable girls (plain or ugly girls, who would be unaccustomed to attention), deceiving them into thinking that the Muslim man was genuinely interested in a relationship and possibly even marriage. The claim was that devout Muslims were instructed to 'be ambiguous about their own backgrounds by for example only describing themselves as Asian,' in order to have greater success with this deception.[62] Perhaps when Sikhs drew the attention of multiculturalists, feminists, or Left-wing activists to this in 2004, these activists could dismiss the claims as being beyond belief: certainly such mendacity and cunning does not accord with what those brought up as Christians would expect from religious people. Nevertheless, by this point there had been multiple reports that fundamentalist Islamic organisations were encouraging behaviour similar to that of the grooming gangs.

3.12 2007 Julie Bindel: a lone voice

In 2007 Julie Bindel was a voice in the wilderness.[63] Bindel drew attention to the fact that the police were doing nothing about the grooming gangs in Yorkshire and Lancashire. Bindel focussed on how the mothers of the victims had taken it upon themselves to gather names and addresses, car registration details, and even photographs of the perpetrators. She quotes one of the mothers saying the police had told her they would not arrest Pakistani men for sexual offences, because it would start 'a race riot' (*i.e.* the Pakistanis would riot).[64] We saw earlier that in 1988 Sikhs made similar claims about supplying intelligence to

---

61 http://www.whyichoseSikhism.com/?p=know&s=10secrets

62 This ambiguity - blurring the distinction between 'Muslims' and 'Asians' - has been continued by the police, media and social services themselves, right up until 2013.

63 Julie Bindel, 'Mothers of Prevention', *op. cit.*

64 *Ibid.*

the police relating to the activities of the grooming gangs. Once again, the law enforcement agencies were apparently refusing to apply the law to Muslims, for fear that they would riot. As we have seen, in 2004 the *Channel 4* documentary about Bradford was also blocked by claims that Muslims would riot if it was shown.

What steps did the police take to stop this lucrative business, a business based on providing schoolgirls to be raped? They sent letters to 70 men who were 'spending an unusual amount of time with young girls', requiring them to sign the letter to indicate that the men knew the girls were beneath the age of consent.[65] Bindel points out that the parents were so angry with the pathetic response by the police, that they were instructing lawyers to seek redress. 'This could result in the biggest civil action ever brought against police for failing to protect children from sexual predators', wrote Bindel.[66] We can find no further record that such legal action took place. We do not know if the case was simply dropped, or if the police settled out of court (in which case a confidentiality clause may well have been incorporated into the settlement agreement).

Since police were so brazenly refusing to enforce the law in order to protect these schoolgirls, what other avenues were open to concerned organisations to stop the grooming activities? We have seen from the events in Bradford in 2003 and 2004, that the Muslim community would not do anything to stop the gangs. Thus, at this stage, the only option left was to educate the schoolgirls about how the grooming gangs work, so that the schoolgirls could possibly protect themselves from being victimised, when everyone else had failed them.

3.13 2008 *My Dangerous Loverboy*

In September 2010, the Serious Organised Crime Agency announced the launch of:

> a film designed to protect children and young people who might be vulnerable to sexual exploitation is launched today. *My Dangerous Loverboy* tells the story of a young girl who is groomed and sexually exploited by an older man before being trafficked around the UK between groups of men. The film is aimed at professionals - including front line police

65 *Ibid.*
66 *Ibid.*

officers, child support workers, and teachers - who are in a position to spot warning signs and to help prevent this kind of exploitation taking place.[67]

This announcement by SOCA is not the success it appears. By any measure, this project has been a failure.[68] The film was first mooted in 2008, and was to be shown to the schoolgirls themselves. But by 2010, we see that SOCA is talking about the film being targeted at teachers, police officers, and social workers. After decades which showed that the police would not protect the victims, the schoolgirls were not even to be provided with the educational materials so that they could protect themselves. To this day, there is no evidence that the film has ever been shown to schoolgirls across England.[69]

The first version of the film was ready by July 2008, but a scene showing drug-taking was removed. The final version was handed over to the UK Human Trafficking Centre (UKHTC) in February 2009. At this point, the film was shown to selected schoolgirls, but was never subsequently shown to the potential victims. Trial screenings took place in a number of Sheffield secondary schools to widespread praise, but viewings have subsequently been restricted to professionals working in the field of child sexual exploitation.

It is understood that the centre, part of the Serious Organ-

---

67 '*My Dangerous Loverboy* film launched to combat child sexual exploitation', 21 Sep 2010, http://www.soca.gov.uk/news/276-my-dangerous-loverboy-film-launched-to-combat-child-sexual-exploitation

68 The website associated with *My Dangerous Loverboy* appears to have come into existence on 24 Jan 2011 (that is the earliest copy of the site to be found in the Internet Archive http://web.archive.org/web/20110124230909/http://www.mydangerousloverboy.com/). Moreover, it appears that this website and the availability of this version of the film is a cut-down version of the original film. See 'Shock at Teesside child trafficking discovery', *Gazette Live*, 12 Feb 2011, http://www. gazettelive.co.uk/news/local-news/shock-teesside-child-trafficking-discovery-3682920. One of the producers, David Grant,

> now believes more needs to be done to get the film into schools and youth centres. He added: "Part of the problem is that in many cases the victims have no idea they have been exploited. We need to educate, and use education, to make young people aware that this is a very real threat." [...] Now, the team behind the project are using social networking and the internet to increase awareness of the issue. Grant added: "A shorter, pop-video-type version of the film is available on our website and we want it to be promoted on twitter and facebook as much as possible."

69 Andrew Norfolk, 'Anger as educational film on grooming withheld', *The Times*, 21 Jan 2011, http://www.thetimes.co.uk/tto/news/uk/article2883087.ece

ised Crime Agency, now hopes to have the film ready to be shown in schools next year.[70]

What is clear from the synopsis of the film, is that by 2008 UKHTC and SOCA were fully aware of the nature of the grooming gang phenomenon: 'The 20-minute drama... examines the relationship between a young white girl and an Asian man who initially poses as her boyfriend before luring her into a world of parties, alcohol and drugs, then sells her to be used for sex by several older men.'[71] The title of the film was taken from the euphemistic concept the Dutch use to describe their country's problem with Muslim grooming gangs.[72] There are 3 significant facets to this:

1. Schools in the Netherlands do at least provide some training to schoolgirls so they can learn how to identify the grooming gangs' activities, and thus schoolgirls can perhaps protect themselves from being entrapped by the gangs:

> Anita visits schools to warn girls exactly what a lover boy looks like, and makes no bones of the fact that most of the gangs are operated by Dutch-born Moroccan and Turkish men. "I am not politically correct. I am not afraid of being called a racist, which would be untrue. I tell the girls that lover boys are young, dark-skinned and very good looking. They will have lots of money and bling as well as a big car. They will give out cigarettes and vodka."[73]

The situation in the Netherlands is clearly less toxic than in Britain, since the schoolgirls are given some warning and instructions (however euphemistic the concept of 'loverboy' might be). It would be better still if parents and society as a whole were given this information, so that

---

70 *Ibid.*

71 *Ibid.* We can infer from this that before 2008 UKHTC were aware of the specific characteristics of the Muslim grooming gangs. The Sikh Awareness Society have posted *My Dangerous Loverboy* on YouTube. They have added captions to strengthen the message, as the video is far too subtle and ambiguous considering the seriousness of the problem. http://www.youtube.com/watch?v=Kjwvo8HlqyM

72 See Chapter 1, section *1.5 International Dimensions* for an overview of the Dutch problem with grooming gangs.

73 Sue Reid 'A Feminist Revolution that Cruelly Backfired', *The Daily Mail*, 23 Nov 2012, http://www.dailymail.co.uk/news/article-2237170/Why-Amsterdams-legal-brothels-lesson-Britain-telling-truth-sex-gangs-race.html

others could keep a watchful eye out for signs that a schoolgirl is being groomed for prostitution.

2. The fact that the British institutions are using the same euphemistic concept employed by the Dutch indicates the child-care professionals and national agencies in Britain know that the problem is not unique to Britain, and these organisations know that in the Netherlands the perpetrators are not Pakistani Muslims but mainly Moroccan and Turkish Muslims. This shows the lie to all the reporting that this is 'Asian gangs' and that the cause of it is 'Asian culture'.

3. Since the Serious Organised Crime Agency (the agency in control of UKHTC) were cognisant of the similarity of the religious characteristics and the modus operendi of the gangs in Britain and Holland, we must ask: why is this not considered to be 'serious organised crime'?[74] Organised criminal behaviour, replicated in a country neighbouring Britain, surely falls within the remit of SOCA: many of the reports on the grooming gangs in Britain point out that the gangs are not only involved in grooming, rape and pimping, but they are also connected with drug-dealing. One is left wondering, just what constitutes 'serious crime' for SOCA? These gangs could be making millions of pounds every year, and there is no indication that any police force is trying to break them up by tracking their finances.

After the first online edition of *Easy Meat* was published, the National Crime Agency (previously known as SOCA) stated:

> The film was on the UKHTC website, sent to every police force and to child protection agencies.

But the NCA admitted the film was never made compulsory for schools and was only ever shown in a handful of classrooms.[75]

According to *The Daily Mirror,* the film was 'suppressed' because of political correctness. Nothing short of a policy of concealment can explain how this film was financed and then allowed to lie unused and forgotten, since it was distributed to all the child protection agencies and to every police force. Who is going to answer for this tragic failure to protect the lives and well-being of tens of thousands of innocent school-

---

74 We will argue later that the pimping activities and other criminal activities of these gangs appear to generate huge amounts of money for the gangs.

75 'Film about grooming gangs suppressed for SEVEN years amid fears it would be branded racist', *The Daily Mirror*, 20 Sept 2014, http://www.mirror.co.uk/news/uk-news/film-grooming-gangs-suppressed-seven-4295910

girls? It's not as though the film showed the unvarnished truth about the grooming gangs, since it barely hints at the tender years of many of the victims, nor does it point the finger squarely at Muslim gangs. But clearly nothing at all was allowed to be said in public discourse about the existence of 'the biggest child protection scandal of our time.'[76]

3.14 2008 *BBC Panorama*: Teenage Sex For Sale

On 27 March 2008, *Panorama* produced a documentary for *BBC TV*, which dealt with the Muslim grooming gangs. All the features that were to be recognised by Parliament in 2013, are to be found in this documentary. However, we can see from the way in which the documentary was summarised and reviewed at the time (and indeed, from the way the documentary was edited), that every effort was being made to ignore the elephant in the room: the gangs in the documentary were Muslim men, and the victims were white girls. For instance, the *BBC*'s own review of the programme does not once mention that the gangs are 'Asian' or 'Muslim', nor does it mention that the schoolgirls being targeted are overwhelmingly white.[77] Nevertheless, this documentary was a significant milestone: unlike the *Edge of the City* documentary, it was not forced into being withdrawn. And unlike the *Edge of the City* documentary, where the grooming gangs were only part of a bigger story; *Panorama* devoted an entire programme to the subject. By making sure that only the most tangential reference was made to 'Asians' in the context of this documentary, it appears that *Panorama* was able to circumvent the pressure heaped on *Channel 4*.

The *Panorama* documentary follows a small, dedicated Lancashire Police unit round Burnley. Significantly, almost no mention is made of the contrast between the ethnicity of the perpetrators and the victims, and where there is the opportunity to draw attention to this, circumlocution is instead used within the narrative.[78] It is not until one-third

76 Andrew Norfolk, 'Police Files Reveal Vast Child Protection Scandal', *The Times*, 24 Sep 2012 http://www.thetimes.co.uk/tto/news/uk/crime/article3547661.ece.

77 See *Panorama*'s own summaries of the programme here http://news.bbc.co.uk/1/hi/programmes/panorama/7302713.stm and here http://news.bbc.co.uk/1/hi/programmes/panorama/7314696.stm

78 'Authorities are already alert to the danger posed by individual paedophiles. But now they are concerned that evidence from some local communities points to an even more sinister threat: organised sexual exploitation of children by ruthless criminal gangs.' http://www.youtube.com/watch?feature= player_detailpage&v=zpD-foDsZU_M&t=324. It seems clear that 'local communities' is some kind of code.

of the way through the documentary, that a throwaway remark from a police officer indicates that there is any significance to the ethnicity of the perpetrators and the victims: 'Within a minute she's changed her story, from waiting for her Dad to waiting for her boyfriend, in an Asian area [...] Police are suspicious - they have intelligence of an Asian man using this name, has been grooming girls.'[79] It is only then, in retrospect, that one remembers that the men shown earlier, convicted for having sex with teenage girls over a prolonged period, were both Asian, and that this might be the theme of this documentary.[80] Thus both the documentary (and the material discussing the documentary) have gone out of their way not to address this contrast in ethnicity.

Mohammed Shafiq is interviewed in this documentary, and in the following years he was to be almost the only Muslim spokesman in Britain to speak out about the gangs. Since the programme again avoids the issue that the gangs are composed almost entirely of 'Asian' (*i.e.* Muslim) men, that they are interviewing a Muslim about this, and that he is pointing out that it is white girls who the gangs are after, this suggests that it is indeed the same phenomenon which CEOP claim to have first 'uncovered' in 2011, and which they named 'localised grooming'. Later on in the documentary, Mohammed Shafiq states that the police are being too cautious in pursuing these criminals because they fear being accused of racism,[81] showing once again how political correctness hinders the police and facilitates the grooming gangs.

The implicit subject of the documentary is that gangs of Muslim men are systematically grooming and pimping young white girls. The money being made from these activities seems considerable. Mohammed Shafiq says that having seen a drop in their income from drug-related crime, the gangs are supplementing their income by prostituting young white girls, where £200 to £300 is charged for the girl.[82] Prof. Barrett, from Bedfordshire University is interviewed,[83] and says he has no doubt that the grooming of the schoolgirls is orchestrated, and that

---

79 http://www.youtube.com/watch?v=zpDfoDsZU_M&t=206

80 At the point where the photographs of the convicted criminals was shown, no mention is made of them being Asian or Muslim, and no mention is made of the ethnicity of the victims. http://www.youtube.com/watch?v=4m55ZCSWQ2M&t=351

81 http://www.youtube.com/watch?v=RFIfcTqBsZc&t=1634

82 http://www.youtube.com/watch?feature=player_detailpage&v=zpD-foDsZU_M&t=345

83 http://www.youtube.com/watch?feature=player_detailpage&v=zpD-foDsZU_M&t=432

the younger the 'woman' the higher the price. He says that he thinks the gangs are earning 'significantly more' than 'tens of thousands of pounds' per schoolgirl each year. The girls describe how they were prostituted on an industrial scale, comparing what happened to them as being made to have sex with a new customer as soon as the previous one had left, being on a metaphorical 'conveyor belt'.[84] When asked if she was paid for any of this, the girl interviewee replied that she wasn't. She also made it clear that if she hadn't done what was required, she would have been imprisoned until she complied. These two factors indicate that this is far more like sex slavery than it is like prostitution. Once again, there were implications here which the documentary could have pursued, but it did not.

The *Panorama* programme states that, at a national level police have concentrated on prosecuting those who traffic young women into the UK for sex, and on internet grooming and pornography; but that the police agencies have ignored British girls being trafficked internally, and ignored the real-world grooming in preference for concentrating on online grooming.[85] A representative from CROP is interviewed in the *Panorama* documentary, and she makes it clear that whenever the problem arises in an area it is treated as a short-term and purely local problem. And once an individual, local case appears to have been resolved,[86] resources are taken away and the problem is then ignored.[87] Detective Whelan states in the documentary, that information is the vital resource needed by the police in order to bring prosecutions.[88] Thus

---

84 http://www.youtube.com/watch?feature=player_detailpage&v=zpD-foDsZU_M&t=377

85 http://www.youtube.com/watch?feature=player_detailpage&v=zpD-foDsZU_M&t=510 They appear to be referring to CEOP.

86 By 'resolved' this almost certainly does not mean the gang has been convicted, since at this time (2008), there had been no more than 14 convictions in 11 years. In the Bradford scandal of 2003, it was reported that 30 white girls had been groomed and raped, over an 18 month period, in that one town. See section 3.8 *2003 Bradford/Keighley*.

87 'This problem is seemingly not taken seriously and not understood, because if it was understood people in authority would realise... it needs long-term investment... these men are in it for the long-run.' Sarah Lloyd, CROP, '*Panorama*: Teenage Sex for Sale', BBC, http://www.youtube.com/watch?v=_VdoT12Fwgw&t=77. This was also observed by Sunny Hundal, in connection with the controversy in Bradford in 2004, see section 3.10 *2005 Radio 5 programme*.

88 http://www.youtube.com/watch?feature=player_detail-page&v=RFIfcTqBsZc&t=1543. It should be obvious that such information needs to be collated and disseminated by a national police agency for the benefit of other forces and agencies, which once again highlights the failings of SOCA and CEOP.

by 2008 it is clear that a sustained national strategy is needed. Yet twenty years since the first stories started to appear in the news media, the only token of a national strategy so far, was the UKHTC film *My Dangerous Loverboy*, gathering dust on the shelves of child-protection agencies and police forces.

After the *Panorama* documentary was broadcast, questions were asked in the House of Lords. Talking about the levels of violence used by the gangs, Lord McColl of Dulwich reiterated: 'Children are much more frightened of the pimps than they are of the law, and the violence that they suffer is terrible. One girl had boiling water held above her throat; another had her tongue nailed to a table.'[89] Sadly, this was in the context of a debate about HIV, rather than a full debate on the grooming gangs; but what this indicates, is that politicians were aware of the contents of this documentary, but still the scandal of the grooming gangs would be ignored by Parliament for another 5 years. The *BBC* reported that 'the government has said it will produce a warning video for use in all schools.'[90] We assume that this refers to *My Dangerous Loverboy*: a video which has never been shown to its intended audience.

At one point in the documentary, the police speak to some of the men in cars hanging around the teenage girls: the men make it clear they blame the parents for allowing these girls out, and that they definitely do not attribute any blame to the adult men having sex with the under-age girls. Whilst the ethnicity of the men remains concealed, we can infer from their stated attitudes that they almost certainly Asian, and very probably Muslim Asians. 'I blame the parents.... they should keep them [the girls] locked up at home... if my sister went out like that I'd kick the fuck out of her and send her back home... That's the proper way, that's how we should be.'[91] This man's cultural values are those of a society where the women are constrained in the home, and where any woman or girl who is outside the home is available for sex. And the way in which the women and girls are to be constrained within the home is by extreme violence should they disobey (so-called 'honour violence'). The interviewee sees these as the 'proper' cultural and moral values.[92]

---

89 http://www.publications.parliament.uk/pa/ld200708/ldhansrd/text/80403-0006.htm

90 'Teenage Sex For Sale: *Panorama*', *BBC* website, http://news.bbc.co.uk/1/hi/programmes/panorama/7302713.stm

91 http://www.youtube.com/watch?v=RFIfcTqBsZc&t=1518

92 Of course, our society does not (yet) have the other values that go with such cultural norms: blood feuds, communal violence and vendettas. Interestingly enough, when Muslims were grooming Sikh schoolgirls in 1988, 2001 and 2013, the Sikhs did

What we are witnessing is the inevitable failure of the cowardly policy of 'multiculturalism': these Asian men are simply applying the traditional values of their culture, in a society which permits them to get away with abusing its tolerance, freedom and openness. If these men found that their daughters and sisters had been groomed and raped, they make it clear they would employ violence, rather than seek a civilised solution. As we will see later, when one examines Islamic morality and the history of Muslim culture, there is a deep tradition of sex-slavery within Muslim culture. Just as the men in the documentary see violence and the oppression of females as acceptable modern values, why should we be surprised if Muslims in Britain also perpetuate Islamic attitudes to sex-slavery? Multiculturalism tells such people: there's nothing wrong with your values.

In connection with the *Panorama* documentary, the *BBC* publicised a list of signs that indicate a child is being groomed:[93] 'change in performance at school in a short time' or 'using street language' or having 'a street name' are given as indicators. Once again, an opportunity is missed: parents and schoolgirls could be informed about indicators that a girl is being entrapped. However, what should perhaps be the most obvious signal - a young white girl having adult 'Asian' male friends - is not listed as a warning sign. Untold thousands of schoolgirls became victims of these gangs, because such opportunities were not taken. The very oddity of an underage white schoolgirl having many older adult Muslim male friends was to be ignored, part of some utopian myth of multicultural integration.

At this time, the *BBC* also distributed a document by Prof. Barrett called, 'Abused Girls: What Do We Know?'[94] In this document he points out:

> 1. That in 1885 W.T. Stead of the *Pall Mall Gazette* exposed how 13 year old girls could be bought and put into a life of prostitution. Even though Stead did this to prove a point and for the sake of the girls, he was imprisoned for this in the 19th century. We will discuss these events further in chapter 9, Victorian Values.
> 2. The Children's Act (1989) enshrined the principle that in

---

initiate 'communal violence', speaking to Muslim grooming gangs in what they would understand as 'the proper way'.

93 http://news.bbc.co.uk/1/hi/programmes/panorama/7314444.stm

94 http://news.bbc.co.uk/1/shared/bsp/hi/pdfs/27_03_08_whatweknow.pdf

a court the welfare of a child must come before those of an adult but that this legal principle 'appears to give way to operational caveats such as wider issues of culture, politics and geography.'

If W.T. Stead were to witness the cowardice of 21st century journalists, he would weep. Would any contemporary journalist risk prison to demonstrate the existence of this modern sex-slavery?

3.15 2009 Rise of English Defence League

In March 2009, a local group formed calling itself 'The United People of Luton', and began to protest against Muslims who had gathered to abuse and spit at soldiers at a homecoming parade in Luton earlier that year. A few months later this group went national, and the United People of Luton became 'The English Defence League' (EDL).[95] Whilst the EDL's original focus had been Muslim extremists who showed loyalty to Muslims globally rather than to the country of which they were citizens, it was not long before the EDL were also campaigning against the Muslim grooming gangs, and the failure of the police and child-care professionals to do anything to stop the gangs. These particular demonstrations focussed on Blackpool, after the 2009 Independent Police Complaints Commission ruling, that the trial against two Muslim men for the murder of schoolgirl Charlene Downes collapsed because 'the investigating team were guilty of a strategic and tactical failure in the management of the audio and video material they obtained...'[96]

None of the official accounts of how the nation woke up to the grooming gang phenomenon mention the effect of the EDL, but it is clear that the EDL were protesting about this issue throughout 2010, yet in 2008 the *BBC* documentary could not bring itself to state that the grooming gangs were made up primarily of Muslim men, and the national police agency could not manage to distribute the film they had financed which euphemistically attempted to broach the problem. On 3 August 2010, the local Blackpool newspaper reported that 'more than 150 members of the English Defence League (EDL), which exists to shun

---

95 Dominic Casciani, 'Who are the English Defence League?', *BBC News*, 11 Sep 2009, http://news.bbc.co.uk/1/hi/magazine/8250017.stm

96 Graham Smith, 'Police rapped for blunders in murder case of girl "turned into kebab meat"', *The Daily Mail*, 16 Oct 2009, http://www.daily mail.co.uk/news/article-1220815/Police-disciplined-blunders-murder-case-girl-turned-kebabs.html

Islam, protested on St Chad's Headland, in South Shore – claiming to be demonstrating for justice for missing schoolgirl Charlene Downes.[97] By May 2011, the EDL had held three of these protests in Blackpool, focussing on the case of Charlene Downes in particular, but also with reference to the wider problem concerning Muslim grooming gangs.[98] The third EDL protest in Blackpool had over 2000 EDL supporters present.[99]

3.16 2011 Andrew Norfolk's pivotal article

In January 2011, Andrew Norfolk wrote an article for *The Times* newspaper which is claimed to have formed a watershed.[100] He went back through all the court cases for convictions of groups of men who groomed schoolgirls for sex. Between 1997 and 2010, he found 56 men who fit this criterion. Only 5 out of the 56 men convicted were not Muslims. Muslims are less than 5% of the population, but in Norfolk's retrospective survey, Muslims were 91% of those convicted. An extraordinary statistical inversion such as this demands further investigation.[101] On the basis of this and related articles, Norfolk received two coveted prizes from his peers for investigative journalism.[102]

It is the evidence from this article by Norfolk which is credited with prompting the government to have a Select Committee investigate the grooming gangs.

There was little media coverage of the issue in the interven-

---

97 'Far right protest in Blackpool', *Blackpool Gazette*, 3 Aug 2010, http://www.black-poolgazette.co.uk/news/local/far-right-protest-in-blackpool-1-1567006

98 'On Saturday 26 March [2011] the EDL will hold a third demo in Blackpool to demand justice for Charlene Downes'. Musings of a Durotrigan, 'Blackpool EDL Demo: Justice for Charlene Downes', 14 Mar 2011, http://durotrigan.blogspot.co.uk/2011/03/blackpool-edl-demo-justice-for-charlene.html. In an ideal world, we would cite references to pages on the EDL's website, but since 2010 their website has been taken down many times by Islamic cyber-terrorists, thus we must turn to secondary websites for information concerning the EDL's activities in these years.

99 '2,000 EDL protesters gather on Blackpool Promenade', *Blackpool Gazette*, 28 May 2011, http://www.blackpoolgazette.co.uk/news/local/2_000_edl_protesters_gather_on_blackpool_promenade_1_3428595

100 Andrew Norfolk, 'Revealed: conspiracy of silence on UK sex gangs', *The Times*, 5 Jan 2011 http://www.thetimes.co.uk/tto/news/uk/crime/article2863058.ece

101 The prosecutions Norfolk used to perform his analysis are almost certainly the tip of the iceberg in relation to the activities of the grooming gangs.

102 http://theorwellprize.co.uk/shortlists/andrew-norfolk/. In 2012 Norfolk also received the Paul Foot Award for his journalism on the grooming gangs. http://en.wikipedia.org/wiki/Paul_Foot_Award

ing years but in [November] 2010 there were two trials which again saw groups of Asian men convicted for sexual offences against white British girls...The first of the series of Andrew Norfolk's Times articles on the subject was published several days before the ringleaders in the Derby case were sentenced and listed 17 trials that had been identified as prosecutions related to localised grooming. In all but one of the trials, the offenders were identified as being Asian, mostly British Pakistani, and the victims were predominantly white.[103]

Naturally, the official parliamentary report does not want the English Defence League to receive any credit for bringing the grooming gangs to national attention. However, between 2004 and 2010, we can find no trace of Andrew Norfolk reporting on these grooming gangs, although Norfolk was certainly aware of the issue in 2004, as he reported on the controversy over *Channel 4's* documentary *Edge of the City*.[104] After reporting on that controversy in 2004, it wasn't until November 2010 that Norfolk again reported on the grooming gangs, and this despite Norfolk stating he lived in Yorkshire, an area where the problem was demonstrably known by the mid 1990s. Perhaps significantly, a few months before breaking this silence, Norfolk reported on the EDL demonstration in Bradford in August 2010.[105] Was it his experience of the EDL demonstration which led Norfolk to investigate whether or not it could be established objectively that Muslim men were hugely over-represented among those convicted in grooming gang trials?

103 Home Affairs Select Committee Report 'Child Sexual Exploitation and the Response to Localised Grooming', 10 Jun 2013, http://www.publications.parliament.uk/pa/cm201314/cmselect/cmhaff/68/68i.pdf p. 53.

104 Adam Sherwin and Andrew Norfolk. 'Police get "race" film postponed', *The Times*, 21 May 2004 http://www.thetimes.co.uk/tto/news/uk/articl e1923155.ece. In an interview with the Sikh Awareness Society in 2012, Norfolk states that he moved back to Leeds around the time of the *Channel 4* controversies over grooming gangs in Bradford. He says that, after reporting on that controversy in 2004, in subsequent years he'd been aware of cases of Muslim grooming gangs across the country, but had not reported on them for fear of 'giving the far-right their dream story.' Andrew Norfolk, 'Reality of Sexual Grooming Gangs in the UK - interview of Andrew Norfolk and Sikh Awareness Society', http://www.youtube.com/watch?v= WbUIfvYbjRc&feature=player_detailpage&t=301. Thus, we see Norfolk concede that it was the fear of aiding the BNP, an abuse of the narrative of racism by pressure groups, which doomed vulnerable schoolgirls to a further decade of violence and forced prostitution.

105 Andrew Norfolk, 'Missiles thrown as far-right rally turns violent in Bradford', *The Times*, 28 Aug 2010, http://www.thetimes.co.uk/tto/news/uk/article2706209.ece

Whilst it is to Andrew Norfolk's credit that he conceived of this pivotal analysis in 2011, more recognition should be accorded to Julie Bindel, for continuing to write about this subject in 2007 and 2010, when no other journalist in Britain was prepared to associate themselves with this controversial problem. As the references throughout our analysis show, since 2011 there have been hundreds of reports on the grooming gangs. But between the furore over *Edge of the City* in 2004 and Norfolk's pivotal article in 2011, the reports on the phenomenon of the grooming gangs could be counted on the fingers of one hand. Only Julie Bindel demonstrated any determination to expose this problem in the years in which every professional body was turning a blind eye.

FOUR
Rotherham: Designated Scapegoat

W HEN THE first online edition of *Easy Meat* was published, we noted how the councils of Rochdale and Rotherham were being singled-out as scapegoats. In the following year the national focus turned to Rotherham alone, with two major reports being published into the failings of the authorities in that borough. However, as Appendix 1: Grooming Gang Convictions shows, the problems were nationwide, with convictions over the past two decades for gangs operating in the following 28 towns: Accrington, Barking, Birmingham, Blackburn, Blackpool, Bradford, Bristol, Burton, Chesham, Derby, Ipswich, Keighley, Leeds, Leicester, London, Manchester, Middlesbrough, Nelson, Oldham, Oxford, Peterborough, Preston, Rochdale, Rotherham, Sheffield, Skipton, Slough, Telford. So why was Rotherham singled out?

Andrew Norfolk's pivotal article (January 2011) demonstrated that there was a pattern where 'Asian' men made up the majority of those convicted of grooming crimes. For a couple of years following this proof, the news media suddenly acted as if the barriers were lifted on the reporting of these trials. However, the national media reporting on the specific details of these trials soon tailed off.[1] For example, between

---

1 By 2015 other commentators were noticing the renewed silence of the national news media in this regard, taking it to be a sign of the strangle-hold of political correctness; see Douglas Murray, 'Child-Rape Crimes Covered Up', 03 June 2015, *Gatestone Institute*, http://www.gatestoneinstitute.org/5879/child-rape-crimes.
Although reported in the local press, the case has warranted only a single, bare-

January 2013 and June 2013, *The Guardian* reported 12 times on the proceedings of the Oxford trial involving Akhtar Dogar; by November 2014, *The Guardian* only reported 3 times on the two lengthy trials in Bristol involving Mohammed Jumale and his accomplices. Effectively, *The Guardian's* editorial policy by 2014 appears to have been to only report the conclusions of these trials. With the Sheffield trial involving Shakeal Rehman in 2014, *The Guardian* only produced a single report, at the conclusion of the trial. No reports could be found of this trial on the *BBC News* website, nor at *The Times*. At the start of 2011, Andrew Norfolk listed some 56 convictions from the previous 14 years. Four years later, the number of comparable convictions across the country had increased by 200%, yet the media seemed to lose interest in keeping the people informed of the national and international dimensions of the problem.

From 2014 onwards the media's attention was focused on Rotherham. In the 18 months from January 2014 *The Times, The Telegraph*, and *The Guardian* reported on Rotherham and the grooming scandal there around 100 times for each newspaper. It's not as if these recent grooming trials which have been neglected by the media shed no light on the grooming phenomenon: what was very significant of the trials in Bristol in 2014, is that all those convicted were Muslims from Somalia, not Pakistan. That these men were not Pakistanis, not Asians, exploded the lie that it was 'Asian' cultural values which were responsible for the grooming gang phenomenon. Instead, throughout 2014 the news media concentrated on Rotherham, where the majority of perpetrators were officially acknowledged to be Pakistanis. The established narrative cannot attend to the Bristol trials because the trials show that the grooming phenomenon has nothing to do with the perpetrators being 'Asian' or even Pakistani. The conviction of Somali Muslims in Bristol shows that the root problem is that these men are Muslims from many different countries.

In August 2014 the report on Rotherham by Prof. Alexis Jay was published.[2] What was significant about this report was that it highlight-

---

bones *BBC* news story in the national press. It may be that the national press is waiting for the trial to commence – or might it be that there are other things going on? And so there are. Crimes of this nature are still being kicked under the carpet – for reasons of 'political correctness' – with no concern for the harm done to the children. The issue is a true tinderbox.

Could it be that the government and the news editors are complicit? Could the National Union of Journalists be behind this?

2 Alexis Jay, 'Independent Inquiry into Child Sexual Exploitation in Rotherham 1997

ed how long the Muslim grooming gangs had been operating in Rotherham with almost total impunity. The scale of the problem, at least for one town, was finally being publicly and officially articulated by someone who had first-hand access to the data and the scale of the problem was shocking: the Jay report made the conservative calculation that there were at least 1,400 schoolgirl victims in that borough alone.[3] There are over 50 urban areas more populous than Rotherham in Britain[4] and it was clear the country found it unimaginable that, in a relatively small town, so many schoolgirls could have been systematically abused over decades, with virtually no-one being punished for this. The scale of this problem sent waves of outrage through the country, and in the subsequent months there was barely a week when Rotherham was not in the news. When *Easy Meat* was first published online, we cited the estimate by CROP of 10,000 victims, a figure which some people found scarcely believable. However, we now consider this figure of 10,000 victims to be a gross underestimate. If the 56th largest borough was recognised as having *at least* 1,400 victims, then the number of historical victims nationally could easily be extrapolated to be 100,000 or possibly even as many as 1 million (a number suggested by the MP for Rotherham). The population of the United Kingdom is around 65 million people, whilst the population of Rotherham is around 260,000; thus the 1400 known victims for Rotherham might be only 1/250th of the total number of victims across the country. It is only when one considers this simple arithmetic, that the idea that there could be as many as 1 million victims across the country ceases to be unbelievable. Mostly the media and experts have shied away from any extrapolations based on the data from Rotherham; in all probability because the implications are simply unconscionable. What does it say about Britain if somewhere between 100,000 and 1 million white schoolgirls were groomed and raped by organised gangs of Muslims? How do child-care professionals, police officers and journalists bear the shame if throughout their professional careers they stood by and allowed this to happen? We can see why those in positions of power and responsibility would have a very strong incentive for the country to believe that Rotherham was not typical of what had gone on elsewhere during the previous 25 years.

It was not just the sheer number of victims in Rotherham which

---

- 2013', http://www.rotherham.gov.uk/downloads/file/1407/independent_inquiry_cse_in_rotherham

3 *Ibid.*, p. 29.

4 https://en.wikipedia.org/wiki/Metropolitan_Borough_of_Rotherham

made the Jay report so shocking. It was that the report officially confirmed there was a huge discrepancy between the ethnicity of the victims and the ethnicity of the perpetrators.[5] Census data showed that in 2011 the white population of Rotherham was around 92%, with the single largest non-white population being Muslims identified as 'Pakistani/Kashmiri' of around 3%.[6] Jay states that 'In Rotherham, the majority of known perpetrators were of Pakistani heritage'.[7] Moreover, as was the case when the matter was brought to national attention in the Bradford area, in Rotherham it was the religious and political 'leaders' of the Muslim community who were asked to help.[8] The pattern remains the same across the years and from different towns. The concept of Muslim grooming gangs, a concept denounced as 'a racist myth' by organisations only 5 years earlier, turns out not only to be true, but to have been known about since at least 1988. Rather than acknowledge the scale and duration of the problem, after 2011 when the problem could no longer be hushed-up the government seemed instead determined to pretend that Rotherham was a unique case.

It turns out the phenomenon was of very substantial size in Rotherham years ago: by 2006 it was admitted by child-care professionals that the Muslim grooming gangs there had now become an industry:

> the appeal of organised sexual exploitation for Asian gangs had changed. In the past, it had been for their personal gratification, whereas now it offered "career and financial opportunities to young Asian men who got involved". [...] Iraqi Kurds and Kosovan men were participating in organised ac-

---

5 'In a large number of the historic cases in particular, most of the victims in the cases we sampled were white British children, and the majority of the perpetrators were from minority ethnic communities. They were described generically in the files as "Asian males" without precise reference being made to their ethnicity.' See p. 35 of Alexis Jay, 'Independent Inquiry into Child Sexual Exploitation in Rotherham 1997 - 2013', *op. cit.*

6 http://www.rotherham.gov.uk/jsna/info/23/people/54/ethnicity_and_cultural_identity

7 Alexis Jay, 'Independent Inquiry into Child Sexual Exploitation in Rotherham 1997 - 2013', http://www.rotherham.gov.uk/downloads/file/1407/independent_inquiry_cse_in_rotherham, p. 92.

8 'There was too much reliance by agencies on traditional community leaders such as elected members and imams as being the primary conduit of communication with the Pakistani-heritage community.' Alexis Jay, 'Independent Inquiry into Child Sexual Exploitation in Rotherham 1997 - 2013', *op. cit.*, p. 91.

tivities against young women.[9]

Whilst *Channel 4* was being accused of racism for reporting on what was going on in Bradford in 2004, just two years later the child-care professionals in Rotherham were privately admitting that this supposedly non-existent phenomenon was operating at an industrial scale. And the Muslims involved in Rotherham were drawing in other (non-Pakistani) Muslims too (it is likely that seeing them get away with these lucrative crimes, other ethnicities would want to join in).

Whilst the grooming problem was decades old and almost certainly national in scope, Muslim organisations, police, and Left-wing political activists were denying that the Muslim grooming gangs even existed. And with rare exceptions the media went along with this. Finally in 2015 the British Prime Minister was admitting that the gangs had been operating on an 'industrial scale'.[10] As we see explicitly from the above

---

9 *Ibid.*, p. 92.

10 'UK children suffered sex abuse on 'industrial scale', *BBC News* website, 03 Mar 2015, http://www.bbc.co.uk/news/uk-31691061

This 2 minuite "interview" of PM David Cameron is very interesting and significant on a number of fronts. Firstly, it's not a press conference, but is rather the UK government using the state broadcaster to issue a stage-managed government statement. Secondly, the interviewer asks the PM why there was nothing in his 2010 manifesto about these problems, and the PM says the events have happened since the General Election. Yet the 2 reports into Rotherham had just been published in the months preceding this interview, disclosing that the events in Rotherham were going on for many years before 2010. This shows how successfully the grooming phenomenon was being concealed, right up to the 2010 General Election, when it was not even obliquely on the agenda of the mainstream political parties. As the BBC journalist says in the text which accompanies the interview: 'It [grooming] is now deemed a national threat akin to terrorism and major civil disorder but the issue of child sexual exploitation was not even a footnote in either the Conservative or Labour manifestos, nor indeed in the coalition agreement, at the last election.' Again, this suggests that without EDL marching through town after town after 2009, this problem would have continued to be kept off the political agenda.

The interview is also significant, as here we have the government making a broadcast statement to say that underage girls cannot give consent to sex, a legal principle conveniently ignored by the judiciary, state prosecutors, police and social workers for decades. When asked if the PM and other politicians had not been 'willfully ignoring' the problem, the PM does not claim that politicians did not know it was going on, but that they have taken measures against it. Finally, we see that rather than accept any blame, the finger of guilt is being pointed by the government squarely at police officers and social workers who have turned a blind eye to the problem; it is claimed that these professionals and local politicians are the people who are going to be criminalised if the problem continues.

Given how many loopholes there are in this statement by the PM, it seems clear why

2006 report from Rotherham, this grooming phenomenon was acknowledged by child-care professionals a decade before the government would publicly admit it. And if we consider that the grooming gangs must have been operating at scale in places like Bradford as far back as the 1990s, then we have every reason to expect a British government to have exposed the level of this sexual abuse more than two decades earlier. Rather than take a role of national leadership, successive governments just ignored the problem. Successive governments pumped money into Muslim organisations up and down the country, but there's no evidence there was any money being given to Muslim groups to try and do something about this problem. Twenty years before a Conservative Prime Minister admitted the scale of the problem, a previous Conservative government had funded a project in Bradford to quietly mop-up the damage caused by the grooming gangs there.

At a national institutional level, any acknowledgement that the grooming phenomenon even existed only occurred between 2011 and 2013, and these were attempts to obfuscate what was going on. This was seen in the reports from CEOP, The Childrens' Commissioner and even the House of Commons select committee: the House of Commons report made no direct acknowledgement that the gangs were overwhelmingly Muslim, with their victims overwhelmingly white. Suddenly in 2014, all attention turned to Rotherham, with it apparently being singled out as exceptionally bad. For the authorities, the idea that Rotherham was typical of what has been going on across England for decades was almost certainly too dangerous to be stated. Rotherham has fewer Muslims as a percentage of its population than does the United Kingdom as a whole. As *Appendix 1* shows, there have been convictions in around 30 different towns across England, and the chronology in Chapter 3 shows that over 25 years the phenomenon was being reported to be going on all over England. There is simply no basis on which it can be argued that what happened in Rotherham was not typical of what had been happening across England for decades.

No sooner had the Jay report come out, than the news media rejected the idea that Rotherham was somehow different from all the other towns where the inhabitants knew there was a grooming problem: 'It's been happening for a long time in lots of our towns and cities where the most vulnerable children are allowed to be pimped out for money

---

this was not conducted as a press conference; the contradictions of the government statement would be too easily exposed in such an environment.

by groups of men – mainly from the Pakistani community.'[11] Following the Jay report, even the *BBC* listed the other towns where these things were also going on: Oxford, Derby, Peterborough, Telford, Rochdale.[12] If it was thought that attention could be focused on Rotherham instead of Bradford, Oxford or Rochdale, throughout 2014 it appeared this manoeuvre was failing. After decades of near total silence, the media were now not letting this story go. The Jay report was published on 26 August 2014, and was immediately followed by such critical news stories as those published above. Then Parliament ordered a second Inquiry into Rotherham, an Inquiry overseen by Louise Casey. The Casey Inquiry began on 10 September 2014, just three weeks after the Jay report was published. The Jay Inquiry was commissioned by Rotherham council itself, and the official explanation for the Casey Inquiry was that Rotherham council appeared to be in denial about what the Jay report had concluded.[13] Perhaps the government realised that the attempt to single out Rotherham as a unique case had failed, and the Casey report was designed to place further emphasis on the supposed uniqueness of what was uncovered in Rotherham. Undoubtedly the Casey report brought the officially-sanctioned narrative into closer alignment with the analysis being propounded in the national media.

The Jay report had resulted in Rotherham council being subjected to enormous media attention. 'Four senior figures in Rotherham council quit shortly after publication of the Jay report. Council leader Roger Stone, council chief executive Martin Kimber and council director of children's services Joyce Thacker all left their posts.'[14] By early 2015, ten police officers from the area were under investigation, with one of them dying in a car crash whilst under suspicion. However, it was the Casey report which appeared to have the biggest impact: because of the report's findings the entire council Cabinet resigned their posts, and cen-

---

11 'Rotherham - The rule rather than the exception', *The Daily Mirror*, 30 Aug 2014, http://www.mirror.co.uk/news/rotherham---rule-exception-4136126. Following the Jay report, the MP for Rochdale stated his belief that Rotherham was the norm.'Rotherham is not an isolated incident, *The Telegraph*, 31 Aug 2014, http://www.telegraph.co.uk/news/uknews/crime/11066244/Rotherham-is-not-an-isolated-incident.html

12 'Rotherham child abuse: Cases in other towns', *BBC News* website, 27 Aug 2014, http://www.bbc.co.uk/news/uk-28953549

13 Louise Casey, 'Report of Inspection of Rotherham Metropolitan Borough Council, Feb 2015', https://www.gov.uk/government/uploads/system/uplo ads/attachment_data/file/401125/46966_Report_of_Inspection_of_Rotherham_WEB.pdf, p. 6.

14 'In numbers: understanding the Rotherham grooming scandal', *Channel 4 News*, 04 Feb 2015, http://www.channel4.com/news/rotherham-grooming-scandal-in-numbers

tral government appointed Commissioners to administer Rotherham council.[15] The media presented this mass resignation as if the councillors were resigning as elected officials, when really the resignation of some of them from their cabinet positions is a minimal action, and in fact was something over which they had no control once central Government decided to take control of administering the local authority. Perhaps what no one anticipated was that the central Government agents sent in to administer the area would soon appeal to the Government to suspend democratic protests in the town if the protests were related to the grooming gang phenomenon.[16]

The Casey report opens with this bald statement:

> Terrible things happened in Rotherham and on a significant scale. Children were sexually exploited by men who came largely from the Pakistani Heritage Community. Not enough was done to acknowledge this, to stop it happening, to protect children, to support victims and to apprehend perpetra-

---

15 "'Not fit for purpose" Rotherham council cabinet resigns', *Channel 4 News*, 04 Feb 2015, http://www.channel4.com/news/rotherham-council-child-abuse-report-louise-casey-eric-pickles

16 Chris Burn, 'Exclusive: Police and council move to ban Rotherham abuse protests', *The Star*, 23 May 2015, http://www.thestar.co.uk/news/local/exclusive-police-and-council-move-to-ban-rotherham-abuse-protests-1-7275252

    Commissioner Ney said... "Whilst we realise that people have a democratic right to assemble and protest under the European conventions, that freedom has been exercised on numerous occasions, by many different groups, all protesting about the same issue. That voice has been heard, and all groups have had the opportunity to protest in Rotherham town centre many times." She said it is "considered legitimate to interfere with that right" on the grounds that it will prevent serious disorder, protect the rights of traders and the public to go about their business and "enable the town to move on following the publication of the Jay and Casey reports".

The attempt to prevent further outbursts of democratic protest by groups like the EDL is another illustration that it was probably these very groups which brought the grooming gang phenomenon out of the shadows and into the glare of media publicity. By scapegoating Rotherham as a singularly bad example of the grooming scandal, central Government had made the town into a focus for protests over this phenomenon. However, let us not forget: these Government-appointed Commissioners were asking to suspend democracy after a mere handful of protests. The lengthiest protest listed by the Commissioners lasted around two weeks and focussed on the refusal of the Police Commissioner to resign. The Commissioners themselves were only able to ask for the suspension of democracy because the council leaders had been forced to give up administrative power and appeared to lament rights granted under European conventions.

tors.[17]

Before 2014, every public report into the grooming scandal had tip-toed around the issues, often not even raising the discrepancy in ethnicity between victims and perpetrators, or if raising the issue of ethnicity, doing so in order to obfuscate the matter by introducing unrelated statistics on other forms of sexual exploitation of children. Focusing on Rotherham alone, the reports by Jay and Casey signify a major shift in the official narrative on the grooming phenomenon. But if the problems are to be acknowledged in Rotherham, why not have inquiries into what has happened in Bradford, which has a much higher Muslim population, and where, according to Andrew Norfolk, the problem can be shown to have been known about by as early as 1991?[18]

One of the things which Casey finds notable about the staff at Rotherham council was that, when it came to the grooming scandal, they claimed: 'They were no worse than anyone else. They had won awards. The media were out to get them.'[19] In this, the council staff will probably be proven right. By early 2015, the local media in Rotherham were fulminating about the refusal by some of the senior officials to give interviews.[20] However, the question should be directed towards the local media in Rotherham, Bradford, Oldham, Oxford: why were you so quiet about the activities of these grooming gangs for the 20 years prior to 2010? The existence and actions of Risky Business in Rotherham for 14 years (an organisation warning of the gangs exploiting schoolgirls) cannot have escaped the attention of the local news media. How was it that parents were reporting shocking events to the police, that the council was conducting investigations, that Risky Business was burgled

17 Louise Casey, Report of Inspection of Rotherham Metropolitan Borough Council, *op. cit.*, p. 5.

18 Andrew Norfolk, 'Reality of Sexual Grooming Gangs in the UK - interview of Andrew Norfolk and Sikh Awareness Society', http://www.youtube.com/watch?v=W-bUIfvYbjRc&t=1385. See section 3.3 1991 *'The earliest case...'*

19 Louise Casey, 'Report of Inspection of Rotherham Metropolitan Borough Council', *op. cit.*, p. 5.

20 James Mitchinson, 'ROTHERHAM CHILD SEX ABUSE SCANDAL - EDITOR'S OPINION: A little girl was raped with a broken bottle, and yet former Council Leader and Police and Crime Commissioner refused to answer questions in interview', *The Star*, 05 Feb 2015, http://www.thestar.co.uk/news/local/rotherham-child-sex-abuse-scandal-editor-s-opinion-a-little-girl-was-raped-with-a-broken-bottle-and-yet-former-council-leader-and-police-and-crime-commissioner-refused-to-answer-questions-in-interview-1-7091999

and then closed down, and the local media did not think these things signified something very news-worthy was going on in their town? Denis MacShane, MP for Rotherham for many years, has admitted that he was aware of problems and discussed issues with another local MP and that he could have done more.[21] It is simply not credible that local news media did not hear of reports over a period of 20 years: if councillors, MPs, social workers, police officers and local imams are all failing the local children and their parents over many years, who else is going to expose such persistent and widespread failures if not the local news media? In the case of Rotherham, it may well be that the editor of the local newspaper only became associated with that town in the last few years. But questions concerning the decades of silence from the local media in towns across England is paramount in understanding how this grooming phenomenon could have been allowed to persist for so long. We can find some evidence that the local newspaper in Bradford was drawing these issues to the public's attention, at least until the near-total news blackout in the wake of the 2004 *Channel 4* documentary on grooming gangs in West Yorkshire. But in general, there is not a single example of a 21st century journalist conducting the kind of investigation or taking the risks of W.T. Stead in the 19th century (see chapter 10: Victorian Values).

It is those who seek to claim that Rotherham was somehow unique whom history will show to have been deluded and misguided. The only significant difference Casey seems to be able to point out between what happened in Rotherham and elsewhere, is that the Rotherham council chose first to ignore, and then close down Risky Business; it appears that Risky Business was providing intelligence to both social workers and the police, shocking events which were repeatedly ignored before the organisation was finally silenced. Child abuse and exploitation happens all over the country, but Rotherham is different in that it was repeatedly

---

21 'Denis MacShane: I was too much of a "liberal leftie" and should have done more to investigate child abuse', *The Telegraph*, 27 Aug 2014, http://www.telegraph.co.uk/news/uknews/crime/11059643/Denis-MacShane-I-was-too-much-of-a-liberal-leftie-and-should-have-done-more-to-investigate-child-abuse.html

Admitting he had been guilty of doing too little, he said he had been aware of the problem of cousin marriage and "the oppression of women within bits of the Muslim community in Britain" but: "Perhaps yes, as a true *Guardian* reader, and liberal leftie, I suppose I didn't want to raise that too hard." He recalled having a "huge row" with another local MP and council grandees because they were complaining about a newspaper investigation into child sexual exploitation in Rotherham, which unearthed uncomfortable truths they did not want to hear.

told by its own youth service what was happening and it chose, not only to not act, but to close that service down.[22]

Time will tell if Rotherham was the only town where social workers and police ignored the information provided to front-line professionals. We have yet to see another council subjected to the level of scrutiny to which Rotherham has been subjected. Given the reports and convictions over the past 25 years, from Yorkshire, Lancashire and the Midlands, there seems no basis on which to differentiate between the grooming phenomenon in Rotherham and anywhere else where it has come to light. If all these other towns were so much better than Rotherham in responding to this criminality, why do those towns with a Muslim population as high as Rotherham not completely dwarf that borough by number of convictions? Why have the grooming gangs been hushed-up in all those towns, if only Rotherham council was in denial? Did these other towns even have an out-reach project like Risky Business which could be ignored and then shut down?[23] Until those other towns are subjected to the same scrutiny as Rotherham, it is wishful thinking to believe the professionals in those towns were any different to the professionals in Rotherham.

The Casey report seems to concede that it was the rise of the English Defence League which finally made the government and media pay attention to the grooming phenomenon:

> By failing to take action against the Pakistani heritage male perpetrators of CSE in the borough, the Council has inadvertently fuelled the far right and allowed racial tensions to grow.[24]

---

22 Louise Casey, 'Report of Inspection of Rotherham Metropolitan Borough Council, Feb 2015', *op. cit.*, p. 4.

23 It is claimed that overnight in 2002, files from the Risky Business offices were stolen, with no sign of breaking and entry. 'National Crime Agency investigation into Rotherham scandal turns attention to missing files', *The Star*, 22 Jan 2015, http://www. thestar.co.uk/news/local/national-crime-agency-investigation-into-rotherham-scandal-turns-attention-to-missing-files-1-7063038. In 2015, it appears these files were finally discovered in Rotherham council offices. Louise Casey, 'Report of Inspection of Rotherham Metropolitan Borough Council, Feb 2015', *op. cit.*, p. 134. After 14 years in operation, Risky Business was shut down in 2011, even though according to the reports by Jay and Casey, it seemed to be doing a good job. 'Rotherham Victim Says Abusers "Untouchable"' *Sky News* website, 29 Jan 2015, http://news.sky.com/story/1416946/rotherham-victim-says-abusers-untouchable

24 Louise Casey, 'Report of Inspection of Rotherham Metropolitan Borough Council, Feb 2015', *op cit.*, p. 10.

If the EDL had not come into existence in 2009, there is no reason to believe that any agency would have taken further steps to curb the grooming gangs. As we have shown, these gangs were in operation for around 20 years before the formation of the EDL. And throughout that time, there had been nothing but accusations that the concept of gangs of Muslim men systematically grooming schoolgirls was a myth spread by racists. Indeed, two pages later, Casey laments how hard it must be for 'the good people of Rotherham' when the EDL 'marches... in their town centre'. It seems that the EDL demonstration in Rotherham in September 2014 was the only demonstration ever held in the town by that organisation.[25] Nevertheless, that Casey should so closely associate the rise of the EDL with the failure of the authorities to take action against the gangs is probably correct. That the EDL marched through many other towns which were not Rotherham, should make it very clear that Rotherham was in no way regarded as unique by the EDL[26]

Within weeks of the Casey report being published, it was disclosed that investigations in Oxford had revealed at least 300 victims of grooming gangs there.[27] Whilst 300 victims in Oxford may seem less significant than 1400 victims cited in Rotherham, let us consider the relative Muslim populations of these towns: as noted above, in 2011 Muslims were 3.1% of the population of Rotherham, whilst at that time Muslims were only 0.75% of the population of Oxford.[28] Thus, *pace* the Casey report, there seems to be no reason to regard the problem in Rotherham to be significantly different from the problem in Oxford. Indeed, in towns where the Muslim population is proportionately higher, one might expect that the grooming phenomenon will be proportionately worse. The Muslim population of Bradford is almost 10 times higher[29] than the Muslim population of Rotherham. And from 1995 to 2006, Bradford was the only town on the map in regards to this problem. Indeed, it may well be that Rotherham has become the focus of attention precisely because the Muslim population there is relatively small compared to towns like Bradford. After all, one of the fears cited by the Rotherham staff was

---

25 'Rotherham EDL child abuse march costs police £750k', *BBC News* website, 15 Sep 2014, http://www.bbc.co.uk/news/uk-england-south-yorkshire-29207140

26 http://en.wikipedia.org/wiki/List_of_English_Defence_League_demonstrations

27 '300 victims groomed and assaulted by Oxfordshire gangs, report finds', *The Telegraph*, 02 Mar 2015, http://www.telegraph.co.uk/news/ukn ews/crime/11443868/300-victims-groomed-and-assaulted-by-Oxfordshire-gangs-report-finds.html

28 http://www.oxford.gov.uk/PageRender/decC/Religionstatistics.htm

29 http://www.bradford.gov.uk/bmdc/community_and_living/population

that there would be riots if the truth about the grooming phenomenon was disclosed.[30] Bradford and Oldham, towns with significant Muslim populations and with proven problems with grooming gangs, already had riots in 2001; it seems likely that if such riots are feared in Rotherham, they are even more feared in Bradford and Oldham. If the prospect of Muslim riots were enough to lead council staff to turn a blind eye in Rotherham, there is even more reason to expect such blindness in towns with a much higher proportion of Muslims.

Like Jay, Casey acknowledges that,

In Rotherham, the phenomenon of CSE [grooming gangs] emerging from the late 1990s onwards concerned a majority of white, female, adolescent or teenage victims and a majority of Pakistani heritage adult male perpetrators.[31]

Casey is highly critical of council staff and police officers for their reluctance to acknowledge the discrepancy in ethnicity between victim and perpetrator, and how their failure to acknowledge this led to the grooming phenomenon continuing and expanding. However, in her report, Casey shows no recognition that for 20 years throughout Britain there had been a failure of child-care professionals and police officers to articulate this discrepancy and a refusal by the media to discuss what was going on. Indeed, from as late as 2011, reports from the House of Commons, CEOP and The Childrens' Commissioner have all been reluctant to acknowledge this discrepancy. Admittedly, it was not within Casey's remit to discuss these national failings; however, she seemed to think that discussing the rise of 'the far right' was within her remit.

The reports by Jay and Casey mark the transition by the establishment in recognizing this discrepancy in ethnicity with the grooming phenomenon, and these reports mark a movement in the officially-approved narrative: the child-care professionals of Rotherham are now being hung out to dry for not having caught up with this change in attitude by the establishment. Over most of the period when the officials in Rotherham were failing, their colleagues throughout Britain in the many other towns with grooming gangs were also failing. There is no reason to believe that there would be different findings if the Jay and Casey reports were conducted into many towns listed in *Appendix 1: Grooming*

30 Louise Casey, 'Report of Inspection of Rotherham Metropolitan Borough Council, Feb 2015', *op. cit.*, p. 40. This fear has been raised of other towns too.
31 *Ibid.*, p. 34.

Gang Convictions. As a senior source said in relation to the revelations about Oxford, published when the Casey report was hot off the printer: 'If you think you haven't got a problem in your city or town, you are just not looking for it.'[32] The situation in Sheffield, a city near Rotherham, does not sound much different to Rotherham: grooming was said to be 'endemic' in Sheffield.[33] And whilst prior to 2014 Sheffield was hardly ever in the news with regard to Muslims grooming schoolgirls for sex, strangely it was the only town to date where it has been reported that the video *My Dangerous Loverboy* (intended to warn schoolgirls of the danger of the grooming gangs), was ever shown in schools. Why would this educational film have been trialled in Sheffield unless the contents would have been of relevance to the schoolgirls there?

It is not only the cities of Bradford, Oxford and Sheffield which seem to have had problems comparable to Rotherham. At the end of 2014 it was also claimed that for more than two decades Birmingham City Council had suppressed a report which showed that there was a connection between 'Asian' taxi drivers and schoolgirls being groomed.

> Dr Jill Jesson was asked by the authority to look at the issue of child prostitution involving girls in care back in 1990.[...] Her report also highlighted claims that some Asian private hire drivers were linked to the sexual exploitation of young white girls in care, including some who had been cautioned for prostitution offences. Yet when Dr Jesson presented her draft findings to a steering group, she was ordered to remove all reference linking ethnicity and the private hire trade. Incredibly, her full amended final report was never published. A meeting planned to discuss it was cancelled – and all copies were to be destroyed.[34]

---

32 'Serious case review slams police failure in serial abuse of Oxford girls', *The Guardian*, 01 Mar 2015, http://www.theguardian.com/society/2015/mar/01/gangs-abused-hundreds-of-oxfordshire-children-serious-case-review

33 'Child sex abuse was endemic in Sheffield, says ex care worker', *BBC News* website, 17 Sept 2014, http://www.bbc.co.uk/news/uk-england-south-yorkshire-29237582

34 'Birmingham City Council hid links between Asian cabbies and child sex victims for 23 years', *Birmingham Mail*, 19 Nov 2014, http://www.birminghammail.co.uk/news/midlands-news/birmingham-city-council-hid-links-8131813. The story goes on to present Birmingham council insisting the full report was published and was discussed some four years after Dr. Jesson wrote it, whilst the local newspaper insists that only part of the report was published. However, when subsequently challenged in a radio programme, it appears that Birmingham council retracted this claim; see 'Child

It is difficult to see how these actions differ from those highlighted in the Casey report, where she points out that Rotherham council was reluctant to allow any connection to be made between 'Asian' taxi drivers and the grooming phenomenon. Casey says about Rotherham:

> Both the Chair of the meeting and the CSE [Child Sexual Exploitation] coordinator pointed out that taxi [sic] and takeaways were identified as a risk nationally and there had been a historic link with CSE in Rotherham. The senior manager did not accept that there was a current problem with CSE and taxis and takeaways.[35]

Moreover, in the above statement the Casey report is making it clear that the grooming behaviour is recognised as following a pattern across the country, and part of that pattern involves 'Asian' taxi drivers and takeaway restaurants. Thus the vectors identified by Dr. Jesson in the West Midlands in 1991 were still being identified by Casey in South Yorkshire in 2015. And there are good reasons to believe that agencies outside of Rotherham are still in denial about the facets of this grooming phenomenon. In a report from 2014, the Birmingham newspaper highlighted a 'confidential' police study which showed that 75% of the perpetrators of 'on street grooming' were 'Asian', whilst 82% of their victims were white. The story concluded that the situation showed that 'children across the region have been failed by police, councils and social services [...which] seemingly mirrors the problem of Asian gangs targeting young girls in places like Oxford, Rochdale and Rotherham'.[36]

Just a couple of months after the publication of the Casey report, a Birmingham newspaper had to use Freedom of Information laws to gain access to a West Midlands Police (WMP) report into the operation of grooming gangs in many towns across the Midlands.[37] The 125 page

---

Sexual Exploitation: We force West Midlands Police to release secret report which confirms "significant similarities" with Rotherham scandal', *Birmingham Mail*, 30 Apr 2015, http://www.birminghammail.co.uk/news/midlands-news/child-sexual-exploitation-force-west-9151006

35 Louise Casey, 'Report of Inspection of Rotherham Metropolitan Borough Council, Feb 2015', op. cit., p. 117.

36 'West Midlands Police report reveals 75 per cent of known on-street child sex groomers are Asian', *Birmingham Mail*, 17 Oct 2014, http://www.birminghammail.co.uk/news/midlands-news/west-midlands-police-report-reveals-7948902

37 'Child Sexual Exploitation: We force West Midlands Police to release secret report which confirms 'significant similarities' with Rotherham scandal', *op. cit.*

report by this police force was heavily-redacted,[38] but even so the local media was able to conclude that the distinctive features of the grooming gang phenomenon from South Yorkshire were to be found in the West Midlands:

> The majority of offenders are typically Asian, of Pakistani origin, aged from 17 to 40.

> A number of Organised Crime Groups associated with CSE exist in the West Midlands. Many are associated with areas of high population densities of Pakistan heritage.

> Victims are typically, but not exclusively, white females aged 13 to 16. Approximately a third are living in care homes and of those living at home, some 25 per cent will have lived in a care home and up to 60 per cent will have an allocated case worker.[39]

Not only was the same disparity in ethnicity between the victims and the perpetrators found, but also the report noted that as with other grooming gangs, 'targeting of victims takes place mainly at children's

---

38 The full report can be found here: 'Child Sexual Exploitation Problem Profile, Oct 2014', http://foi.west-midlands.police.uk/wp-content/uploads/2015/04/724_ATTACH-MENT_011.pdf. Even the pages of the Executive Summary at the start of the report contain blackened-out redactions. WMP claimed that 'the small amount of information that is withheld in these redactions would not add to the public's knowledge sufficiently to warrant the possible compromise of the police role' (see http://foi.west-midlands.police.uk/wp-content/uploads/2015/04/724_PUBLIC_INTEREST_TEST.pdf. It is hard to believe that the bullet points within the two-page Executive Summary contains any operational information which could possibly compromise the criminal investigations of WMP. Perhaps most significantly, the two bullet points in this Summary which are redacted are the two points relating to the ethnicity of the victims and the ethnicity of the perpetrators. This looks far less like an attempt to conceal operational data, and more like an exercise in propaganda. Later on in the report, the authors bemoan the lack of data relating to the ethnicity of perpetrators. This complaint about lack of data is then immediately followed by their own data pertaining to ethnicity being redacted in this report (p. 15).

It should be remembered that West Midlands Police failed in a criminal prosecution against *Channel 4*, when that TV company broadcast a documentary exposing Muslims in mosques across Britain fomenting hatred and subversion.

39 'Child Sexual Exploitation: We force West Midlands Police to release secret report which confirms "significant similarities" with Rotherham scandal', *op. cit.*

homes and schools'.[40] That is, according to this report, the majority of the victims have been living 'in the care' of the state, and have a state-funded allocated child-care professional. The gangs were found to be operating not just in Birmingham, but also in the nearby towns of Wolverhampton, Coventry, Solihull, Sandwell, Dudley, Lye, Brierley Hill, Tipton, Smethwick, Willenhall and Walsall.[41] Moreover, the police report notes that in many cases the local councils seem to know of only a fraction of the victims. In being forced to release this report, West Midlands Police bemoan the lack of data[42] - four years after CEOP also bemoaned the lack of data. The grooming gang phenomenon was first publicly observed in Wolverhampton in 1988 and 1989, but until the local newspaper forced the police to release this report in 2015 the West Midlands was almost never again publicly identified with this grooming phenomenon. Since West Midlands Police only released this report following a demand under Freedom of Information laws, we conclude this police force would have preferred that this report remained unavailable to the general public.[43] Indeed, a few months later, the local newspaper was able to reveal that a 2010 report by this police force had drawn comparisons between a grooming trial in Derby in 2009 with similar criminal activities going on in the West Midlands.[44]

---

40 'Child Sexual Exploitation Problem Profile, Oct 2014', http://foi.west-midlands.police.uk/wp-content/uploads/2015/04/724_ATTACHMENT_011.pdf, p. 9.

41 'Sex abuse gangs in Black Country: "Significant similarities" to Rotherham scandal, say police', *Express & Star*, 02 May 2015, http://www.expressandstar.com/news/crime/2015/05/02/sex-abuse-gangs-in-black-country-significant-similarities-to-rotherham-scandal-say-police/. See also the towns listed here: 'Child Sexual Exploitation: We force West Midlands Police to release secret report which confirms "significant similarities" with Rotherham scandal', *op. cit.*

42 https://foi.west-midlands.police.uk/cse-problem-profile-724_15/

43 Subsequently the UK government has mooted restrictions to these Freedom of Information laws. 'Freedom of Information laws "misused" by journalists, says Chris Grayling', *The Independent*, 29 Oct 2015, http://www.independent.co.uk/news/media/press/freedom-of-information-laws-misused-by-journalists-says-chris-grayling-a6713866.html

44 According to the local newspaper, the police report,
> highlights in shocking detail how young girls in care were being failed by police and Birmingham City Council. Other reports show how predators targeted both children in care and those living at home, virtually unheeded for years. One city outreach worker with the Children's Society had told the 2009 report: "I have no doubt that every girl living in a childrens home in Birmingham is being sexually exploited, has been a victim of sexual exploitation or is being groomed for sexual exploitation." And a "senior stakeholder" in Birmingham Children's Services had said: "There is not a childrens home in Birmingham where a twelve year

Casey's criticism is not confined solely to the officials of Rother-ham council, but also incorporates criticism of the police of South Yorkshire. For example, she draws attention to the police imposing caps on the number of people they would bring to trial, even when vastly more men were implicated.[45] And similar charges as those relating to Birmingham and Rotherham were made last year against the police in Greater Manchester.[46] The problem in Manchester is thought to dwarf Rotherham by the scale of the sexual abuse in what is a much larger city than Rotherham: 'Campaigners fear that the true figure may be far high-er and could exceed the 1,400 victims identified in a report on child sex-ual exploitation in Rotherham over a 16-year-period.'[47] We pointed out that Casey is attributed with exposing that political correctness was of over-riding importance in Rotherham, yet a retired police officer from Greater Manchester has made similar accusations against that force:

> just as political correctness was partly blamed for failing abuse victims in Rotherham [...] "They didn't want to class the abuse as Asian on white girls. They didn't want to cause a fuss," she said. "I took the view that this wasn't about racism, it was about child abuse – but political correctness and cul-tural sensitivities were important to management."[48]

---

old child who has been placed will not come out more sexualised and criminal-ised than when they went in." Meanwhile, a report from 2010 said of suspects, the majority identified were from an Asian background - a large proportion of whom were of Pakistani origin. The majority of suspects in the force area were likely to be from a Muslim background, the report said.

Jeannette Oldham, 'Confidential police reports reveal "threats to life" to failed child sex-ual exploitation victims', *Birmingham Mail*, 23 Jun 2015, http://www.birminghammail. co.uk/news/midlands-news/confidential-police-reports-reveal-threats-9514835

45 Louise Casey, 'Report of Inspection of Rotherham Metropolitan Borough Council, Feb 2015', op. cit., p. 48.

46 'Police "put cap on arrests" in Rochdale sex abuse inquiry: Social worker whis-tleblower says dozens of offenders are still on streets', *The Daily Mail*, 30 Oct 2014, http://www.dailymail.co.uk/news/article-2815055/Police-cap-arrests-Roch-dale-sex-abuse-inquiry-Social-worker-whistleblower-says-dozens-offenders-streets. html

47 'Hundreds of child victims in new sex abuse scandal', *The Times*, 06 Oct 2014, http:// www.thetimes.co.uk/tto/news/uk/crime/article4227800.ece.

48 'Child sex gangs? We are too busy trying to catch car thieves... That's what tar-get-driven police told head of their abuse unit', *The Daily Mail*, 14 Sept 2014, http:// www.dailymail.co.uk/news/article-2755020/Child-sex-gangs-We-busy-trying-catch-car-thieves-That-s-target-driven-police-told-head-abuse-unit.html

So even now it appears that local politicians, council workers and police forces in towns other than Rotherham, are more concerned about their public image and about what cannot be said because of political correctness.[49]

If the attempt to scapegoat Rotherham succeeds in the face of all this evidence, then it will be a testimony to the power of the state to control the truth. The grooming phenomenon is probably endemic to many towns in England, and this was allowed to happen because of failures from the top down, at a national as well as a local level. Only time will tell if the state is able to continue to conceal evidence relating to the grooming gang phenomenon. The statutory funding of the *Barnardo's* project in Bradford in 1995 shows that government Ministers and civil servants must have been aware of the grooming phenomenon for decades. After the Casey report was published, a government panel found that the authorities responsible for scrutinising child-protection failures have

> a deep reluctance in some instances to conduct SCRs [Serious Case Reviews] and the panel has on occasion found the logic tortuous and considerable intellectual effort expended on finding reasons why an SCR is not required.[50]

When such case reviews were held, half of the reviews disclosed failings on the part of the authorities. As was seen with Rotherham, the authorities seemed more concerned with protecting their own reputation rather than revealing their failures in protecting children. Until Rochdale, Oxford, Birmingham, Leicester, Bradford, etc. are subjected to the same level of scrutiny as Rotherham, it is almost certainly just wishful thinking to claim that Rotherham was exceptional.

After decades where the media failed to properly investigate and publicise the grooming phenomenon, from 2011 to 2014 it appeared that journalists have finally acquired the determination to expose the

---

49 The National Crime Agency, which replaced SOCA (the Serious Organised Crime Agency), has said that they have 300 potential suspects to prosecute in Rotherham, including some current and previous local politicians. 'Rotherham sex abuse inquiry identifies 300 potential suspects', *BBC News* website, 24 Jun 2015, http://www.bbc.co.uk/news/uk-england-33256405

50 'How officials invent "tortuous" excuses to block child abuse inquiries', *The Telegraph*, 03 Mar 2054, http://www.telegraph.co.uk/news/uknews/law-and-order/11445772/How-officials-invent-tortuous-excuses-to-block-child-abuse-inquiries.html

long-term failures of police authorities and child-care professionals. Sadly, there is still almost no sign of 21st century journalists acquiring the courage and determination of the 19th century journalist who exposed the child prostitution scandal in Victorian London. Throughout 2015 a new pattern of reporting on the grooming phenomenon emerged: the national media acted as if the official reports into Rotherham and Oxford represented the end of the problem. Local news media would report on the gruesome details of trials in their area, and the national media might report on the conclusion of such trials. If there were any evidence from such trials which refuted the idea that the grooming phenomenon was anything other than some rogue Pakistanis in Rotherham, it was ignored or discounted. Such were the cases in Bristol where the gangs were Somali Muslims. The perpetrators even cited religious motivations for their crimes, yet the national media virtually ignored these trials and the implications from them which showed the inadequacy of focusing on the failings of Rotherham alone. The idea that this was a problem with national and international dimensions was put to bed: no comparisons were to be made with the situation in the Netherlands, no comparisons were to be made with devout Muslim terrorist groups in Nigeria, Iraq and Syria who were abducting schoolgirls and subjecting them to sex-slavery.

FIVE
Systemic Institutional Failure

*There's a culture here of denial and cover-up and a refusal to
accept the reality that we have men ... who treat young girls as
objects for their sexual pleasure. It's time to tell the truth. We
must root out this evil.*
— Denis MacShane MP, *The Times*, 2012

THE PARLIAMENTARY report published in 2013 acknowledges
that here had been a decade of silence and inaction concerning
the Muslim grooming gangs.

> Ann Cryer was right. Since that time [2003], many more chil-
> dren have been abused because of the failures of the agencies
> and of the communities to address what was happening.[1]

We disagree with this simplistic analysis. Ann Cryer was not entirely
right: she blamed 'Asian culture', instead of Islam. Yet it is very rare that
a non-Muslim Asian has been convicted for grooming gang activities.
And furthermore, non-Muslim Asians have counted far more significantly among the victims of the grooming gangs than among the perpe-

---

1 Home Affairs Select Committee Report 'Child Sexual Exploitation and the Response
to Localised Grooming', 10 Jun 2013, http://www.publications.parliament.uk/pa/
cm201314/cmselect/cmhaff/68/68i.pdf p. 52.

trators.[2] There is not one case where it was non-Muslim men grooming
Muslim girls, and that despite the fact that 95% of the men in Britain
are not Muslims. Recently the Muslim Women's Network produced a
report on the Asian children who were victims, and even this Muslim
organisation had to admit that 'Asian/Muslim female victims are most
vulnerable to offenders from their own communities as the overwhelming majority of the offenders were from the same background as the victims.'[3] There is thus no evidence at all that non-Muslim men are grooming Muslim children, but ample evidence that Muslim men are directing
their grooming at non-Muslim schoolgirls.

The first time we can find Ann Cryer making any public statement
about the Muslim grooming gangs was in August 2003, once *Channel
4* began to mention this problem in their news report. It appears that
there was already an officially recognised problem with the grooming
gangs in West Yorkshire in 1995,[4] but we can find no evidence that Ann
Cryer discussed this problem publicly until *Channel 4* broke the story in
2003. As we have shown, by 2003 the problem with Muslim grooming
gangs was known not only in West Yorkshire, but also in Derbyshire
(see section 3.7 *2001 Derby and 'Real Caliphate'*), and the Midlands (see
section 3.1 *1988 Sikh/Muslim violence*), and in those reports it was not
white schoolgirls who were being groomed, but Sikh girls.

In their 2013 report, the Home Affairs Select Committee claims
that 'communities' failed to deal with it. This cannot be interpreted as
anything other than code for the phrase 'the Muslim community failed
to deal with it.'[5] As we have seen, in 1988 Sikhs risked prison sentences
to deal with it when the police failed to constrain the Muslim grooming
gangs. In 1998, a full decade after these first reports of Muslim gangs
grooming Sikh girls, Sikhs created the Sikh Awareness Society in an-

2 'Though most of the girls targeted have been white, among the victims of a Pakistani
gang in one city were several Bangladeshi Muslim girls.' Andrew Norfolk, 'Revealed:
conspiracy of silence on UK sex gangs', *The Times*, 5 Jan 2011, http://www.thetimes.
co.uk/tto/news/uk/crime/article2863058.ece

3 Shaista Gohir MBE, 'Unheard Voices: The Sexual Exploitation of Asian Girls and
Young Women', September 2013, http://www.mwnuk.co.uk//go_files/resources/Un-
heardVoices.pdf, p. 23.

4 See section 3.4 *1995 Bradford: Streets and Lanes*.

5 In 2013, Parliament concluded that the perception that it was 'Asians' (*i.e.* Muslims)
who were principally responsible for these crimes was not inaccurate. Shortly after this,
the Muslim community was applauded in the national media for having 'a sermon'
against grooming gangs. However, the vast majority of the mosques in Britain did not
take part in reading this sermon.

other attempt to stop their girls from falling prey to these gangs. More-over, it is not beyond the realm of possibility, that the 'race riots' which occurred in Bradford and Oldham in 2001 were initially caused by the indigenous working-class British communities trying to protest about these grooming gangs or protesting about the total failure of the state to stop these things.[6] Thus, the only community who failed is the Muslim community. How could the community of the victims be accused of fail-ure? Does this mean that the British government wanted the indigenous population to resort to vigilante violence? The families of the victims often tried to get help for their daughters, but no one would help. No one was prepared to warn parents that their 11 to 14 year old daughters would be targeted by cunning criminals whom the police would not touch. Were those parents (privy to no public information film and no news reports about the gangs' activities) supposed to ferry their daugh-ters to and from school every day, and ensure they were in the company of a trustworthy adult at all times after school? And if they were to im-pose these restrictions on their daughters, didn't the nation have a right to be told why these restrictions were necessary?

We will now turn to examine the various local and national agen-cies and what role they appear to have played in ensuring that the groom-ing gangs were able to go about their predatory business with impunity for so long. Even when the state started to take the problem seriously from 2011 onwards, both the CEOP report and The Children's Commis-sioner report emphasised that many local authorities and other agencies involved in child protection did not respond to requests for data.[7] We have seen that as late as 2010 council officials and police officers were so scared of accusations of racism they would not even speak about the grooming gangs to a respected journalist from *The Times*. This suggests that the campaign of fear orchestrated by the Left and racism groups still holds sway over many of those professionals whose principal concern should be the children for whom they are legally obligated to care.

5.1 Schools

The 2013 parliamentary report noted:

---

6 Given the lack of objective historical research on this subject, there is no indication that we will ever know the truth about those 'race riots.' But one thing is clear: by the time of the 2001 'race riots', Muslim grooming gangs had been operating with impunity in Bradford for 10 years.

7 Home Affairs Select Committee Report, *op cit*. p. 10.

Teachers are more likely to see victims on a regular basis than almost any other professional. They will notice recurrent or prolonged absences and significant changes in behaviour. They are therefore key in identifying children at risk at an early stage and, by raising concerns at an early stage, being able to potentially stop the grooming process before the sexual exploitation has begun.[8]

As the reproductions in *Appendix 4: Leeds School Warning* and *Appendix 5: Sheffield School Warning* show, even in 2013 schools are still noticing Muslim grooming gangs hanging around school gates, with the implied fear that these "Asian men" are waiting to prey on schoolgirls during the transition between the safety of school and the safety of home. Muslim gangs hanging around in cars outside of schools is an identifiable pattern that goes as far back as 1988[9] in Wolverhampton; yet we can think of no national campaign by teachers' unions to publicise such risks. As the parliamentary report said: 'The anecdotal evidence provided to the Committee indicates that teachers are often aware of child sexual exploitation and yet they do not seem to be raising concerns either with social services or the police.'[10] Serious questions need to be asked about the failure of schools and teachers' unions and organisations in this regard.[11]

The accounts of the Sikh vigilante groups in the 1980s report that Muslim grooming gangs would wait in flashy cars outside schools. The report in *The Telegraph* of the incidents in Derby in 2001 also claims that Muslims were being encouraged to mount a systematic campaign of seduction aimed at non-Muslim schoolgirls, where schools were to be considered an 'ideal place' for Muslim men to meet, deceive and seduce non-Muslim girls.[12] Many other reports relate how the gangs use the pe-

---

8 *Ibid.*, p. 48.

9 See section 3.1 *1988 Sikh/Muslim violence*   .

10 Home Affairs Select Committee Report, *op. cit.*, p. 48.

11 A quick glance at the website of the National Union of Teachers shows they are involved in campaigns for children and schools from Greece, to Columbia and Burma: http://www.teachers.org.uk/international/campaigns. There is every reason to have expected them to have initiated campaigns to protect schoolgirls in Britain from being groomed, raped, tortured and prostituted. A search of the NUT website for the term 'grooming' only returned pages referring to children being groomed as consumers by advertisers. In an attempt to find any document by the NUT referring to the grooming gangs, searching their website for the term 'sexual exploitation' was equally futile.

12 See *Appendix 6: Real Khilafah - Letter to Moslem Youth.*

riod when schoolgirls travel from school to home, seeing this as a time of vulnerability where they can get access to the girls. Yet we are unable to find any evidence of schools mounting campaigns to stop this from happening.[13] We can find no evidence that educational organisations or teaching unions have ever done anything to stop the grooming gangs or to draw public or state attention to the threat to these girls from the gangs. If our inability to find such campaigns is not due to failure on our part, then this shows a remarkable dereliction of duty on the part of teachers and their unions over several decades.

There is also evidence that even when it was impossible for teachers to fail to notice that groomed schoolgirls had had prolonged absence or were dishevelled in the classroom, teachers apparently did not act on the evidence in front of their eyes. Before the parliamentary committee, the Deputy Children Commissioner cited

> a case of a victim who was being regularly abducted who was held for several days at a time and sometimes more than a week, without access to food, water or washing facilities. As a result, when released she would be dirty, covered in sores and ill, but on her return to school, nobody would question her about her physical state.[14]

School teachers have a legal duty to act *in loco parentis*. If this had been the story about a child whose parents ignored her absence for a week, and ignored her physical state on return, we would say they were unfit parents. If we view the teachers by this same standard, we must conclude that many of them are unfit to be *in loco parentis*.

In 2008, a government agency tasked with preventing human trafficking, commissioned the film *My Dangerous Loverboy*, with the intention that this film be shown to 13 to 14 year old schoolgirls.[15] This film

---

13 Andrew Norfolk cites a single instance from around 2001, when the headmaster of a Rotherham secondary school sent a letter to parents warning that some of his pupils were being used by adults for sex. 'Shocking facts are beginning to emerge regarding the systematic sexual exploitation of 13 to 16-year-old girls in our care,' he wrote. Andrew Norfolk, 'Police Files Reveal Vast Child Protection Scandal', *The Times*, 24 Sep 2012, http://www.thetimes.co.uk/tto/news/uk/crime/article3547661.ece. However, whilst we should be thankful that this headmaster was at least doing this, we can find no evidence of any campaign by any school about what was going on outside their school-gates in the last 25 years.

14 Home Affairs Select Committee Report, *op. cit.*, p. 48.

15 See section 3.13 *2008 My Dangerous Loverboy*.

was never shown in schools (the only reported viewings of this film were in schools in Sheffield, on some kind of test run). It is not clear to us if the national failure to distribute and show this film is because of ideological objections by teachers and/or teachers' unions, but that seems a possible explanation. We do not believe that non-Muslim Asians found the film objectionable, since the Sikh Awareness Society not only distribute the film, but have gone to the trouble of adding sub-titles to make the message more emphatic. Some of the biggest teachers' unions in Britain, such as the NUT (National Union of Teachers) and the NASUWT (National Association of Schoolmasters Union of Women Teachers), are major sponsors of Unite Against Fascism, an organization which has been associated with attempts to block publicity about the grooming gang phenomenon and the role played by Muslims.[16] Since teachers' unions are so heavily involved with this pressure group, it seems not implausible that the policies espoused by Unite Against Fascism strongly correlate with views of these teaching unions. When it came to stopping the major TV documentary which first clearly addressed the problem of the grooming gangs, it was reported that 'Colin Cramphorn, the then Chief Constable of West Yorkshire, joined groups such as Unite against Fascism in calling for the [2004] documentary to be withdrawn. *Channel 4* complied...'[17]

What part was played, if any, by teachers' unions or the UAF or individual teachers in preventing the distribution/viewing of *My Dangerous Loverboy*? With this video, the national police agencies responsible for child protection rightly made an attempt to stop the supply of

---

16 A list of those supporting unions, representing professional employees in the media and in education, can be found on the UAF's website. http://uaf.o rg.uk/about/ our-supporting-organisations/. To see that this support is more than just financial, one can see evidence of the active involvement of the NUT in the work of the 'anti-fascist' Unite Against Fascism across Britain: in London, http://uaf.org.uk/2012/04/nut-leader-Christine-blower-joins-election-campaign-against-fascists/, in Ipswich, http://www. ipswichnut.org/2013/06/unite-against-fascism-public-meeting.html, in Derby, http:// cityofderbynut.blogspot.co.uk/2013/08/derby-uaf-relaunch-meeting-scheduled.html and in Bolton, http://justice4bolton.org/2010/08/nut-complain-to-police-and-uaf-demand-disclosure-from-police-authority/. The General Secretary of the NASUWT (another teachers' union) speaks at UAF conferences http://uaf.org.uk/2013/02/speakers-announced-for-conference/, and national officers of both NUT and NASUWT are among the 13 officers of the UAF http://uaf.org.uk/about/our-officers/. The NUJ (National Union of Journalists) are also listed as major sponsors of Unite Against Fascism.
17 Julie Bindel, 'Gangs, Girls and Grooming: The Truth', *Standpoint*, Dec 2010, http:// www.standpointmag.co.uk/node/3576/full. See also http://www.telegraph.co.uk/news/ uknews/1462413/Race-fears-halt-film-on-Asian-sex-grooming.html

victims to the grooming gangs. We must demand explanations why this educational film from 2009 was never seen in schools. Who knows how many thousands of schoolgirl victims could have been saved from rape and prostitution if the film had been widely seen by the intended audience? In this whole scandal, the failure to educate schoolgirls about the techniques of the gangs, something that the Netherlands has been doing for years, must rank as the single worst failure by child-care professionals. To the extent that the pool of victims have had any idea about the techniques of the gangs, and how to avoid entrapment, this knowledge would have been acquired in a haphazard way from other schoolgirls or from those parents lucky enough to have an idea about the gangs' techniques. CEOP reports that it trains thousands of child-care professionals every year, but no training was ever passed on to the supply of victims, even though this was clearly seen by national police agencies as an important step in solving this problem.

5.2 Local Councils

When the parliamentary committee reported on localised grooming in 2013, they singled out two local councils in particular for criticism: Rotherham and Rochdale.

> Both Rochdale and Rotherham councils were inexcusably slow to realise that the widespread, organised sexual abuse of children, many of them in the care of the local authority, was taking place on their doorstep... That it took so long for anybody, at any level from the Chief Executive downward, to look at reports of young girls with multiple, middle-aged "boyfriends", hanging around takeaways, drinking and taking drugs, and to think that it might be worth investigating further, is shocking.[18]

In our opinion, this smacks of damage limitation at best, and government cover-up at worst. As we have pointed out, there are far more councils who are blameworthy, not just Rotherham and Rochdale. Furthermore, we maintain there is every reason to believe that local agencies needed the assistance of national agencies and pressure groups, not only to provide them with intelligence and guidance, but also to enable them to withstand the political pressure they would face at a local and

---

18 Home Affairs Select Committee Report, *op. cit.*, p. 27.

national level, should the local agencies attempt to clamp down on the grooming gangs. Having spent decades failing to execute any national policy, it looks like the government is attempting a damage-limitation exercise, holding out that the problem is under control everywhere except Rotherham and Rochdale. The evidence which has emerged about the failings at Rotherham and Rochdale councils will no doubt be found elsewhere if other councils are subjected to scrutiny. It was not just the Chief Executives of these two councils who claimed ignorance of the grooming gangs or showed no interest in responding to them. Let us look at some of the criticisms around Rochdale council.

The Parliamentary inquiry reported that:

> Roger Ellis, who was Chief Executive of the Council [in Rochdale] for 12 years, told us that the first he had heard of the issues around child sexual exploitation in Rochdale was in 2010 following arrests which had been made in December as part of Operation Span.[19]

And the Assistant Director for Children's Social Care said he was unaware of the scale of the grooming problem until arrests in 2010; yet he had worked for Rochdale Social Services for 11 years.[20] A group was set up in 2007 to analyse information about the scale of localised grooming in the borough, and led to the prosecution of three men. Following this investigation, in 2008 it was recommended that 'a multi-agency team' be set up 'as a matter of urgency'. This team did not become operational until 2010, allegedly because of 'funding and staffing' issues.[21] Yet there were staff who gave evidence to the parliamentary inquiry who said that social services in Rochdale knew about the problem as far back as 2004, and nothing was done. It appears that the staff at Rochdale were busy claiming they knew nothing until the last few years: yet this behaviour mirrors the Parliamentary report, which claims that at a national level nothing was known until the last few years, yet significant amounts of funding from 'statutory agencies' was being given to *Barnardo's* in Bradford decades ago, and a few years after funding the *Barnardo's* project in Bradford, the Home Office was involved in complex reports into the activities of grooming gangs in other local authorities.

In 2012, the mother of one of the victims testified at the trial of Ro-

---

19 *Ibid.*, p. 22.
20 *Ibid.*, p. 23.
21 *Ibid.*, p. 21.

chdale men accused of grooming offences, and she said that the council social services team knew of the problems as far back as 2002.[22] She went on to say:

> I wanted the three of them [my daughters] to be put into child protection but they wouldn't do it. I must have called in to social services eight or nine times and phoned them lots of times.

As we saw with the *Channel 4* controversy about Bradford in 2003, and with Julie Bindel's report about Blackburn, Leeds and Sheffield in 2007 and the major trial in Oxford in May 2013, parents across the country were trying in vain to get the councils and the police to take action. Thus, inaction and denial by staff at Rochdale were by no means unique to that area.

In a local inquiry into what had gone wrong in Rochdale, they found that the council did not seriously discuss the issue of grooming until 2010, and then only once 4 arrests had been made:

> Social workers weren't sure how to tackle the problem. "Staff advised they did not know what to do about CSE and how to deal with it".[23]

The report goes on to say that one of the police inspectors involved in Rochdale 'concluded the abuse could have been stopped if only the authorities had stepped in sooner.' For 6 years after the council's child-care professionals were first informed about the Muslim grooming gangs, they and the police did not act. And having been scared into inaction, councils then tried to conceal the fact that they had failed in their duty of child protection. Both Ofsted and the Home Affairs Select Committee found that some of the councils who have come under scrutiny have deliberately tried to conceal information in order to defend themselves and their staff from criticism over their failure to protect the children in

---

22 Nigel Bunyan, 'Rochdale Grooming Trial: Police Knew about Sex Abuse in 2002 but Failed to Act', *The Telegraph*, 9 May 2012, http://www.telegraph.co.uk/news/uknews/crime/9254982/Rochdale-grooming-trial-police-knew-about-sex-abuse-in-2002-but-failed-to-act.html

23 Chris Jones, 'Rochdale grooming scandal: "Lack of care that shames our town"', *Manchester Evening News*, 24 May 2013, http://www.man chestereveningnews.co.uk/news/greater-manchester-news/rochdale-grooming-scandal-lack-care-4011687

their care.[24] The failings by those councils and police forces are just part of a much bigger problem. Before 2011, where was the national debate about this problem? Where was the analysis and guidance from national agencies? With no fear of exposure, no fear of censure, councils and police forces could just ignore what was going on.

Let us now consider some of the events around Rotherham council. Following the murder of Laura Wilson in 2010 by the Muslim man who made her pregnant, Rotherham Council's "Safeguarding Children Board" produced a report into the murder.[25] In Rotherham, council staff were adhering to the politically-correct line, which had been used to rule out *a priori* any consideration that cultural/ethnic values could play any part in this new phenomenon. Andrew Norfolk got access to an unpublished 2010 report into "four victims, aged from 13 to 16, [who] suffered relentless sexual abuse over months and even years before a criminal investigation was launched." But once again, political correctness blinkered the staff, who concluded in the report that:

> although the alleged perpetrators are of Asian origin and the victims are white, this is the factuality of these cases alone; nothing more can be drawn from that. It is imperative that suggestions/allusions of a wider cultural phenomenon are avoided. These assertions are without foundation.[26]

Thus, facts on disparities in ethnicity were admitted, but it is commanded that these facts about disparities must be shorn of all significance. Imagine a criminal investigation, or a medical procedure, where facts are observed and admitted, but it is commanded that they must not be allowed to have any meaning or any implications. There was a conscious refusal to follow where the facts might lead.[27]

---

24 Home Affairs Select Committee Report, *op. cit.*, pp. 18-19.

25 Daniel Miller, 'Social workers hid fact they knew teenage mother was at risk from sex grooming gangs SIX YEARS before she was brutally murdered', *The Daily Mail*, 7 Jun 2012 http://www.dailymail.co.uk/news/article-2155823/Social-workers-hid-fact-knew-teenage-mother-risk-sex-grooming-gangs-SIX-YEARS-brutally-murdered.html

26 Andrew Norfolk, 'Police Files Reveal Vast Child Protection Scandal', *The Times*, 24 Sep 2012, http://www.thetimes.co.uk/tto/news/uk/crime/ article3547661.ece

27 We are confident that this behaviour can be found throughout the agencies responsible for the impunity with which the grooming gangs operated. When the facts could not be ignored, they would be deemed to have no significance. There may not be a paper trail proving this throughout all the agencies, but nothing short of willful blindness can explain the decades of inactivity.

In another instance, it is claimed that Rotherham Council went so far in covering their tracks, they initiated legal action to prevent a leaked copy of a report from being used by *The Times*. The uncensored copy of the report showed that the council had known that from the age of 11, Laura Wilson was at risk of being groomed by Pakistani men. They failed to act on information they had which could have protected her from grooming. Then they actively attempted to stop anyone making any connection between grooming gangs and Muslim men. They concealed this information, and even initiated legal action to maintain the concealment when it looked like it was to become public knowledge.[28]

But it wasn't just Rotherham Council where political correctness served to blinker the staff. A report at the end of 2013 into the failings of child-care professionals at Rochdale council stated that the staff were obsessed with the politically-correct notion that race could not be considered as a factor:

> What is absent is any evidence that practitioners attempted to understand why the fact that the men were "Asian" might in fact have been relevant and legitimate for consideration. There is little evidence that practitioners asked questions as to why quite well established social and racial boundaries were being crossed so frequently. Questions could have been legitimately asked as to whether "friendships" between middle aged "Asian" men and predominantly socially disadvantaged and "challenging" white teenagers required further examination.[29]

Moreover, grooming gang cases have gone to trial as far afield as Oxford, Bristol, Newcastle, and Ipswich. And in some of these cases, the victims and their families have claimed that they notified the child-care services in their area, but nothing was done. There are very strong reasons to believe that the behaviour of child-care professionals in Rochdale and

---

28 'The council went to court in an attempt to tried [sic] to suppress the hidden information after a uncensored copy of the report was leaked to *The Times* newspaper but they have now abandoned legal action.' Daniel Miller, 'Social workers hid fact they knew teenage mother was at risk from sex grooming gangs SIX YEARS before she was brutally murdered', *op. cit.*

29 John Bingham, '"Colour blind" social workers couldn't see glaring racial clues to Rochdale sex abuse', *The Telegraph*, 20 Dec 2013, http://www.telegraph.co.uk/news/uknews/crime/10529794/Colour-blind-social-workers-couldnt-see-glaring-racial-clues-to-Rochdale-sex-abuse.html

Rotherham was replicated across the country for years. CROP estimated that there were 10,000 victims of child sexual exploitation. Yet, over the past 3 decades, only around 177 men have been convicted in grooming gang cases. If CROP's estimates are accurate, then it seems likely that at most councils political correctness led to staff not seeing, not speaking, not acting. If what went on in Rotherham was typical of England as a whole, then we may extrapolate from what is known there to conclude that the total victim count is 100,000 or more. Central government and the local authorities would have a strong incentive to keep a scandal of this magnitude from being explored.

What could possibly motivate child-care professionals to allow schoolgirls to suffer this abuse for so many years, and then be so deeply in denial that these professionals would demand that no-one even discuss the ethnicity of the gang members? Did the pressure brought to bear on *Channel 4* over the documentary *Edge of the City* scare child-care professionals into compromising their integrity? Were the officials of public-service trade unions, supporters of UAF, putting pressure on social workers to turn a blind eye? Did the theoretical framework taught in social work degrees/in-service training encourage these child-care professionals to view the schoolgirls as willing sexual agents and to view the Muslim grooming activity as part of the rich diversity of multicultural Britain? Was it that Muslim or other councillors encouraged the child-care departments to implement a policy of 'see no evil' where the Muslim grooming gangs were concerned? These are not rhetorical questions. Across Britain, thousands of government and local government services ask people racial profiling questions every single day, but when it comes to understanding a new and very serious form of organised crime, it was not an option for child-care professionals to even observe a glaring dichotomy between the ethnicity of the perpetrators and the victims. As the local MP for Rotherham said: 'There is a culture here of denial and cover-up.'[30] A thorough investigation is needed into what forces were responsible for child-care professionals abandoning schoolgirls to be systematically groomed and raped by Muslim gangs across Britain.

For more than a decade, this kind of refusal to acknowledge specifics was to be found not just in council staff, but also across police forces, national agencies, children's charities, and the media. When the *BBC* reported on the banning of *Edge of the City* they reported it as a 'race documentary', thus aligning themselves and most of the national debate with the ideology that only a racist would observe that the victims were

30 Andrew Norfolk, 'Police Files Reveal Vast Child Protection Scandal', *op. cit.*

overwhelmingly white, and the perpetrators overwhelmingly Muslim. The first prosecution in Bradford did not occur until 2005, fourteen years after Andrew Norfolk says that the child-care professionals there knew that 'British Pakistani men' were collecting girls from a children's home, and prostituting them.[31] It is a staggering catalogue of failure, and sometimes even deception, across many councils in Britain.

The claims made by *Channel 4* in 2003 about what was going on in Bradford, should have meant that Bradford council too became the subject of inquiry. The situation in Bradford from 1991 to 2013 has not come in for any of the scrutiny to which Rochdale and Rotherham were subjected. Yet given the assertions of Bradford Council and West Yorkshire Police in 2004 that 'there was no evidence' to support the claim that there were Muslim grooming gangs in operation, it is clear that they too were probably involved in denial just as much as agencies in Rotherham and Rochdale. Once the controversy over the 2004 *Channel 4* documentary died down, the following year West Yorkshire Police closed down the special investigative unit. And just as the Home Affairs Select Committee wound down its investigations (March 2013) singling out the councils of Rotherham and Rochdale for blame, we saw a major grooming gang from Oxford convicted (May 2013). The evidence that came out in that case showed that the local council had been passive for years when it came to the Muslim grooming gangs.[32] And the behaviour of that grooming gang set a new standard in the public recognition of how horrific the treatment of the girls had been. Yet the councils and chief executives of Bradford and Oxford have not been pilloried. Moreover, in 2013 Muslim women in the West Midlands claimed there was extensive grooming going on in that area, yet the West Midlands has come in for no criticism and the local authorities have not been mentioned in relation to this problem in decades, even though the West Midlands is where the Sikh Awareness Society started in the 1990s in order to stop the grooming gangs, and it was the West Midlands where the first news reports of grooming were to occur in the 1980s.

---

31 'Reality of Sexual Grooming Gangs in the UK - interview of Andrew Norfolk and Sikh Awareness Society' http://www.youtube.com/watch?v= WbUIfvYbjRc&-feature=player_detailpage&t=1323. Rotherham council staff first knew about this phenomenon in 1996.

32 Harriet Arkell, "'My mother begged Oxford social services to rescue me from sex abuse NINE YEARS AGO'", *Daily Mail,* 15 May 2013, http://www.dailymail.co.uk/news/article-2324790/My-mother-begged-Oxford-social-services-rescue-sex-abuse-NINE-YEARS-AGO-Victim-known-Girl-C-13-says-claims-dismissed-inappropriate.html

So, we do not believe that what was happening in Rochdale and Rotherham was very different from the rest of the country. *The Daily Mirror* investigation in 2013 regarding which police forces currently have active investigations into grooming gangs, showed that Thames Valley police had 14 current investigations. We believe that the records of child protection services in Bradford, Derby, Wolverhampton and Oxford should be subjected to scrutiny for evidence of indifference, denial, or concealment. From 1988 to 2008 there were scarcely any prosecutions, and those who spoke about the grooming gangs were either ignored or were accused of being racists. In this toxic atmosphere is it any wonder that council staff would decide to turn a blind eye to schoolgirls and parents begging for help, or that council staff would rationalise to themselves why they should ignore the glaring difference between the ethnicity of the perpetrators and the victims? If the CPS would not prosecute, and the council staff would be subject to allegations of 'racism' or even disciplinary action, are we surprised that they chose to conceal this problem?

We cannot find evidence of any council or police force which, under the scrutiny of a public inquiry, could be singled out as having had an appropriate response to the problem during these years. The greater the size of the local Muslim population, the greater likelihood not only that grooming gangs were in operation, but also that there would be Muslim councillors and 'community leaders' who would denounce anyone who spoke about these gangs. And the more Left-wing councillors or MPs an area had, with their commitment to political correctness and multiculturalism, the more likely it would be that they too would join in with such a witch-hunt. At the conclusion of one of the biggest grooming gang trials, Ann Cryer explained that inactivity by police and social services was because they 'were petrified of being called racist and so reverted to the default of political correctness.'[33] We shouldn't be surprised by this, as the furore over *Edge of the City* showed in 2004, even the *BBC* were ready to imply that racism was involved in any allegations that Muslim grooming gangs were seducing and raping schoolgirls.[34]

33 Nigel Bunyan, 'Rochdale grooming trial: Police accused of failing to investigate paedophile gang for fear of appearing racist', *The Telegraph*, 8 May 2012, http://www.telegraph.co.uk/news/uknews/crime/9253250/Rochdale-grooming-trial-Police-accused-of-failing-to-investigate-paedophile-gang-for-fear-of-appearing-racist.html.

34 The *BBC News* website reported that the documentary 'alleged the girls are showered with gifts then given heroin or crack cocaine and some allegedly subjected to rape', but then described this in the headline as a 'race documentary'. 'Campaign to Stop Race Documentary', *BBC News* website, 17 Aug 2004, http://news.bbc.co.uk/1/hi/

The parliamentary investigation seems determined to single out a handful of senior staff in just two councils for responsibility.

> It is no excuse for Rochdale and Rotherham managers to say they had no knowledge of what was taking place, as they are ultimately responsible and must be held accountable for the appalling consequences of their lack of curiosity. Early retirement or resignation for other reasons should not allow them to evade responsibility and they must be held to account. In particular, we are deeply shocked by Roger Ellis' receiving £76,798.20 in redundancy payout. He should be required to repay it.[35]

By all means, hold up the staff of these two councils as examples of the failure. But it should be recognised that all indicators point to this being a failure across the board, a systemic failure. Singling out individual Chief Executives is looking for scapegoats. We have national organisations who should have been paying attention when these claims were made between 1988 and 2003.[36] In fact, there is evidence to suggest that at a national level aound 2007 there was a very good understanding of how these gangs were operating.[37] Individual local councils and council staff are being blamed when there was clearly a lack of determination, a lack of direction, and a lack of support at a national level. Council staff and managers were able to assuage their guilt by telling themselves 'the problem in our area is no worse than in other areas.'[38] They have been telling themselves that for decades. And it might well be true. What the councils needed was direction and support at a national level.

entertainment/3572776.stm

35 Home Affairs Select Committee Report, *op. cit.*, p.28.

36 In 2004, Anna Hall who made the *Channel 4* documentary, was commenting that the grooming gangs were nationwide. See 'Child victims who believe it's about love', *Telegraph & Argus*, 25 Aug 2004, http://www.thetelegraphandargus.co.uk/archive/2004/08/25/7999581.Child_victims_who_believe_it_s_about_love/

37 As we discussed earlier, in 2008 the UK Human Trafficking Centre began the production of a cautionary video (*My Dangerous Loverboy*), to be shown to schoolgirls to warn them of the ways in which grooming gangs work.

38 'Child sexual exploitation "no worse than other town and cities"', *Asian Image*, 21 Nov 2012, http://www.Asianimage.co.uk/news/10061493.print/. Cf. 2004 statement by Bradford's Director of Social services in '"This sexual abuse is not unique to Bradford"', *Telegraph & Argus*, 26 Aug 2004, http://www.thetelegraphandargus.co.uk/archive/2004/08/26/7999558._This_sexual_abuse_is_not_unique_to_Bradford_/

When councils have admitted any fault, it was to argue that any negligence had only occurred in the last few years, rather than admitting that they had failed to respond for probably a decade or more.

> Cheryl Eastwood, the [Rochdale] authority's executive director for Children, Schools and Families, said: "We, along with other agencies working with the young women involved in the recent court case are now aware, with the benefit of hindsight, recent local learning and national safeguarding initiatives, that we missed some opportunities to offer more support and assistance to them in 2008 and 2009."[39]

We think that, should these cases come to civil or criminal litigation, it would be difficult for institutions to claim that they did not know about the underlying realities. This would apply most particularly to councils in the areas of Lancashire and West Yorkshire, and the West Midlands, where evidence of the grooming gangs dates back not just to 2008, but as far as 1998 and even 1988. It appears that such legal action is now beginning, with between four and fifteen girls and women from Rotherham instructing solicitors over the failure of the council to protect them as children, failures dating back to the 1990s.[40] Indeed, it is reported that the deputy leader of Rotherham council, Jahngier Akhtar, has stood down, 'over claims he knew about a relationship between a girl in care and a suspected child abuser.' Mr. Akhtar was also Vice Chair of the Police and Crime Panel.

5.3 Police

We have seen how the parliamentary investigation singled out a few senior individuals of a couple of councils for blame. Almost no other blame is apportioned in the parliamentary report. Neither racism groups, nor police forces, nor national agencies/charities receive any

39 Nigel Bunyan, 'Rochdale Grooming Trial: Police Knew about Sex Abuse in 2002 but Failed to Act', *op. cit.*

40 Caroline Davies, 'Rotherham council faces legal action from alleged abuse victims', *The Guardian*, 23 Aug 2013, http://www.theguardian.com/uk-news/2013/aug/23/rotherham-council-legal-action-alleged-abuse. By January 2014 there were reports that another 11 victims were taking legal action against Rotherham council. 'Rotherham Council to be sued over child sexual exploitation', *The Star*, 1 Jan 2014, http://www.thestar.co.uk/ news/crime/rotherham-council-to-be-sued-over-child-sexual-exploitation-1-6345919

blame. Some blame is apportioned to South Yorkshire Police (in whose patch is the town of Rotherham).[41] However, there is good reason to believe that South Yorkshire Police are not alone in failing to investigate the grooming gangs. As Julie Bindel pointed out in 2007, 'organisations such as Crop continue battling with the police to act on the intelligence they [CROP] have built up.'[42] CROP (Campaign for the Removal of Pimping) was based around Leeds, and as we saw with *Channel 4's Edge of the City*, the Chief Constable of West Yorkshire Police played a major role in getting the documentary withdrawn, joining with Bradford Council to deny that there was any evidence at all for the existence of grooming gangs: 'West Yorkshire Police and Bradford Council said that they had spent the past two years investigating the allegations, but found "no evidence of systematic exploitation."'[43] They could get away with this claim, because most people in Britain had no idea that by 2004 *Barnardo's* had spent almost a decade working with the victims of the grooming gangs in Bradford.[44] If the media had shown courage at this time, they would have brought up the evidence for the existence of this systematic exploitation and challenged these statements. But the majority of journalists were only too ready to bury any discussion of this grooming phenomenon.

In 2011 Detective Chief Inspector Alan Edwardes of West Mercia Police stated that 'to stop this type of crime you need to start everyone talking about it but everyone's been too scared to address the ethnicity factor' and that this was a 'damaging taboo'.[45] Telford falls within the area of West Mercia Police, and it was not until 2012 that a grooming gang from Telford was successfully prosecuted. The newspaper report in which Alan Edwardes was quoted also contained this observation: 'Charities and agencies working in conjunction with the police to help victims of sexual abuse in such cases have publicly denied there is a link between ethnicity and the on-street grooming of young girls by gangs

41 Home Affairs Select Committee Report, *op. cit.*, pp. 34 & 36.

42 Julie Bindel, 'Mothers of Prevention', *The Sunday Times*, 30 Sep 2007, http://www.thesundaytimes.co.uk/sto/news/uk_news/article72310.ece

43 'Campaign to Stop Race Documentary', *BBC News* website, 17 Aug 2004, http://news.bbc.co.uk/1/hi/entertainment/3572776.stm

44 A project which was started with almost £700,000 of money from statutory agencies. See section 3.4 *1995 Bradford: Streets and Lanes*.

45 Chris Brooke, 'Top detective blasts "culture of silence" that allows Asian sex gangs to groom white girls... because police and social services fear being branded racist', *The Daily Mail*, 5 Jan 2011 http://www.dailymail.co.uk/news/article-1344218/Asian-sex-gangs-Culture-silence-allows-grooming-white-girls-fear-racist.html

and pimps.' We can thus see that even as late as 2011, the professional child-care experts were in a state of denial about the Muslim grooming gangs.[46] The actions of these charities also requires investigation.

The 2013 parliamentary report stated that Lancashire Police were among the most accomplished in the country at dealing with child sexual exploitation.[47] However Mick Gradwell, a retired senior officer from the Lancashire Police force, stated that even when he joined that police force in 1979, 'one of the issues was Asian men cruising around in BMWs and Mercs trying to pick up young drunken girls' outside nightclubs.[48] He is reported to have said, 'the targeting of under-age and vulnerable girls had been going on for decades.' Gradwell went on to say that senior officers would not comment on it, for fear of being accused of racism, and went on to ask: 'How many young girls have been abused and raped because of the reluctance of the authorities to say exactly what is happening?' The mother of one of the victims in the 2012 Rochdale case stated that 'over the years both police and social services turned a blind eye to the abuse.'[49]

Numerous examples have come to light illustrating incredible behaviour by police forces. One story that came before the Home Affairs Select Committee went like this: at 5am a mother found her 13 year old daughter in their home with a 32 year old man.

> Her mother phoned the police, reporting that Child S had been burnt by the man. Upon arrival, the police were told by Child S that she had burnt herself and so the police took no further action and failed to inform social services of the event. This was despite the fact that she had been considered to be at risk of child sexual exploitation since she was ten.[50]

In his analysis of hundreds of unpublished reports from police and social services on grooming gangs, Andrew Norfolk relates some more incredible stories:

---

46 See section 5.9 *Barnardo's*.

47 Home Affairs Select Committee Report, *op. cit.*, p. 32.

48 Jaya Narain, 'Police chief: "We couldn't speak out on Asian sex gangs for fear of appearing institutionally racist"', *The Daily Mail*, 12 Jan 2011 http://www.dailymail.co.uk/news/article-1346291/Police-chief-We-speak-Asian-sex-gangs-appearing-racist.html

49 Nigel Bunyan, 'Rochdale Grooming Trial: Police Knew about Sex Abuse in 2002 but Failed to Act', *op. cit.*

50 Home Affairs Select Committee Report, *op. cit.*, p. 34.

Two girls aged 14 and 15 were allegedly being sold for sex by a man known to police for criminal activities including pimping. He charged £10 a time to Asian men who collected the girls in cars and taxis, returning them to their home neighbourhood after each sexual encounter.[51]

A girl's mother copied the names, numbers and text messages of 177 Asian men, including a police officer, from her daughter's mobile phone after the 13-year-old went missing for five days. Police said that using the information would infringe the girl's and the men's human rights.[52]

Two terrified girls, who were dragged into a car and driven to Bristol to be used for sex as part of a drugs deal, phoned support workers to seek help. Officers from Avon and Somerset Constabulary rescued them and returned them to Sheffield on a train. South Yorkshire Police did not question them about the incident.[53]

If Lancashire Police are considered among the best in the country at tackling child sexual exploitation, yet a former senior officer from that force says they had turned a blind eye to the grooming for decades, that force might only be considered 'the best' because the standard has been set so low. One man claims he has been trying to extract information from various police forces concerning their behaviour in relationship to the grooming gangs, and the police have even refused to honour Freedom of Information requests.[54] At the end of a major grooming gang prosecution in Lancashire, Assistant Chief Constable Steve Heywood denied sweeping the issue of Asian sex gangs under the carpet.[55] Yet as we have shown from the statements of retired police officers, police in Lancashire have apparently known about grooming gangs since the

51 Andrew Norfolk, 'Police Files Reveal Vast Child Protection Scandal', *op. cit.*

52 *Ibid.*

53 *Ibid.*

54 Tony Shell, 'The Culpability of the State in the Gang-Related Sexual Exploitation, Abuse, and Murder of Young English Females', 2013, http://www.darklake-synectics.co.uk/ithilien-web/docs/special_projects_19.pdf, p. 10.

55 Nigel Bunyan, 'Rochdale Grooming Trial: Police Knew about Sex Abuse in 2002 but Failed to Act', *op. cit.*

1970s and that the senior officers would refuse to discuss the problem. At a national level, the Serious Organised Crime Agency knew enough about the grooming gangs to commission *My Dangerous Loverboy* in 2008. If South Yorkshire Police are to come in for severe criticism, then so should the police forces of Lancashire, Manchester, West Yorkshire, West Midlands, East Midlands, Thames Valley and probably many other areas. The failure of police to investigate and prosecute Muslim grooming gangs resulted in vigilante violence in Wolverhampton in 1988, and in Leicester in 2013. It may well be that the oft-reported cause of the Muslim riots which occurred in Oldham and Bradford in 2001, were only proximally 'caused' by a demonstration by 'nationalists'. We are never told what those 'nationalists' were demonstrating about: it is just possible that the protests were brought about by the failure of the police to prosecute Muslim grooming gangs.[56]

In effectively exonerating police forces around the country, the parliamentary report stated that victims would often reveal information to 'youth workers' but would then refuse to make those statements to the police, and that success often comes from building a case that does not rely on the schoolgirl's testimony, but which is instead built a on objective evidence, such as evidence from CCTV.[57] Yet in 2007, Julie Bindel reported how mothers were gathering evidence that the police would then dismiss: it wasn't the case that the police used that evidence to subsequently set up surveillance operations. They simply dismissed the mothers and their concerns.

We are always being told that 'lessons have been learned', but it seems quite clear that this is meant to placate the public and is a deceit. In the heart-breaking story from 2007, of mothers having to do the de-

---

56 It is interesting to note, that the nationalist demonstration was banned, yet still Muslims rioted. http://en.wikipedia.org/wiki/2001_Bradford_riots. The report does not state why the 'nationalists' wished to hold a demonstration in Bradford, a city where *Barnardo's* had been running a project to help the victims of grooming gangs for the preceding five years. Two months before Muslims rioted in Bradford, they rioted in Oldham. Once again, the causes of these riots are vague, but one of the causes cited was the disproportionate amount of racist violence towards white people: 'In the year leading up to the riots, there were 572 reported ethnicity related crimes in the Oldham area, and in 62% of these, white persons were recorded as being the victim.' http://en.wikipedia.org/wiki/2001_Oldham_riots. In Oldham in 2001, white British were 71% of the population, 27% were Asian. http://en.wikipedia.org/wiki/Oldham. In the case of Oldham, it seems that the 'nationalists' were demonstrating about the racist violence towards white people. However, this may not be the full story with these riots in Oldham and Bradford.

57 Home Affairs Select Committee Report, *op. cit.*, p. 31.

tective work the police would not do, Julie Bindel points out that:

> Recommendations following the Soham murders clearly state that police should arrest in cases where older males have sex with a child under the age of 16. However, police rarely take action unless the victim complains, thereby allowing the pimps and their customers to act with impunity.[58]

Over and over again, it is manifest that police forces from South Yorkshire, to Lancashire, West Mercia to West Yorkshire have not followed these recommendations. The blame for this crisis escalating over the last 25 years does not just lie with one or two councils or police forces, it seems clear that there has been a pattern of neglect across the board, on both a local and a national level.

5.4 Criminal Justice System

One of the reasons why council staff and police officers have turned a blind eye to the Muslim grooming gangs, was that they feared being accused of racism. However, if the criminal justice system had been sufficiently attuned to this new form of criminal behaviour, it may have been easier for police forces to secure convictions, thus providing a positive feedback mechanism for police officers and council staff to continue to pursue the exploitative gangs. It must make it easier for childcare professionals to deal with the false accusations of racism, when the details of the grooming activities come out in open court, and a jury decides to convict the child rapists. However, as if the schoolgirl victims have not suffered enough, it has been observed that 'some victims... found the court process worse than the actual exploitation.'[59] After one day of giving evidence in a recent trial, one of the victim's who was testifying attempted suicide.[60] Whilst it might be hard to compile a criminal case across agency and regional boundaries, and whilst it might be hard to get the schoolgirls to realise that they were victims from the time the grooming was initiated, surely facilitating the trial process is something

---

58 Julie Bindel, 'Mothers of Prevention', *op. cit.*

59 Home Affairs Select Committee Report, *op. cit.*, p. 41.

60 Hayley Dixon, 'Teenager giving evidence against sex gang accused attempted suicide', *The Telegraph*, 6 Aug 2013, http://www.telegraph.co.uk/news/uknews/crime/10224527/Teenager-giving-evidence-against-sex-gang-accused-attempted-suicide.html

that is within the power of national agencies? If the trial procedure is even worse than being tortured and sexually abused, there is something very wrong with the criminal justice system.

It's not just the trial procedure which is at fault. The Crown Prosecution Service (CPS) seems to have been reluctant to prosecute, and at times has been downright obstructive. In 2009, Police in Rochdale carried out a four month investigation into grooming and sexual exploitation in that area. Greater Manchester Police arrested six 'Asian' men, and sent the details of the investigation to the CPS. The CPS refused to take any further action, saying that the victim lacked credibility as a witness:

> [I]t took them [Greater Manchester Police] 11 months to send a file on the case to the Crown Prosecution Service, which decided in July 2009 that Girl A would not be a credible witness in court and did not, therefore, go ahead with a prosecution. The police decided not to contest the decision even though Ahmed had no explanation for how his DNA had been found on Girl A's underwear.[61]

After complaints to the Home Office two years later, this decision by the CPS was overturned and led to the conviction in 2012 of nine Muslim men from Rochdale for a variety of crimes relation to grooming and sexual abuse.[62] As the Home Affairs Select Committee noted in 2013, the CPS 'has readily admitted that victims had been let down by them and have attempted... to discover the cause of this systematic failure.'[63] The parliamentary investigation offers no indication as to what could be the cause of the CPS 'systematic failure' with regard to these cases. When this case in Rochdale went to trial, it turned out to be far more shocking than any of the grooming trials which had preceded it in the previous 15 years: in fact, it was probably the single most significant grooming trial in those 15 years, not just because of the number of men convicted, but also for the number of schoolgirls they had groomed. And yet this key trial almost fell by the wayside, as the CPS refused to proceed with

---

61 Nigel Bunyan, 'Rochdale grooming trial: how the case unfolded', *The Telegraph*, 21 Jun 2012, http://www.telegraph.co.uk/news/uknews/crime/9347305/Rochdale-grooming-trial-how-the-case-unfolded.html

62 Tony Shell, 'The Culpability of the State in the Gang-Related Sexual Exploitation, Abuse, and Murder of Young English Females', 2013, http://www.darklake-synectics.co.uk/ithilien-web/docs/special_projects_19.pdf, p. 6.

63 Home Affairs Select Committee Report, *op cit.*, p. 33.

it. Without complaints to the Home Office about the failure of the CPS, this significant gang (who had been abusing 50 girls for many years), would have continued unhindered. Yet Parliament did not think that the CPS merited any particular censure for their role in the failures to stop the grooming gangs.

A brief examination of the case of 12 year old Samantha shows how the criminal justice system treats these kinds of cases, even when the CPS has actually decided to proceed with a prosecution. On October 27th 2006, Samantha:

> was abducted by two Asian men who drove her around Old-ham for hours and then raped her. They then threw her out of a moving car in the Chadderton area of Oldham. She ran away and asked another man for help. He invited Samantha inside and then dragged her upstairs and sexually assaulted her. She ran away whilst he was calling his friends to come and join him. At that point a taxi driver and his passenger pulled up beside her to ask her if she was okay, they said she looked very upset and like she'd been through hell, and so offered to take her to the police station and then home... They then took Samantha to a house on Attock Close, took her inside and then locked her in a room where 5 Asian men went on to rape her over and over for nearly 24 hours. The ringleader, was Shakil Choudhury, and he received a three year sentence for leading this extraordinary attack.[64]

Whilst this case is not included in our list of grooming gang convictions, it has all the hallmarks: multiple 'Asian' men abducting and raping a non-Muslim schoolgirl. In fact, she seems to have been abducted and raped by three separate Muslim groups on the same day. We have not included this case in our list of grooming convictions, as there is no indication that a 'grooming' process was involved. Nevertheless, it gives us some idea of just how common it is for disparate groups of men in some Muslim communities in Britain to consider abducting, raping and sharing a non-Muslim schoolgirl amongst their friends and relatives. The

---

64 http://www.youhavenotdefeatedme.co.uk/Featured/what-happened-to-sammi.
html. Shakil Choudhury actually received a sentence of six years, but was released after three years. The website dedicated to this case is apparently conflating this distinction. Nevertheless the end result is shocking: a man responsible for multiple rapes of a 12 year old schoolgirl only spends three years in prison for his crimes.

men in this report clearly have little fear of being caught and convicted of any crime, and seeing a schoolgirl in a vulnerable situation clearly sets off ideas in their minds which most of the population of Britain would never contemplate.

And what happened when this case entered the criminal justice system simply reinforces the belief of these abusive men that they can behave like this without any significant punishment. Of all those men involved in the abduction and sexual abuse of this 12 year old girl, *just one was prosecuted*. And this lone man, Shakil Choudury, served only 3 years (of a 6 year sentence) for these crimes, despite sentencing guidelines that should have ensured he got a custodial sentence of between 11 and 17 years.[65] Appeal judges refused to extend the sentence (apparently because violence was not used, and the girl had consumed alcohol.) Even though he refused to name his accomplices, Choudury was released after 3 years.[66] Thus, even if the CPS decided to proceed with a prosecution, trial and appeal judges give derisory sentences. It appears as though the blindness of political correctness extends as far as the judiciary, who think that a (possibly) wayward 12 year old girl is somehow asking to be abducted, raped and abused. One has to wonder: would the perpetrators have escaped so lightly if they had been non-Muslims? Could it be that the judiciary have been systematically lenient to Muslim men? Could 'the racism of low expectations'[67] be so pervasive, that the judiciary are unaware of what they are doing? Do they operate a form of 'reverse racism' where they expect 'Asian' men to conform to lower standards of behaviour than others?

One of the most incredible parts of the 2013 parliamentary report, is that the MPs involved felt it necessary to spell out that these under-age girls cannot legally consent to sex. That the sex takes place at all is a

---

65 Tony Shell, 'The Culpability of the State in the Gang-Related Sexual Exploitation, Abuse, and Murder of Young English Females', *op. cit.*, See p. 5 and note 23.

66 'Six years for paedophile "is long enough"', *Manchester Evening News*, 28 Dec 2007 http://www.manchestereveningnews.co.uk/news/local-news/six-years-for-paedophile-is-long-1015378

67 The 'racism of low expectations' is when people expect lower moral or intellectual standards from people from ethnic minority backgrounds; the assumption being that people from those ethnic minorities are actually incapable of attaining the same moral or intellectual heights as white people. Those who suffer from this form of racism are often even unaware that they are lowering the bar for ethnic minorities, resulting in them implicitly having the same view of the relationship between white people and ethnic minorities as explicitly avowed by racial supremacists. See Sunny Hundal, 'The soft racism of low expectations', *The Guardian*, 30 Jun 2006, http://www.theguardian.com/commentisfree/2006/jun/30/panderingtocrackpots

criminal offence, especially if the men involved know that the girl is under 16 (or under 18 in the case of someone paying for sex).

> It is widely acknowledged that the criminal justice system has failed to adequately protect and support victims of local-ised grooming and child sexual exploitation... The confusion about whether or not these children were "consenting" to sexual activity (though the law clearly says that they cannot) was also a factor which influenced police decisions.[68]

Considering the amount of training undergone by police officers, so-cial workers, teachers and state prosecutors it is truly staggering that any of them should have attempted to defend their inaction by saying they thought the schoolgirls had consented. *These schoolgirls could not consent to sex with these men any more than they could consent to buy a house or take out a bank loan.* That Parliament felt this needed to be explicitly spelt out is a strong indication of how much courts, police and child-care professionals have abandoned recommendations laid down for child protection. With that in mind, we must wonder at the decisions of the judges involved in the Shakil Choudary case, who thought that the rape victim not attempting to escape was an indication that she was consenting[69]—something that parliament has now spelt out was impos-sible, even if she had been propositioned and agreed to sex, never mind being abducted and raped.

Another betrayal of the victims occurs when a schoolgirl goes to the police to make an allegation: if she is not prepared to support an immediate prosecution the case is dropped. Parliament stated that 'it may take many years for victims to disclose the full extent of their abuse and for them to trust the criminal justice system to treat them with the sensitivity they require and deserve.'[70] In such circumstances, the alle-gations should be recorded and kept on file. Whilst the Home Affairs Select Committee did not spell it out, it is clear that given the complex-ity of these cases, the police should start to investigate the accused and

---

68 Home Affairs Select Committee Report, *op. cit.*, p. 34.
69 'Six years for paedophile "is long enough"', *op. cit.*
  ...despite the "disgusting" nature of his crime, there was no evidence that force was used to make her comply, the judge noted. Despite the lengthy sex sessions with the four men lasting all through the night, the [12 year old] girl had not objected...
70 Home Affairs Select Committee Report, *op. cit.*, p. 29.

start to put him under surveillance, as other objective evidence could be discovered, implicating him in something far larger than the abuse of one girl.

It is quite often the case that the sexual exploitation of the school-girl takes place years before a prosecution, and any prosecution may take place years after the young woman has escaped the clutches of the gang. In such circumstances the victim receives no special protective measures during the trial process (such as having the help of an inter-mediary in the court).[71] Parliament also noted that even when a victim was eligible for special protective measures in court, these special mea-sures often failed or were missing 'leading to the victim either feeling unable to give evidence or being so shaken that their evidence presents as being unreliable.'[72] It does not serve justice if parliament mandates that special measures be offered to young people in a trial, but the trial then continues when these measures have failed to be put in place by the court.

In the Youth Justice and Criminal Evidence Act (1999) it was agreed that video recording of cross-examination or re-examination should be available to young and vulnerable witnesses. Yet in 2013, Par-liament stated 'we are at a loss to understand why the Ministry of Justice, fourteen years after the Act was passed, has still failed to implement this measure.'[73] If this advance had been implemented in the early years of the 21st century (along with the other provisions intended to help young witnesses), more prosecutions of grooming gangs could have succeeded, because the witnesses would have been less intimidated by the proceedings. And if more convictions had succeeded, then parents, schools, social services and police forces would not have felt powerless, and would have been more likely to take action when presented with evidence of grooming gang activities. Furthermore, successful prosecu-tions, and the details which came out during the trial process, would have made it impossible for allegations of 'racism' to stop this phenom-enon from becoming public knowledge, and a wide-scale public debate would have taken place years ago. The public outcry over the activities of the grooming gangs across the country would have meant that the years of inactivity by the national crime organisations could not have gone unchallenged.

As the Home Affairs Select Committee said in 2013: 'the balance

71 *Ibid.*, p. 42.
72 *Ibid.*, p. 41.
73 *Ibid.*, p. 40.

is skewed too strongly in favour of protecting the defendant's rights as opposed to the very vulnerable witnesses in cases of child sexual exploitation.[74] It is a bitter irony that it should have taken these eminent politicians, with their expert witnesses, and the ruined lives of perhaps 100,000 vulnerable schoolgirls to grasp what the mothers were saying a decade earlier.

> The mothers say the fact the men are Asian isn't an issue for them -- they say they just want this abuse stopped. They met David Blunkett in person to argue that if criminal proceedings can't be brought because their daughters won't make complaints to the police then the law needs changing.[75]

Moreover, if the politicians were not prepared to listen to the mothers, then one might have hoped they would have listened to Prof. Barrett, who in 2008, pointed out that intent of The Children's Act (1989) was being ignored.[76]

The narrative of racism has been horribly abused, to prevent justice being done. The case of Samantha, outlined above, shows that the decades in which these gangs have been able to get away with their child abuse has made the gangs very sure that the odds are stacked in their favour. The mothers' intuition is probably correct: new laws will be required in order to undo the damage of three decades of inactivity. Localised grooming will need to be identified as a specific crime, with a very heavy penalty. The judiciary will need to be instructed to put the child's interests first. And the CPS needs to be investigated to see why it was

---

74 *Ibid.*, pp. 44-45.

75 'Asian Rape Allegations', *Channel 4 News*, 27 Aug 2003, (from archive.org) http://web.archive.org/web/20100620042427/http://www.channel4.com/news/articles/society/law_order/Asian+rape+allegations/256893

76 'Abused Girls: What Do We Know?', http://news.bbc.co.uk/1/shared/bsp/hi/pdfs/27_03_08_whatweknow.pdf.

> The 1989 Act received all-party support in its drafting stages and enshrines "the welfare of the child shall be the court's paramount consideration"; this implies it takes precedence over that of adults. The current "children versus adults" battles, regarding various forms of abuse cases, which are regularly played out in the legal system, have become a power see-saw which undermines this bedrock principle of the 1989 Act. Moreover, it also appears to give way to operational caveats such as wider issues of culture, politics and geography, because we continue to see regional variations in the application of the child protection laws despite ample safeguarding guidance to the contrary, which requires consistency and transparency.

so reluctant to proceed with major prosecutions, such as the Rochdale trial, where the police appealed above the CPS.

The regional police forces and the judicial system have failed these children so spectacularly and for so long, that some council lawyers are being praised for their resourcefulness in using 'Medieval' laws simply in order to obtain injunctions to stop a group of men from approaching girls, without needing to prove any guilt of these men in a court of criminal law.[77]

5.5 Child Exploitation and Online Protection Centre

The Child Exploitation and Online Protection Centre (CEOP) has existed since 2006, and is a cross-agency department of the Serious and Organised Crime Agency.[78]

The centre is split into three faculties; Intelligence, Harm Reduction and Operations. Each faculty is supported by teams covering governance, communications, partnerships and corporate services. The intelligence faculty receive intelligence of online and offline offenders; all reports made through the centre's website, [sic] and ThinkUKnow are dealt with at any time of day so that law enforcement action can be taken. The Harm Reduction faculty manage Public Awareness campaigns and educational programmes, including the ThinkUKnow education programme, which is currently being used in UK schools.[79]

Considering that CEOP is principally about the gathering and dissem-

---

77 'How a local authority is using the law to protect girls from sexual exploitation', *The Guardian*, 19 Nov 2014, http://www.theguardian.com/l aw/2014/nov/19/local-authority-using-law-protect-girls-exploitation-birmingham. The men were named as: Omar Ahmed, Mohammed Anjam, Sajid Hussain, Nasim Khan, Shah Alam, and Mohammed Javid. 'Six men named as subject of anti-grooming orders', *The Guardian*, 19 Nov 2014, http://www.theguardian.com/uk-news/2014/nov/19/six-men-anti-grooming-orders-high-court-birmingham. West Midlands Police had attempted to stop their names being made public.

78 Since we first wrote this report, the Serious Organised Crime Agency has been wound up, and replaced with a new agency call the 'National Crime Agency'. However, CEOP still exists as a part of the NCA.

79 http://en.wikipedia.org/wiki/Child_Exploitation_and_Online_Protection_Centre#-Faculties

ination of information about offenders, and about discerning international patterns of child exploitation, it is reasonable to have expected them to have been intervening with the grooming gang problem from the inception of CEOP in 2006. At the very least, we could have expected them to be assembling intelligence from local services, and using this to build up an idea of what was going on nationally (or within regions). From this intelligence, they could then have devised training programmes for professionals in the field, and provided advisory services to government and other national agencies (*e.g.* the CPS, the Ministry of Justice), concerning the scale of the problem and the complexity involved in curtailing the gangs. But until 2011, there appeared to be no intelligence analysis nor 'harm reduction' strategy from CEOP in this regard.

In June 2011, CEOP released a report on the spate of gangs being convicted for grooming schoolgirls.[80] In this report, CEOP invents the term 'localised grooming'. This term cannot be found on their website before 2011.

> CEOP has carried out a rapid assessment of "localised grooming" in the UK. This is a form of sexual exploitation, previously referred to as "on street grooming" in the media, where children have been groomed and sexually exploited by an offender, having initially met in a location outside their home, usually in a public place (such as a park, cinema, on the street or at a friend's house). Offenders often act in concert, establishing a relationship with a child or children before sexually exploiting them. Some victims of "street grooming" may believe that the offender is in fact an older "boyfriend", introducing peers to the offender group who may also be sexually exploited. Abuse may occur at a number of locations within a local area and on several occasions. "Localised grooming" has been subject to considerable media attention following a number of prosecutions of adult males for the grooming and sexually exploitation of children and young people in various towns and cities in the UK. Several NGOs have reported that large numbers of victims of this type of child sexual exploitation have accessed their services across the UK. However, there have been comparatively few prosecutions, and

---

80 CEOP, 'Out of Mind, Out of Sight - Breaking Down the Barriers to Understanding Child Sexual Exploitation', Jun 2011, http://ceop.police.uk/Publications/

> there is a general lack of knowledge of grooming and sexual
> exploitation in the UK and the threats posed to children and
> young people.[81]

Significantly, CEOP qualify 'grooming' to be 'localised grooming', betraying that their interest is with internet-related grooming and child
pornography on the internet, and on cross-border trafficking. In the
CEOP definition of 'localised grooming' they excluded 'peer-on-peer
exploitation, online grooming, familial child sexual abuse, stranger
abduction and the trafficking of non UK nationals for sexual exploitation.'[82] Yet if they had been focussing on real-world grooming of schoolgirls, then it would have been the 'online grooming' which became a
qualified term. In setting up CEOP it was not called 'The Online Child
Exploitation Protection Centre', yet apparently, when it came to British
children, they were only interested in 'online protection': the child exploitation component of CEOP's remit covered the trafficking of foreign
children into the UK, but not the exploitation of British children within
Britain. Could it be that when CEOP was set up, they were explicitly told
that their concern was only to focus on internet-related issues and international issues? Was it made clear when CEOP was established, that
it was to ignore the Muslim grooming gangs? Or were the staff at CEOP
also victims of political correctness, who dared not study or report on
the Muslim grooming gangs? Questions need to be asked of what went
wrong at CEOP.

That CEOP had to carry out a 'rapid assessment' of a problem that
was known by the general public to exist since the first few years of the
21st century, a problem that was known by organisations like *Barnardo's*
since before 1995, shows that CEOP had ignored this aspect of 'child
exploitation'. No doubt the grooming gang phenomenon was known to
journalists, social workers and police officers long before 2003; SAS was
founded in 1998, to deal with the grooming of Sikh girls. Thus CEOP
seems to have been set up principally to protect children who have com-
puters in their own bedrooms from being groomed by online paedophiles. It appears CEOP had scant regard for children who are drugged,
raped and pimped-out in the real world. If CEOP had been actively
gathering information, they would have known there was a very real
problem. Yet it is 5 years after the creation of CEOP before they issue a
report which even touches on the grooming gangs. Why would Parlia-

---

81 *Ibid.*, p. 5.
82 *Ibid.*, p. 10.

ment ask CEOP to produce a report if it was not part of their remit? And if it was part of their remit, why were they doing a 'rapid assessment' and who are they to bemoan the lack of data? If it was part of their remit, then they should have had this information-gathering in hand years earlier. In 2008 the United Kingdom Human Trafficking Centre (UKHTC), which like CEOP was part of SOCA, was already commissioning an educational video to warn schoolgirls about the gangs, yet it was another 3 years before CEOP considered what their information-gathering and advisory responsibilities were in this area.[83]

CEOP's 2008 self-congratulatory Annual Report says:

> The coordination of online police resources is delivering not only an economy of scale but a more effective assault on predators. Six major paedophile rings have been dismantled in the last twelve months and our tracker teams have traced more missing sex offenders than ever before. With a large and varied number of investigations now underway, the child abuser is facing an increasingly hostile environment both on and offline.[84]

So CEOP saw it as their business to destroy organised groups who were sexually exploiting children. Yet they gave a wide birth to the grooming gangs in Britain. There seems to be no justification whatsoever for CEOP's investigative and analytical and training failures. They were proudly breaking up paedophile rings, but not when those paedophile rings consisted of Muslim men.

CEOP was not only concerned with gathering of intelligence in order to gain criminal convictions. The CEOP 2008 report goes on to say that in the previous year '2,600 law enforcement and child protection professionals have attended specialist CEOP training courses.'[85] This was a year in which a mere six 'localised groomers' were convicted. It's not even as though 2009 fared much better with these 2,600 newly-trained child-care professionals: again, only six 'localised groomers'

---

83 It seems very strange that one part of SOCA was so aware of the problem it was commissioning an educational video to warn the victims, but years later another part of SOCA was claiming to have only just discovered the problem existed.

84 'CEOP Annual Review', 2008, http://ceop.police.uk/Documents/ceopannualreview2008.pdf p. 7.

85 *Ibid.*, p. 9.

were convicted.[86] Where are the economies of scale in this? It is great that six paedophile groups were broken up, but there could be hundreds of Muslim grooming gangs in operation.

In 2007 Julie Bindel had reported in *The Times* on how the mothers of the victims of grooming gangs had been amassing chronological and photographic evidence by themselves, only to have the police then refuse to look at the evidence. The 2008 CEOP report goes on to say how important it is to listen to children, and to explain the role CEOP played in creating an International Youth Advisory Congress. Yet thousands of schoolgirls might have been saved from the exploitation of the grooming gangs, if CEOP had spent time training social workers and police officers about the specific characteristics of the grooming gangs, and the signals that a child was in their clutches, or that children in an area were being targeted outside schools or takeaways, in shopping malls and shopping centres. CEOP could have been measuring the progress of different police forces, and pointing out those whose prosecution rate lagged behind the intelligence reports indicating grooming gang activity.

Based on other documents produced by CEOP, the organisation's principle concerns in 2009 were internet technology and digital imagery, criminal finances from child pornography, and the international travel of sex offenders. In 2009 there is no mention whatsoever of 'localised grooming' within their list of 'key intelligence requirements'.[87] When they break down their investigations into offender behaviour, fully 48% of it is dedicated to grooming, but once again, apparently it is only in the sense of 'online grooming' with which CEOP is concerned. There seems to have been an astonishing blind-spot when it comes to the Muslim grooming gangs. Let us remember, the Association of Chief Police Officers says there are tens of thousands of grooming gang victims every year, and extrapolating from the Rotherham statistics there could easily be as many as 100,000 victims spanning recent decades.

Having ignored the issue of real-world grooming and sexual exploitation happening within Britain, when CEOP came to write its 'rapid assessment' of the situation, it was clear that they were going to be writing a report that would at most provide a rough idea of what was going on. The report 'aimed to determine the known extent of child sex-

---

86 See *Appendix 1: Grooming Gang Convictions*.
87 'CEOP Strategic Overview, 2008-2009', http://ceop.police.uk/Documents/strategic_overview_2008-09.pdf. p. 10.

ual exploitation.'[88] The CEOP report says:

> Given the pace with which relevant data was collated, agencies had a limited timeframe to interrogate their data storage systems, extract relevant information and configure data into a format suitable for submission to CEOP. Agencies from each sector faced particular difficulties in submitting a comprehensive response.

What was the rush? Why would the national crime agency tasked with providing this report not have the data? The problem of the grooming gangs got national publicity almost a decade before this report was produced. Why the sudden rush? Because suddenly in 2011, people across Britain were asking questions, and MPs must have found that they did not have the answers. However, the key question is: why would a dedicated cross-agency child sexual exploitation group have not been collating this information about this major form of child sexual exploitation over the previous five years? And having rushed to get an inadequate report out, why have two years elapsed without CEOP returning to this problem and doing a professional and thorough analysis? At what point will CEOP have adequate data?

The sample data in this 2011 report has perpetrators and victims classified on racial rather than religious grounds. That is probably all the data they had, since police forces are not compelled to record the religious beliefs/background of perpetrator and victim. But it means that the question and the answer are going to be off-kilter. If CEOP had been attending properly to this problem, they would have known that almost identical problems with gangs of Muslims grooming young non-Muslim girls for sexual exploitation was occurring in Holland too. Indeed, since UKHTC, the sister organisation of CEOP, commissioned a documentary based on what was going on in Holland, it is literally unbelievable that CEOP could not have known that the issue has far more to do with religion than with race. With that knowledge, from 2006 when CEOP was created, they could have been training and advising police forces about the nature of this crime and about the kind of data which needed to be recorded to establish the patterns. Religion was clearly far more relevant than race when it comes to this kind of child sexual exploitation. Some national agency needed to make this explicit so that local agencies

---

88 CEOP, Out of Mind, Out of Sight - Breaking Down the Barriers to Understanding Child Sexual Exploitation, *op. cit.*, p. 6.

could gather this kind of information. Perhaps it would have required legislation to mandate that police forces and social services record if the perpetrator was Muslim or not. This is the kind of thing which CEOP should have been investigating from its inception.

In reading this report, you can sense their embarrassment: an organisation that was set up to provide intelligence and training on child sex exploitation cannot provide any kind of useful information about a massive problem going on under their nose. CEOP begin the report by highlighting the limitations:

> (i) Child sexual exploitation is often hidden from view. The thematic assessment sought to determine and assess the known scale of "localised grooming" based on information held by relevant agencies. (ii) All agencies faced particular difficulties in responding to the information request. As a result, information submitted to CEOP during the rapid assessment is incomplete, and does not represent the totality of information relating to child sexual exploitation or "localised grooming" held by relevant agencies. (iii) Of those agencies which were able to respond, many were unable to provide information relating to the complete study period, from 1 January 2008 to 1 March 2011. Instead, agencies submitted a snapshot of relevant data.[89]

But this begs the question: if the police forces listened to the children (as CEOP claims is so important), then the crime would not have been 'hidden'—victims and their parents were trying to draw the attention of social workers and the police to what was going on (as were a couple of brave journalists), but the majority of the professionals were neither listening nor seeing. As one of the mothers of the victims stated in 2007: 'We parents are doing more to investigate these criminals than the police...'[90] If the various agencies involved had received guidance by CEOP from 2006 onwards, then the agencies would have known to listen to the victims and their parents. CEOP was supposed to pull all these agencies together and to guide them; yet here we have CEOP trying to blame the local agencies for not having the information that CEOP has been tasked with collating, when there is no sign that between 2006 and 2011 CEOP made any attempt to train police forces and child-care profes-

---

89 *Ibid.*, p. 9.
90 Julie Bindel, 'Mothers of Prevention', *op. cit.*

sionals in the methods of these criminals or the extent of their criminal networks. If the data is unavailable surely only CEOP are to blame for this? How could police forces or other agencies know to collect this specific data if they have never been instructed to do so?

The major recommendations of the CEOP report are:

a) experience of past victims should be used to design prevention messages and to design early intervention
b) local agencies (child services, police, etc.) must meet their responsibilities under existing (2009) statutory guidance
c) local agencies must ensure that children who are at risk are identified early on.[91]

This emphasizes once more the failures of CEOP. In 2011 their principal recommendation is that education based on the experiences of victims should be used for early intervention. CEOP was stating this 3 years after their sister organisation had already commissioned an educational video designed to do this, an educational video that still has not been seen by prospective victims. From 2009, had any of those thousands of child-care professionals trained by CEOP even seen *My Dangerous Loverboy*? This would have enabled those professionals to fulfil the other two recommendations made by CEOP. Viewings of that educational video could have been made compulsory in schools: whilst children are taken to mosques as part of the National Curriculum, there was no effort by schools to ensure that a video such as *My Dangerous Loverboy* was seen by potential victims.

CEOP is basically trying to pass the blame onto the local agencies (children's services and police), rather than accepting that they had a guiding role, and they failed in this role. The gangs were operating across regions, and multiple local agencies were failing to deal with them. There is even an international dimension.[92] It is clear that local agencies were mostly paralysed when it came to dealing with this kind of criminality. CEOP could not have been unaware that even at a national level, the media were too scared to discuss the subject of grooming gangs, because they would be accused of 'racism' by the Left and racism groups: the furore over the *Channel 4* documentary *Edge of the City* only preceded the creation of CEOP by two years. National leadership was required, but it was not forthcoming. Moreover, if local agencies

91 *Ibid.*, p. 95.
92 See Chapter 1, section 1.5 *International Dimensions.*

were failing to adhere to statutory guidelines (in the Panorama documentary of 2008, Prof. Barrett pointed out this was also the case with courts failing to enforce recommendations protecting the interests of children), didn't CEOP have a role in identifying this earlier, reporting these failures to the Home Office or Ministry of Justice? Is it acceptable for CEOP to have been silent whilst child exploitation occurred because local agencies or courts were failing to follow statutory guidelines?

Whilst refusing to ever recognise that being Muslim and male is the single most common factor among the perpetrators, CEOP goes on to conclude:

> The offenders within our dataset are younger with almost half of them being under 25, where age is known. There is a noticeable level of networking and particular behavioural characteristics among many offenders in that they appear to derive satisfaction from the status and power of exerting control over victims, not only to commit sexual offences, but also as an end in itself.[93]

In refusing to acknowledge the most glaring objective characteristics of the perpetrators, CEOP concentrates on mind-reading the emotions of these men during their criminal activities (satisfaction), and asserting that this emotion came not from sex, or from money, or from religious belief, but from the pure exercise of power as its own reward. In what way do these characteristics help the victims, parents or child-care professionals to identify that grooming may be going on? Describing the physical or cultural characteristics of the perpetrators is far more important than speculating about their emotions. And whilst the will to power might sound like a grand notion, no attempt is made to consider whether or not Islamic doctrine might be a more concrete and identifiable form of motivation for these gangs.

Far more significant characteristics can be found from our dataset (see *Appendix 1: Grooming Gang Convictions*). In our dataset, 90% of the men were Muslims. Almost 20% of them had the same first name (Mohammed). It appears that about 20% of those convicted are blood relatives, many being brothers (even those with different surnames may actually be related, so this characteristic could be stronger). The 'localised grooming' did not just happen anywhere: it did not feature school

---

93 CEOP, Out of Mind, Out of Sight - Breaking Down the Barriers to Understanding Child Sexual Exploitation, *op cit.*, p. 93.

teachers exploiting their students, it did not feature parents exploiting their role as voluntary workers. It featured gangs of Muslim men, exploiting social environments where girls would be vulnerable, where the schoolgirls would be out of view of those adults who would have responsibility for them. And the gangs were protected by a wall of silence from within their own community, and protected by the fact that people outside their communities were too scared to identify them more precisely, for fear of accusations of 'racism'. These are more significant characteristics than those identified by CEOP.

The 'profiling' data provided to CEOP was extremely inadequate. However, as that is the only data that is offered in this report, we should look at the data.[94]

Ethnicity of Perpetrators

Unknown	White	Asian	Black	Chinese
38%	30%	28%	3%	0.16%

It is immediately obvious from this data that white people are significantly under-represented as perpetrators, whilst Asians are significantly over-represented (87% of the UK population are white, 7% of the population are Asian). Asians are very significantly over-represented. As the list of convictions shows, the 'Asians' involved in these crimes are almost entirely Muslim by religion.[95] Moreover, it is also significant that the single biggest ethnic category in the CEOP data for perpetrators is 'Unknown'. That such information is missing, highlights the fundamental failings of a national agency for exploitation, created just after the controversy over the 'racism' of *Edge of the City*. Since that documentary had brought the grooming gang phenomenon to the awareness of the nation for the first time, and since this debate was immediately shut

---

94 *Ibid.*, p. 87.

95 The CEOP data produces some significant anomalies compared with the data we find from actual convictions, where the names betray that 90% of those convicted for these types of crimes have Muslim names. Whilst CEOP claim that their data shows that around half of the perpetrators of grooming are white men, that does not tally with the data from convictions (see *Appendix 1: Grooming Gang Convictions*). Either the police and CPS are refusing to prosecute white non-Muslim men for these crimes (a very unlikely scenario), or the 'data' connecting white men with these crimes is of such low quality that it would have no chance of standing up in court. As time goes on, if this anomaly between data from convictions and data from organisations like CEOP continues, then the data from CEOP is going to look increasingly unreliable.

down by accusations of 'racism', it seems obvious that the factor of 'race' and even religion should have become an even more important data point with regard to sex crimes against children.

Significantly, when we come to look at the ethnicity of the victims in the CEOP data, the relationship between Asian people and white people is reversed: there are very few Asian victims, and most of the victims are white.

Ethnicity of Victims

Unknown	White	Asian	Black	Chinese
33%	61%	3%	1%	

This data on victims is consistent with the reports that the majority of the victims are white or Sikhs. However, even when there are victims who are Sikh or Muslim Asian schoolgirls, the perpetrators in such cases have never been shown to be white non-Muslims.

The CEOP slogan is 'making every child matter... everywhere.' Yet clearly they were more focussed on the abuse of Vietnamese children being trafficked into Britain than they were with the non-Muslim girls within Britain being exploited and trafficked around the country. If any single child protection agency should be considered central in the failure of agencies to fulfil their duty, CEOP is that agency. They had the responsibility to guide the other regional policing agencies, yet it was only in 2011 (two years after the English Defence League started conducting high profile demonstrations) that CEOP performed their 'rapid assessment' of the problem of 'localised grooming'. This report by CEOP was created some 15 years after *Barnardo's* had started their *Streets and Lanes* project in Bradford and after *Risky Business* was started in Rotherham, and 7 years after the furore over *Channel 4's Edge of the City* documentary. The CEOP report came out several years after the production of an educational film by UKHTC (a sister organisation to CEOP), a film to warn schoolgirls of the ways in which the grooming gangs work, a film in which the main villain is 'an Asian'. And yet in 2011 CEOP had to scramble to collect data in order to ascertain whether or not localised grooming was almost entirely associated with 'Asians' or not. Along with their parent organisation, the Serious Organised Crime Agency, CEOP had the remit and the resources of no other national agency. But instead of leading the other agencies on this issue the Child Exploitation and Online Protection Centre seemed to only take notice of this crisis following umpteen demonstrations by the English Defence League.

5.6 Serious Organised Crime Agency

CEOP is a subsidiary agency of the Serious Organised Crime Agency (SOCA). Another of the governmental organisations we have come across, the UK Human Trafficking Centre (UKHTC), is also a subsidiary agency of SOCA. Since we began writing this report, SOCA has been wound up. This means that documents to which we refer on the SOCA and CEOP websites are likely to disappear. SOCA has been replaced by the National Crime Agency. We do not know if the closure of SOCA is an intentional cover-up. SOCA came into existence on 1 April 2006 and was closed on 7 October 2013. SOCA was an amalgamation of various policing agencies, including the National Criminal Intelligence Service. At first glance it might seem strange that SOCA should oversee CEOP and UKHTC. However, these agencies are concerned with stopping organised crimes of sexual exploitation/slavery, crimes of great seriousness, and these criminal activities generate large amounts of money for the criminals, who operate on a national (and possibly even international) level. That SOCA should control CEOP and UKHTC, means that SOCA too must be considered at fault.

Recently journalists have claimed that the gangs were pimping out girls to clients for £200 a time.[96] Mohammed Shafiq, one of the few Muslims to speak out against the grooming gangs in Rochdale, commented: "some of these men were making between £600 - £1000 a day."[97] This accords with what Julie Bindel pointed out in 2007:

> Pimping is lucrative. According to the Metropolitan Police Vice Squad, a pimp can make £300,000 to £400,000 a year selling a 16-year-old girl.[98]

Official reports as far back as 2006 stated that some Muslim men in Rotherham saw grooming and pimping schoolgirls as a career.[99]

---

96 Allison Pearson, 'Oxford grooming gang: We will regret ignoring Asian thugs who target white girls', *The Telegraph*, 15 May 2013, http://www.telegraph.co.uk/news/uknews/crime/10060570/Oxford-grooming-gang-We-will-regret-ignoring-Asian-thugs-who-target-white-girls.html

97 http://www.mohammedshafiq.net/grooming---the-men.php

98 Julie Bindel, 'Mothers of Prevention' *op. cit.*

99 Angie Heal's 2006 report, quoted in Alexis Jay, Independent Inquiry into Child

Some of the girls would be pimped out for 15 years, into their mid to late twenties.[100] The average person would never conceive of the kinds of money that might be involved. When we consider that each year the pimp could be making well in excess of £100,000 for each girl, and he might control a girl for 5 to 10 years, we can see that vast amounts of money could be made from this crime. Which makes it clear why SOCA should have been very heavily involved in monitoring these crimes. Furthermore, the international dimension should also be the concern of a major national crime agency: the similarities between the Muslim grooming gangs in Britain and the gangs in Holland, are obvious, and lead us to ponder whether or not the gangs are actually conferring, and maybe even trafficking the victims across national borders. Yet all the indicators are that SOCA has done almost nothing to investigate and stop these crimes. The most that SOCA appears to have done, is to have commissioned (through UKHTC) the film *My Dangerous Loverboy*.

This film has never been shown to its intended audience. UKHTC claim that 'racial sensitivities' have nothing to do with this failure.[101] By 2015 this film was the only national educational project to warn and educate girls about the gangs' grooming techniques – and yet it has not even been shown to its intended audience. In 2011, David Dillnutt, head of UKHTC was quoted as saying UKHTC was working closely with CEOP, to get the film shown in schools.[102] Several years later, and there is still no sign of this happening. It looks like the government has decided there is to be no attempt to cut off the supply of victims to the grooming gangs. The film was quietly 'announced' at the end of 2010 as a DVD (which could be obtained directly from SOCA or UKHTC):

for use by people who have regular contact with children

Sexual Exploitation in Rotherham 1997 - 2013, http://www.rotherham.gov.uk/downloads/file/1407/independent_inquiry_cse_in_rotherham, p. 92. Why would these men not consider this lucrative industry desirable? They were able to earn very substantial amounts of money, with the authorities doing nothing to curb these activities and the media ensuring that no attention was drawn to what they were doing.

100 'Grooming: a Life Sentence', *File on Four* (*BBC Radio 4*), 11 Jun 2013, http://news.bbc.co.uk/1/shared/bsp/hi/pdfs/11_06_13_fo4_grooming.pdf p. 17.

101 'Film on dangers of Asian sex gangs commissioned by Government agency... then withheld for three years', *Daily Mail*, 22 Jan 2011, http://www.dailymail.co.uk/news/article-1349354/Film-dangers-Asian-sex-gangs-commissioned-Government-agency--withheld-years.html

102 Andrew Norfolk, 'Anger as educational film on grooming withheld', *The Times*, 21 Jan 2011, http://www.thetimes.co.uk/tto/news/uk/article2883087.ece

and are in a position to notice any changes in behaviour and physical signs which may indicate sexual exploitation. This includes front line professionals such as police officers, social workers, teachers, doctors, school nurses, sexual health practitioners and youth workers, in addition to parents and carers. The UKHTC is working with CEOP to develop a schools package for the film so it can be used in secondary schools.[103]

There is no later announcement from SOCA to say that any version of the film is being shown routinely to schoolgirls. It seems from this 'announcement' by SOCA that the only schoolgirls who are going to be given advice warning them about Muslim grooming gangs, are the girls who have already been ensnared by the gangs, and who are displaying signs that they are already being raped, signs obvious enough for a teacher or police officer or doctor to notice, and that they would then perhaps show the video to the victim.[104] It is obvious to any reasonable person, that this is far too late to try and warn such children. The horribly euphemistic 'Loverboy' concept of the title comes from the Netherlands, but at least that country has a programme where schools warn children and educate them about the tactics of these 'Loverboys'.

---

103 http://www.soca.gov.uk/about-soca/about-the-ukhtc/prevention/my-dangerous-loverboy

104 In March 2015 *Channel 4* broadcast a documentary entitled, *Things Which We Won't Say About Race Which Are True*, about the pernicious role which political correctness has played in Britain in the preceding decades. It would seem the entire documentary was in fact a way to talk about the grooming gangs, since the programme ends saying 'we might save some children's lives and we might save others from abuse'. Andrew Norfolk was interviewed in that documentary and it was again claimed that *My Dangerous Loverboy* had been suppressed specifically because the main groomer was shown to be Asian. The production team behind *My Dangerous Loverboy* responded to the Channel 4 documentary, and said 'the UKHTC, and the bodies it was subsequently incorporated into [...] did not have a coherent, national plan to distribute the film to young people around the UK' (http://www.mydangerousloverboy.com/the-truth-about-my-dangerous-loverboy/). Their response went on to say that another organisation had distributed the film and that they 'estimate that up to 400,000 young people will have watched the film'. They do not say what the timescale this number is based on, nor how they estimate it. There are 8 million children in schools in the UK (https://www.gov.uk/government/publications/number-of-schools-teachers-and-students-in-england/number-of-schools-teachers-and-students-in-england). At most only a minority of children can have seen this video. Since the original expectation was that the video would be only shown to schoolgirls exhibiting signs they had been ensnared by the gangs, this number of 400,000 viewings would be higher than we would expect from reports that the Association of Chief Police Officers estimates there are tens of thousands of victims each year).

The SOCA web page where one can ask for a copy of *My Dangerous Loverboy* says 'To obtain copies of *My Dangerous Loverboy*, please send an e-mail to UKHTC@soca.x.gsi.gov.uk Your details will be added to a waiting list and copies will be issued when they become available.' It has said this from 4 Jul 2011 until 4 Sep 2013.[105] Other than a pilot project in Sheffield, there is no evidence that any school has been using this DVD.

At the end of 2013, CEOP – now under the aegis of the National Crime Agency, which replaced SOCA – released a new film about 'sexual exploitation'.[106] This 'educational video' shows the principal victim as black, and the perpetrators as white, and it shows the sexual exploitation happening between school children of the same age. If it was supposed to inform schoolgirls about the risks from Muslim grooming gangs, it must be judged completely inadequate: it's as if CEOP is in denial concerning all the information that has come out about the peculiarities of this crime spree. This latest 'educational' film

- doesn't show the victim as a barely pubescent 11-year-old,[107] rather than the 16 year old in the video
- doesn't show that 90% of those convicted for these crimes are Muslims[108]
- doesn't show that the average age of those convicted is 29 years old,[109] rather than the 18 year old shown in the video
- doesn't show gangs of men hanging around schools and shopping malls and preying on schoolgirls[110]
- doesn't show the girls being intentionally addicted to alco-

---

105 http://www.soca.gov.uk/about-soca/about-the-ukhtc/contact-ukhtc

106 http://www.ceop.police.uk/Media-Centre/Press-releases/2013/School-best-place-to-learn-about-sexual-exploitation/. Again, it seems as though there is no attempt to draw any connection between sexual exploitation and Muslim grooming gangs, even as the conviction of Muslim men for these crimes are at an all-time high. The film is available on YouTube http://www.youtube.com/watch?v=qORv-TgI4JI Bizarrely, CEOP has adverts prefacing the video. It seems extraordinary that a national police agency would seek to supplement their income by taking a slice of Google's advertising revenue.

107 Sandra Laville and Alexandra Topping, 'Oxford child sex abuse ring: social services failed me, says victim', *The Guardian*, 15 May 2013, http://www.theguardian.com/society/2013/may/14/oxford-abuse-ring-social-services

108 *Appendix 1: Grooming Gang Convictions*

109 *Ibid.* To a 17 year old, someone around 30 seems very old.

110 'Child grooming still a problem in Derby, say police', *BBC News*, 12 Dec 2011, http://www.bbc.co.uk/news/uk-england-derbyshire-16137593

hol and drugs by the gangs[111]

· doesn't show the victim as white, when even CEOP's own data shows that most of the grooming gang victims are white[112]

· doesn't show the gangs using accusations of racism against the girls' parents to drive a wedge between the child and those who want to protect her[113]

· doesn't show schoolgirls having their tongues nailed to the table when they want to escape from the gangs[114]

· doesn't show the death threats being made by the grooming gangs against the victim's siblings and parents[115]

The video bears even less relationship to the techniques and threat of the grooming gangs than does the 2009 film, *My Dangerous Loverboy*. CEOP seem to have ignored their own data, and the 20 or so major criminal cases from 6 years preceding this video. It seems like CEOP and SOCA/NCA have learned nothing. Only extended political pressure will make these agencies face up to their responsibilities.[116]

---

111 Sandra Laville and Alexandra Topping, 'The nasty truth about rape: To those of you who think a 12-year-old girl from Rochdale in a short skirt can't be raped - you're very wrong', *The Mirror*, 11 May 2012, http://www.mirror.co.uk/news/uk-news/rochdale-grooming-gang-to-those-o f-you-828599

112 See the analysis of the CEOP data above. If the 33% of victims whose ethnicity is "unknown" are discounted from the CEOP data, then there are 60 white victims for every black victim. There is evidence that grooming gangs are at least partially motivated by racism against white girls - see *Racist Aspects of Grooming* below.

113 Julie Bindel, 'Mothers of Prevention', *op. cit.*

114 Kathryn Knight, 'Is political correctness stopping police ending the misery of the teenage sex slaves?', *Daily Mail*, 27 Mar 2008, http://www.dailymail.co.uk/femail/article-546809/Is-political-correctness-stopping-police-ending-misery-teenage-sex-slaves.html

115 Arthur Martin, 'Faces of True Evil: Judge Jails Depraved Sex Gang for 95 Years After they Committed Grotesque Abuse on Girls as Young as 11', *The Daily Mail*, 27 Jun 2013 http://www.dailymail.co.uk/news/article-2349784/Sadistic-paedophile-sex-gang-brothers-given-lengthy-prison-sentences-exploiting-underage-girls.html

116 When SOCA was transformed into the National Crime Agency, the head of CEOP resigned, saying that submerging CEOP within NCA would be bad for children. If the inactivity of CEOP and SOCA with regard to the grooming gangs had led to these agencies being censured by the media, child-care professionals and politicians, one could see why a new agency might be created, and why CEOP might be controlled by that new agency. Instead, with no criticism of either CEOP or SOCA, a new agency was created, even when the head of CEOP resigning over 'government plans to merge

It is remarkable that the Home Affairs Select Committee did not have anything to say about this astonishing failure at the heard of national policing. They offered no criticism of national agencies like CEOP, UKHTC nor SOCA. If the number of victims quoted are even remotely accurate, and the amount the gangs earned from prostituting/trafficking one girl are close to accurate,[117] then our country is looking at criminal activity with a possible value of maybe £300 million per year. That is for the pimping activities alone. If all the other related criminality of these gangs was tallied, their gains could be far greater.

In the first edition of *Easy Meat* we asked the following questions: How has SOCA (and its various subsidiary organisations) evaded censure? What other crime agency should have been pursuing these criminal gangs and their highly lucrative criminal activities? Recently the UK government said that grooming gangs were to be 'treated in a similar way to serious and organised crime.'[118] But no new national policing initiative was announced in relation to this supposed new serious attitude to the grooming gangs. We must thus conclude that this statement was probably pre-election tub-thumping.

5.7 Children's Commissioner

One year after the CEOP 'rapid assessment', where CEOP bemoaned the lack of data with which to provide a proper analysis of 'localised grooming', the Children's Commissioner for England, wrote a report following a year-long investigation.[119] This report from The Chil-

---

CEOP into a National Crime Agency. [saying] "I have resigned because I think it is not best for children"', 'CEOP chief: National Crime Agency would be bad for children', *Channel 4 News*, 12 Oct 2010, http://www.channel4.com/news/ceop-chief-national-crime-agency-would-be-bad-for-children. This video looks like he was right: despite CEOP's own data showing major disparities in ethnicity with 'localised grooming', their new educational video does nothing to inform schoolgirls of the true nature of the risks they face.

117 It is often quoted that the gangs charged around £600 to those who wished to rape these under-age victims. Sandra Laville and Alexandra Topping, 'Oxford gang skilfully groomed young victims then sold them for £600 a time', 14 May 2013, *The Guardian*, http://www.theguardian.com/uk/ 2013/may/14/oxford-gang-groomed-victims-hell

118 'Jail terms proposed for those who "neglect" sex abuse victims', *BBC News* website, 03 Mar 2015, http://www.bbc.co.uk/news/uk-31691061

119 The report was called '"I thought I was the only one. The only one in the world": The Office of The Children's Commissioner's Inquiry into Child Sexual Exploitation In Gangs and Groups', Nov 2012, http://www.childrenscommissioner.gov.uk/info/cseggl. The vast majority of victims in the data contained in this report are the victims of what

dren's Commissioner also complained about a lack of data. And given their complaints about a lack of data, we cannot see that this report from the Children's Commissioner added anything of significant value to the CEOP report. It merely confirmed that the data had considerable gaps when it came to the recording of race (never mind the lack of data on religion).

The purpose of this second report seemed to be intended to ameliorate the findings of CEOP: where CEOP had data, it confirmed that 'Asians' were massively over-represented amongst the perpetrators involved in grooming. The report from the Children's Commissioner was used by people to deny the relevance of ethnicity to the grooming phenomenon,[120] as if the report somehow refuted the claims of organisations like CROP:[121] namely, that the vast majority of the perpetrators in the grooming gangs were Muslim men.[122] As the Sikh Awareness Society said, there was 'Anger as sex abuse report "turns blind eye to Asian

---

CEOP called 'localised grooming'. Since the schoolgirls who were being groomed by Muslim gangs were often used to lure other schoolgirls into the gang's control, we have to assume that the title of the Children's Commissioner's report is 'poetic'. The report even contradicts its own title by page 6:

> The abuse takes place in private houses, warehouses, transportation vehicles, public spaces, parks, schools, hotels and hostels. [...] Victims are linked to each other through schools, the internet, mobile phones, social gatherings, children's homes, neighbourhoods and public spaces such as shopping centres, funfairs, take away shops and coffee shops.

A thorough inquiry into the ways the grooming gangs operate might well show that it was totally inaccurate and misleading for The Children's Commissioner to choose this title, which stresses victim isolation as the fundamental feature of the exploitation: it is very likely that those victims who thought they were 'the only one' were the exception rather than the rule. No doubt it suits child-care professionals to make the public think that no-one could have known what was going on with these schoolgirl victims, and it is harder to sell that myth when the grooming was often going on in public, in broad daylight.

120 Steve Doughty, 'Sex gangs report "will play down threat of Pakistani men targeting white girls"', *The Daily Mail*, 16 Nov 2012 http://www.dailymail.co.uk/news/article-2234004/Sex-gangs-report-play-threat-Pakistani-men-targeting-white-girls.html; see also 'Children's commissioner defends controversial grooming report', *The Yorkshire Post*, 16 Dec 2012 http://www.yorkshirepost.co.uk/news/main-topics/general-news/children-s-commissioner-defends-controversial-grooming-report-1-5215737

121 The charity which was dedicated to working with the schoolgirl victims and their families.

122 Paul Vallely, 'Child Sex Grooming: the Asian Question', *The Independent*, 10 May 2012 http://www.independent.co.uk/news/uk/crime/child-sex-grooming-the-Asian-question-7729068.html

Pakistani gangs'".[123] We will proceed to show that the report from the Children's Commissioner does nothing to diminish the claims of the victims, their families, nor CROP: most of the perpetrators were 'Asians' (and the conviction data shows they were almost entirely Muslims).

Whilst most people will be able to understand what a national agency like SOCA or CEOP is, who or what is the Children's Commissioner?

> The Children's Commissioner for England... her team makes sure adults who work with children think about the needs of children and young people and listen to their views to make their lives better. They speak up for *all children and young people, especially those who are not often asked for their views or who might be vulnerable.* For example, children who miss out on education, disabled children, those who have just arrived in this country, young people with emotional difficulties and those who get in trouble with the law. *The Commissioner's job was created in 2004 by the Children Act. The Children Act is a law created by the Government to keep children safe from harm.*[124] (emphasis added)

Since local authorities, local police forces, and national agencies were ignoring what was going on, it was even more important that the Children's Commissioner speak out for the rights of these vulnerable children, who were being ignored by virtually every agency and failed by every safeguard supposedly put there to protect children.

The office of the Children's Commissioner came into existence in 2004. At the time that this office was created, surely the most notorious issue in child welfare was the grooming/pimping gangs being disclosed by *Channel 4* reports? Remember that in 2006, the Sikh Awareness Society became a national organisation, stating as a reason that the grooming gangs were operating nationwide. Yet we can find no evidence that between 2004 and 2012 the Children's Commissioner paid any attention whatsoever to the thousands of schoolgirls being groomed by these gangs. In *The Times* in 2007, Julie Bindel pointed out that the parents were having to do the detective work, that the police were then dismissing what they did, and that social workers were not listening to the girls or their parents. And then in 2008, *Panorama* did their exposé of the grooming gangs. How could it be that the Children's Commissioner, an office specifically set up to champion the views of children who were being ignored, could not know that these grooming gangs existed and that these children were being failed by virtually every agency that was there to protect them?

When the Children's Commissioner came out with its report on child sexual exploitation in 2012, rather than attempt to acquire more data consistent with the definition set out by CEOP, the Commissioner report conflates two distinctly different forms of child sexual abuse: 1) gang-related, and 2) group-related (where the latter definition closely matches the phenomenon of localised grooming). It is clear from looking at the data accompanying the Children's Commissioner definitions,[125] that with gang-related CSE, there are very few Asian perpetrators and very few Asian victims. However, with group-related CSE (*i.e.* what was designated by CEOP as 'localised grooming'), there are relatively few black victims, and (in absolute terms) most of the perpetrators are white, but in proportional terms white people are hugely under-represented as perpetrators; yet even in this data, 'Asians' are hugely over-represented as perpetrators. Since the Children's Commissioner still used separate terms for these different forms of Child Sexual Exploitation, we can compare the two reports in this regard (see *Appendix 8: Children's Commissioner Charts*): allowing us to remove the conflation introduced by the Children's Commissioner. The results are really not significantly different from the problem represented in the data from CEOP.

With regard to 'localised grooming', CEOP found that Asian men were 28% of the perpetrators whilst white men were 30% of the perpetrators; the Children's Commissioner report found that around 21% of the perpetrators were Asian, whilst white men were 27% of the perpetrators. When it came to the victims of 'localised grooming', CEOP found that Asian girls were 3% of the victims, but white girls were 61% of the victims; whilst the Commissioner's report found that 4% of the victims were Asian, whilst 50% of the victims were white. In effect, the Children's Commissioner ended up re-confirming the findings of CEOP.[126]

---

125 Where there is racial data, see *Appendix 8: Children's Commissioner Charts*.

126 The only significant aspect of the Children's Commissioner's intervention into this area, is to highlight that 'localised grooming' is a far more significant form of Child Sexual Exploitation than that conducted by street gangs.

If we express this in tabular form, it will be clearer.[127]

Ethnicity of Perpetrators (Localised Grooming)

Source	Unknown	White	Asian
CEOP	38%	30%	28%
CC	16%	27%	21%

Ethnicity of Victims (Localised Grooming)

Source	Unknown	White	Asian
CEOP	33%	61%	3%
CC	15%	51%	4%

Despite the Children's Commissioner spending a year on their study, and despite them getting data from more sources and with a higher response rate than did CEOP, The Children's Commissioner's report serves to reconfirm what the data available to CEOP showed: among perpetrators of 'localised grooming', 'Asians' (Muslims) are very significantly over-represented, whilst white men are very significantly under-represented. Yet when it comes to the victims, it is white children who are the majority of the victims. Whether it was planned or not, what the Children's Commissioner's report does is perform tricks with statistics. By merging two distinctly different forms of child sexual exploitation, the report manages to make it look like there are fewer

---

127 We are extracting from *Appendix 8: Children's Commissioner Charts*, the equivalent data to that extracted from the 2011 CEOP report, in our earlier discussion in section 5.5 *Child Exploitation and Online Protection Centre* of our analysis. Obviously, in none of the tables here do the rows add up to 100%; that is because we are simplifying the presentation to concentrate principally on 'localised grooming' and the disparity between the ethnicity of the perpetrators and the victims. If the Children's Commissioner had chosen not to obfuscate matters, they would have made it easier for anyone to do a mapping between their data and the CEOP data, with regard to ethnicity and 'localised grooming'. For our purposes, we are ignoring those perpetrators and victims who are black, as race is only a secondary factor when considering the characteristics that identify a perpetrator or a victim in this crime (as the evidence concerning the Sikh victims shows). A far more significant identifying factor is the *religion* of the perpetrator and the victim. Since the authorities have chosen to ignore this factor for the last 10 to 25 years, where we cannot ourselves infer religion from data (see *Appendix 1: Grooming Gang Convictions* and *Appendix 3: Name Distribution of Convicts*), we must use the secondary indicators of 'Asian' and 'white' for 'Muslim' and 'non-Muslim' respectively. We want to acknowledge that doing this means that the Sikh victims of the Muslim grooming gangs are ignored, but we must work with the conflated information provided. This is one of the tragedies of the authorities insisting on seeing this in racial terms all these years.

'Asians' involved as perpetrators, and fewer white girls as victims: this is because the proportions are altered, simply by including more black and white perpetrators, and including more black victims. If the Children's Commissioner had kept these two forms of exploitation separate (as simple as having two different sections in the report), then their findings regarding the discrepancy in ethnicity between perpetrator and victim in 'localised grooming' would have been indistinguishable from those of CEOP. It is as if the Children's Commissioner took some acidic mixture, and added some alkali, then said: 'Look, this mixture is less acidic than people say': the most significant outcome is that they distorted the procedure, not that the facts (as far as they are known) were proven to be any different.

In *Appendix 9: Victims to Perpetrators* we have taken the Children's Commissioner data concerning the incidence of Asian and white people in the categories of victim and perpetrator, put this data on the same chart so to remove the confusion of scale introduced by the statisticians working for the Children's Commissioner, and also included the percentages of the entire population who are either Asian or White.[128] In doing this, we have removed those white and black victims and perpetrators connected to street gangs.[129] Using our simplified chart, it is indisputable: white men are still significantly under-represented as perpetrators in this type of crime, and Asian men are still significantly over-represented. Just on the data from the Children's Commissioner, Asian men are 6 times more likely to be involved in grooming gangs than white men (Asians are 3 times over-represented, white men are 3 times under-represented). Since the presentation of the 'data' in the Children's Commissioner report leads people to believe[130] that there are roughly equal numbers of white men and Asian men involved in the grooming gangs, where are the prosecutions and convictions against these white men? The police and child-care professionals who ignored

---

128 According to 2011 Census data, Asians are 7% of the UK population, white people are 87% of the UK population. See https://en.wikipedia.org/wiki/Ethnic_groups_in_ the_United_Kingdom#Ethnic_Groups_-_2011_Census_data

129 It goes without saying, that form of criminality should be pursued and reported (separately) by the media.

130 In the Interim Report, the two charts we have put together in *Appendix 8: Children's Commissioner Charts* are in fact separated by 12 pages of text, tables and other charts - see pp. 92-105 at http://www.childrenscommissioner.gov.uk/info/cseggl. If the Children's Commissioner had been interested in examining the disparity in ethnicity between victims and perpetrators in localised grooming, surely they would not have presented this data so badly?

the grooming gangs because they were mostly 'Asian' have good reason to ensure that prosecutions of white men take place instead. Given that the child-care professionals and police have been ignoring these crimes for 25 years, the public can have little confidence in the data which was fed to the Children's Commissioner.[131] Moreover, let us reiterate: the conviction data, where evidence is rigorously assessed first by police, then CPS, and finally in a court, is of a known quality. And the data from convictions shows that these 'Asians' are almost always Muslims. Furthermore, there is an ideological and cultural background which would explain this over-representation of one specific ethnic group in these crimes (see chapter 7 Islamic Cultural Background). The data from convictions also shows that when it comes to the evidence rigorously assessed in the trial process, the presence of Muslims and the absence of non-Muslims in this form of criminality is even greater.

Our single chart removes much of the extraneous information included by the Children's Commissioner's analysis and this shows not only that 'Asians' are 6 times more likely than white men to be involved in these crimes, it shows that Asian children are far less likely than white children to be victims. This simplified chart thus reveals things concealed by the analysis by the Children's Commissioner: if there was not an ethnic dimension to these crimes, if Asian men were grooming Asian children, and if white men were grooming white children, then one would expect that there would be an equivalence between the ethnicity of the perpetrators and the ethnicity of victims.[132] But when The Children's Commissioner data is rendered in this more intelligible form, it is clear that the proportion of white victims is far greater than the proportion of white perpetrators, yet the proportion of Asian victims is far less than the proportion of Asian perpetrators. What the Muslim Council of Britain was calling "a racist myth" in 2009, was not only contradict-

---

131 The agencies who supplied this data to the Children's Commissioner have powerful incentives to find, fudge or lose data, to ensure that the public do not realise that there has been a specific, new form of criminality, which these agencies had studiously ignored for decades. There is already evidence that local councils would go to considerable lengths to ensure that their negligence would not be uncovered. See section 5.2 *Local Councils*.

132 The Muslim Women's Network admits that, at least for Asian victims, the perpetrators are also Asians: 'Asian/Muslim female victims are most vulnerable to offenders from their own communities as the overwhelming majority of the offenders were from the same background as the victims.' Shaista Gohir MBE, 'Unheard Voices: The Sexual Exploitation of Asian Girls and Young Women', September 2013, http://www.mwnuk. co.uk//go_files/resources/UnheardVoices.pdf, p. 23.

ed by the reporting of Andrew Norfolk in 2011, but also by The Children's Commissioner's data in 2012: this data shows that "Asian" men are grooming white children. Asian children are not even found among the victims in proportions in which Asians are found among the general population. Asians are 7% of the UK population, but only 4% of the victims are Asian. Moreover, not only are the Asian perpetrators almost certainly Muslims, but it is likely that among these Asian victims, most of the victims are not Muslims but are Sikhs or Hindus. So, if 'Asian' men are 3 times over-represented as groomers, and 'Asian' children are 2 times under-represented, from which community are these 'Asian' men getting their non-Asian victims? All of this supports what the director of *Edge of the City* learned from *Barnardo's* back in 1996: the perpetrators are mostly 'Asian', and the victims are mostly white.[133] The evidence from convictions, evidence which is of a far higher quality than the 'evidence' supplied to the Children's Commissioner makes things even clearer: Muslim perpetrators out-number non-Muslim perpetrators by 9 to 1, whereas the Children's Commissioner analysis claims Asian and white men are to be found in almost equal numbers (see Figure 1 of *Appendix 8: Children's Commissioner Charts*, where the 'choices' made by the Children's Commissioner's expert advisers results in a chart which suggests there is no ethnic dimension whatsoever to this form of criminality). This highly-publicised analysis by the Children's Commissioner was used by others to dismiss the idea that there was any ethnic dimension to these crimes.

One of the few Muslims who chose to speak out about the Muslim grooming gangs, was Yasmin Alibhai-Brown, who took apart the report by the Children's Commissioner, saying the report writers 'try hard to side-step some difficult facts and even warn the rest of us from going where they have chosen not to tread.'[134] As we have pointed out throughout our analysis, the agencies who should have listened to the victims

---

133 Anna Hall 'Hunt For Britain's Sex Gangs, C4' *Broadcast* 2 May 2013, http://www. broadcastnow.co.uk/in-depth/hunt-for-britains-sex-gangs-c 4/5054504.article

In October 1996... I met Sara Swann, who ran Bradford's *Barnardo's Streets and Lanes* project. Barnardo's was interested in making a film to warn teenagers and educate parents ... the girls were white and living in multi-cultural Bradford and the perpetrators were Asian... everybody wanted to pretend it wasn't happening. All anyone seemed concerned about was the risk of a race riot if we mentioned it.

134 Yasmin Alibhai-Brown 'Why as a Muslim and a Mother I Believe it's so Damaging to Hide from the Truth about Asian Sex Gangs', *The Daily Mail*, 21 Nov 2012, http://www.dailymail.co.uk/debate/article-2236081/Why-Muslim-mother-I-believe-damaging-hide-truth-Asian-sex-gangs.html

and their parents frequently ignored what they heard and saw, as much of the evidence attests. And now that the issue was gaining publicity, the Children's Commissioner chose to write a report that seemed designed to confuse matters. Serious questions must be raised about decisions made by the Children's Commissioner.

By failing to recognise the specifics of 'localised grooming', the Children's Commissioner 'generalised' these crimes, putting the Muslim grooming gangs in with all other child abusers.[135] Ms. Alibhai-Brown points out that The Children's Commissioner report disguises that:

> [I]n some British cities... circles of sexual hell for young girls are run by gangs of Muslim men (most of Pakistani or Bangladeshi heritage) who mostly prey on white girls.[136]

It is bad enough that the Children's Commissioner should have failed from its inception to identify these crimes and the victims who were being ignored by police and social services. But once this crime was no longer deniable, the Children's Commissioner instead set about confusing the specific details, rather than concentrating on unearthing them. Who is the Children's Commissioner supposed to represent? Is this not a fundamental failure of this office? As Ms Alibhai-Brown states,

> It is easy to loathe the abusers, but much harder to ask what it is about some Asian cultural assumptions that make the paedophiles feel no guilt or shame about what they do... the Children's Commission report needed to attend to specifics, and not vague generalities about perpetrators.[137]

Once again, we conclude that it is the fear of being accused of being 'racist' by Muslim organisations, by the racism groups, by Leftist organisations which made an office such as the Children's Commissioner

---

135 It goes without saying that the Children's Commissioner should have also been speaking out for the victims of, what they chose to call, 'gang CSE'. Was 2012 the first time that the Children's Commissioner office bothered to address this problem of 'gang' CSE too? Let us remind ourselves of the purpose of the Children's Commissioner: to 'speak up for all children and young people, especially those who are not often asked for their views or who might be vulnerable'.

136 Yasmin Alibhai-Brown 'Why as a Muslim and a Mother I Believe it's so Damaging to Hide from the Truth about Asian Sex Gangs', *op. cit.*

137 *Ibid.* We note that Ms.Alibhai-Brown is still pushing the idea that it is 'Asian culture' rather than Muslim culture which is the problem.

abandon its core directives and create confusion when what was needed was clarity. Ms. Alibhai-Brown reaches the same conclusion: that 'the committee in charge of the report are nervous of causing offence to community leaders, of being thought racists.'[138]

However, we should not make Ms. Alibhai-Brown into a saint. As a journalist of many years standing, she too could have chosen to lend her support to the likes of Anna Hall and Julie Bindel, the only journalists who spoke out about these Muslim grooming gangs between 2004 and 2010. Ms. Alibhai-Brown did admit she was partly motivated to speak out now because see was worried about matters 'rebounding' on 'Asians' and 'Muslims'.

> The reason I feel compelled to write about these particular groomers and rapists is because I am Asian, and I know how their repugnant activities are rebounding on all of us and on good Asian men. The internet is rife with horrifying stories about such gangs. They are a mix of fact and fiction. Every Asian and Muslim I know, including some imams, want these monsters exposed, named and put away.[139]

Ms. Alibhai-Brown did at least, finally, take this stand and subject this obfuscation by the Children's Commissioner to criticism. However, if it is true that all the Muslim leaders known by the well-connected Ms. Alibhai-Brown wanted the groomers exposed, then we must ask: Why were prominent Muslim leaders at the beginning of this century denouncing people like Ann Cryer for speaking out? Why were Muslim 'elders' refusing to get involved when Ms. Cryer asked for their help before it all became public in 2003?[140] Why have the Muslim organisations and Muslim leaders not defended those who were denounced as 'racist' who dared to speak about this? Where were the Muslim groups coming out in support of Mohammed Shafiq, when he was receiving death threats from those who sought to conceal the activities of the Muslim grooming

---

138 *Ibid.*

139 *Ibid.*

140 We might also note, that following the Parliamentary investigation into the grooming gangs, it was widely publicised that mosques around the country were going to read out a sermon condemning these crimes. Yet most of the mosques in Britain did not read the sermon condemning the grooming gangs. We must wonder just what section of the Muslim community it is which she claims 'want these monsters exposed, named and put away'. In 2009, the Muslim Council of Britain, which represents hundreds of Islamic organisations, said that the grooming gangs were 'a racist myth'.

gangs?[141] Was it loyalty to the Muslim community (the Ummah) which prevented Ms. Alibhai-Brown's Muslim friends from speaking out? Or was it the fear that they would be subject to death threats, as Mr. Shafiq apparently was?

What is clear from the Children's Commissioner report, is that in a country which is overwhelmingly white, white people are no more than 40% of the perpetrators of the groups and/or gangs involved in child-sexual exploitation (CSE), and non-white people are responsible for 40% of the CSE, and most of these were Asian. When it comes to the 'race' of the victims, 60% were white, about 25% were non-white (and most of those were not Asian).[142] Black men feature far more prominently in the Children's Commissioner report because the report specifically included (mostly black) street gangs, who use sexual exploitation as an initiation rite/control structure within the gangs.[143] Thus, if we consider the project that the Children's Commissioner has undertaken, they have re-confirmed one fundamental idea: when it comes to groups or gangs who exploit children sexually, white children are far more likely to be victims, and non-white adults are far more likely to be perpetrators. If the office of the Children's Commissioner set out to prove that the idea of Muslim grooming gangs was a myth, then the Commissioner failed spectacularly.[144] The report more or less confirms

141 Julie Bindel, 'Girls, Gangs and Grooming: The Truth', *Standpoint Magazine*, Dec 2010, http://www.standpointmag.co.uk/node/3576/full.
  'I was one of the first within the Muslim community to speak out about this, four years ago,' says Shafiq, 'and at the time I received death threats from some black and Asian people. But what I said has been proved right — that if we didn't tackle it there would be more of these abusers and more girls getting harmed.'
142 Compare figure 1 and figure 2, in *Appendix 8: Children's Commissioner Charts*. For about 15% of cases, there was no racial data for either the perpetrator or the victim. When you compare figures 1 and 2, bear in mind that the scale for figure 2 is half the scale of figure 1 (*i.e.* the top of the scale for figure 1 is 60%, the top of the scale for figure 2 is 30%). If the charts used the same scale for victims and perpetrators, then the report would have been less misleading.
143 Mark Townsend, '"Being raped by a gang is normal – it's about craving to be accepted"', *The Guardian*, 18 Feb 2012, http://www.theguardian.com/society/2012/feb/18/being-raped-by-gang-normal
144 What we need to bear in mind with regard to the 'data' from CEOP report and from the Children's Commissioner report, is that their data is gathered from disparate sources, and the quality of much of that data will not stand up in court. The principles of the Norfolk analysis mean that the data has gone through weeks of rigorous questioning in court, leading to convictions despite this contestation. Thus, the Norfolk analysis is based on data which has been subjected to the most rigorous of questioning - and this data shows that where the evidence is strong enough to bring about a

what the CEOP data showed with regard to Muslim grooming gangs. Indeed, all the Commissioner's report managed to do was to highlight that there is also a significant over-representation of black men in other forms of child-sexual exploitation than 'localised grooming'. The Children's Commissioner report did little to arrest the growing awareness in the UK, that the majority of those perpetrators in the grooming gangs were Muslim men.

Sikh organisations reported that it was 'difficult to overstate the contempt' in which government ministers held the Children's Commissioner's report.[145] Yet apart from Yasmin Alibai-Brown it was hard to find commentators who took the report apart to show that even merging localised grooming with the crimes of street-gangs did not manage to conceal the huge over-representation of 'Asian' men as perpetrators. Indeed, the report was used by Left-wing journalists/activists to claim that this official report supported the idea that race was not relevant to the grooming phenomenon. When the Parliamentary inquiry concluded, there was no censure of the Children's Commissioner for the report or even for failing to take up the problem of the schoolgirls being ignored by agencies from 2004 to 2012. Indeed, the Parliamentary inquiry did not censure the Children's Commissioner but thanked her, twice.[146] Whilst in private government ministers might have expressed their contempt for this obfuscatory report, in public the government was giving its stamp of approval to obfuscation. Yet another example of parliament's determination to ensure that no blame should fall on any national organisation for the decades of failure in tackling the grooming gangs. The only people to scapegoat would be individuals in Rotherham and Rochdale. By 2015, it was clear that Rotherham was being held out as a singularly bad example.

This 2012 report was described as an 'interim' report, part of a 2-year project called Child Sexual Exploitation in Gangs and Groups (CSEGG), which began in October 2011,[147] the final report being completed by Autumn 2013. Did the "final" report show that The Children's

---

conviction, the vast majority of those involved in 'localised grooming' are Muslim men. Thus, even if the reports from CEOP and the Children's Commissioner had in fact demonstrated that most of the perpetrators were not Muslims, and that 5% of the victims were Muslims, this would still be less reliable data than the data provided by the convictions in court.

145 http://www.sasorg.co.uk/anger-as-sex-abuse-report-turns-blind-eye-to-asian-pakistani-gangs/

146 Home Affairs Select Committee Report, *op. cit.*, p. 10, p. 62.

147 http://www.childrenscommissioner.gov.uk/info/csegg1

Commissioner had taken on board the (supposed) contempt of government ministers, the critique of Muslims like Ms. Alibhai-Brown, or the critical perspective from the Sikh Awareness Society? No. The data and conclusions from the 'interim' report were used by many commentators to argue that there was no relevance to discrepancies between the ethnicity of the perpetrators in the grooming gangs and the ethnicity of the victims.[148] Yet when the Children's Commissioner's final report came out in 2013, supposedly with more complete evidence since it was to be the 'final report', it offered no additional evidence to that contained in the 'interim report'.[149] Indeed, the 'final report' makes up for none of the short-comings in data, bemoaned by CEOP in 2011, and by the Children's Commissioner's own interim report of 2012. What can we conclude from this? Did the 'interim report' serve a purpose in confusing the data regarding the disparity in ethnicity between perpetrators and victims? Did they collect more data, but found that it proved even more categorically that white men are under-represented amongst perpetrators?

In the years leading up to the 2012 report, the Commissioner's office was mostly concerned with issues like bullying at school, stopping parents smacking their children, the housing conditions of the children of asylum seekers. There was no evidence of any interest in the grooming gangs, who operated with impunity because the victims were failed by schools, police, social services, the CPS and the courts. The Children's Commissioner has some specific powers that are not shared by other agencies 'to demand answers from statutory bodies and to interview in private any child in a location (other than the family home) where he or she is being looked after.'[150] The Commissioner chose to prioritise other issues, and did not use those powers to investigate the controversial topic of the grooming gangs. When Dr. Maggie Atkinson applied for

---

148 Sunny Hundal, 'Oxford gang-rape case: were the girls exploited because they were white?', *Liberal Conspiracy*, May 14 2013, http://liberalconspiracy.org/2013/ 05/14/oxford-gang-rape-case-were-the-girls-exploited-because-they-were-white/

149 The Children's Commissioner, 'If Only Someone Had Listened', 2013, http:// www.childrenscommissioner.gov.uk/force_download.php?fp=%2Fclient_assets%2F-cp%2Fpublication%2F743%2FIf_only_someone_had_listened_Office_of_the_Childrens_Commissioners_Inquiry_into_Child_Sexual_Exploitation_in_Gangs_and_Groups.pdf

150 Peter Wilby, 'Young at heart: The choice of the next children's commissioner has been mired in controversy, but what legacy does the incumbent, Sir Al Aynsley-Green, leave his successor?', *The Guardian*, 3 Nov 2009, http://www.theguardian.com/education/2009/nov/03/children s-commissioner-aynsley-green

the post of Children's Commissioner, she declared that the most distinctive feature of her career to date was her ability to lead.[151] Readers must judge for themselves the extent to which, between 2009 and 2012, her office displayed leadership when it came to advocating for the rights of the schoolgirl victims of the grooming gangs. Local authority staff and police officers faced being branded as 'racists' if they pursued these gangs. It was up to organisations like CEOP, SOCA and the Children's Commissioner to show leadership at a national level.

In May 2015 it was reported that Sue Berelowitz, the Deputy Children's Commissioner behind this report, took voluntary redundancy and was awarded a payment of £134,000. Within 24 hours she was then reportedly hired at almost £1,000 per day as a consultant.[152]

5.8 Home Affairs Select Committee

In June 2012, the Home Affairs Select Committee started a 6 month investigation into 'localised grooming', the term coined by CEOP in 2011. The findings of this parliamentary investigation were published in the summer of 2013.[153] If we were to summarise this report it could be best summed-up by the failed attempt by one of the committee members (David Winnick, Labour MP for Walsall North) to get the committee to insert the rider that 'the perception, that grooming perpetrators are largely of Asian, British Asian or Muslim origin' was false. The committee rejected the claim that this was a false perception.[154] We can take it from the rejection of this proposed amendment, that the majority of the MPs on the Committee now concluded that the perception that these gangs were predominantly 'Asian' or 'Muslim' was accurate. It had taken Parliament 10 years from the original *Channel 4* disclosure to admit this; it was 15 to 20 years since projects to deal with mopping up the damage caused by the grooming gangs had been created in Rotherham and Bradford. And all the indications are that every year, thousands of

151 'Appointment of The Children's Commissioner for England - Children, Schools and Families Committee Contents', http://www.publications.parliament.uk/pa/cm200809/cmselect/cmchilsch/998/99808.htm

152 Julie Bindel, 'Child protection boss paid off with £134k after failing to speak out about abuse by Pakistani gangs is rehired as a consultant within 24 hours on £1k a DAY', *The Daily Mail*, 23 May 2015, http://www.dailymail.co.uk/news/article-3093642/Child-protection-boss-paid-134k-failing-speak-abuse-Pakistani-gangs-rehired-consultant-24-hours-1k-DAY.html

153 Home Affairs Select Committee Report, *op. cit.*

154 *Ibid.*, p. 73.

vulnerable schoolgirls continue to be raped by Muslim grooming gangs.

The Home Affairs Select Committee singles out 'the investigative journalism' of Andrew Norfolk as a pivotal event in the recognition of the grooming phenomenon.[155] This parliamentary investigation blamed front-line services for the failure to bring Muslim grooming gangs to justice: 'police, social services and the Crown Prosecution Service must all bear responsibility for the way in which vulnerable children have been left unprotected by the system.'[156] However, we think that given the systematic, long-standing exploitation by the gangs, given that they were trafficking children around the country, and given the international similarities with what was happening in the Netherlands, central, government-led organisations such as the Children's Commissioner and CEOP should have been the central object of criticism for their failures to investigate, analyse, coordinate and educate the front-line services. The Ministry of Justice as well as the CPS should be in the dock concerning the failure of the criminal justice system to implement procedures which would have enabled the exploited victims to give successful testimony. And finally, SOCA and the UKHTC should be held responsible for their failure to treat these gangs as traffickers and serious, organised criminals.[157] Behind closed doors, the Home Office is also likely to have known by 2007 about the characteristics of these Muslim grooming gangs, as by that time the Home Office were already funding CROP.[158] A former minister, 'responsible for tackling child sexual exploitation', stated that there had been 'three working groups on child sexual exploitation that he established, none of which had produced any practical actions.'[159] Are we to believe successive governments knew nothing?

Thus, we have two major government departments whose Ministers cannot feign ignorance of these grooming gangs prior to the Home

---

155 *Ibid.*, p. 27. However, as we have pointed out above: even though Norfolk has admitted to knowing about the grooming gangs since he moved to Yorkshire in 2003, we cannot find evidence of him reporting on this until October 2010: we cannot find any report by him of the two major grooming cases in 2009 that led to convictions (including one case near him in Yorkshire, in which 75% of the convicted men were named 'Mohammed').

156 *Ibid.*, p. 10.

157 That SOCA produced *My Dangerous Loverboy* in 2008 when Parliament only came to accept 'that grooming perpetrators are largely of Asian, British Asian or Muslim origin' shows that SOCA and/or UKHTC were aware of the truthfulness of this perception back in 2008 or 2007.

158 Julie Bindel, 'Mothers of Prevention', *op. cit.*

159 Home Affairs Select Committee Report, *op. cit.*, p. 11.

Affairs Select Committee's investigation, Ministers who were aware of the success or failure of various initiatives. It is a catalogue of failures. Failures can be attributed to agencies at every single step of the way. It is hard to think of an agency which is not culpable of neglect. As the report states:

> The failure of these cases has been both systemic and cultural. Rules and guidelines existed which were not followed. People employed as public servants appeared to lack human compassion when dealing with victims. Children have only one chance at childhood. For too long, victims of child sexual exploitation have been deprived of that childhood without society challenging their abusers. Such a situation must never happen again.[160]

Yet the report zones in on the management of the councils of Rochdale and Rotherham, and of South Yorkshire Police, because (to date) they have apparently performed worse than their peers. But the blame must be spread far and wide. As the Parliamentary inquiry was drawing to a close, a court case relating to Oxford exposed that the police and social services in that area had also been neglectful in protecting schoolgirls from a Muslim grooming gang. Yet failures by councils and police relating to the Oxford case are not addressed in the Parliamentary report (the horrors and longevity of the abuse uncovered in the Oxford trial surpassed even those which came out of the 2012 Rochdale trial). That the problems are national and persistent was clear from the time the controversy over these gangs first erupted in Bradford in 2003 and 2004: those at the heart of the controversy stated that the problems were nationwide. By 2006 there were two charities which specifically focused on the grooming gang phenomenon who had moved from local actions to national operation: namely, Sikh Awareness Society (SAS) from the West Midlands, and the Coalition for the Removal of Pimping (CROP) from Leeds. Considering that the Home Office was quietly funding the national organisation CROP by 2007, we have to regard the Committee's singling out of Rotherham and Rochdale with some suspicion. Moreover, when the *Barnardo's* project was started in Bradford in the mid 1990s, it was stated that it was funded by statutory agencies.[161] With TV

---

160 *Ibid.*

161 Sara Swann, 'Helping girls involved in "prostitution": a Barnardo's Experiment', in *Home Truths About Child Sexual Abuse: Policy and Practice*, Catherine Itzen (ed.),

programmes being withdrawn because of controversy, with statutory agencies funding projects, and with charitable organisations reaching out to solve national problems, how credible is it that government departments did not know about this problem?

There is one tier of child-care professionals on which which we have not focussed: the Local Safeguarding Children Boards (LSCB). These were established by the 2004 Children's Act. Tasked with 'co-ordinating between and scrutinising the work of agencies, the LSCB is responsible for providing safeguarding training, undertaking serious case reviews and publishing an annual report on the effectiveness of safeguarding in the local area.'[162] Considering the furore caused by the BNP campaigning on the issue of Muslim grooming gangs, and that surrounding the *Channel 4* documentary, there is every reason why it should have been a major focus of these LSCBs. Yet we can find no evidence that most of them made it a priority to safeguard schoolgirls from the Muslim grooming gangs. The parliamentary report states the unbelievable statistic that only 1 in 4 of the LSCBs were correctly implementing requirements to monitor the prevalence of, and responses to, child sexual exploitation within their area.[163] This is another indicator that future events will reveal Rotherham and Rochdale to be far less exceptional than the Parliamentary inquiry would lead us to believe: 75% of the local authorities were not even following the legal requirements in safeguarding children from sexual exploitation such as grooming. Rochdale and Rotherham might have been worse than some, but such statistics reveal that negligence in this area of social policy was to be found across the country. A full public inquiry would probably produce even more shocking statistics.

The Home Affairs Select Committee claims that the concept of 'localised grooming' was only recognised following the successful convictions from Operation Retriever, which began in Derbyshire in 2009.[164] However, that the Home Office was funding CROP in 2007, and that SOCA and UKHTC commissioned *My Dangerous Loverboy* in 2008 makes this claim look uninformed at best, and at worst, deliberately misleading. The controversy in 2003 and 2004 around the grooming of schoolgirls in Bradford could not have been unknown to the committee, since Ann Cryer testified before them about this. How could the nation-

Routledge, London, 2000, pg. 277.

162 Home Affairs Select Committee Report, *op cit.*, p. 16.

163 *Ibid.*

164 *Ibid.*, p. 4.

al media permit this revisionism to go unchallenged? When the controversy erupted in Bradford in 2003 concerning *Channel 4*, the documentary in question was claiming that police and social services in that area had been conducting an investigation since 2001. It seems as if the Home Affairs Select Committee is involved in re-writing history: how could government departments have been unaware of *Barnardo's Streets and Lanes* project, started in Bradford in 1995?[165] It is quite simply astonishing that the government can claim a problem was not identified until after 2009, when for more than 20 years governments had been funding projects and reports dealing with the damage of this phenomenon. Significantly, whilst this parliamentary committee was hearing evidence and even when its final report was published, the media barely mentioned that the committee was sitting. Was this by design?

It is true that until 2010, no local or national child-care organisation was publicly discussing what they knew was going on. The parliamentary report says:

> those involved in child protection were more used to dealing with cases of familial abuse and so the recognition of localised grooming as a form of abuse was not recognised by professionals. They were therefore unable to piece together the different parts of a puzzle in order to create a clear picture of what was happening.[166]

Was the *Barnardo's* project which started in Bradford in 1995 a secret? References to it can be found in sundry news articles and books. CEOP was training thousands of child-care professionals every year, and UKHTC was commissioning a video in 2008, which was distributed to all police forces and child-protection agencies. But is it the case that these child-care professionals were unable to recognise 'localised grooming' until after 2009? Again, if this is the line that Parliament wishes to take, then this points to the failure of national organisations like SOCA, CEOP, UKHTC and The Children's Commissioner. It must surely have fallen to them (and to a lesser extent, academics and child-care charities) to have informed and shaped the professional under-

---

165 We have shown that between 1995 and 2000, staff comments and news reports about that project were describing the phenomenon which came to be known as 'localised grooming', and the project was funded by almost £700,000 from statutory authorities.

166 Home Affairs Select Committee Report, *op. cit.*, p. 7.

standing of the specific features of 'localised grooming'. Yet as *The Times* journalist Andrew Norfolk pointed out in 2011:

> For more than a decade, child protection experts have iden-
> tified a repeated pattern of sex offending in towns and cities
> across northern England and the Midlands involving groups
> of older men who groom and abuse vulnerable girls aged
> 11 to 16 after befriending them on the street. Most of the
> victims are white and most of the convicted offenders are of
> Pakistani heritage, unlike other known models of child-sex
> offending in Britain, including child abuse initiated by on-
> line grooming, in which the vast majority of perpetrators are
> white.[167]

It appears that the Parliamentary inquiry wanted to re-write history. And as proof that child-care professionals had recognised this phenomenon long before 2009, the description of grooming given by Sara Swann in 2000, showed that the professional understanding of the phenomenon then was no different then than in 2010.[168]

The most staggering admission by the committee was that the committee felt it necessary to spell out to child-care professionals that children cannot consent to sex, it is a legal impossibility:

> it should be the fundamental, working assumption of all
> front-line staff working with children and young people that
> sexual relations between an adult and a child under the legal
> age of consent are non-consensual, unlawful and wrong.[169]

 The committee failed to point out that the judiciary also needed to be reminded of this. Too often it has been claimed these cases are diffi-cult are to prosecute, because the girls appeared to be consenting. For decades it should have been impossible to mount that as a successful defence.

The committee found that the only reason why children from care homes were disproportionately represented among the victims was be-

167 Andrew Norfolk, 'Revealed: conspiracy of silence on UK sex gangs', *The Times*, 5 Jan 2011 http://www.thetimes.co.uk/tto/news/uk/crime/article2863058.ece

168 Sara Swann, 'Helping girls involved in "prostitution": a Barnardos Experiment', *op. cit*. See our discussion of this project in section 3.4 *1995 Bradford: Streets and Lanes.*

169 Home Affairs Select Committee Report, *op. cit.*, p. 14.

cause these children were in fact more vulnerable to the gangs. Thus, the greatest defence of a child against these gangs was to have caring parents (yet as we saw in Bindel's 2007 report, these parents were ignored by the police even when the parents had done the initial detective work).[170] The parents and schoolgirls were failed by so many agencies. In many ways, this Parliamentary report also fails the victims and their parents.

5.9 Barnardo's

In section 3.4 *1995 Bradford: Streets and Lanes*, we briefly discussed the Streets and Lanes project, which *Barnardo's* began in 1995, in order to help schoolgirls lured into a life of 'prostitution'. In 2011, *Barnardo's* referred to this project in their acclaimed 'Puppet on a String' report, which demanded 'urgent action' on child sexual abuse.[171]

This 'child prostitution' project was started by *Barnardo's* in Bradford in 1995. The priority of this project seems to have been about freeing the girls from the gangs, preventing the gangs claiming new victims, or even just providing sexual health checks to the victims. Those are all commendable aims, but given how much *Barnardo's* and their staff knew about the grooming phenomenon, doesn't the public have the right to ask why they weren't taking an active campaigning role, back in 1995? Parliament and national agencies are purporting that nothing was known about 'localised grooming' until 2011. What was *Barnardo's* doing between 1995 and 2011 to draw this phenomenon to the attention of government, national agencies and the media? Did *Barnardo's* not think that the gangs needed to be stopped by law enforcement, or at the very least, that the supply of potential victims should be forewarned?

By the time that the Child Exploitation Online Protection Centre (CEOP) was created in 2006, the charity *Barnardo's* had more than a decade of experience dealing with the victims of the grooming gangs, with the Director of *Barnardo's* Bradford project precisely describing the 'localised grooming' process by the year 2000. How could it be that CEOP did not discover this grooming phenomenon for more than a decade after Sara Swann had adequately described it in print? Did *Barnardo's* not think it important to lobby CEOP between 2006 and 2011? Where was *Barnardo's* support for *Channel 4* in 2003 and 2004? Why was *Barnardo's* silent when the Chief Constable of West Yorkshire Police per-

---

170 *Ibid.*, p. 12.

171 'Puppet on a String: the Urgent Need to Cut Children Free From Sexual Exploitation', 2011, http://www.barnardos.org.uk/ctf_puppetonastring_report_final.pdf pg. 1.

suaded *Channel 4* to withdraw their documentary? Why was *Barnardo's* not loudy supporting local MP Ann Cryer in 2003 and 2004? Why did *Barnardo's* remain silent in 2004 when Bradford Council and West Yorkshire Police stated there was 'no evidence' that these grooming gangs existed? How did *Barnardo's* respond in 2005 when West Yorkshire Police closed down their investigation into the grooming gangs? Why did *Barnardo's* not lend support to CROP in Leeds, or to Julie Bindel in 2007? We cannot find any information that will allow us to answer these questions. It seems strange that *Barnardo's* started to demand 'urgent action' in 2011, when for 15 years they had been helping the victims of the gangs, but had not run high-profile publicity campaigns.

Despite being cited by the Parliamentary investigation in 2012, the 30 page *Barnardo's* report from 2011 barely mentions 'localised grooming'. As we have found is typical of reports from *Barnardo's* over many years, they never address any characteristics of the men who do the grooming. The *Barnardo's* report does spend a lot of time talking about online grooming, a facet of grooming which CEOP had focussed on to the point of eliminating any discussion of localised grooming. One would expect that with the grooming phenomenon moving to centre stage in 2011 and 2012, a report from *Barnardo's* would actually discuss this phenomenon. When the 2011 *Barnardo's* report talks about 'trafficking' they cite a case in 'the south west', an area where there has been no evidence at all of localised grooming. The only time the *Barnardo's* report does talk about localised grooming is when they report on the highly publicised cases from Rochdale and Derby, cases which the whole country would already have known about. Where was the expert information from *Barnardo's* experience in Bradford from 1995 onwards? According to Anna Hall (who made the 2004 documentary for *Channel 4*), it was from her encounters with *Barnardo's Streets and Lanes* project in 1996 that she learned about the 'overwhelmingly Asian' grooming gangs.[172] *Barnardo's* seems to have gone out of its way to avoid identifying the glaring and specific patterns concerning the ethnicity of the grooming gangs, although *Barnardo's* does go into detail about 'the characteristics of children at risk of sexual exploitation'.[173]

Yet even in 2002, with no mention of the contrast in ethnicity between the majority of the perpetrators and the majority of the victims,

---

172 Anna Hall 'Hunt For Britain's Sex Gangs, C4', *op. cit.*

173 'Effective Work with Sexually Exploited Children and Young People', http://www.barnardos.org.uk/effective_work_with_sexually_exploited_children_young_people_2008-2.pdf p. 3.

publications were mentioning that the *Barnardo's Streets and Lanes* project was exposing:

> a "grooming" process which is undertaken by the "boy-friend" or "pimp" in producing a child prostitute. This process not only draws young women/girls into prostitution; it creates complete dependency, which perpetuates their abuse through prostitution. They are almost always lead into prostitution by a man, often aged 18 to 25, who begins a relationship with a vulnerable girl... The pattern of control typically involves four stages: 1. Ensnaring 2. Creating dependency 3. Taking control 4. Total dominance The end result of this grooming process is that the "boyfriend" who has become the all important person in the girl's life, has created a willing victim in a completely dominating relationship.[174]

Thus, it is clear that sometime between 1995 and 2000, the 'localised grooming' pattern of exploitation was recognised by *Barnardo's*, and by those talking to the charity about their work in Bradford (*contra* the claims of CEOP, the Children's Commissioner and the Home Affairs Select Committee that this grooming phenomenon was not identified until 2011).

In early 2011, following the sentencing of those convicted in a major grooming trial at the end of the previous year, former Home Secretary Jack Straw said some Pakistani men saw white girls as 'easy meat'.[175] What was so surprising about this admission, was that since the controversy over the *Edge of the City* documentary in 2004, no-one in the public eye (apart from Julie Bindel and Mohammed Shafiq) had dared to make any explicit connection between 'Asians' and the grooming gangs. In reporting the remarks of Jack Straw MP, the media presented the Chief Executive of *Barnardo's* as saying 'the case was more about vulnerable children of all races who were at risk from abuse', with the media implying that ethnicity was basically irrelevant.[176] Let us remember that

---

174 Suzanne Knight 'Children Abused through Prostitution', *Emergency Nurse*, vol.10, no.4, 2002, pp. 27-30. http://rcnpublishing.com/doi/abs/10.7748/en2002.07.10.4.27. c1069

175 'White girls "easy meat" to Pakistani men, says Straw', *The Independent*, 8 Jan 2011, http://www.independent.co.uk/news/uk/crime/white-girls-e asy-meat-to-pakistani-men-says-straw-2179347.html.

176 'Jack Straw: Some White Girls are "Easy Meat"', *BBC News* website, 8 Jan 2011 http://www.bbc.co.uk/news/uk-england-derbyshire-12141603. In many reports

Jack Straw had successfully represented one of the areas in Britain with a very high proportion of Pakistanis; yet when he pointed out that being male and Pakistani were significant features in this criminality, the media ensured that *Barnardo's* Chief Executive is widely quoted in such a way as to appear to undermine what Jack Straw had stated. Were the remarks of *Barnardo's* Chief Executive taken out of context, or is it really *Barnardo's* policy to discourage people from considering the ethnicity of the perpetrators?

After releasing the 'Puppet on a String' report in 2011, the Chief Executive of *Barnardo's* made a point of stating that ethnicity should be marginalised:

> From our experience, we know that in some areas ethnicity is a factor, but in many other areas it isn't... If you focus on one model of sexual exploitation, children who are being exploited in different circumstances won't see that it's an issue for them as well. Young people who need support won't come forward because they don't fit the model that's being presented.[177]

---

of Straw's comments, Martin Narey, the Chief Executive of *Barnardo's* is quoted as disagreeing with Straw that there is any ethnic or racial dimension to this crime. However, if we read carefully what the Chief Executive of *Barnardo's* says in some of these reports, it is entirely consistent with our thesis that it is not race that is the significant factor in these crimes, but religion. Thus in David Batty, 'White girls seen as "easy meat" by Pakistani rapists, says Jack Straw', *The Guardian*, 8 Jan 2011, http://www.theguardian.com/world/2011/jan/08/jack-straw-white-girls-easy-meat. It says:

> The Barnardo's chief executive, Martin Narey, said the case was more about vulnerable children of all races who were at risk from abuse. Street grooming was "probably happening in most towns and cities" and was not confined to the Pakistani community. "I certainly don't think this is a Pakistani thing. My staff would say that there is an over-representation of people from minority ethnic groups – Afghans, people from Arabic nations – but *it's not just one nation*," said Narey. (emphasis added)

Whilst being reported as disagreeing that being a Pakistani is a salient fact in being a perpetrator in these crimes, Narey is actually saying that salience is reduced, because the other (Muslim) men who perpetrate this crime are from countries other than Pakistan *e.g.* Afghanistan and Arabic countries. Once again, the media conflate race and religion and sow confusion.

177 'Barnardo's: focus on race in sexual exploitation cases could lead to more risk', 18 Jan 2011, http://www.communitycare.co.uk/articles/18/01/2011/ 116089/focus-on-race-in-grooming-cases-could-lead-to-more-risk.htm. This was the newly appointed Chief Executive speaking.

Yet this is exactly what *Barnardo's* has done. It has focused on one model: a generic model, where it is every adult who is a possible perpetrator, and every child who is a possible victim. What is different about the Muslim grooming gangs has been totally obscured. This is precisely the point that Andrew Norfolk made: 'most of the victims are white and most of the convicted offenders are of Pakistani heritage, unlike other known models of child-sex offending in Britain.' Despite being on 'the front-line' dealing with the victims in Bradford since 1995, despite much research, we can find no evidence of *Barnardo's* drawing attention to this singular difference, and many statements from them indicating that ethnicity is not relevant (or at least, only relevant when it comes to considering victims, to ensure non-white victims are considered, even when they are a minority of the victims). All the signs were that the problem with the Muslim grooming gangs had massively increased: as Mohammed Shafiq predicted, if the questions of ethnicity were ignored the problem would get worse.

We have searched the *Barnardo's* website to see if at any time between 1995 and 2015 we can find some mention by them of the contrast in ethnicity between the perpetrators and the victims. In a two year study by *Barnardo's* (ending in 2006), 13 out of 32 cases reported were 'young women' who were sexually exploited. In 21 cases the 'young woman' identified the exploiting man as her 'boyfriend'. In 13 cases this fits the model of a pimp deliberately grooming a teenage girl for prostitution.

> In five cases a much older male was involved; in each case he was a known or convicted sex offender and appeared to be primarily interested in the girl for his own use – although issues of being "shared" or sold to "friends" also appeared, this was not in a pimping arena. At 12 and 13 these were the youngest girls in the sample, and despite the fact that the men involved were in their 30s, 40s and 50s, they too considered their abuser to be their "boyfriend."[178]

In this report there is no indication of the 'ethnicity' of the exploitative adult men. And this is not because *Barnardo's* works in a world unaware of political correctness and oblivious to the politics of ethnicity: the re-

---

178 Sara Scott and Paula Skidmore 'Reducing the Risk: Barnardos Support for Sexually Exploited Young People', 2006, http://www.barnardos.org.uk/reducing_the_risk_report.pdf p. 25.

port did consider ethnicity in ensuring that the cases examined should represent a spread of ethnicities in Britain.[179] This piece of 'research' looks more like promotional material for the *Barnardo's* way of doing things, why '*Barnardo's* works', and as such, it seems to have steered away from any information which could have confirmed the existence of the (overwhelmingly Muslim) grooming gangs. It is bizarre that a mere 5 years later, their 'Puppet on a String' report should complain about 'a shocking lack of awareness', when this 2006 report from *Barnardo's* addresses the ethnicity of the victims, but ignores the ethnicity of the perpetrators. Before 2011, when had *Barnardo's* ever spoken out about the reality of these grooming gangs? Just the year before, the Muslim Council of Britain (MCB) was presented as endorsing leaflets in the general election of 2010, which claimed the grooming gangs were a 'racist myth'.[180]

In a 2004 joint project between *Barnardo's* and Dutch organisations, *Barnardo's* clearly had knowledge of the 'Loverboys' project in the Netherlands.[181]

> Through a number of exchange visits and meetings, the implementation of a specially designed monitoring tool and collection of case study materials, the project set up a systematic comparative evaluation of the work of UK and NL schemes. This enabled schemes in both countries to compare their assessments of young people at risk of sexual exploitation. Through this method, common ways of working to prevent and intervene against child sexual exploitation were clearly identified, as well as some national differences.[182]

This 2004 report makes no mention of the ethnicity/religion of the perpetrators, even though one of the principal focuses was on liaison and comparison between staff from *Barnardo's* *Streets and Lanes* project which started in Bradford, and the 'Loverboys' project in the Nether-

---

179 *Ibid.*, p. 16.

180 See *Appendix 12*. If they were aware of such political claims, organisations like *Barnardo's* and the NSPCC had the perfect opportunity to contradict such claims and to make the grooming phenomenon an issue in that election.

181 Paula Skidmore, 'What Works in Child Sexual Exploitation: Sharing and Learning', July 2004, http://www.barnardos.org.uk/final_report_by_paula_skidmore_in_english. pdf p. 5. This 'Loverboy' concept became the foundation for the UKHTC video *My Dangerous Loverboy*, commissioned in 2008.

182 *Ibid.*, p. 17.

lands. This document focuses on identifying the characteristics of children who are likely to be vulnerable to sexual exploitation and pimping without ever focusing on the characteristics of the perpetrators. Yet there *were* significant points of comparison between the grooming problems in the UK and those in the Netherlands: namely, the majority of the perpetrators were Muslim men.

In 2007 *Barnardo's* undertook another partnership project, comparing the UK with the Netherlands and Estonia. This project did not involve any focus on the 'Loverboys' project in the Netherlands, nor the *Streets and Lanes* project in Bradford. However, there was a plenary presentation from a Dutch representative 'on the loverboy problems' in Amsterdam, but no mention is made of *Barnardo's Streets and Lanes* project.[183] There was also a presentation from an imam from Eindhoven 'on the issues and recognition of the problem within the Muslim community and the different attitudes towards girls and boys involved in prostitution activities.'[184] We cannot imagine that there is much of a problem with young Muslim men being prostituted in the Netherlands, so we conclude that this talk concerned the Muslim boys being involved in prostitution as pimps. The report does refer to the analysis of 32 young women being sexually exploited, as in *Barnardo's* 2006 report, but as we noted above, in that analysis *Barnardo's* expressed no interest in the ethnicity of the perpetrators.[185] This 2007 report also records that a presentation was held by the Platform of Islamic Organisations in Rijnmond (Holland), where '1 project was started on the "loverboy" problem due to the fact that a number of victims and perpetrators have Muslim backgrounds.'[186] Another presentation from Holland that was part of the 2007 report stated:

> Social control has no effect. That is why the awareness and condemnation of the social problem and the danger of the loverboys needs to be encouraged in the Moroccan community. For instance, mosques to state that it is unacceptable.[187]

---

183 'Blueprints of Experience: working to prevent and reduce child sexual exploitation in the United Kingdom, Netherlands and Estonia', January 2008 http://www.barnardos.org.uk/blueprints_reduce_child_sex_exploit_2007.pdf p. 17.

184 *Ibid.*, p. 18.

185 *Ibid.*, p. 13.

186 *Ibid.*, p. 20.

187 *Ibid.*, p. 21.

Two further presentations in the 2007 project concerned the Loverboy problems in the Netherlands. Whilst the Dutch participants in the project focussed almost exclusively on the Loverboy problem, the *Barnardo's* team did not appear to mention the overwhelming role that Muslim men in Britain play in grooming gangs. It is truly astonishing that in so many international meetings between two countries who both suffer from gangs who groom schoolgirls, *Barnardo's* should not talk about their *Streets and Lanes* project, and the points of similarity or contrast. The Dutch participants were clearly aware of an Islamic connection (at the very least in terms of demography, even if they had not articulated that there might well be doctrinal motivations). What did *Barnardo's* do to make the British public aware of the 'Loverboys' in Holland, and the similarities with the grooming gangs in Britain?[188] Did *Barnardo's* staff really fail to notice that there was an Islamic connection in both these forms of sexual exploitation?

Year after year, *Barnardo's* projects do not mention the grooming gangs. Throughout these reports, *Barnardo's* seems to be more concerned with self-promotion than with drawing attention to this shocking phenomenon. The only time *Barnardo's* gave any indication that they knew there was a problem with Muslim grooming gangs in Britain was the 2011 report, which came out after a year in which, in 6 different trials around England, a total of 32 Muslim men were convicted for crimes in which they groomed schoolgirls. After such a run of conclusive evidence, it was frankly unnecessary for *Barnardo's* to say anything, and what they did say added nothing to the debate. And one has to wonder: did *Barnardo's* only come out with this report in 2011 because they were aware that Norfolk was working on an analysis that would prove the existence of the grooming gangs? It would have reflected very badly on *Barnardo's* if Norfolk's report came out, and the organisation which had been working with the victims of the gangs over 16 years ago had never issued any kind of report about this phenomenon.

Despite *Streets and Lanes* from 1995 being the origin of what eventually became *Channel 4's* controversial 2004 documentary, we cannot find any evidence that *Barnardo's* have ever mounted any kind of overt publicity campaign about the Muslim grooming gangs. None of this is to say that any of the other children's charities come out of this any better. We are not aware of any children's charity, with the exception of

---

188 We think it likely that *Barnardo's* were one of the principal sources informing SOCA and/or UKHTC about the Loverboy problem in Holland, leading to the commissioning of *My Dangerous Loverboy* in 2008.

CROP, which went out of the way to state who in particular was committing this kind of crime.

5.10 Academic Experts

We wanted to make sure that we were not missing any instances of courageous academics who had used their academic freedom to research and report on the grooming gangs, even when the child-care professionals and the media were too politically correct to do so. On the NSPCC website we found a 'reading list of key research into child sexual exploitation', and a glance at the titles of this 'key research' is enough to demonstrate how academics and other child protection experts have fundamentally ignored the grooming gangs.[189] There are two main academic institutions whose work we can examine to see how much they have done to speak out about the grooming gangs: the International Centre for the Study of Sexually Exploited and Trafficked Young People (Bedfordshire University) and the Jill Dando Institute of Security and Crime Science (University of London). If one consults the NSPCC 'list of key research', one will see that the bulk of the list is made up of documents from *Barnardo's*, Bedfordshire Centre, or the Jill Dando Institute.

It was at the end of 2011 that Sue Jago and Professor Jenny Pearce from Bedfordshire University published research into the failings of Local Safeguarding Children Boards.[190] Once again, it seems that it was after the spate of successful prosecutions in 2010, and when CEOP, *The Times* newspaper and *Barnardo's* started to address this hitherto unspoken problem, that the University of Bedfordshire academics also became involved. We have to ask: what research was this centre (or its staff) doing on this subject between 1988 and 2011? We can understand that there are reasons why charities may want to tread within the borders of safety when it comes to political correctness, as bad publicity could affect their funding, and charities can be forgiven for fearing that some pressure groups might be ruthless enforcers of the ideology of political correctness. However, when it comes to academics, here is a group of professionals supposedly guided by truth, not by the ideological dogma of political correctness.

In 2009 Prof. Pearce (Director of this Centre at Bedfordshire Uni-

---

189 NSPCC 'Research on child sexual exploitation' Jul 2013 http://www.nspcc.org.uk/Inform/resourcesforprofessionals/sexualabuse/sexual_exploitation_research_wda85130.html

190 http://www.beds.ac.uk/news/2011/october/exploitationstudy

versity) authored a book on sexual exploitation.[191] In that book Prof. Pearce was perfectly capable of describing the phenomenon of 'localised grooming', which CEOP went on to supposedly discover two years later. According to Prof. Pearce:

> the "grooming model for sexual exploitation", explained the process whereby an abusive adult entices a young person into becoming dependent upon them. Invariably, this involved the young person believing they are in love with their abuser. The pattern moves through a process where the abuser flatters the young person, giving them attention, accommodation and other gifts. The young person increasingly becomes dependent upon the abuser who invariably isolates them from family and friends and encourages them to become reliant upon drugs and alcohol. The young person is then forced or coerced into swapping or selling sex to raise money for the "boyfriend."[192]

This is the form of grooming which the Home Affairs Select Committee claimed was only recognised following the successful convictions in Derbyshire in November 2010. It also clearly matches what *Barnardo's* staff were describing as happening in Bradford in 1995[193] and 2000.[194] The repeated occurrence of descriptions of this phenomenon before 2011 shows that Parliament and CEOP were involved in a cover-up, trying to claim that what was going on was a new phenomenon, when it had been identified by child-care professionals years earlier.

Although she does refer to *Barnardo's Streets and Lanes* project, Prof. Pearce does not make any comparison between the Dutch 'Loverboy' phenomenon and the British grooming gangs. Her book does not even discuss the controversy around *Channel 4's Edge of the City*, or Julie Bindel's 'Mothers of Prevention'. This is not because Prof. Pearce is oblivious to ethnicity: in her book she goes on to complain that 'the domi-

191 Jenny Pearce, *Young People and Sexual Exploitation: It's not Hidden, you Just Aren't Looking*, Routledge, 2009.

192 *Ibid.*, p. 21.

193 'Scandal of child-sex on Bradford streets', *Telegraph & Argus*, 14 Jul 1998, http://www.thetelegraphandargus.co.uk/archive/1998/07/14/ 8075434.Scandal_of_child_sex_on_Bradford_streets/.

194 Sara Swann, 'Helping girls involved in "prostitution": a Barnardos Experiment', *op. cit.*

nant image of a sexually exploited child... is of them as a white young woman.' She urges the agencies involved not to adopt these race (and gender) blinkers, in case it 'has a negative impact... on the service provision to Black and minority ethnic communities.'[195] This is, of course, very commendable. However, there is no injunction to say that such race-awareness should also be extended to considerations of the perpetrators or the motivations of the abusers. In several places she discusses the ethnicity of the victims. But we can find no attempt to discuss the ethnicity of the perpetrators. So, just as court cases were coming to light in 2009 and 2010, showing that grooming gangs were disproportionately Muslim (as Anna Hall had come to realise in Bradford in 1996), Prof. Pearce is advising that professionals should be searching out minority ethnic victims; but there is no indication that minority ethnicities might be found in hugely disproportionate numbers amongst the perpetrators. It seems that once again ethnicity can only be considered salient when it comes to the victims of crime, but must not be mentioned when it comes to the perpetrators.

Whilst Prof. Pearce may have made significant omissions in her work with regard to what some experts are calling 'the biggest child protection scandal of our time',[196] the work of academics associated with the Jill Dando Institute of Security and Crime Science is worse. Cockbain and Brayley, are described in *The Independent* as the 'authors of the first independent academic analysis looking at "on-street grooming", where young girls, spotted outside, including at the school gates, have become targets.'[197] *The Independent* report goes on to say of the research by Cockbain and Brayley that their most recent work studies just five cases – though of the 52 offenders involved, 83 per cent are Asian Pakistani, 11 per cent Asian other and 6 per cent white.[198] This hugely disproportionate presence of 'Asians', particularly those from the Islamic state of Pakistan, is entirely in keeping with our analysis of the CEOP data, the Children's Commissioner data, and all the convictions for this type of

---

195 Jenny Pearce, *Young People and Sexual Exploitation: It's not Hidden, you Just Aren't Looking, op. cit.*, p. 21; see also, p. 121.

196 Andrew Norfolk, 'Police Files Reveal Vast Child Protection Scandal', *op. cit.*

197 Caroline Davies and Karen McVeigh, 'Child sex trafficking study sparks exaggerated racial stereotyping', *The Guardian*, 6 Jan 2011 http://www.theguardian.com/law/2011/jan/06/child-sex-trafficking-racial-stereotyping.

198 *The Independent* does not give the publication details of this report by Cockbain and Brayley.

crime in Britain since 1997.[199]

At least Cockbain and Brayley have not ignored the phenomenon; but what they did was to attempt to claim that the perpetrators could not be Muslims, even if they described themselves as 'Muslims'. Cockbain and Brayley are quoted as saying:

> ...religion seems to be a red herring here, in that many offenders seem to be Muslim only in a nominal sense. Prior to arrest many drank alcohol, took drugs, did not have beards, and all engaged in extramarital sex with underage girls. Hardly the hallmarks of a strict Muslim.[200]

It seems extraordinary that non-Muslim academics such as Cockbain and Brayley should set themselves up as the people who can define who is or is not a Muslim: a Muslim man without a beard is only a 'nominal' Muslim? How many times must some Muslim man go to the mosque each day before he is considered more than a Muslim in name only? Whilst the Koran may have some restrictions on the consumption of alcohol, where does the Koran say that Muslims cannot sell or take drugs? That a major supplier of hashish is Morocco, and the major suppliers of heroin are Afghanistan and Pakistan should show that this is an extremely flawed understanding of the restrictions of Islam and the behaviour of Muslims. Iran has the world's worst problem with heroin addiction.[201] Does this mean that the 3.5 million heroin addicts in the Islamic Republic of Iran are not Muslims? Cockbain and Brayley seem to be saying that only those Muslims who conform to the most extreme image of a fundamentalist Muslim are to be regarded as Muslims. Does this mean that only Muslim women who wear a burka or niqab are to be considered Muslims, and that the majority of Muslim women who wear only a hijab are not real Muslims? Yasmin Alibhai-Brown does not even wear a hijab, which many fundamentalist Muslims would say means she is not a Muslim. It seems very strange that two female academics from the Jill Dando Institute should be supporting the idea that only the most

---

199 Whether or not the non-Pakistani Asians in their analysis were Muslims is hard to know.

200 Paul Vallely, 'Child Sex Grooming: the Asian Question', *op. cit.*, Whether these remarks were spoken directly to the journalist, or are quotations from a paper authored by Cockbain and Brayley is hard to determine.

201 'Iran and heroin: a lesson for the west?', *Channel 4 News*, 10 Mar 2006, http://www.channel4.com/news/iran-and-heroin-a-lesson-for-the-west

overtly fundamentalist Muslims are a genuine measure of what it means to be a Muslim. Should we extend this, and say that the 57% of British Muslims who don't want to have apostates killed[202] are 'Muslim only in a nominal sense'?

This is not the only incident where Cockbain and Brayley declare what is and is not the behaviour of genuine Muslims. In an article on *The Guardian* website, authored by Cockbain and Brayley, they state: 'The defendants in question are at most nominally Muslim. Practising Muslims certainly aren't supposed to have sex with children.'[203] Here Cockbain and Brayley seem to be going further, suggesting that it may be appropriate to regard the perpetrators as non-Muslims (considering that 31% of British Muslims think that those who leave Islam should be killed,[204] it is dangerous to say that a Muslim is not a Muslim). It would seem that it is precisely the issue of these men having sex with children which would discount them from eligibility to be Muslims. However, if Cockbain and Brayley paid attention to the legality of sex with children according to manuals of sharia law (manuals which are found in public libraries in Britain), perhaps these academics would notice reports from feminists in London of under-age Muslim girls[205] being married off by imams in mosques to devout old Muslim men, not 5 miles from the Jill Dando Institute at University College London.[206] If we adopt the criteria which seem to inform the work of Cockbain and Brayley, we would have to declare that these devout old Muslim men were not Muslims, and maybe even declare that the imams who married the old men to

---

202 Munira Mirza, Abi Senthilkumaran and Zein Ja'far, 'Living apart together: British Muslims and the paradox of multiculturalism', *Policy Exchange*, 2007, http://www.policyexchange.org.uk/images/publications/living%20apart%20together%20-%20jan%20 07.pdf, p. 47.

203 Ella Cockbain and Helen Brayley, 'The truth about "Asian sex gangs"' (*Comment is Free*), *The Guardian*, 8 May 2012 http://www.theguardian.com/commentisfree/2012/may/08/Asian-sex-gangs-on-street-grooming. This article was on *The Guardian* website until late 2013, but has now been removed.

204 Munira Mirza, Abi Senthilkumaran and Zein Ja'far, 'Living apart together: British Muslims and the paradox of multiculturalism', *Policy Exchange*, 2007, http://www.policyexchange.org.uk/images/publications/living%20apart%20together%20-%20jan%20 07.pdf, p. 47.

205 See Pavan Amara, 'Islington Girls Forced into Marriage at the Age of Nine', *Islington Tribune*, 27 Jan 2012, http://www.islingtontribune.com/news/2012/jan/islington-girls-forced-marriage-age-nine. The 'moderate' imam quoted in that story 'explained that Sharia law stated an individual can marry when they begin puberty', and it is clear that the Muslim schoolgirls were providing sexual services to their 'husbands'.

206 Paul Vallely, 'Child Sex Grooming: the Asian Question', *op. cit.*

the under-age children were not Muslims. Even if the evidence of their own study shows that the gangs in Britain are mostly Pakistani Asians (Muslims), Cockbain and Brayley rule that race and religion are to be considered irrelevant: if necessary, the men must be designated as being Muslim in name only, even if these men were brought up as Muslims, and define themselves as Muslims.

In the article on *The Guardian* website, entitled 'The Truth about "Asian sex gangs"', Cockbain and Brayley describe themselves as 're-searchers specialising in this crime'.[207] As such, we should expect them, more than anyone else, to have understood the history of this phenomenon, and to have investigated any connection with Islamic doctrine and the historical behaviour of Muslims (particularly since these academics have decided to list criteria that differentiate 'strict Muslims' from 'nominal Muslims'). Cockbain and Brayley offer no evidence to show that the behaviour of the grooming gangs is un-Islamic, other than their own assertions. That so many sources of evidence demonstrate that Muslim men are hugely over-represented as the perpetrators in the grooming gangs should have been a signal to Cockbain and Brayley that they need to examine the history and doctrine of Islam. Indeed, Cockbain and Brayley are knowingly rejecting the claims by others that there is an Islamic dimension to this crime: they explicitly refer to Nick Griffin of the BNP and to the EDL. This was the opportunity for 'researchers specialising in this crime' to start looking at Islamic doctrine and the behaviour of other Muslims in Britain and around the world, to see if men having sex with children had any foundation in Islam. Cockbain and Brayley criticise others for 'generalisation', but they work with a fantasy version of Islam.

Rather than concentrate on 'racial profiling', Cockbain and Brayley suggest improved detection and prevention techniques:

> there are plenty of things to be getting on with that don't depend on offender profiling. The best bits of policing nationwide need to become more widely adopted: innovative anti-exploitation teams, training programmes for front-line officers and brave approaches to covert investigations. Often dubbed the missing part of the jigsaw, healthcare and education have a crucial part to play in spotting and supporting victims...[208]

207 Ella Cockbain and Helen Brayley, 'The truth about "Asian sex gangs"', *op. cit.*
208 *Ibid.*

We would draw the attention of Cockbain and Brayley to the *Barnardo's* staff, who in 1996 were talking to Anna Hall about 'overwhelmingly Asian'[209] grooming gangs in Bradford. That *Barnardo's* project had an anti-exploitation team who were involved in supporting victims with healthcare and education. There is no indication that such activities managed to stop the grooming gangs: ten years later, it was still reported that the problems were just as bad in Bradford. If the *Barnardo's* project had succeeded between 1996 and 2003 in eliminating Muslim grooming activities, *Channel 4* would have had no basis for making *Edge of the City* there in 2004. And just a year after Cockbain and Brayley espoused their naïve views, West Yorkshire Police arrested 45 men in the largest grooming case so far.[210] Or perhaps Cockbain and Brayley might like to read the section 3.13 *2008 My Dangerous Loverboy*, about the educational film commissioned by UKHTC in 2008, and which has yet to receive distribution. CEOP were reporting that they trained thousands of front-line staff every year. These activities have been tried (or at least suggested) before, and none of them have shown any effectiveness at stopping the gangs. It is truly astonishing to see these experts trot out such naïve opinions, apparently unaware of the history of this problem.

These experts advise against any focus on the most clear characteristic of this crime: groups of 'Asian' (Muslim) men with non-Muslim schoolgirls; such focus supposedly risks targeting the 'non-deviant majority'. Yet we have had 25 years in which the ethnicity of the perpetrators of these crimes has been denied. And all the indicators are that this did nothing to stop the crime nor to improve detection and conviction rates. It achieved the reverse: it allowed the subset of men who groom, rape and pimp schoolgirls to hide among the 'non-deviant majority', that is, the population of white men, who are vastly under-represented in this type of crime. To ignore the distinctive features of this type of crime, means that instead of focusing on a group who are maybe 1% of the UK population (Muslim men), police forces are to be focusing on 100% of the UK population (*i.e.* everyone, Muslims and Christians, men

209 Anna Hall, 'Hunt For Britain's Sex Gangs, C4', *op. cit.*

210 Suzannah Hills, 'UK's biggest child sex gang uncovered as 45 men are arrested over abuse of girls as young as 13', *Daily Mail*, 18 Aug 2013, http://www.dailymail.co.uk/news/article-2396486/UKs-biggest-child-sex-gang-uncovered-45-men-arrested-abuse-girls-young-13.html. The report states that some of the men are white, some are Asian. Let's hope for the sake of the reputation of Cockbain and Brayley, that this case reverses the trend, and is 95% white and 5% Muslim, which is what one would expect if there were no other factors.

and women, the old and the young). This is nonsense, and would stretch police and social service resources enormously, making it harder for the police to separate signal from noise. Ignoring the astonishing fact, that a group who are a tiny percentage of the population should make up almost all the perpetrators of a horrific yet highly lucrative criminal operation, would do nothing to help the victims. It is a recipe for continuing to leave schoolgirls vulnerable, something which has persisted for over 25 years.

Cockbain and Brayley assert that since conclusions are being drawn from small samples, it could be misleading.

> There have been so few investigations of large offending groups that a few cases involving big non-Asian groups could easily shift these offender profiles in a whole new direction. Whether this happens or not remains to be seen, but entrenched stereotypes have a nasty habit of persisting, even when the evidence moves on.[211]

These 'specialists' made this observation in 2012. Yet as our list of convictions for the subsequent years shows,[212] the proportion of Muslims convicted of these crimes has continued to remain at around 90%. Thus, the evidence continues to show that the pattern demonstrated by Andrew Norfolk in 2011, a pattern which was observed as long ago as 1995 by staff working for *Barnardo's*, is still to be found in the data. At the time these academics wrote this piece, Andrew Norfolk had identified 56 convictions over a period of 14 years. But within a few years of Norfolk's analysis, the number of convictions has nearly tripled in that short time, and the pattern still obtains. The truth about the grooming gangs is that all the evidence so far indicates that they are overwhelmingly Muslim men.

Cockbain and Brayley attack racial profiling. But this is a straw man: the question is not about 'racial profiling', but about 'religious profiling' or 'cultural profiling'. Cockbain and Brayley attempt to employ a *reductio ad absurdum*, invoking the idea of fingerprinting all the Pakistanis in Britain.[213] Yet they shy away from the far more reasonable process, of investigating what it is about Islamic doctrine and Muslim culture that could have led to the formation of this new kind of crimi-

---

211 Ella Cockbain and Helen Brayley, 'The truth about "Asian sex gangs"', *op. cit.*

212 *Appendix 1: Grooming Gang Convictions.*

213 Ella Cockbain and Helen Brayley, 'The truth about "Asian sex gangs"', *op. cit.*

nality (both in Britain and in the Netherlands). And in terms of cutting down the incidence of this crime, these academics should be asking why is it that the Muslim community have protected these criminal gangs in full knowledge of what these gangs were doing. Until there is a recognition of the history and scale of this problem, until there are signs that the perpetrators are more likely to be convicted, what is required is an education programme warning schoolgirls what the profile of this kind of perpetrator is, and the techniques the criminals use to entrap the schoolgirls into becoming sex slaves: seduction, addiction, subjugation, prostitution. In chapter 7, Islamic Cultural Background, we will examine the parts of Islamic doctrine and Muslim culture which could produce this grooming phenomenon. This is the very thing from which academic researchers, child-care professionals, journalists and politicians have shied away for decades.

SIX
Abuse of the Narrative of Racism

It's a real shame when votes come before young girls' lives.
                      – groomed victim's mother, *Standpoint*, 2010

6.1 Political Correctness

COULD political correctness really be so powerful that it could allow this child-care scandal to persist and flourish for decades? We should not underestimate the power of this mental straight-jacket. People often refer to political correctness in humorous terms, but in reality it is no laughing matter. Political correctness is a sinister device constructed by the Left to ensure that negative outcomes of Left-wing ideology are never subject to criticism.[1] One might argue that surely those who oppose the Left would be able to use these failures as a corrective to Left-wing policies, but this does not appear to have any con-

---

1 As long ago as 1995, Prof. Thomas Sowell was documenting how the implementation of many Left-wing policies led to negative consequences for those whom the policies were supposed to help. He shows how, despite failure after failure, the Left refuse to acknowledge that the consequences of their policies are detrimental to the intended beneficiaries. See Thomas Sowell, *The Vision of the Anointed: Self-congratulation as a Basis for Social Policy*, Basic Books, 1995.

194

sequence. As Nobel prize-winning economist and political philosopher Friedrich Hayek pointed out back in the 1960s, it is the Left who set the agenda, and mostly their 'Conservative' opponents just follow along in the trajectory set by the Left.[2]

Political correctness is nothing less than an implementation of Newspeak, a tendency identified by George Orwell in his dystopian novel *1984*. Whilst Orwell probably considered himself a socialist to the end of his days, this is how he characterizes Newspeak:

> Newspeak was... devised to meet the ideological needs of Ingsoc, or English Socialism... The purpose of Newspeak was... to make all other modes of thought impossible.[3]

Orwell clearly identified the mental straight-jacket of Newspeak with English Socialism, and the only significant criticisms of political correctness have come from those who would be seen as opponents by the Left,[4] and the greatest advocates of political correctness in the West have been socialists, government employees, trade union organisers, teachers, etc.

The implementation of political correctness emerged in American universities in the 1980s, and by the early 1990s was sufficiently well advanced to prompt collections of essays discussing the phenomenon.

> The new ideology tends toward nihilism, erasing any distinction between truth and falsity... In the name of "sensitivity" to others and under pain of being denounced as a sexist or racist... radicals require everyone around them to adhere to their... codes of speech and behavior.[5]

From the universities in the 1980s and 1990s, political correctness spread to journalism and public bodies: "'Politically Correct" was originally an approving phrase of the Leninist Left to denote someone who

---

2 Friedrich Hayek, 'Why I Am Not a Conservative', http://object.cato.org/sites/cato.org/files/articles/hayek-why-i-am-not-conservative.pdf.

3 See Appendix in George Orwell, *1984*, http://msxnet.org/orwell/print/1984.pdf

4 Anthony Browne, *The Retreat of Reason: Political Correctness and the Corruption of Public Debate in Modern Britain*, Civitas, 2006; Bruce Bawer, *Surrender: Appeasing Islam, Sacrificing Freedom*, Doubleday, 2009.

5 Paul Berman, 'The Debate and its Origins', p. 2 in Paul Berman (ed) *Debating P.C. - The Controversy Over Political Correctness on College Campuses*, Dell Publishing, New York, 1992.

steadfastly toed the party line'.[6]

Given the extent to which the far Left was in control of British trade unions during the 1980s, it is no surprise that political correctness should have come to rule the working lives of those working for central and local government in Britain: teachers, social workers, civil servants, police officers, etc. From being a phenomenon only spoken of in the 1980s by Leftists and academics, political correctness spread out to become a pervasive phenomenon, just as Hayek predicted: 'conservatives' would be pulled along by the impetus of the Leftist agenda. Government by parties which ostensibly supported freedom of speech would implement laws which made people fearful of speaking the truth. At this point in time, one would struggle to find any divergence between the political correctness of the Left, the Right or the Centre of British politics.

In the UK, the definitive example of the push by the Left to control what can be said, was the behaviour of the socialist government in Britain, immediately following the terrorist attack on the World Trade Center in New York in 2001: the British government introduced the first in a series of determined attempts to make it illegal for anyone to publicly criticise Islam. When the government finally succeeded in passing this law on a third attempt in 2005, it was only at the repeated insistence of The House of Lords that there was any concern for the principle of freedom of speech.[7]

Having encouraged Muslim immigration to the UK without any national debate concerning the nature of Islam and how Islamic values conflict with those of the indigenous population, the socialist govern-

---

6 Paul Berman, 'The Debate and its Origins', *op. cit.* p..5.

7 'Government beaten on hatred bill', *BBC News* website, 25 Oct 2005, http://news.bbc. co.uk/1/hi/uk_politics/4376314.stm. That it was the House of Lords' version of the Bill which became law was down to the socialist government being defeated by just one vote in the House of Commons.

> MPs voted either for or against government attempts to overturn a Lords amendment to the bill that said 'abusive and insulting' behaviour should not be criminalised, merely 'threatening' behaviour; and that people should not be prosecuted for 'recklessly' stiring up religious hatred - that is, without intent.

'Religious hatred: How MPs voted', *BBC News* website, 01 Feb 2006, http://news.bbc. co.uk/1/hi/uk_politics/4668266.stm. If the socialist government had prevailed, if someone had even unintentionally said or written something which Muslims found insulting, then that person could have faced up to 7 years in prison. In this sort of political climate, is it any wonder that public service employees in Labour-dominated towns or highly-unionised professions should have feared imprisonment or professional suicide, should they have articulated their observations that most of the members of the grooming gangs were Muslims or Asians?

ment determined that Islam should not be criticised in the wake of Islamic terrorist attacks.

> In June 2005 the Government introduced the *Racial and Religious Hatred Bill 2005-06* in the House of Commons. The Bill represented the Government's third attempt to outlaw incitement to religious hatred. Provisions had been included in both the *Anti-Terrorism Crime and Security Bill* and the *Serious Organised Crime and Police Bill*. These previous attempts fell as a result of Parliamentary opposition, particularly in the House of Lords. This note sets the attempts to outlaw religious hatred following the attacks on 11 September 2001...[8]

In 2001 it fell to former Left-wing writers such as Melanie Philips to highlight how the socialist government's censorship proposals conflict with freedom of speech:

> the new law will criminalise not deeds that threaten life and liberty but thought itself... If we are properly to defend our liberal values, it's essential to realise what freedom of speech entails. It is the freedom to say things that cause offence; it is the freedom to say things that may cause people to dislike others.[9]

Originally the socialist government intended that even saying something which Muslims found insulting, was to be a criminal offence. As the Parliamentary record of the transition of this legislation through the House of Lords in 2005 records:

> We have therefore tabled amendments that would maintain the criminal offence of threatening, but would remove the words "abusive" and "insulting".[10]

---

8 Lucinda Maer, 'Religious Hatred: Attempts to legislate 2001-2005', 10 Jun 2008, House of Commons Library, http://www.parliament.uk/briefing-papers/SN03189.pdf

9 Quoted in 'Why a religious hatred law would harm religious liberty and freedom of speech', *The Christian Institute*, http://www.religionlaw.co.uk/reportbb.pdf

10 http://www.publications.parliament.uk/pa/ld200506/ldhansrd/vo051025/text/51025-04.htm#51025-04_head2

Moreover, not only was the socialist government determined to make it a criminal offence to insult Muslims, but from 2001 to 2006 the socialists wanted to conflate race with religion.

> Religion is all about ideas, beliefs and philosophies. Religion (and irreligion) governs the choices people make between doctrinal, philosophical or moral alternatives. Race and national origin, on the other hand, are immutable...[11]

The Home Secretary of this socialist government between June 2001 and December 2004, was David Blunkett (then MP for Sheffield Brightside).[12] He made it clear that the proposed criminalisation was intended not only to those who incited hatred, but also those who provoked 'dissension'.[13] Therefore, thinking in a way which did not conform to what was considered 'correct' was to become a crime, if such thought should be made public. Why should anyone be surprised then, following the enactment of this law in 2006, that the allegation of 'racism' could be used to silence anyone who wanted to draw attention to the observable fact that most of the members of the grooming gangs were Muslims? In relation to the 2005 Bill, such fear was observed at the time:

> Proponents of this law argue that there are significant safeguards placed within the proposed legislation – including the fact that the Attorney General must provide his consent before a prosecution is brought. However, even if this supposed safeguard does mean that not many individuals are actually prosecuted each year, it will not stop suspects having to go through the stress of lengthy investigations before the Attorney General makes his decision and is therefore bound to have a chilling effect on people's willingness to engage in

---

11 Quoted in "Why a religious hatred law would harm religious liberty and freedom of speech", *op. cit.*, p..7.

12 http://en.wikipedia.org/wiki/David_Blunkett

13 '[B]earing in mind the fact that the existing law in relation to race provides for those religions that have a direct relationship with the race of the individual concerned. We want to extend that facility to people who follow Islam and Christianity. The measures will also enable us to deal with those who deliberately use the current law to stir up dissention [sic] and hate, which we would all find unacceptable.' David Blunkett, quoted in House of Commons Library Research Paper, 'The Anti-Terrorism, Crime And Security Bill: Introduction And Summary', 19 Nov 2001, http://research-briefings.files.parliament.uk/documents/RP01-101/RP01-101.pdf, p. 14.

controversial religious debate for fear of the process itself, if not the outcome.[14]

As the government exhibited over a number of years its determination to criminalise statements (however truthful) which Muslims might find offensive, then censorship and self-censorship by journalists and public officials could be expected from 2001 to 2006 and beyond. It may be that child-care professionals and journalists would censor themselves or turn a blind-eye without such laws. But there can be no doubt that the implementation of political correctness in the form of repeated attempts to criminalise criticism of Islam must have contributed to a climate of fear.

The socialist government had not only conducted a sustained campaign to make it illegal to criticise Muslims and Islam, but had done much to merge the concepts of race and religion throughout these campaigns. That the final Bill in 2005 should have been called 'The Racial and Religious Hatred Bill' should make this clear, even though Islam is a proselytizing religion, a religion which commands that its followers convert others to this set of beliefs (thus ensuring that Muslims can be Asian, African, Chinese or white). As far as the socialist government was concerned, these white Muslims were to be considered to be of a different race to white atheists. And if people were wary of the accusation of racism for noting that the grooming gangs were predominantly Muslim, they were going to be far, far more reluctant to speculate as to whether or not the Islamic cultural background of these Muslims could explain why this hitherto unknown phenomenon had appeared in Britain as the proportion of the population who were Muslim increased. As far as the general public was concerned, from 2001 onwards the government was determined to brand as 'racist' and imprison for up to 7 years, those who even published written material which Muslims found insulting.[15]

---

14 Mark Mullins, 'Religious Hatred Law', http://www.cmf.org.uk/publications/content. asp?context=article&id=1693

15 In a discussion on the second attempt to make criticism of Islam a criminal offence, in 2005 in the House of Lords, Lord Desai noted that it was incorrect when existing laws which had conferred the status of a race on the adherents of Judaism and Sikhism, and that to confer racial status on Muslims was to compound this error.

As to Sikhs being a mono-ethnic group, I am absolutely astonished. Footnote 12 on page 8 of the Select Committee report cites the case of Mandla v Dowell Lee, which is about wearing turbans. Only Sikh men wear turbans; Sikh women do not. So I presume that Sikh women do not have protection under this law and that only Sikh men will. Sikh men also have a right to wear a dagger. Is that

So, following religiously-motivated mass-murders by devout Muslims who flew passenger jets into the World Trade Center, between 2001 and 2006 the socialist government of the UK made repeated and determined attempts to criminalise criticism of Islam and Muslims, despite protests that such censorship was in direct conflict with our supposedly fundamental freedom of speech.[16] Meanwhile, in those same years, in towns and cities throughout England, even those police officers, teachers and social workers who would want to draw attention to the Muslim grooming gang phenomenon were already fearful of being accused of racism. Rather than criticise individual council employees or police officers from failing to risk their careers by speaking out on the grooming gangs and being charged with 'racism', attention should be focussed on the local media and the politicians in these towns, who must explain why they were silent on the scandal of local children being groomed for prostitution and drug addiction.

Between 2001 and 2004, could this socialist government have known about the grooming gang phenomenon? It is almost certainly the case that members of that government knew of the problem. Al-

---

allowed? I doubt it very much.

But Sikhs are not a mono-ethnic group. The noble Baroness, Lady Flather, already has said something about that. But worse than that, a number of Canadians have converted to Sikhism. Are they—good, strong, white, tall, blonde people—covered by this? Sikhism is a religion: it is not a race.

Perhaps I may even accuse the Law Lords of being ignorant—maybe I will get it for contempt of court. People get intimidated when judging other races and religion. They say, "Oh dear, my God, if I don't say this I will be looked on as racist" or something like that. Only profound ignorance, in the face of another religion and another culture, could have allowed this to get into our law books. If I was smart enough, I would like to move an amendment to remove the protection for Sikhs and Jews on the grounds of religion.

Serious Organised Crime and Police Bill HL Deb 14 March 2005 vol 670 cc1106-98, http://hansard.millbanksystems.com/lords/2005/mar/14/serious-organised-crime-and-police-bill-1

16 It was quite clear in 2001, that even the first attempt to introduce what became the Racial and Religious Hatred Act, was legislation intended to protect Islam, rather than any other religion, from criticism. Briefings by 'human rights' organisations such as Liberty in response to the 2001 Bill, made it clear that Muslims were the group being targeted by the anti-terrorism provisions of such legislation. See BRIEFING ON ANTI- TERRORISM, CRIME AND SECURITY BILL 2001, https://www.liberty-human-rights.org.uk/sites/default/files/nov.pdf, p. 5. The 2001 Bill makes multiple references to Muslims in relation to terrorism - see House of Commons Library, The Anti-Terrorism, Crime and Security Bill: Introduction & Summary, 19 Nov 2001, http://researchbriefings.parliament.uk/ResearchBriefing/Summary/RP01-101, p. 10, p. 41.

ready by 1997 when the socialist government came to power, the previous Conservative government had been funding projects to treat the
victims of the grooming gangs operating in towns in West Yorkshire and
South Yorkshire (both areas strongholds for socialist MPs).[17] In 2001,
when the MP for Sheffield was proposing the first attempt at a law which
would make it a criminal offence to provoke 'dissension' (implicitly)
with regard to Islam, his department was funding a report into grooming gangs in Rotherham, a town a few miles from his own constituency.[18] Not only was his department commissioning reports into one of the
towns with a grooming problem, but South Yorkshire Police were also
commissioning reports into 'child prostitution' in Rotherham.[19] These
reports by Dr. Heal and commissioned by a public body, were eventually released following a Freedom of Information request by the local
newspaper, *The Sheffield Star*. These reports covering the period 2003 to
2006, 'also highlighted child sexual exploitation in Sheffield',[20] the very
city which the Home Secretary represented in Parliament. In addition to
Dr. Heal's reports from the years covering 2003 to 2006,

> similar information about suspected abusers in Rotherham
> being provided to South Yorkshire Police in 2002 by Home
> Office researcher Adele Gladman.[21]

It thus appears highly doubtful, whilst introducing repeated attempts
to criminalise those who provoked 'dissension' on the topic of Islam or
who 'insulted' Muslims, that the Home Secretary and the Home Office
could have been oblivious to the claims regarding the phenomenon of

---

17 See section 3.4 and section 3.5.

18 'Between 2001 and 2002, *Risky Business* participated in a Home Office research pilot
whose aim was to find out the most effective approaches to street prostitution.' Alexis
Jay, *Independent Inquiry into Child Sexual Exploitation in Rotherham 1997 - 2013*,
http://www.rotherham.gov.uk/download s/file/1407/independent_inquiry_cse_in_
rotherham, p. 4.

19 'In addition to the unpublished 2002 Home Office research report, other significant
reports relating to the exploitation and abuse of children in Rotherham included two
reports by Dr Angie Heal in 2003 and 2006...' Alexis Jay, *Independent Inquiry into Child
Sexual Exploitation in Rotherham 1997 - 2013, op. cit.*, p. 5.

20 'Rotherham abuse warning reports released', *BBC News* website, 5 May 2015, http://
www.bbc.co.uk/news/uk-england-south-yorkshire-32586558

21 'EXCLUSIVE: South Yorkshire Police given list of key Sheffield and Rotherham
abuse suspects in 2003', *The Star*, 5 May 2013, http://www.thestar.co.uk/news/local/
exclusive-south-yorkshire-police-given-list-of-key-sheffield-and-rotherham-abuse-
suspects-in-2003-1-7243228

Muslim grooming gangs operating in Bradford, Rotherham and Shef-field. These three towns all returned prominent socialist MPs between the years 2001 and 2006. And as we saw with our discussion of *Channel 4's* investigations in the Bradford area in 2003, only Ann Cryer spoke out on the issue; but even she was claiming that the problem was not related to Muslims or Islam, but was due to 'Asian culture'.[22]

It is interesting to note that in the House of Commons report on the history of these attempts to introduce legislation protecting Islam from criticism, it is stated that around 2004, the time when grooming gangs were first being exposed to national attention around Bradford, the Muslim Council of Britain (MCB) was associated with this censor-ship: 'The Muslim Council of Britain has also linked its calls for a change in the law to the activities of the British National Party.'[23] The MCB doc-

---

22 See section 3.8.

23 Lucinda Maer, 'Religious Hatred: Attempts to legislate 2001-2005', 10 Jun 2008, House of Commons Library, http://www.parliament.uk/briefing-papers/SN03189. pdf, p.3). The 2004 document from The Muslim Council of Britain cited by Mair is still to be found on the MCB website (http://www.mcb.org.uk/bnp-documentary-un-derlines-urgent-need-for-incitement-legislation/); interestingly, the MCB has since removed from their website the document from 2009 where they described the groom-ing gangs as 'a racist myth'.

The second attempt of the socialist government to introduce the provisions which became the Racial and Religious Hatred Act, was the Serious Organised Crime and Police Bill of 2004. This Bill gave rise to the Serious Organised Crime Agency (SOCA), which with its subsidiary organisations CEOP and UKHTC, have singularly failed the thousands of victims of the grooming gangs - see section *5.6 Serious Organised Crime Agency*. The controversial provisions concerning religious hatred were dropped from this Bill as an election approached, but in the 2005 General Election the Labour Party made a commitment to introducing a separate law proscribing religious hatred. It is quite clear that this 2004 Bill was entirely focused on the creation of SOCA, and the topic of religious hatred was scarcely relevant to the purpose of the Bill. The first attempt to provide laws protecting Islam from criticism appeared directly after Sep-tember 11th 2001. When that failed, the Labour government seemed determined to get this law passed, even shoe-horning it into a Bill where it was irrelevant.

The House of Commons Library document on the Racial and Religious Hatred Act 2006 notes that the socialist government had attempted to introduce laws against reli-gious hatred from 1997, although the document does not give any details about these attempts between 1997 and 2001. See Lucinda Maer, 'The Racial and Religious Hatred Act 2006', 06 Nov 2009, House of Commons Library, http://researchbriefings.files. parliament.uk/documents/SN03768/SN03768.pdf, p.1), where she refers to a docu-ment entitled 'Religious Hatred: Attempts to legislate 1997-2005' and identified by the reference "SN/PCC/3189". This is the same reference number by which her document 'Religious Hatred: Attempts to legislate 2001-2005' is identified. It is unclear whether this document SN/PCC/3189 has been re-written and the information about attempts between 1997 and 2001 have been removed.

ument cited by the House of Commons library specifically refers to a BBC documentary where the leader of the British National Party in 2004 is addressing the issue of the grooming gangs, and how these gangs might well be ideologically driven by Islamic doctrine and history.[24]

As Orwell pointed out in his discussion of Newspeak, the purpose of the Left's policy of making concepts and events unsayable is to ultimately make them unthinkable. The population becomes increasingly scared of criminal convictions, losing their jobs or of becoming social outcasts because they said something 'politically incorrect' or even noticed something that was 'politically incorrect'. And despite the supposed 'defeats' for the socialist government in criminalising criticism of Islam between 2001 and 2006, during an election campaign in 2014 the leader of a legitimate political party in the UK was arrested merely for reciting a statement on Islam from a book by Winston Churchill.[25] The end goal of Newspeak/political correctness is to make it impossible to think outside the ideology propounded by the Left. In a society where a politician cannot recite a passage on Islam from a book by a past Prime Minister without fear of arrest, how are ordinary employees supposed to draw attention to the observable fact that most of the men grooming schoolgirls are followers of Islam?

When one considers the admitted scale of abuse in the town of

---

24 'The Secret Agent', *BBC* website, 15 Jul 2004, http://news.bbc.co.uk/1/hi/programmes/newsnight/3896921.stm. Nick Griffin, the leader of the BNP, faced a criminal trial in 2006 for statements at a BNP meeting in 2004, statements which were only brought to the public's attention by covert filming by the BBC.

> Four charges deadlocked the jury, including the pub speech where Mr Griffin used the 'vicious, wicked faith' lines. The trial followed a six month undercover assignment by reporter Jason Gwynne for a *BBC1* programme, 'The Secret Agent', which was watched by an audience of 5m last July. The speeches were recorded during the 2004 run-in to local and European elections in West Yorkshire when the BNP appeared to be riding high. The party has since been accused of hijacking a local campaign in Keighley against pimps who targeted schoolgirls, which led to police action and successful prosecutions. Martin Wainwright, 'Retrial ordered after Griffin walks free', *The Guardian*, 03 Feb 2006, http://www.theguardian.com/politics/2006/feb/03/uk.race

It is interesting to note that *The Guardian* trumpets 'police action and successful prosecutions' between 2004 and 2006: in 2005 a mere two men were convicted for grooming offences in that area, and the police unit was then promptly shut down.

After the failure of this first trial of the leader of the BNP, the Crown Prosecution Service promised a retrial, and at this retrial at the end of 2006, the jury would still not find Griffin and his co-defendant guilty.

25 'Euro candidate Paul Weston arrested over Islam remarks', *BBC News* website, 28 Apr 2014, http://www.bbc.co.uk/news/uk-england-hampshire-27186573

Rotherham, it is easily conceivable that as many as 100,000 schoolgirls may have fallen victim to these gangs. The girls' lives, and those of their families, were wrecked by the gangs. Based on these reports, and others we have discussed, we cannot think of a worse child-care scandal in Britain in the last 40 years; indeed, it is hard to think of a worse child-care scandal in Britain in the last 100 years. The schoolgirls and their families were failed by thousands of professionals who were supposed to take care of children. Successive child-protection laws from the 1980s onwards were made to play a subservient role to maintaining the doctrine of multiculturalism. A climate of fear was fostered by the Left's agenda of political correctness. And as Hayek observed in 1960, it is the Left's agenda which dominates politics in Britain: it is thus no surprise that the supposedly Right-wing Conservatives were also quiet on the scandal of the grooming gangs. The schoolgirls were abandoned, sacrificed for the doctrine of multiculturalism.

The narrative of racism has held such sway in Britain for the last 30 years, that it has enabled the Muslim grooming gangs to extend their operations with 'virtual impunity'.[26] It was the accusations of 'racism', and the fear of what that could to do the career of social workers and police officers, which was used to silence all discussion of the predominantly Muslim grooming gangs between 1995 and 2009.[27] In some of the trials, the perpetrators even tried to allege that they were only being prosecuted because the police were racist.[28] Yet it has taken almost two decades to finally get the police to bring these criminals to justice. Some of those going through the courts are being prosecuted for criminality

---

26 Andrew Norfolk, 'Police Files Reveal Vast Child Protection Scandal', *The Times*, 24 Sep 2012 http://www.thetimes.co.uk/tto/news/uk/crime/article3547661.ece.

27 Even when the Jay report came out in August 2014, 'newspapers' like *The Huffington Post* were publishing articles ridiculing the idea that political correctness could have played a significant role in protecting the gangs from scrutiny and punishment. 'Was "Political Correctness" Really To Blame For Unthinkable Rotherham Inaction?', *The Huffington Post*, 27 Aug 2014, http://www.huffingtonpost.co.uk/2014/08/27/rotherham-abuse-political-correctness_n_5721112.html. Whilst newspapers like *The Telegraph* publish articles saying that Casey blamed 'political correctness', there is nowhere in Casey's report where she comes out and says things like 'Political correctness protected abusers'. Her report says it was tasked with seeing if political correctness was to blame, but when Casey looks like she blames it she does not: political correctness is put inside scare quotes (*e.g.* in her Executive Summary).

28 'Rochdale Grooming Trial: Police Knew about Sex Abuse in 2002 but Failed to Act', *The Telegraph*, 9 May 2012, http://www.telegraph.co.uk/news/uknews/crime/9254982/Rochdale-grooming-trial-police-knew-about-sex-abuse-in-2002-but-failed-to-act.html

that occurred between 10 and 30 years ago.[29] This shows how much political correctness has benefited the criminals at the expense of the children. Fundamentally, it is not the 'race' of the perpetrators or the victims which is pivotal to these cases, but the religion of both. We will argue that the religious/cultural heritage of the perpetrators can explain how the actions of the grooming gangs could be considered acceptable by the gang members and their wider community. But it was the doctrine of multiculturalism, enforced by political correctness and the abuse of the narrative of racism which allowed these gangs to operate with impunity. After discussing the abuse of the narrative of racism, we will then turn our attention to the Islamic cultural background of the gangs.

If the police, the social services, children's charities, the media, the Left had all spoken out more bravely and more explicitly against the Muslim men prostituting schoolgirls, then the British National Party (BNP) would only have been one voice amongst many, and the BNP's views on the matter would have been of no importance. It was the silence of so many on this issue, the false racialisation of the problem, which meant that the problem could be seen as serving the political goals of the BNP. According to Anna Hall, her *Edge of the City* documentary was taken up by the BNP *only* after the BNP found out that there were calls to ban the documentary:

> After the council viewed it, West Yorkshire's chief constable asked for the film to be postponed amid fears of more riots. All hell broke loose. The BNP got hold of the story and used the film as propaganda. Police and social services said noth-

---

29 The Oxford gang convicted in 2013 were being tried for some offences that happened 9 years earlier. Harriet Arkell, "'My mother begged Oxford social services to rescue me from sex abuse NINE YEARS AGO'", *Daily Mail*, 15 May 2013, http://www.dailymail.co.uk/news/article-2324790/My-mother-begged-Oxford-social-services-rescue-sex-abuse-NINE-YEARS-AGO-Victim-known-Girl-C-13-says-claims-dismissed-inappropriate.html.

At the end of 2015 there was a prosecution of a grooming gang in the North West of England, relating to offences which occurred in the 1990s. 'Three East Lancashire men charged with raping teen girl', *Lancashire Telegraph*, 30 Dec 2015, http://www.lancashiretelegraph.co.uk/news/14172387.Three_East_Lancashire_men_charged_with_raping_teen_girl/. A trial proceeding in Rotherham concerned offences from the 1980s. 'Gang "forced girl of 11 to have sex with three men a day": Rotherham care home girls were repeatedly raped by groups of Asian men after being enticed by two women accomplices, court hears', *Daily Mail*, 10 Dec 2015, http://www.dailymail.co.uk/news/article-3354286/Teenage-girls-Rotherham-targeted-sexualised-instances-subjected-acts-degrading-violent-nature.html

ing.[30]

The attempts to suppress information about this grooming phenomenon turned the gangs into an issue the BNP could appropriate: it was the refusal of child-care and policing agencies to acknowledge the truth, the willingness of pressure groups to censor the truth, which gave the BNP a platform for this story. We conclude that the failure of local and national agencies to fulfil their responsibilities meant they were unintentionally aiding the BNP, providing the party with a campaign that could not fail to gain support for the party. Whilst every other organisation refused to tackle this crime because of the fear of being labelled 'racist', they gifted the scandal of the Muslim grooming gangs to the BNP. And if society continues to marginalise this problem, then there is always the possibility that the grooming gang phenomenon will provide future support to an organisation like the BNP. Whilst the scandal of the grooming gangs might well have brought supporters to the BNP, it seems clear that the BNP taking up this issue did not lead to increased prosecutions. As late as 2009, organisations like the Muslim Council of Britain were able to insist that the idea of gangs grooming white girls was a 'racist myth',[31] a position supported by the near total lack of news stories about the grooming gangs in the 5 years after which the BNP campaigned about the phenomenon. But by 2013, the Muslim Council of Britain was behind the effort to get mosques in Britain to deliver a sermon denouncing grooming gangs.[32] The BNP's adoption of the issue of the grooming gangs in 2004 didn't bring about this change. Something else happened between 2009 and 2013.

If the media and the authorities had paid attention to the grooming of Sikh schoolgirls in the 1980s, 1990s and beyond, then the issue of Muslim grooming gangs could have been tackled without the issue of 'race' ever being raised. Instead, the authorities shirked their responsibilities to protect the Sikh schoolgirls, leaving Sikh men (initially Sikh street gangs like Shere Punjab, and latterly, the Sikh Awareness Society) to deal with the problem as best they could, given the lack of action and the denials by child-care professionals and the police. To the extent that the BNP could exploit these Muslim grooming gangs, it was because of

30 Anna Hall 'Hunt For Britain's Sex Gangs, C4' *Broadcast*, 2 May 2013, http://www.broadcastnow.co.uk/in-depth/hunt-for-britains-sex-gangs-c 4/5054504.article.

31 http://www.mcb.org.uk/vote2009/stopfarright.html

32 Vikram Dodd, 'Imams in 500 mosques to denounce grooming and abuse of children', *The Guardian*, 28 Jun 2013, http://www.theguardian.com/world/2013/jun/28/imamas-500-mosques-denounce-grooming

15 years of systemic failures by the authorities and the media. As the Sikh Media Monitoring group said, efforts to tackle the problem needed to focus on the Muslim community: 'it's a small element who treat white and Sikh girls as sexual playthings, and we aren't going to tackle it successfully unless the politically correct lobby stop putting up a smokescreen to hide the fact that this issue is about the Muslim community.'[33] If the child-care professionals, the police and the media had been acting on the evidence (from 1988 onwards) that Sikh girls were being groomed, then the BNP could not have made this a case about 'Asian gangs' preying on white children. But because of the indifference of the elite to the cultural conflict between Muslims and Sikhs, the criminal behaviour of Muslim men preying on Sikh girls (and white girls) was ignored. Whilst propounding multiculturalism, the metropolitan elite refuse to learn anything about Islam; the elite give lip-service to 'diversity' but refuse to countenance the idea that other cultures might have radically different values to those held by the vast majority of Britons.

6.2 Muslims, not 'Asians'

Sikh Media Monitoring are not the only group to have criticised the media and the authorities for misdirecting attention, and pretending these gangs were 'Asian' rather than 'Muslim'. In May 2012, a joint statement was released by three community groups (the Network of Sikh Organisations UK, The Hindu Forum of Britain, and The Sikh Media Monitoring Group UK) denouncing the use of the word 'Asian' to describe these grooming gangs.[34] They said the word 'Asian' was used in order to stop people from realising that the vast majority of the criminals were Muslims, and that the vast majority of the victims were non-Muslim girls. And as was the case with most of the white victims, the cases where the victims were Hindu or Sikh, also never reach the courts.

Even in 2013, despite the fact that the evidence has been mounting for a decade that these groups are overwhelmingly Muslim in both Britain and the Netherlands, the parliamentary inquiry seems to be deliberately ignorant or profoundly racist:

---

33 Rebecca Camber & James Tozer, 'Teenager who Lured Girls into House to be Raped by Asian Gang is Jailed for Seven Years', *The Daily Mail*, 3 Sep 2011, http://www.dailymail.co.uk/news/article-2033022/Teenager-lured-girls-house-gang-raped-Asian-gang-jailed-seven-years.html

34 'Complaints over use of "Asian" Label in Grooming Cases', *BBC News* website, 16 May 2012, http://www.bbc.co.uk/news/uk-18092605

...many of those involved in investigating the issue of localised grooming have warned against citing race as a key factor
in these cases, [and] it is not difficult to see why the British Pakistani community might feel that the suggestion that
this is an "Asian problem" is inaccurate and unfair. There is
certainly evidence of localised grooming being carried out
by offenders from other ethnic groups. Tim Loughton cited
cases involving offenders from central Africa.[35]

It is as if the politicians think that only Asians can be Muslim, even when
the British media were talking up Mo Farah (a Muslim Olympian from
East Africa) at every opportunity. There are black and Asian Muslims
who are outstanding sportsmen. There are white and black and Asian
Muslims who are terrorists. Are our elected politicians so stupid and so
racist that they cannot see that Cat Stevens, Mohammed Ali, Malcolm
X, were all Muslims who were not Asian? Moreover, not all Asians are
Muslims. Or are the elite just playing word-games, thinking the public
are so stupid they can be easily misled?[36] 'Muslim' is not a racial category, but the committee members seem to find this concept exceedingly
difficult to grasp. Showing that there are black members of grooming

---

35 Home Affairs Select Committee Report 'Child Sexual Exploitation and the Response to Localised Grooming', 10 Jun 2013, http://www.publications.parliament.uk/
pa/cm201314/cmselect/cmhaff/68/68i.pdf p. 55. Notice how there is no concern for
Sikhs, Hindus, etc. who have been tarred for at least a decade with the association that
the grooming gangs are 'Asian'. There only seems to be concern for Muslims.

36 Strangely, even a Left-wing, Asian commentator like Sunny Hundal, whose parents
are Sikhs, conflates ideology (religion) with biology (race). In claiming that there was
no relevance to the huge over-representation of 'Asian' men among the grooming
gangs, Hundal states:

> During the Rochdale case the Judge said: "You preyed on girls because they
> were not part of your community or religion" — this is repeatedly cited by some
> people. But it's also untrue. As was revealed after the ring-leader in the Rochdale
> case also "repeatedly raped an Asian girl over many years." Sunny Hundal,
> 'Oxford gang-rape case: were the girls exploited because they were white?', May
> 14 2013, http://liberalconspiracy.org/2013/05/14/oxford-gang-rape-case-were-
> the-girls-exploited-because-they-were-white

The judge pointed out that the (all Muslim) grooming gang on trial targeted people
outside their religion, and Hundal then conflates religion with race. Hundal provides
no evidence that the Asian girl who was raped by this Asian Muslim was also 'part of
his religion'. Perhaps Hundal thinks that all Asians in Britain form one community? He
seems unaware of the long history of Sikhs resisting the Muslim gangs grooming Sikh
girls. See Chapter 2 *Sikh Victims of Grooming Gangs*, section 3.1 *1988 Sikh/Muslim violence*, section 3.6 *1998 Sikh Awareness Society starts*, section 3.7 *2001 Derby and 'Real
Caliphate'*, and section 3.11 *2005 Luton and 'Real Caliphate'*.

gangs tells us nothing about the religion of those black people.

This generic use of the word 'Asian' not only enabled Muslim criminal behaviour to be concealed amongst the law-abiding behaviour of Sikhs, Hindus and Buddhists, but meant that Sikh and Hindu men would end up being associated with the criminal behaviour of Muslim men, even when their own sisters and daughters were among the victims targeted by these Muslim gangs. Moreover, by commentators and pressure groups insisting that the issue involved 'Asian' rather than 'Muslim' gangs, it concealed what could turn out to be the specific motivation for this crime: Muslim culture and Islamic doctrine. And this is why Andrew Norfolk's work was so pivotal: by analysing the names of those convicted (which were mostly Islamic names), he was able to demonstrate the association between being convicted of a grooming offence and being a Muslim man.

6.3 'Racism' Protected the Rapists

When politicians finally came to discuss the issue of grooming gangs, almost a decade after these first came to the nation's attention in the *Channel 4* documentary, Parliament attributed the objective nature of Norfolk's 2011 analysis with having finally made people realise that there was undeniable proof that the public were not wrong to associate 'Asian' men with these gangs.[37] However, Norfolk attributed the BNP championing the cause of the vulnerable schoolgirls as the reason why people ignored the problem for the following decade:

> The far right leapt on the story... I think that it almost acted as a brake for several years on anybody seriously looking at whether there was any truth in what she [Ann Cryer, the MP in that area] was saying but, as the years passed, I noticed cases cropping up from time to time across Yorkshire and Lancashire with a very similar pattern.[38]

Norfolk, the journalist who received investigative awards for his reporting on the grooming gangs, appears here to voluntarily admit that

---

37 Section 1.1 of the Home Affairs Select Committee's Report discusses Norfolk's analysis from January 2011. Home Affairs Select Committee Report, *op. cit.* In this way they indicate that his report was fundamental to their investigation.

38 Home Affairs Select Committee Report 'Child Sexual Exploitation and the Response to Localised Grooming', *op. cit.*, p. 52.

he noticed cases cropping up but did not write about them.[39] We have shown that there were even numerous occasions in the twelve years preceding *Edge of the City*, when Sikhs were warning about Muslim grooming gangs preying on Sikh schoolgirls.[40] Perhaps not surprisingly, the BNP showed no interest in those cases with Sikh victims; that the media, sociologists and the advocates of multiculturalism also ignored these reports is noteworthy. The extent to which the BNP could claim the long-standing problem of Muslim grooming gangs as positive publicity for their agenda was directly related to the preceding 10 to 20 years in which politicians, police, social services and the Muslim community refused to do anything about the grooming gangs.

The decisive period when the narrative of racism was used to shut down discussion and investigation into the Muslim grooming gangs was around the *Channel 4* documentary in 2004. It was widely reported that a variety of pressure groups, along with West Yorkshire Police, attempted to block the broadcast of *Edge of the City*.[41] As *The Guardian* reported at the time:

> Groups such as Unite Against Fascism, the 1990 Trust, and the National Assembly Against Racism began to flood Channel 4 with requests to delay transmission. The Chief Constable of West Yorkshire, Colin Cramphorn, joined the call, and Channel 4 complied.[42]

However, in 2004 *Channel 4* said that their decision to withdraw the documentary was unrelated to any attempt by the BNP to make political

---

39 See Andrew Norfolk's pivotal article from 2011 and Norfolk's interview with the Sikh Awareness Society http://www.youtube.com/watch?v= WbUIfvYbjRc&feature=player_detailpage&t=301

40 See the following sections, covering events from 1988 to 2001: *1988 Sikh/Muslim violence, 1989 Sikhs convicted, 1998 Sikh Awareness Society* starts, *2001 Derby and 'Real Caliphate'*,

41 'Campaign to Stop Race Documentary', *BBC News* website, 17 Aug 2004, http://news.bbc.co.uk/1/hi/entertainment/3572776.stm; Julie Bindel, 'Girls, Gangs and Grooming: The Truth', *Standpoint Magazine*, Dec 2010, http://www.standpointmag.co.uk/node/3576/full; Matt Born, 'Race fears halt film on Asian sex "grooming"', *The Telegraph*, 21 May 2004, http://www.telegraph.co.uk/news/uknews/1462413/Race-fears-halt-film-on-Asian-sex-grooming.html

42 Anthea Milnes, '"The BNP hijacked my film"', *The Guardian*, 9 Aug 2004, http://www.theguardian.com/media/2004/aug/09/channel4.otherparties.

capital from it.[43] Thus, we can accept the judgement from *The Guardian*, that the TV company paid more attention to the combined efforts of these pressure groups and the Chief Constable of West Yorkshire, than to any advantage the BNP might have gained from addressing the documentary.

The BNP only championed *Edge of the City* when the police wanted to suppress it on the basis that it might cause Muslims to riot, and that the riots and/or the grooming scandal might influence how people voted in the up-coming elections. Yet that is what it means to live in a liberal democracy. Issues are discussed, facts are debated; issues should not be suppressed because of the threat of mob violence. In a civilised society democracy is used to bring about change peacefully and gradually. Instead, the threat of mob violence, a form of cultural terrorism, triumphed over democracy: 'Channel 4 has pulled a documentary about social workers in Bradford from its schedule after police warned it could increase racial tension.'[44] The Police, the very group under the spotlight for failure to prosecute these grooming gangs, were able to use the threat that Muslims might riot as an excuse to put pressure on *Channel 4* not to show its documentary. Even though *Channel 4* stated that the BNP's interest in the issue did not affect their decisions, for many years afterwards, most journalists refused to pay any attention to the problems faced by thousands of schoolgirls across the country. It would seem that journalists avoided reporting on the grooming gangs because it had been turned into an issue about race, and the journalists did not want to do anything to assist the BNP. However, even if the BNP wanted the scandal to be about race, there was nothing stopping journalists from learning about the Sikh victims, and thus concluding that race was not the issue. No organisation seemed to spend any effort finding a way to deal with the grooming gang phenomenon, whilst not helping the BNP. So they left the gangs to prey on schoolgirls, and (with a couple of notable exceptions) journalists left the BNP alone to raise the issue of the grooming gangs, with the BNP having no positive impact on the problem.

When the *Channel 4* documentary was withdrawn from the schedule in 2004, it was to be screened some months after the election. But even when the election was over, pressure groups began another

---

43 *Channel 4* said 'the party's attempt to capitalise on the documentary had not influenced its decision.' Matt Born, 'Race fears halt film on Asian sex "grooming"', *op. cit.*

44 'Documentary pulled over race fear', *BBC News*, 20 May 2004, http://news.bbc.co.uk/1/hi/entertainment/tv_and_radio/3733215.stm

campaign to stop it from ever being shown (demonstrating that the contradictions of multiculturalism are something that the Leftist pressure
groups do not want to be aired).

> An online campaign has been launched to try and stop
> *Channel 4* from airing a documentary that features claims
> Asian men are grooming white girls for sex. *Edge of the City*,
> set in Bradford, had been shelved in May after police warned
> it could incite racial violence ahead of local and European
> elections. The Black Information Link website asks readers
> to lobby *Channel 4*, police and the Culture Secretary to stop
> the film.[45]

The documentary was eventually shown, very late at night. Following
this low-key broadcast, West Yorkshire Police and Bradford Council
were able to further diminish claims made in the documentary, implying that the claims made by the documentary were groundless: 'they had
spent the past two years investigating the allegations, but had found "no
evidence of systematic exploitation".'[46] Moreover, one year after these
pressure groups helped to stop the documentary being shown, West
Yorkshire Police quietly closed the investigative unit at the heart of this
documentary.[47] The police, the council and local MPs were saved the
embarrassment of having to face elected representatives who could have
held the police and social workers to account for their failures and inactivity. After 2005, the grooming gangs in Bradford were brushed under
the carpet, even though their activities in that city had been officially
known about for more than a decade.[48] There wasn't to be another prosecution there until 2012.[49]

---

45 'Campaign to Stop Race Documentary', *BBC News*, *op cit*.

46 'Race documentary broadcast on C4', *BBC News* website, 27 Aug 2004, http://news.
bbc.co.uk/1/hi/entertainment/3600730.stm

47 See section 3.10 *2005 Radio 5 programme*.

48 See section 3.4 *1995 Bradford: Streets and Lanes*.

49 In August 2013, almost a decade after claiming there was 'no evidence' for the
existence of these gangs in West Yorkshire, 45 men in that area, aged between 20 and
60, were arrested in an operation apparently against one gang. '45 arrested in police
probe into "biggest ever child sex abuse gang"', *Halifax Courier*, 20 Aug 2013, http://
www.halifaxcourier.co.uk/news/crime/45-arrested-in-police-probe-into-biggest-ever-
child-sex-abuse-gang-1-5967618. The men arrested were from the three towns in the
area, and are reportedly all connected to the rape and sexual assault of under-age girls:
'All the allegations are said to be "historic", having taken place at least two years ago.'

Even in reporting on this controversy in 2004, the *BBC* unproblematically designated the documentary as a 'race documentary', and in the article in *The Telegraph* by Matt Born in 2004, he puts quotation marks around 'grooming' but not around 'race'. The media too were incapable of separating being Muslim (a religious belief, open to white, Asian and black people) from the racial categorization of most of the Muslims in Britain. If the separation of religious belief from nationality and skin colour had been articulated, and the Asian Sikh girls being groomed by Asian Muslim men had not been ignored, there would be no difficulty in understanding that the core issue here is religious belief and culture, not racial or national origin.

Before the end of 2010, Julie Bindel was the only journalist we can find who repeatedly investigated the grooming gangs, despite being castigated as an anti-Muslim bigot by Left-wing websites dedicated to opposing criticism of Islam:

> When I first wrote about the issue of Asian grooming gangs in 2007, my name was included on the website *Islamophobia Watch: Documenting anti-Muslim Bigotry*. So was that of Ann Cryer, the former Labour MP for Keighley in Yorkshire, who had been at the forefront of attempting to tackle the problem, after receiving requests for help from some of the parents of children caught up with the gangs in her constituency.[50]

Bindel was not alone in being castigated by Left-wing supporters of Muslims. Ann Cryer had also been criticised before by prominent Muslims within her own political party. In July 2002 Shahid Malik, a Muslim member of Labour's National Executive Committee (and later Home Office Minister under a Labour Government), criticised Cryer after she spoke out about the criminal behaviour of 'Asian' gangs in her constituency whose criminality and violence was 'out of control'.

In relation to that incident, Shahid Malik was quoted

calling on Ms Cryer's constituents to "stand up against" her. "She has failed the ethnic minority community in Keighley,"

'Britain's biggest child sex grooming gang thought to have been busted after cops arrest 45 men', *The Mirror*, 18 Aug 2013, http://www.mirror.co.uk/news/uk-news/britains-biggest-child-sex-grooming-2181438.

50 Julie Bindel, 'Girls, Gangs and Grooming: The Truth', *Standpoint Magazine*, Dec 2010 http://www.standpointmag.co.uk/node/3576/full

he said. "Her comments are offensive and I do not think she should be the MP in Keighley under the Labour Party."[51]

These 'Asian' gangs in the constituency she represented were getting away with criminal behaviour because of the fear generated by political correctness.[52] When one considers that in her remarks, Ms. Cryer had gone to the trouble of exonerating most 'Asians', it is surprising to see her come in for such criticism.

In the light of these previous attacks on her in 2002, it was brave of Ms. Cryer to speak out again in 2003 and 2004.[53] Some Muslims did offer Ann Cryer their support on the issue of lawless gangs in her constituency. Dr Ghayasuddin Siddiqui, of the Muslim Parliament, was one of the Muslims who supported her: 'Ann Cryer is the local MP and she knows her own community.'[54] In 2010, Julie Bindel was noting that there were Muslims who were prepared to speak out about the grooming gangs. Mohammed Shafiq, of the Ramadhan Foundation was advocating that imams and community leaders speak out about sexual exploitation, and for doing this 'black and Asian people' threatened to kill him.[55] Shafiq had the foresight to see that without intervention, the grooming gangs would expand and more schoolgirls would be victims: 'But what I said has been proved right — that if we didn't tackle it there would be more of these abusers and more girls getting harmed.' Julie Bindel pointed out

---

51 'Asian Gangs "Out of Control"', *BBC News*, 6 Jul 2002, http://news.bbc.co.uk/1/hi/uk_politics/2102470.stm.

52 *Ibid.*

53 It seems very likely that there is more to this story than the public were told at the time. That Shahid Malik should have criticised her, suggests the gangs were probably Muslim (and another Muslim is quoted in Cryer's defence). The story reported that the gangs

> are resorting to turf wars and totally disregarding the law.... she has criticised leading representatives of the Asian communities... burying their heads in the sand and not acknowledging there is a problem... "These young men and their appalling behaviour are becoming role models...They are the ones with the fast cars and smart suits.If we do not defeat them their children will become part of the problem."

Also, it is plausible that these gangs were involved in the network of criminal activities around drug-dealing and grooming. Clearly these gangs are involved in something lucrative, hence the turf wars. As with reports about the grooming activities, there's no indication that the Muslim leaders were going to show any leadership. It's even possible that there was gang violence with Sikhs or Hindus, attempting to stop their female relatives from being groomed. 'Asian Gangs "Out of Control"', *BBC News, op. cit.*

54 Asian Gangs "Out of Control", *BBC News, op. cit.*

55 Julie Bindel, 'Girls, Gangs and Grooming: The Truth', *op. cit.*

that Zlakha Ahmed from Rotherham also spoke out in 2010, saying:

> this abuse is appalling and needs to be raised within the community. There are still people denying that it happens so the more of us who speak out about it the better.[56]

Unfortunately, it seems for every Muslim who supported those who spoke out about the grooming gangs, there were Muslims and proponents of multiculturalism who criticised or threatened to kill those who confirmed the existence of the grooming gangs. Sometimes it is worth reminding oneself of the wider historical and cultural context: in 21st century Britain, considered one of the most open and lawful countries on earth, people were threatened with death for criticising gangs of men systematically seducing and prostituting schoolgirls. Furthermore, for decades the political class and the media ignored not just the brave critics being threatened with death, but also the thousands and thousands of schoolgirl victims. We can get so caught up in the minutiae of this problem that we fail to notice we have adjusted our framework of what is considered acceptable behaviour.

6.4 Racist Aspects of Grooming

We have pointed out that the narrative of racism was used to protect the perpetrators. However, there is an aspect of racism involved in these grooming gangs, but it is the reverse of what the racism groups would have us believe: that is, the gangs can have racist motivations. In 2011, it was again Mohammed Shafiq who was prepared to point out that it is the Muslim grooming gangs who exhibit anti-white racism:

> There is a perception that some of these young men do not see white girls as equal, as valuable, of high moral standing as they see their own daughters, and their own sisters, and I think that's wrong...It's a form of racism that's abhorrent in a civilised society.[57]

It is no surprise that Mohammed Shafiq was getting death threats from

---

56 *Ibid.*

57 'Jack Straw: Some White Girls are "Easy Meat"', *BBC News*, 8 Jan 2011, http://www.bbc.co.uk/news/uk-england-derbyshire-12141603. Here Mohammed Shafiq is saying that it is the racist behaviour of these grooming gangs which is wrong.

black people and Asians alike, when he stated: 'it is clear that they [the grooming gangs] do not value white teenagers because they think they are less valuable or honourable than their own daughters or sisters and by targeting white girls there would be no fall back in the community'.[58]

Julie Bindel took this point further, and argued that what the gangs were doing was more than 'simple opportunism', and that there was a racist motivation *driving* some of the gangs: 'pimping of white females by black and ethnic-minority men can be a type of revenge against whites'.[59] In one of the prosecutions, the judge even brought this up in the trial, saying of the gang:

> [T]hose girls were raped, callously, viciously and violently. Some of you acted as you did to satiate your lust, some of you to make money, all of you treated them as though they were worthless and beyond respect... I believe that one of the factors that led to that was that they were not of your community or religion.[60]

Finally by 2012 it was revealed in the statements from the perpetrators, witnesses and even the judiciary that there was a 'racist' motivation for the activities of these gangs. However, since Sikh Asian girls were also targeted by the gangs, and since the gang members were sometimes Muslims who came from places other than Asia, it is the disparity of ethnicity between the perpetrators and the victims, rather than differences in race, which should be considered fundamental to this phenomenon.

Journalists, politicians and child-care professionals have often tied themselves in knots trying not to acknowledge the disparity in ethnicity between the perpetrators and the victims. Some time after the trial where the judge made the above statement, Simon Danczuk, the MP for Rochdale (the town with the greatest number of convictions at that point in time) was reported discussing these crimes in terms of 'ethnicity' and 'race'. Mr. Danczuk is quoted saying, 'He dismissed suggestions made by Greater Manchester Police that the case was not about race, la-

58 Mohammed Shafiq, 'Untitled Article on Rochdale Trial for MEN' http://www.mohammedshafiq.net/grooming---the-men.php

59 Julie Bindel, 'Mothers of Prevention', *The Sunday Times*, 30 Sep 2007, http://www.thesundaytimes.co.uk/sto/news/uk_news/article72310.ece

60 '"You preyed on girls because they were not part of your community or religion", says judge as he jails Rochdale sex gang for 77 years', 15 May 2012, *Manchester Evening News*, http://www.manchestereveningnews.co.uk/news/local-news/you-preyed-on-girls-because-they-were-687987

belling the force's attitude on the subject as "just wholly and completely wrong." While he stated, 'there is no doubt about it, ethnicity is a factor in this type of abuse', he then went on to say 'nine Asian men convicted for grooming and abusing white girls in his constituency was *not a racial issue* and said similar abuse was still continuing' (emphasis added).[61] He is quoted saying that 'the Asian community' (he deploys a racial categorisation) is in denial about these crimes, whilst failing to highlight that since all of those convicted in his town were Muslims, 'ethnicity' is a far more appropriate categorisation than 'race'.[62] It is amazing that one single report in a 'quality' newspaper should be able to mix up claims about ethnicity and race so thoroughly in so few words. Extracting what Mr. Danczuk truly believes from that report is impossible.

We try to maintain a distinction between 'ethnicity' and 'race' in the discussion of this phenomenon. One aspect of racism which has been ignored, is the way in which the grooming gangs themselves deployed the narrative of racism to break families apart and stop them from protecting their own children. The group which has articulated the clearest understanding of the Muslim grooming gang phenomenon points out:

> What is missing here is an understanding of the emotional dynamics of grooming. For grooming to work, the child needs to be trapped into a coercive relationship with their abuser, and then forced to perform sex with growing numbers of older men. But why don't the schoolgirls just run away from this abusive and exploitative situation? Why do they keep going back for more abuse? Because the grooming has driven a massive wedge between child and parent.[63]

---

61 Rosa Silverman, 'Asian communities "in denial" about grooming, says Rochdale MP', *The Telegraph*, 9 Dec 2013, http://www.telegraph.co.uk/news/uknews/crime/10507023/Asian-communities-in-denial-about-grooming-says-Rochdale-MP.html

62 When one looks at the range of ethnicities of those convicted for grooming gang crimes, there are as many non-Pakistani Muslims as there are non-Muslims. Moreover, on the rare occasion when a gang had no Muslim members at all, these gangs were operating in heavily Islamised towns (Blackburn, Blackpool), where Muslims had been getting away with these crimes for years. Most often when non-Muslims were part of a gang, Muslims were either the majority of the gang, or certainly the ring-leaders.

63 PACE, 'The grooming of children for sexual exploitation is largely misunderstood', 21 Jan 2013, http://www.paceuk.info/the-grooming-of-children-for-sexual-exploitation-is-largely-misunderstood/

It might be easy to understand how the groomers could insert themselves into the affection of schoolgirls who were in the care of social services (by gang members offering the girls gifts, attention, 'love', an entry into the world of adulthood, etc.). But it is more difficult to understand how the groomers manage to insert themselves between a schoolgirl and her loving parents. One of the ways in which the gangs did this was to exploit the narrative of racism, and accuse the parents who tried to intervene of being 'racists'.

> The pimps are adept at trading on teenage rebellion and use similar methods...of convincing the girls all white people are racist. This is part of the controlling process, to instil guilt in the girls. "Like most teenagers, I was going through a phase of arguing with my mum," says Gemma. "Amir told me they didn't understand me and were racist and ignorant. I believed him." Gemma was given an Asian name by Amir, and told she had to read the Koran, a story support workers tell me is not uncommon. "They erode the girls' identities," says Kosaraju, "to make them more compliant and needy."[64]

Thus, the narrative of racism was used by the gangs to prevent the schoolgirls from believing their parents: the gangs could use allegations of racism as a tool to make the girls estranged from their carers, and thus make the schoolgirls even more vulnerable. A schoolgirl's parents were probably the single strongest line of defence between the gang and their prey: teachers were doing nothing about the cars full of men outside the school-gates, police officers were returning the victims to their captors, social workers were turning a blind-eye, the local and national news media were enforcing self-censorship. If anyone was to be able to stop the girl falling into a life of addiction and prostitution it was the parents. It is no wonder Julie Bindel entitled her 2007 plea 'Mothers of Prevention'. The details from recent trials show many examples of parents being ignored by social workers, of police arresting parents for trying to save their daughters.[65] The narrative of racism proved a powerful tool in the hands of the gangs.

---

64 Julie Bindel, 'Mothers of Prevention', *op. cit.*

65 This is the kind of situation one might expect in a totalitarian state, where the institutions of the state would readily penalise parents who resisted abuse of their children by the Nomenklatura. It is also reminiscent of the situation of non-Muslims living under Islamic domination, for example in countries like Pakistan.

Even when facing a judge and jury, members of these gangs tried to accuse the police, the judiciary and even the state of racism, rather than concede that their actions were wrong. In a major grooming trial centred round crimes in Rochdale, one of those convicted addressed the court:

> "We are the supreme race, not these white b******s (pointing to police officers in court)." He continued: "You will not get a CBE. You will not get an MBE. You will get a DM, a destroyer of Muslims. You were born one thousand years too late. You f***ed my community. You destroyed my community and our children. None of us did that. White people trained those girls to be so much advanced in sex. They were coming without hesitation to Rochdale, Oldham, Bradford, Leeds and Nelson and wherever." He said the jury in Liverpool has been "taking instructions" from BNP leader Nick Griffin and later pointed to Rachel Smith, who prosecuted both cases on behalf of the Crown, saying: "I curse you at night. I curse you and your family. You will understand (pointing at Judge Khokhar). I curse the juries. I curse the media and most of you b******s. Your family will get it."[66]

Rather than accept that, in the value framework of the British legal system, he had committed serious offences the gang leader asserted Muslim supremacism, Muslim victimhood, used accusations of racism, and issued violent threats. Rather than accept that this network of adult men, united by a religious and ethnic identity, had preyed on schoolgirls, he accuses the British state of sending alluring and sexually precocious schoolgirls to corrupt Muslims. He deploys the narrative of racism to claim he is the victim, whilst simultaneously making racist insults and asserting that he and other Muslims are a superior race.

---

66 'Leader of Rochdale sex grooming gang found guilty of 30 rapes in new trial', *Manchester Evening News*, 21 Jun 2012, http://www.manchestereveningnews.co.uk/news/local-news/leader-of-rochdale-sex-grooming-gang-689930. Consider the decades of silence by the British media and politicians, and the refusal of experts to recognize that these grooming gangs represent a new cultural phenomenon in Britain. In a single case about a specific town and a (supposedly) isolated group of men, unmotivated by a shared ideology: this co-defendant speaks of the perpetrators operating as a group, whose activities span many different towns (Rochdale, Oldham, Bradford, Leeds, Nelson, etc.) Here we see the grooming phenomenon as seen from the perspective of the perpetrators.

Mohammed Shafiq is one of the few Muslims who was prepared to speak out about the grooming gangs and the disparity in ethnicity of the victims,[67] In 2010 Shafiq told Julie Bindel that he was

> "disgusted" to hear some perpetrators refer to their victims as "white trash". He adds: "I say to them, would you treat your sister or daughter like this?"[68]

Shafiq claims that these crimes are nothing to do with Islam and are even opposed to Islam. His solutions are unworkable.

> There needs to be more honest and open dialogue with the Police and authorities where these issues are addressed, a local marketing campaign with advertisements and leaflets talking [sic] detailing the crimes and what happens if you are involved in this evil.[69]

This kind of thing was done years earlier in similar situations, and it appeared to change nothing. In 2007 Julie Bindel pointed out that police in Lancashire and Yorkshire had sent letters to Muslims suspected of grooming, warning them they were with under-age girls, and getting them to sign the letters to show they knew the girls were under the age of consent. This achieved nothing.[70] How would 'a local marketing campaign' change the racist and supremacist views quoted from the Rochdale trial above? What is needed is to pour resources into an objective, uncompromising analysis of the problem, to determine why it is that 90% of those convicted for these crimes are Muslim men. Instead the narrative of racism was deployed to stop the grooming phenomenon from being discussed and analysed. Later we will determine if these crimes have any relationship to Islamic values, and we will see whether or not there is any basis for Shafiq's claim that these crimes are un-Islamic.

---

67 'Rochdale grooming trial: Mohammed Shafiq, the campaigner who stood up to the abusers', *The Telegraph*, 08 May 2012, http://www.telegraph.co.uk/news/uknews/crime/9252003/Rochdale-grooming-trial-Mohammed-Shafiq-the-campaigner-who-stood-up-to-the-abusers.html

68 Julie Bindel, 'Girls, Gangs and Grooming: The Truth', *op cit.*

69 Mohammed Shafiq, 'Untitled Article on Rochdale Trial for MEN', http://www.mohammedshafiq.net/grooming---the-men.php

70 Julie Bindel, 'Mothers of Prevention', *op. cit.*

The narrative of racism was not just deployed by the grooming gangs as a tool and as a justification for their activities. This narrative was misused by Left-wing organisations and the media ever since the grooming gang phenomenon was raised in the national media: *Channel 4's* 2004 documentary was casually and easily dismissed as a 'racist' documentary, and its contents could therefore be dismissed by 'right-thinking' people without further thought. Framing the issue in this way meant that many people did not bother to research more deeply into the conflation between religion and race, nor into the relative proportions of Asian men (really, Muslims) who were to be found among the gang members and their customers. And the narrative of racism could be used as a self-justification by the police to excuse why they were not pursuing these gangs. These oft-used narratives can becomes so familiar that we no longer question their applicability to individual cases, and just let them lead us along well-trodden mental paths, where we supply missing information using familiar assumptions. Throughout the existence of the Muslim grooming gangs, this narrative of racism has done immense harm to the schoolgirls (and the use of this narrative also stopped the Asian victims from getting the help they needed).

Mohammed Shafiq's warning, that left unchallenged the grooming gangs would extend their operations, shows he had more insight on this subject than any of the journalists or academic experts. However, we don't think he foresaw that permitting these grooming gangs to get away with this for so long would in turn start to fuel racist views in the parents of the victims and perhaps even in the wider public.

> One of the many tragedies resulting from this phenomenon is how it is fuelling racism and mistrust of whites towards Pakistanis where little existed previously. Although racism can be rife in towns such as Blackburn, Jean claims that before her daughter's life was ruined she bore no animosity towards the Asian community. Things have changed. When ordering a taxi, Jean spends several minutes looking through the telephone directory, explaining she is looking for a "white-run firm."[71]

It seems not unreasonable to assume that even those whose own family are not the immediate victims of the 'Asian' grooming gangs might become wary of those of other races. In 2008, it was reported the *BBC*

---

71 Julie Bindel, 'Mothers of Prevention', *op. cit.*

sacked a presenter who repeatedly asked a taxi company not to provide Asian drivers.[72] It would be interesting to know what *BBC* staff say to each other off-air, when discussing these Muslim grooming gangs, and what they say about the relationship of grooming gangs to taxi firms and takeaway food businesses.

The following year, the English Defence League (EDL) was formed. This organisation was not specifically formed in response to the grooming gangs, but in response to Muslim fundamentalists in Luton attacking British troops. If EDL were just violent thugs as claimed by the media, then we might expect to have seen EDL leading violent attacks against Muslim grooming gangs (as Sikhs did in 1988, 2001, and 2013). Instead, the English have been surprisingly quiescent concerning the activities of the grooming gangs, and the failure of the institutions to deal with them for so many years. We can find no instances of the indigenous population using communal violence to deal with grooming gangs, the way that Sikhs in Britain have on a number of occasions.[73]

However, through their 50 or so demonstrations and their internet presence, the EDL did much to educate people about the grooming gangs, and were probably pivotal in forcing the authorities to finally start a concerted effort to bring the grooming gangs to court. Considering the anger felt by most people in Britain about the evidence emerging about this grooming phenomenon, it is good fortune that the EDL were not promoting racist or fascist views.[74] Within the first six months of

---

72 'BBC Radio host sacked after call to taxi firm requesting "non-Asian" driver', *Daily Mail*, 12 Nov 2008, http://www.dailymail.co.uk/news/article-1084702/BBC-Radio-host-sacked-taxi-firm-requesting-non-Asian-driver.html

73 Examples of this 'communal violence' (the euphemistic term used in India to refer to violent conflicts between Muslims and Sikhs and Hindus), resulting in criminal prosecutions for the Sikhs, can be found as early as 1988 and as late as 2013. See section 3.1 *1988 Sikh/Muslim violence* and section 3.2 *1989 Sikhs convicted*. See also the case in Leicester in 2013: 'Peace talks held after rampage at Moghul Durbar restaurant', *Leicester Mercury*, 17 Jan 2013, http://www.leicestermercury.co.uk/Peace-talks-held-rampage-Moghul-Durbar-restaurant/story-17880361-detail/story.html

74 The EDL's policies are clearly not racist, as their 'Mission Statement' makes clear: http://www.englishdefenceleague.org/mission-statement/. With Sikh, LGBT and Jewish 'Divisions', it seems clear they welcome diversity within their organisation, and within the concept of 'Englishness' with which they operate. The media have consistently ignored photographs and videos of non-white people in EDL demonstrations. In fact, when the media have reported on EDL inviting Jews, Sikhs, Gays to EDL protests, the media spun it in such a way that they presented EDL as a white supremacist organisation: Robert Verkaik, 'Jewish? Gay? Join us, white extremists say', 27 Nov 2010, *The Independent*, http://www.independent.co.uk/news/uk/politics/jewish-gay-join-us-white-extremists-say-2145003.html. Throughout the EDL's existence to date, we

its existence, a group of black men and white men from EDL were interviewed on the *BBC's* premier news programme, where they burned a swastika to demonstrate the opposition of their organisation to Nazism.[75] Much to the chagrin of the far Left, a year later the police National Domestic Extremism unit spent months studying the EDL and concluded that the EDL was not a far-right organisation.[76] As a society we should be relieved that EDL has not been a racist or Nazi organisation, which could grow powerful from the failure to address decades of sexual exploitation of schoolgirls by Muslim gangs. Nevertheless, the possibility that the EDL's ranks might grow, and that the EDL might resort to the violent tactics used by some Sikhs in Britain, must serve to keep the authorities focussed on showing that steps are being taken against the grooming gangs. It is hard to say whether or not it was the formation of the EDL which led to the sudden increase in prosecutions against grooming gangs, but we cannot find another event in 2009 which could have brought about the revolution in our society's response to this problem.[77] The sudden increase in convictions began in July 2009, some 4 months after EDL started demonstrating across England. It seems likely

---

found not one photo or video of an attack on a minority supporter of the organisation, nor any evidence of racist or homophobic chanting. However, after years of the media misrepresenting EDL as a racist/fascist organisation, the leader of the EDL resigned, saying that he was spending too much time trying to keep racists out of the EDL. http://news.sky.com/story/1151663/tommy-robinson-stands-down-from-the-edl. Should some racists turn up to EDL demonstrations that would hardly be surprising, since most of the media and state-sponsored or socialist-sponsored organisations keep telling racists that the EDL is the place for them. Whether or not EDL survives, and whether or not it manages to keep racists at bay, is yet to be seen.

75 Paraic O'Brien 'Under the skin of English Defence League', *BBC Newsnight*, 12 Oct 2009, http://news.bbc.co.uk/1/hi/programmes/newsnight/8303786.stm. In the Summer of 2013, the EDL leader once again made clear, in front of thousands of supporters and the assembled media, that Nazis were not welcome at EDL demonstrations: http://www.youtube.com/watch?v=8I1QpjSIbJ0. Thus, from 2009 to 2013, within the forms of communication under their control, they were sending a clear message that they were opposed to Nazism and they welcomed non-white supporters. As is typical, the media did not report on what strikes us as significant statements by the EDL.

76 John Millington, "'EDL not far-right", says police extremism chief', *The Morning Star*, 23 Nov 2010, http://www.morningstaronline.co.uk/index.php/news/content/view/full/98004. Strangely, the *Morning Star* article has now disappeared from that Communist organisation's website. A screenshot of it can be seen in *Appendix 10: Police Report on EDL*. We can find no trace of any national news organisation in Britain which reported the findings of the National Domestic Extremism unit, despite these findings going against all media reporting on the EDL.

77 See *Appendix 2: Grooming Gang Chronology*. Also see this chapter: *Chronology: Cover-up to Collapse*.

that the threatening image of EDL portrayed in the media will be serving to keep the attention of the authorities on how easily the grooming problem could lead to violence.

Without this sudden increase in convictions from 2009 onwards, Andrew Norfolk would have struggled to find the evidence which provided the basis for his pivotal article at the start of 2011. It was the pattern revealed by his article which led to Norfolk testifying before the Parliamentary committee. The evidence for the criminal activities of these gangs could be found in the 20 years preceding the rise of the EDL. Yet in those two decades there had been very few prosecutions and very little reporting on this phenomenon. No matter how often the English Defence League were cast as 'racists' and 'fascists' by Left-wing and Muslim organisations, from 2009 the EDL kept on marching. They may well have been instrumental in putting the grooming gangs onto the national agenda.

SEVEN
Islamic Cultural Background

I will never ever understand what has made them so evil and ignorant that still to this day they think they've not done anything wrong.

— grooming gang victim, *BBC News*, 2010

W E HAVE shown that it is now widely accepted, even by the parliamentary investigation, that for more than a decade, a new phenomenon has existed in Britain: gangs made up almost entirely of Muslim men who are luring schoolgirls into a life of drugs, rape and prostitution. Where this much has finally been recognised, it has been 'Asian culture' which has been blamed rather than Islamic culture. That Islam could be the basis for this criminality has always been ruled out of consideration, but with no investigation of Islamic theology, the history of Islam, or the rulings of sharia law.[1] Yet we cannot afford to dismiss

---

1 For example, William Oddie, 'The Oxford "Asian grooming gang" were not in fact all Asian. But they were all Muslim: is this a problem we are afraid to face?', 15 May 2013, *Catholic Herald*, http://www.catholicherald.co.uk/commentandblogs/2013/05/15/ the-oxford-Asian-grooming-gang-were-not-in-fact-all-Asian-but-they-were-all-Muslim-is-this-a-problem-we-are-afraid-to-face/. Oddie recognises that Asians are being unfairly blamed for this crime, when Islam is the common factor for 90% of the perpetrators, not their country of origin.

I am not saying that the problem is Islam per se, any more than I am saying that it's the racial origin of the perpetrators (which in this case it can't be). But there is one generalisation that can safely be made: it is that Muslim men tend to

this question out of hand: not only are non-Muslim Asian men (*e.g.* Sikhs) almost entirely absent from these gangs, but non-Muslim Asian schoolgirls (Sikhs, Hindus) are targets of the gangs.[2] The presence of these characteristics in such extreme opposition indicates that there is almost certainly not a random explanation for these events. When one introduces the similarities between Muslim gangs in the UK and the organised child-sexual exploitation in the Netherlands, then the pattern becomes even clearer.

We have shown a number of instances over the past 20 years in the UK where it was reported that devout, pro-Caliphate Islamic groups were encouraging Muslims to deceive and seduce non-Muslim girls. We must look at Islamic doctrine and the history of Islam to see if there are things which are deeply-rooted in Islam which could account for the reported activities of these pro-Caliphate groups. From 2014 onwards, reports spread around the world of devout jihadi groups in Iraq, Syria and Nigeria taking girls as sex-slaves. These groups justified their actions by reference to the core texts of Islam. If these groups had come to prominence 20 years ago, it would have been far more difficult for people to claim that the Muslim grooming gangs in the UK and the Netherlands had nothing to do with Islam or even that these gangs were un-Islamic.

7.1 'Asian gang': racist duplicity

When the story of the grooming gangs in the UK first burst into

---

have a low opinion of, how shall I put this, the general level of chastity of white women.

Where do Muslim men (from widely dispersed Muslim countries) get this attitude to women, if not from Islam? Furthermore, Oddie is left looking somewhat uninformed on this subject, when one considers the long history of claims that Muslim men were grooming Sikh schoolgirls in Britain. When this is taken into account, it is clear that the skin colour of the victims is not a general explanation: focusing on the gangs' attitudes to the 'chastity' (*i.e.* morality, behaviour, availability) of their Asian or Caucasian victims, and the fact that the victims are overwhelmingly non-Muslims, leads us back to the need to look at Islam more closely. Oddie might expect Sikh and Hindu men to have similar attitudes to chastity, yet Muslims make up 90% of all those convicted for these type of crimes, while non-Muslim Asians are not found among the perpetrators in significant proportions. See *Appendix 1: Grooming Gang Convictions*.

2 Even when the victims of a grooming gang are Muslim, the perpetrators were still Muslim men. 'Asian/Muslim female victims are most vulnerable to offenders from their own communities as the overwhelming majority of the offenders were from the same background as the victims.' Shaista Gohir MBE, 'Unheard Voices: The Sexual Exploitation of Asian Girls and Young Women', September 2013, http://www.mwnuk.co.uk//go_files/resources/UnheardVoices.pdf p. 23.

the national media in 2003, Ann Cryer (then Labour MP for Keighley, outside Bradford) said 'I believe there is a very strong cultural reason, it's nothing to do with the religion lets [sic] make it quite clear, its [sic] to do with the Asian culture, which wants these young men to marry these very young girls from their village...'[3] Ten years later, Andrew Norfolk (who had lived in that area for most of that time) is quoted in the parliamentary report saying:

> If you come from a rural Mirpuri, Kashmiri community, where, whatever state law says, village tradition and sharia says that puberty is the green light for marriage—as it does—and if you recognise that most girls in this country are hitting puberty at 11 or 12, perhaps one begins to understand why it is not just lone offenders. *There has to be something, given that so often this is a normalised group activity—not among a major criminal gang, but among friends, work colleagues and relatives—that does not have the same sense of shame attached to it as would be the case for your typical White offender*, who works alone because if he told too many people, somebody would report him.[4] (emphasis added)

So, in 2003 Ann Cryer was blaming 'Asian culture', and a decade later, award-winning journalist Andrew Norfolk is still scratching round, blaming 'village tradition'. In 10 years the national debate has moved on by just one small step: instead of blaming the culture of an entire continent, the spokesmen given voice by the media are blaming the culture of single villages. But the doctrines and history which shape this culture cannot be stated. Whilst politicians and the media offer no explanation, it would appear that it is commonly accepted by the general public that Islam and Muslims are to blame for this phenomenon. However, there is still no attempt in the media or among academics to explain why this phenomenon of schoolgirls being systematically groomed for prostitution should have appeared in Britain and in Holland (and probably other European countries with significant Muslim populations). Norfolk gives some indication that he might think it is more than just 'village

---

3 'Asian Rape Allegations', *Channel 4 News*, 27 Aug 2003, (from archive.org) http://web.archive.org/web/20100620042427/http://www.channel4.com/news/articles/society/law_order/Asian+rape+allegations/256893
4 Home Affairs Select Committee Report 'Child Sexual Exploitation and the Response to Localised Grooming', *op. cit.* p. 54.

tradition', when he mentions (and passes by) the concept of 'sharia' in the quotation above.[5]

By 2011 Jack Straw (then MP for Blackburn) characterised the problem thus: 'there is a specific problem which involves Pakistani heritage men... who target vulnerable young white girls. We need to get the Pakistani community to think much more clearly about why this is going on.'[6] However, there is little evidence that 'the Pakistani community' is giving any thought to why this happens with Pakistani Muslim men in Britain, even though there is no evidence of Pakistani Christians or Pakistani Hindus in Britain who are involved with the gangs: that the perpetrators are mostly Pakistani is far less pertinent than that they are Muslim. It seems that many of those journalists and public figures who point out other races and nationalities in the grooming gangs, rely on the public not realising that such people from Iraq, Afghanistan, North Africa, Central Africa are more than likely to be Muslims. These spokes-

---

5 On at least two occasions, Andrew Norfolk has made statements implicating 'village tradition' and sharia law as an explanation for why Muslims find these crimes less objectionable. See also https://www.youtube.com/watch?v=RZCQ9ZWfCuQ#t=388. Andrew Norfolk glosses over the enormous difference between a village tradition (like clog-dancing) and the idea that certain behaviour is likely to get a Muslim man into Heaven (due to the Muslim man closely following the behaviour of Mohammed). And it is not just illiterate peasants who arrived in Britain 5 years ago who want sharia law: 40% of Muslim university students in Britain want sharia law - see 'The latest WikiLeaks revelation: 1 in 3 British Muslim students back killing for Islam and 40% want Sharia law', *Daily Mail*, 22 Dec 2010, http://www.dailymail.co.uk/news/article-1340599/WikiLeaks-1-3-British-Muslim-students-killing-Islam-40-want-Sharia-law.html. Moreover, there would have to be more to this grooming phenomenon than the idea that sharia law says that a Muslim can marry a girl who has reached puberty: these gangs were not marrying these non-Muslim schoolgirls, but were consciously luring schoolgirls into sex-slavery, and prostituting the schoolgirls to other men. This was not some kind of misguided, inter-generational, cross-cultural *Love Story*. If it was just a question of the implementation of village tradition/sharia, meaning that Muslim men married under-age girls in Britain, that too happens in Britain and is bad enough - see Pavan Amara, 'Islington Girls Forced into Marriage at the Age of Nine', *Islington Tribune*, 27 Jan 2012, http://www.islingtontribune.com/news/2012/jan/islington-girls-forced-marriage-age-nine. The pro-Caliphate groups, like those which have been associated with efforts to seduce/groom non-Muslim girls, are very serious about implementing full sharia law. Manuals of sharia law advocate morality far unlike our own, *e.g.* that homosexual people are to be executed - see Section o12.2, *Reliance of the Traveller: a Classic Manual of Islamic Sacred Law*, Keller translation, 1991.

6 'Jack Straw: Some White Girls are "Easy Meat"', *BBC News*, 8 Jan 2011, http://www.bbc.co.uk/news/uk-england-derbyshire-12141603 We think that 'the Pakistani community' know that Islamic doctrine is the reason the grooming gangs exist, but that they do not want non-Muslims to realise this.

men will use these ethnic details as a way of 'proving' that the gangs have many ethnicities, and that it is thus irrelevant that most of those convicted are Pakistani Muslims. If this was part of a conscious process of concealment, it could hardly have been better executed.

Despite the experts knowing that not all the Muslims in Britain who do this are Asian, despite knowing that an almost identical pattern of criminality has been going on in Holland (and that the Muslims in Holland who are doing it are from Turkey and Morocco), the experts refuse to look at Islam as a causal factor, even when there is no other cause that can be seen: 'All except two of the men were of Pakistani origin. The Karrar brothers were from north Africa.'[7] One would expect that the fact that one of those north African brothers in the Oxford trial in 2012 was called 'Mohammed', and that 'Mohammed' is the most common name of all the men in Andrew Norfolk's original overview from 2011, should have signalled that the names of these men are more significant than the countries from which their parents came.[8] Yet even in his 2012 interview with the Sikh Awareness Society, Norfolk claims what is going on is 'not an Islamic issue'. How can he make this emphatic claim? Simple: Norfolk says that since not all Muslim men are involved, Islam cannot be a factor.[9] This argument seems to be that Islam cannot command that these men exploit young girls, or else the exploitation we see from the grooming gangs would be universal wherever there were Muslims in Britain. However, this is analogous to arguing that Christianity could not have been a factor in the Crusades, since Christianity forbids killing, and not all Christians took part in the Crusades. Moreover, Andrew Norfolk's claim that Muslims from Gujarat have not been involved could quite simply be based on a lack of evidence for the involvement of Gujarati Muslims (we have been told by both CEOP and the Children's Commissioner that the evidence about these crimes has not been consistently gathered). It seems that the experts will try to split hairs, rather

---

7 Arthur Martin, 'Faces of True Evil: Judge Jails Depraved Sex Gang for 95 Years After they Committed Grotesque Abuse on Girls as Young as 11', *The Daily Mail*, 27 Jun 2013, http://www.dailymail.co.uk/news/article-2349784/Sadistic-paedophile-sex-gang-brothers-given-lengthy-prison-sentences-exploiting-underage-girls.html

8 Andrew Norfolk, 'Revealed: conspiracy of silence on UK sex gangs', *The Times*, 5 Jan 2011, http://www.thetimes.co.uk/tto/news/uk/crime/article2863058.ece

9 Norfolk points out that in Blackburn, a hotspot for these grooming gangs, men involved in grooming all come the area of Kashmir; the Muslim men in that area who hail from Gujarat have not been involved. http://www.youtube.com/watch?feature=player_detailpage&v=WbUIfvYbjRc&t=799

than actually look at what aspects of Islamic doctrine *could* lead some Muslims to find this kind of horrendous crime acceptable. It would help the argument of those who wish to exonerate Islam if they could even find some injunctions from Islam which would forbid or outlaw these crimes (such evidence is never forthcoming).

There is tacit admission from Parliament that Islam is fundamentally connected to this crime. Why did the Home Affairs Select Committee have input from a Sheikh, but not from a Bishop? Because Pakistani Christians in Britain are not involved in this criminality? If there is no connection with Muslims/Islam, why was there to be a sermon in mosques in June 2013, instructing Muslims that grooming schoolgirls for prostitution was against Islam?[10] No similar sermon was to be read out in Christian churches, Sikh gurdawaras, or Jewish synagogues. This tacit admission goes all the way back to the first time this crime got national media attention, that is, when Ann Cryer's constituents came to her about their daughters being groomed, she did not go to the police, she reportedly contacted 'village elders' and asked them to tell the Muslim men to stop doing it, because 'it is un-Islamic'. She did not go to the Sikh or Hindu temples, or to the local church, or the local working-men's club. Perhaps more significantly than most people realise, the Muslim leaders *refused* to tell their fellow Muslims: this behaviour is un-Islamic.[11]

We also have the confirmatory behaviour of the British judiciary, who give light sentences to devout Muslim men who rape under-age girls, excusing the men's behaviour if they have had a very Islamic upbringing. As late as May 2013, the media were reporting that a Muslim man in Nottingham who:

> had "raped" an underage girl, was spared a prison term after the judge heard that the naïve 18-year-old attended an Islamic faith school where he was taught that women are worthless. Rashid told psychologists he had no idea that having sex with a willing 13-year-old was against the law; besides,

---

10 Vikram Dodd, 'Imams in 500 Mosques to Denounce Grooming and Abuse of Children: Co-ordinated Effort to Deliver Same Sermon Across the Country Follows Convictions of Muslim Men for Series of Horrific Cases', *The Guardian*, 28 Jun 2013, http://www.theguardian.com/world/2013/jun/28/imamas-500-mosques-denounce-grooming

11 This occurred in 2003 in Keighley, and then occurred again nationally in 2013, when the vast majority of mosques did not read the sermon condemning the grooming gangs.

his education had taught him to believe that "women are no more worthy than a lollipop that has been dropped on the ground."[12]

So, Islamic religious values are being used by judges in British courts, as extenuating circumstances for child-rape. But Islamic religious values are not to be mentioned as an explanatory factor with the grooming/pimping gangs, where Muslims who are less than 5% of the population make up anywhere from 28% to 90% of the perpetrators of a distinct and new kind of crime?[13] This is double-think.

Setting themselves up as the arbiters of who is or is not a Muslim, some non-Muslim academics claim that the Muslim men convicted are Muslims in name-only. But there is a significant amount of evidence to show that some of those convicted were indeed devout Muslims. In one of the trials, one of the gang members was a mosque official.[14] In another trial, the gang were caught after abducting and raping girls as part of their Eid celebrations.[15] In a case where six men were convict-

---

12 Allison Pearson, 'Oxford grooming gang: We will regret ignoring Asian thugs who target white girls', *The Telegraph*, 15 May 2013, http://www.telegraph.co.uk/news/uknews/crime/10060570/Oxford-grooming-gang-We-will-regret-ignoring-Asian-thugs-who-target-white-girls.html. In a similar vein, Libyan soldiers on training in England reportedly went on a spree of rapes and sexual assaults in Cambridge, and a spokesman for them blamed the British authorities, saying 'They didn't tell us about British law and what's the difference between right and wrong here.' 'Libyan cadet in Bassingbourn claims "poor treatment"', *BBC News* website, 05 Nov 2914, http://www.bbc.co.uk/news/uk-england-cambridgeshire-29923770

13 The figure of 28% comes from the CEOP 'rapid assessment' - see section 5.5 *Child Exploitation and Online Protection Centre*. The figure of 90% comes from our analysis of those convicted - see *Appendix 1: Grooming Gang Convictions*. What we need to bear in mind with regard to the 'data' from CEOP report and from the Children's Commissioner report, is that their data is gathered from disparate sources, and the quality of much of that data will not stand up in court. The principles of the Norfolk analysis mean that the data has gone through weeks of rigorous questioning in court, leading to convictions despite this contestation. Thus, the Norfolk analysis is based on data which has been subjected to the most rigorous of questioning - and this data shows that where the evidence is strong enough to bring about a conviction, the vast majority of those involved in 'localised grooming' are Muslim men.

14 'Profiled: Guilty members of Rochdale sex grooming gang', *Manchester Evening News*, 9 May 2012, http://www.manchestereveningnews.c o.uk/news/greater-manchester-news/profiled-guilty-members-of-rochdale-sex-687971

15 Katherine Faulkner, 'Muslim gang jailed for kidnapping and raping two girls as part of their Eid celebrations', *The Daily Mail*, 21 Apr 2012, http://www.dailymail.co.uk/news/article-2132985/Muslim-gang-jailed-kidnapping-raping-girls-Eid-celebrations.html. A few years later, another group of Muslim men were jailed after they raped a 16

ed in Leicester of crimes relating to paying a 16 year old Sikh girl for sex and/or prostituting her, the media did not report that 5 of the 6 men were Muslim. Almost no report carried an artist's impression of the accused, one of whom was in the dock in the clothing and beard of a devout Muslim.[16] When Ashtiaq Asghar decided to murder a groomed girl whom he had made pregnant, he said 'I'm gonna send that kuffar [non-Muslim] bitch straight to Hell', showing he was viewing the victim and her 'punishment' in Islamic terms.[17] Some of those who have worked extensively with the victims of the gangs, report how the gangs give the schoolgirls 'Muslim' names, and force them to read the Koran.[18] As the Muslim journalist Yasmin Alibhai-Brown states: 'The rapists are all probably considered very good Muslims, praying and fasting in the daytime, then prowling and preying at night on girls they think of as barely human.'[19] Thus, there are plenty of reasons to regard the mem-

---

year old girl as part of their Eid celebrations. 'Pictured: Men who gang raped schoolgirl after luring her to hotel room during sinister game of "hide and seek"', *Manchester Evening News*, 30 Jan 2016, http://www.manchestereveningnews.co.uk/news/greater-manchester-news/hotel-schoolgirl-gang-rape-rusholme-10811461. After the trial it was reported that significant harassment had been directed towards the family of the victim by a very large group of Muslim relatives of those convicted.

16 This report on the *BBC News* website is one of the few to display this image. http://www.bbc.co.uk/news/uk-england-23896937

17 Paul Sims, 'Groomed for sex then thrown into a canal and killed: Life for man who murdered white girl for "shaming" Asian family', *Daily Mail*, 22 Dec 2011, http://www.dailymail.co.uk/news/article-2077205/Teenage-mother-stabbed-death-thrown-canal-bringing-shame-family.html

18 'Gemma was given an Asian name by Amir, and told she had to read the Koran, a story support workers tell me is not uncommon.' Julie Bindel, 'Mothers of Prevention', *The Sunday Times*, 30 Sep 2007, http://www.thesundaytimes.co.uk/sto/news/uk_news/article72310.ece

19 Yasmin Alibhai-Brown, 'Asian Grooming Gangs', 21 May 2012, http://alibhai-brown.com/Asian-grooming-gangs/. We noted that the grooming gangs were the talk of the town among Muslim taxi drivers in Rochdale. It has also come to light that in Rotherham, the activities of the gangs were discussed in mosques, but that people did not go to the police.

> Pakistani community leaders in Rotherham were complicit in hushing up the shocking "ethnic" dimensions of the sexual exploitation rather than speaking out [...] Parveen Qureshi, director of the United Multicultural Centre in Rotherham, revealed the shocking issue was widely discussed between leaders who were privately "trying to resolve the problem". She refused to name those who kept quiet, but was certain the problem of Asian men abusing white girls was known "for a long time".

'"Muslim leaders fully aware of problem but did nothing": Pakistani community worker makes explosive claims on Rotherham's religious leaders who "talked in mosques but not

bers of these grooming gangs as practising Muslims. Furthermore, a Muslim leader has finally come out and stated that imams in Britain are responsible for this new phenomenon of grooming gangs, because Muslim men are taught in mosques that women are 'second-class citizens, little more than chattels or possessions over whom they have absolute authority.'[20] We saw earlier how a leader of a grooming gang in Rochdale held forth at his trial with a rant about Muslim supremacism.

Even if the Muslim men who are involved in these crimes had never set foot in a mosque in their adult lives, we believe that Islamic culture must still be examined as a motivating factor. Indeed, we have nothing else to look at for motivation, since being Asian, being Sikh, being Hindu has nothing like the correlation that being Muslim has with these crimes. Those who wanted to use the problem of the Muslim grooming gangs to talk up the issue of racism, were simultaneously turning a blind eye to the suffering not just of white schoolgirls, but also the suffering of Asian schoolgirls.

7.2 Islamic Morality, Muslim Culture

Over hundreds of years the stories, morality and principles from the Koran, the Hadiths, and the *Sira* (*The Life of Mohammed*) must have passed into Islamic culture.[21] These principles, values and narratives

---

to police"', *Daily Mail*, 28 Aug 2014, http://www.dailymail.co.uk/news/article-2736995/Muslim-leaders-fully-aware-problem-did-Pakistani-community-worker-makes-explosive-claims-religious-leaders-talked-mosques-not-police.html

20 Hayley Dixon, "'Imams promote grooming rings", Muslim leader claims', *The Telegraph*, 16 May 2013, http://www.telegraph.co.uk/news/uknews/crime/10061217/Imams-promote-grooming-rings-Muslim-leader-claims.html. Taj Hargey also castigated the political correctness of the groups we have taken to task in our study:

> [T]he reason this scandal happened at all is precisely because of such politically correct thinking. All the agencies of the state, including the police, the social services and the care system, seemed eager to ignore the sickening exploitation that was happening before their eyes. Terrified of accusations of racism, desperate not to undermine the official creed of cultural diversity, they took no action against obvious abuse...

Also, let us not forget the claims, reported by the media and by Sikh organisations, that from the 1990s until 2005, that there was evidence of devout, pro-Caliphate Muslim organisations in Britain, not only instructing Muslim men to groom non-Muslim women, but Sikh organisations and even reports in national newspapers claimed these Muslim fundamentalist organisations were issuing instructions on how to do this.

21 We realise that these three different categories of religious texts in Islam may be confusing to the layman. The Koran is the core text of Islam, believed by Muslims to be the direct word of their God, communicated to Mohammed. However, in Islam the

have affected what Muslims view as right and wrong. These things shape their view of the world. This is not to say that the whole of these textual corpuses would have passed into the store of knowledge of any particular Muslim, or Muslim family, or Muslim community in Britain. But it is inevitable that parts of them would. Even with Islam being a recent addition to British society, most non-Muslims in Britain now 'know' that halal meat, the burka, 'honour killing', and even terrorist violence are associated with Islam (knowing where any of these are mandated/ forbidden in any particular texts is something even most Muslims could not provide).

The culture in countries which have majority Muslim populations is 'Islamic culture'; quite often these countries define themselves as 'Islamic states'. But even when they do not go as far as that, a country which was subjugated by the armies of Islam 1000 years ago or more, cannot have escaped 'Islamic values' from pervading the culture of the country. Indeed, we would contend that even those who remain as non-Muslims in those countries may also have acquired some Islamic values. Whilst Muslims may not be able to cite chapter and verse for particular beliefs they have (such as beliefs about genies), those beliefs have suffused their upbringing and their world-view (and the very fact that most non-Muslims reading this book would know about genies testifies to how ideas both travel and 'sediment' down within a culture). It is astonishing to see how glibly supposed experts in sociology, politics or theology will conveniently create an impermeable barrier between religion and culture, as if the two can never affect each other.

To understand this in the context of 'Christian countries' (even those which are not legally defined as 'Christian states'), consider the concept of 'a crusade'. It is 1000 years since the actual Crusades took place, yet the flags of many countries still bear a cross, and there can be 'crusades against crime', 'crusades against poverty', and so on. Organisations from the time of the Crusades still exist (*e.g.* St. John's medi-

---

behaviour of Mohammed is considered to be exemplary, to be followed by all Muslims. Thus, the *Sira* and the Hadiths are of secondary importance. However they are still of great importance, as they allow Muslims to know how Mohammed behaved, so that they might copy his behaviour. The *Sira* is a narrative biography of Mohammed; the Hadiths are collections of short reports of Mohammed's behaviour, from a variety of different people. The *Sira* and the Hadiths also serve as the chronological framework, against which contradictory verses in the Koran can be resolved. If a later verse contradicts an earlier verse, then the later verse countermands the earlier verse. Thus, Muslims need Hadiths and *Sira* not just for detailed information about Mohammed's behaviour, but also to order the Koran's verses chronologically.

cal services, from the Order of St. John). Yet the actual Crusades are a tiny and almost insignificant part of Christian history (there were only 9 Crusades, compared to over 500 Muslim Holy Wars against Christian countries). We have many stories where Richard the Lionheart is a key figure (such as the re-tellings of Robin Hood), and in the 21st century, the English Defence League is once again using the iconography of the Crusades. If something like the Crusades can still resonate and shape the culture and world-view of a secular Britain, it is obvious that stories, morals and values from Islamic theology and Islamic history must shape the world-view of Muslims; these things have been passed down in mosques and Muslim homes since the time of Mohammed.

We will look at values and stories from the Koran, the Hadiths, and The Life of Mohammed (the *Sira*) to see how these texts and stories could make Muslims in Britain and Holland take part in, or excuse, the activities of the grooming gangs. We are not offering this as proof that Muslims were specifically and consciously implementing these values: although there is evidence that there are Sikhs and Hindus who believe that these grooming activities were motivated by Islamic values.[22] We are going to look at the elephant in the room, which everyone else has been determined to ignore for the preceding 25 years: are there aspects of Islamic doctrine which could have shaped Muslim culture, such that these crimes seem acceptable to some Muslim men? These are pressing questions, and it is shameful that they have not been articulated in the first 25 years of this grooming phenomenon.

7.3 Koranic Instructions

The Koran[23] instructs Muslim men to make their women and girls

---

22 "'The attitude of showing disrespect towards non-Muslim girls by a small minority of Muslim men through some confused religious sanction needs to be tackled head on by the mosques,' said Anil Bhanot of Hindu Council, UK", Yudhvir Rana, 'Sigh of relief among Hindu, Sikh communities in UK', *The Times of India*, Jul 2 2013, http://articles. timesofindia.indiatimes.com/2013-07-02/other-news/40328466_1_hindu-council-an-il-bhanot-uk

23 Historically, and even in some Muslim countries today, non-Muslims were not allowed to touch the Koran nor speak about what it contains. This is in keeping with the principle in Islam that non-Muslims are considered inferior to Muslims (some Muslims even put non-Muslims into the same category as faeces - see http://islam-ic-laws.com/tawzeh/najisthings.htm). Consequently, many Muslims are outraged to have a non-Muslim argue with them about what is in the Koran. Also, with this new development in history - non-Muslims being able to find out that Islam seeks to subjugate non-Muslims - there are translations of the Koran which do their best to make

cover up, and those women and girls who are not covered are liable for abuse: 'tell your wives and your daughters and the women of the believers to bring down over themselves [part] of their outer garments. That is more suitable that they will be known and not be abused.'[24] Any woman who commits sexual intercourse outside the limits permitted by Islamic rules is to be killed according to the canonical texts: 'Those who commit unlawful sexual intercourse of your women - bring against them four [witnesses] from among you. And if they testify, confine the guilty women to houses until death takes them.'[25] The Koran lays down strictures as to how a decent Muslim woman must dress, and restricts her sexual freedom. And if she dresses inappropriately, or is sexually liberated, then she is to expect abuse and even death, with no legal repercussions for the husband who kills her (or for the people who abuse her for being 'immodestly' dressed). We can see from this, that Muslim men in Britain and Holland would distinguish between virtuous women (Muslim women) and immodest or 'lewd' non-Muslim women. Indeed, in London a devout Muslim man, named Sunny Islam, set about raping and beating non-Muslim women because they were, in his judgement, behaving lewdly simply by being out at night without a controlling father, husband or brother.[26]

This is all reprehensible, to say the least. However, there are worse things in Islamic doctrine. We know it will come as a shock[27] to many

---

the Koran sound softer (and even confusing) to non-Muslims. In the light of this, we think it advisable that non-Muslims do not rely on just one translation of the Koran, but where necessary they should use websites which offer many different translations of the Koran side by side, for example http://www.usc.edu/org/cmje/religious-texts/quran/

24 The Koran, surah 33, verse 59 http://quran.com/33/59

25 The Koran, surah 4, verse 15 http://quran.com/4/15

26 Nick Enoch, '"Strict Muslim" raped four women at knifepoint to "punish them for being on the streets at night"', *Daily Mail*, 25 Jan 2012, http://www.dailymail.co.uk/news/article-2091669/Sunny-Islam-Strict-Muslim-raped-4-women-knifepoint-punish-them.html

27 Political activists in the west have been very selective in their opposition to slavery. They consistently emphasise a few hundred years of white European Christians trading black African slaves, but are virtually silent on the much longer and much larger trade in slaves by Muslims. Even academics have a terrible record of concealing this trade. See John Alembillah Azumah, *The Legacy of Arab-Islam in Africa*, Oneworld, Oxford, 2001, pp.14-17. These academics and activists not only ignored the Islamic slave-taking and trading of white and Asian slaves, but also of black African slaves. The conclusion one must draw is that these activists and academics were not interested in the horror of slavery *per se*, but were instead merely interested in denigrating European values.

untrained individuals to discover that Islam has a very accepting attitude concerning the morality of slavery, and so we will provide references to books by black British academics (Azumah), African American professors (Thomas Sowell), anti-Apartheid campaigners (Ronald Segal), Indian historians (K.S. Lai) and Islamic scholars (Sultan Tabandeh) to show that the morality and legality of slavery in Islam is not some fiction. Perhaps talking of slavery in the context of the grooming gangs may seem exaggerated: however, that is how Sikhs were describing these gangs back in the 1980s (see section 3.2 *1989 Sikhs convicted*), and some of the victims in recent trials have been described as 'sex slaves'.[28] These values must be considered if we are to look at how Islamic doctrine and tradition could have made this crime seem acceptable to many of those brought up as Muslims.

From before the start of Islam until just after World War II, slavery was not only legal in Islamic countries: it was an all-pervasive part of Islamic history, actively and extensively practised throughout their culture:[29] slave-taking and trading was practised as part of Islam from before Britain was even officially a Christian country, right up until men were walking on the moon. Indeed, one could argue that throughout history Islamic society has been based on subjugation and slave-taking. Whilst the Koran does not contain injunctions telling Muslims they can have slaves, laying that out explicitly was not necessary: the morality and legality of slavery was taken for granted at the time of Mohammed, and he himself had slaves and took women as slaves, and he is viewed as exemplary. Whilst Mohammed is credited by Muslims with ending extant but immoral practices such as infanticide,[30] he did not seek to end slavery. The conditions under which Muslims can acquire slaves are not specified in the Koran. Having said that: the Koran contains no in-

---

28 Moreover, the police are now describing the victims of these gangs in these terms: Vicky Smith, 'Child sex slave gangs in EVERY city in Britain: Police chief's warning after Oxford grooming horror', *The Mirror*, 15 May 2013, http://www.mirror.co.uk/news/uk-news/child-sex-slave-gangs-every-1891898. The association of slave-taking with these grooming gangs was also made back in 2008; see Kathryn Knight, 'Is political correctness stopping police ending the misery of the teenage sex slaves?', *Daily Mail*, 27 Mar 2008, http://www.dailymail.co.uk/femail/article-546809/Is-political-correctness-stopping-police-ending-misery-teenage-sex-slaves.html

29 See Emmet Scott, *The Impact of Islam*, New English Review Press, 2014, pp. 16-18, pp. 61-74, pp. 142-153.

30 'Mohammed and Women', http://www.pbs.org/muhammad/ma_women.shtml. See also p. 3 of 'Khutba - Tackling Street Grooming in the UK', 2013, http://www.mcb.org.uk/uploads/Khutbah%20-%20Street%20Grooming%20final%20version.pdf

junctions telling Muslims that slavery is immoral or illegal. But the Koran does contain instructions telling Muslims how they can treat their slaves.

The Koran makes a distinction between legal wives and slaves, and instructs Muslim men that they can have sex with either their wives or their slaves: 'We have made lawful to you your wives whom you have given their dowries, and those whom your right hand possesses out of those whom Allah has given to you as prisoners of war.'[31] Whilst Muslim men cannot have sex with the wives of other Muslim men, they can have sex with enslaved women, even if the enslaved woman has a husband: 'all married women (are forbidden unto you) save those (captives) whom your right hands possess.'[32] Not only are Muslim men permitted legally and morally to rape their slaves, but they are also forgiven if they turn a slave girl into a prostitute: 'do not compel your slave girls to prostitution, when they desire to keep chaste, in order to seek the frail good of this world's life; and whoever compels them, then surely after their compulsion Allah is Forgiving, Merciful.'[33] It is clear, that these kind of Islamic views easily lend themselves to Muslim men seeing women as objects, to be controlled and dominated by men. It would lead them to believe that if some non-Muslim woman within their control could be prostituted, there would be no moral or legal consequences for them within an Islamic world-view.[34]

There are also features of Islam which are supremacist and which look with contempt at non-Muslims. According to the Koran, non-Muslims are the worst of all living creatures, thus sub-human: 'The disbelievers among the People of the Book and the pagans will dwell for-

---

31 The Koran, surah 33, verse 50 http://www.usc.edu/org/cmje/religious-texts/quran/verses/033-qmt.php. It might not be immediately obvious to the untrained reader, but 'right hand possesses' is a metaphor for 'slave', as can be found in contemporary discussions of this phrase on Islamic websites. http://forums.understanding-Islam.com/showthread.php?7663-Who-are-women-whom-your-right-hand-possess

32 The Koran, surah 4, verse 24 http://www.usc.edu/org/cmje/religious-texts/quran/verses/004-qmt.php

33 The Koran, surah 24, verse 33 http://corpus.quran.com/translation.jsp?chapter=24&verse=33. Since any woman who does not wear a hijab/burka is considered to be 'lewd' in Islamic doctrine, the Muslim grooming gangs could quite easily rationalise their pimping as being in accord with Islam, *i.e.* they were not pimping out slave girls who 'desire to be chaste'. Some might argue that this verse says that it is the woman who is compelled who is forgiven; we argue that the forgiveness applies to the slave-owner, since all non-Muslims are destined for hell, according to Islamic doctrine.

34 It is not uncommon to find someone who is described as 'a moderate Muslim' who insists that they will only obey English law that does not conflict with Islamic law.

ever in hell; they are the worst of all creatures.'[35] Some Muslims take the Koranic description of infidels as the worst of creatures, and put non-Muslim into the same category of dirty things as faeces and dead bodies.[36] One of the police officers who managed to get convictions for a gang in Bradford in Leeds in 1997 said 'The men held those young girls in extremely low esteem; they thought that this somehow justified the violation that was taking place.' The Koran refers to non-Muslims as animals, and the standard term for a non-Muslim in Arabic is 'kafir', a highly derogatory term.[37]

Furthermore, we should not be surprised when Muslims who said they disapproved of the grooming/raping gangs still said 'they would never have dreamt of going to the police about it, because you do not turn on your own community',[38] as this too is part of Islamic theology. The Koran tells Muslims that they must always band together against non-Muslims: 'Let not the believers Take for friends or helpers Unbelievers rather than believers.'[39] As one of the few Muslims who has been prepared to speak (anonymously) about the grooming gangs said to Andrew Norfolk:

"a lot of people" knew of the abuse but that he and others were "too scared to do anything about it." He points to a widespread view that betraying members of one's own community to the police would be an even greater sin than child sexual exploitation.[40]

We know it sounds incredible, but there is so much evidence to show that the vast majority of Muslims put their loyalty to other Muslims (the Ummah) above all else. It is a part of Islam, a concept that weaves

35 The Koran, surah 98, verse 6 http://corpus.quran.com/translation.jsp?chapter=98&verse=6 'People of the Book' means 'Jews and Chrstians'.

36 This Islamic website explains this view of non-Muslims: http://www.al-Islam.org/laws/najisthings.html

37 http://alquranwasunnahislamicsiteoflearning.yuku.com/topic/888#.UjDwHsasio8

38 Home Affairs Select Committee Report 'Child Sexual Exploitation and the Response to Localised Grooming', 10 Jun 2013, http://www.publications.parliament.uk/pa/cm201314/cmselect/cmhaff/68/68i.pdf, p. 53.

39 The Koran, surah 3, verse 28. http://corpus.quran.com/translation.jsp?chapter=3&verse=28

40 Andrew Norfolk, "'Some of these men have children the same age; they are bad apples"; Sexual grooming; The grooming of white girls by gangs of Pakistani heritage is an issue that few in the community will address', *The Times*, 5 Jan 2011.

through Islamic texts. The Islamic world-view is so deeply ingrained in many Muslims, that they would rather allow schoolgirls to be raped, drugged, and pimped than tell the police that it was going on.

Whilst most of what we have covered so far in Islamic theology sounds like it only relates to adult women, it is time to turn to the issue of what constitutes a woman under Islamic law and morality. Aisha was Mohammed's favourite wife, and she was only aged 6 years old when he married her. It is on the basis of Mohammed marrying her when she was 6 years old and him consummating that marriage when she was 9 years old, that girls around the ages of 9 to 15 are married off in many Muslim countries (Iran, Saudi Arabia, Malaysia, Yemen, etc.) In the chapter where divorce is discussed in the Koran, it contains provisions for the divorce of a wife who has not yet begun to menstruate: 'And those who no longer expect menstruation among your women - if you doubt, then their period is three months, and [also for] those who have not menstruated. And for those who are pregnant, their term is until they give birth.'[41] This is a subject which many western Muslims will dispute or deny; whether that is out of shame or ignorance we cannot say. But that 'Islamic states' (*e.g.* Saudi Arabia, Yemen) permit 9 year old girls to be married cannot be denied (some of these child-brides die giving birth shortly after they are married).[42]

Some Muslims will point out that in medieval Europe, Kings took young wives. That might very well be true, but our societies have laws and morals which evolve. This is a problem when a group of people insist on holding onto an unchanging morality that is supposedly the direct and eternal word of god. This is how we end up with a situation like that in 2012 in London, where 9 year old Muslim girls were being married off to old men, and trapped in primary school in the day whilst

41 The Koran, surah 65, verse 4 http://quran.com/65/4

42 See Sara Nelson, 'Bride Aged 8 Dies After Suffering Internal Sexual Injuries During Wedding Night With Man, 40', *Huffington Post*, 9 Sep 2013, http://www.huffington-post.co.uk/2013/09/09/bride-aged-8-dies-internal-sexual-injuries-wedding-night-_n_3892892.html; Ali al-Ahmed, 'Why is no one protecting Saudi Arabia's child brides?', *The Guardian*, 8 Nov 2011, http://www.theguardian.com/commentisfree/2011/no v/08/saudi-arabia-child-brides-marriage; 'Child bride, 12, dies in Yemen after struggling to give birth for THREE days', *Daily Mail*, 17 Mar 2010, http://www.dailymail.co.uk/news/article-1213168/Fawziya-Abdullah-Youssef-dies-labour-Child-bride-12-dies-Yemen-struggling-birth-THREE-days.html; Emma Graham-Harrison, 'Afghan judges free three jailed for torture of child bride Sahar Gul', *The Guardian*, 11 Jul 2013, http://www.theguardian.com/world/2013/jul/11/afghan-judges-free-sa-har-guls-torturers; 'Contemporary Paedophilic Marriages in Islam' http://wikiIslam.net/wiki/Contemporary_Pedophilic_Islamic_Marriages

providing sexual services to the old man in the evening.[43] It also explains how it could be that so many of the Muslim men in the grooming gangs were interested in girls as young as 10:

> The youngest identified victim was 10, with 14 and 15 the peak ages for exploitation... "Offenders tend to prefer younger victims. The exploitation tails off in most cases as the children get older and offenders identify and groom new, younger victims."[44]

Even in the last few years, primary schools in England (where the oldest child is 11 years old) were sending home letters to parents warning them of groups of Asian men sat in cars outside the school gates (one of the classic behaviours of the Muslim grooming gangs).[45] If one examines websites providing coverage of Islamic countries, one can find contemporary stories of 'child prostitution in the guise of marriage.'[46] According to UNICEF in Pakistan 'child marriages accounted for 32 per cent of all marriages.'[47] When multiculturalism encourages immigrants to keep their own cultural values, why should we be surprised if they maintain a preference for sex with girls whom our culture consider to be children, whilst their culture and religion consider such children to be legitimate candidates for sex and marriage?

That Aisha was 6 years old when Mohammed married her was not disputed for 1300 years. It was only in India in the 1920s that a new

---

43 Pavan Amara, 'Islington Girls Forced into Marriage at the Age of Nine', *Islington Tribune*, 27 Jan 2012, http://www.islingtontribune.com/news/2012/jan/islington-girls-forced-marriage-age-nine

44 Andrew Norfolk, 'Police Files Reveal Vast Child Protection Scandal', *The Times*, 24 Sep 2012, http://www.thetimes.co.uk/tto/news/uk/crime/article3547661.ece

45 'Worryingly members heard that the risk was not only to secondary school pupils and that incidences of primary school pupils being targeted had been picked up in the transition process from primary to secondary school.' See 'Middlesbrough primary school children "targeted for sex"', *BBC News* website, 02 Oct 2014, http://www.bbc.co.uk/news/uk-england-tees-29467029. Also see the photographic copies of letters sent to parents of primary school children in Leeds and Sheffield, *Appendix 4: Leeds School Warning* and *Appendix 5: Sheffield School Warning*.

46 Cam McGrath, 'Underage Girls Are Egypt's Summer Rentals', *Inter Press Service News Agency*, http://www.ipsnews.net/2013/08/underage-girls-are-egypts-summer-rentals/

47 'Underage victims: "To stop child marriages, state needs to step in"', *The Express Tribune*, http://tribune.com.pk/story/434512/underage-victims-to-stop-child-marriages-state-needs-to-step-in/.

interpretation arose: these Indian Muslims claimed that Aisha was 10 years old when Mohammed married her.[48] Any Muslims who claim that Aisha was significantly older than 10 years of age on marriage are making a claim contradicted by the marriage laws of various Muslim countries. And to Muslims, Mohammed is regarded as the perfect man; it is part of their religion that they should emulate his behaviour.[49]

We can imagine many readers struggling to comprehend how the Koran's statements about slavery could be taken seriously by Muslims in the 21st century. Surely only an extreme Muslim would refuse to condemn such things? However, it is cultural blindness to assume that Muslims feel the same way about the literal interpretation of their religious texts as the Christians and ex-Christians in Britain feel about the Old Testament and the New Testament: it is a refusal to see that people from different cultures can do things differently and can believe different things. To remedy this incomprehension, we would remind people of the statements of Mehdi Hasan, who was then political director of *The Huffington Post* and a frequent guest on the *BBC TV's Question Time*, who allegedly contrasted Muslims and non-Muslims thus: 'Once we lose the moral high-ground we are no different from the rest, of the non-Muslims; from the rest of those human beings who live their lives as animals...'[50] Another example is a discussion on Twitter between historian Tom Holland and Mohammed Ansar. Mohammed Ansar is presented by the media in Britain as a moderate Muslim, yet it is reported that in one discussion he asked: 'If slaves are treated justly, with full rights, and no oppression whatsoever... why would anyone object?'[51]

---

48 This was at a time when Muslims also started to claim that Islam was 'the religion of peace', when Muslims started to re-write history. http://www.Muslim.org/Islam/aisha-age.htm

49 See Koran 33:21. The reader should note that the name 'Mohammed' is by far the most common first name among the men listed in the tables compiled using the Norfolk definition: *Appendix 1: Grooming Gang Convictions*. Of the 177 convicts listed in this table, 27 have some variant of the name 'Mohammed'.

50 Here is the video where you can see a version of Islam which the multiculturalists would have us believe does not exist: http://www.youtube.com/watch?v=h4hp-fqFt-0Q#t=30.

> We know that keeping the moral high-ground is key. Once we lose the moral high-ground we are no different from the rest, of the non-Muslims; from the rest of those human beings who live their lives as animals, bending any rule to fulfil any desire.

See also Douglas Murray, 'Mehdi Hasan and the EDL', 30 Jul 2013, http://blogs.spectator.co.uk/douglas-murray/2013/07/mehdi-hasan-and-the-edl/

51 http://twitter.com/MoAnsar/status/224553175858954240. This tweet has now dis-

By a slave having 'full rights' and being 'treated justly', we presume this moderate Muslim means that the slave is granted the rights which slaves are granted in Islam, such as being able to work outside their owner's business. In another discussion, we can see this moderate Muslim state that he would never denounce any part of the Koran.[52] Equally, it is hard to imagine a modern-day devout Christian, touted by the media for his moderation, asking what is wrong with slavery, or saying that no part of the Bible can be criticised nor denounced. It is hard to imagine a moderate Christian associating non-Christians with animals.

It is clear from this, that even the most moderate, most integrated Muslims have very different values from Christians (and post-Christians) in Britain, including areas of morality where we non-Muslims might assume all people think the same. But even in more contentious moral areas such as homosexuality, there are surveys where 61% of Christians in Britain support equal rights for gay people.[53] Contrasting surveys show that 61% of Muslims in Britain want to see people criminalised for being gay.[54] Across many different topics, it seems that the moral views of Muslims in Britain are very different from the moral views of Christians in Britain. Yet the proponents of multiculturalism deny there are any significant differences, whilst praising diversity. When we look not at the views of moderate, integrated Muslims but at the views of those popularly described as 'extremists' or 'fundamentalists', things look much darker.

Those who propound and defend multiculturalism say that people from different cultural backgrounds have different values, and that we must all accept these values as being of equal validity. But when it comes to examining what those different values are, multiculturalists

---

appeared. However, a discussion about this tweet is here: https://homoeconomicusnet. wordpress.com/2013/03/10/mohammed-ansar-on-islam-and-slavery-poverty-within-oic/

52 https://twitter.com/MoAnsar/status/340930760271884290

53 Stephen Gray, 'UK study: 61% of Christians back equal rights for gay couples', *Pink News*, 14 Feb 2012, http://www.pinknews.co.uk/2012/02/ 14/uk-study-61-of-christians-back-equal-gay-rights/

54 Munira Mirza, Abi Senthilkumaran and Zein Ja'far, 'Living apart together: British Muslims and the paradox of multiculturalism', *Policy Exchange*, 2007, http://www. policyexchange.org.uk/images/publications/living%20apart%20together%20-%20 jan%2007.pdf, p. 47. 'Poll reveals 40pc of Muslims want sharia law in UK', *Telegraph*, 19 Feb 2006, http://www.telegraph.co.uk/news/uknews/1510866/Poll-reveals-40pc-of-Muslims-want-sharia-law-in-UK.html. Manuals of sharia law state that the criminal penalty for homosexuality is death.

suddenly lose interest in the details of these differences and lose interest in the consequences which follow from these different values. Yet we have seen, that even those Muslims who are classed as liberal or moderate have views which would be considered extreme if those views were espoused by a non-Muslim in Britain. Are we really surprised that conflicts and problems arise when communities with these different values are living side-by-side? These conflicts and problems are just concealed by the advocates of multiculturalism. Proponents of multiculturalism dare not examine the views of Islamic fundamentalists, views carried by a significant minority of Muslims in Britain.

What multiculturalists do not seem to understand is that pre-Islamic Arabia was a multicultural society: the pagan Meccans permitted Mohammed to preach this new religion, which denigrated the prevailing religion. After 13 years of listening to Mohammed criticise and denigrate their religion, the Meccan pagans finally drove him out. Mohammed went to Medina, a Jewish and pagan settlement, and the multiculturalist Jews and pagans of Medina permitted Mohammed to preach his new religion there. But since these cities fell to Muslim domination, Jews and pagans were not even allowed to set foot in either Mecca or Medina, let alone pray, proselytise or denigrate the religion of Muslims. Mohammed and his army of Muslims used assassination, mass murder, rape and slavery to destroy any set of values other than Islam.[55] Multiculturalism died, and Islamic totalitarianism supplanted it.

Multiculturalists think that Muslims will embrace multiculturalism; yet Islam was established 1300 years ago to destroy multiculturalism. Muslims even have a contemptuous Arabic word for democratic multiculturalism, *Jahiliyyah*:

> *Jahiliyyah*... takes the form of claiming that the right to create values, to legislate rules of collective behavior, and to choose

---

55 These atrocities are well-documented in Ibn Ishaq's *The Life of Mohammed*, the most authoritative biography of Mohammed, a biography written by a devout Muslim. The most tolerance that the Islamic world ever showed to non-Muslims was to allocate 'Dhimmi' status to Jews and Christians: at best, this was a form of apartheid, where the Dhimmis were third-class citizens. We can be sure that Muslims in contemporary secular society would be outraged if we imposed third-class citizenship on them as Islam does on non-Muslims. See Bat Ye'or, *The Dhimmi: Jews and Christians under Islam*, Associated University Presses, New Jersey, 1985. It is truly amazing that the media and schools in Britain seek to 'educate' the non-Muslim majority in Britain about Islam, without telling the public that in Islam we non-Muslims are denigrated.

any way of life rests with men...[56]

In a lack of awareness of philosophy, of history, and of Islam, the advocates of multiculturalism see their ideology as superior to Islam, ignorant of the fact that Islam arose in a multicultural society and destroyed that multicultural society. And since the 1920s, Muslims across the world have been involved in a return to the roots of Islam, the fundamentals of Islam. In the view of Muslim fundamentalists, non-Muslims are inferior beings.[57] *Jahiliyyah* is not just a word for democracy, secularism, or multiculturalism. It applies to any values that are not Islamic. Thus, societies based on Christianity and Judaism, or Buddhism or Hinduism, and even atheistic societies like those of Communist countries are regarded as *Jahiliyyah* by Muslim fundamentalists: 'the Islamic society is... the only civilised society, and the *jahili* societies, in all their various forms, are backward societies.'[58] It is clear from this: the Islamic society

---

56 Sayyid Qutb, *Milestones*, Islamic Book Service, New Delhi, 2001, p. 11 . Qutb's book contains chapters with title such as 'The Universal Law', 'Islam is the Real Civilisation', not to mention 'Jihad in the Cause of God', which show that Muslim fundamentalists have nothing but contempt for the ideology of multiculturalism. *Milestones* was written in 1964, and Sayyid Qutb was not some minor figure in the history of 20th century Islam, but was the major theoretician of The Muslim Brotherhood.

> During most of his life, Qutb's inner circle mainly consisted of influential politicians, intellectuals, poets and literary figures, both of his age and of the preceding generation. By the mid-1940s, many of his writings were officially among the curricula of schools, colleges and universities. http://en.wikipedia.org/wiki/Sayyid_Qutb

Whilst one might think that Qutb's influence was confined to Egypt, we must note that the importance of the concept of *Jahiliyyah* was something which Qutb took from the theologian Maulana Maududi. Maududi is probably the most significant 20th century Muslim as far as Muslims in Britain are concerned. 'How Islam got political: Founding fathers', *BBC News,* 10 Nov 2005, http://news.bbc.co.uk/1/hi/4424208.stm

57 Those who think that talk about the Dhimmi status of Jews and Christians under Islam is fanciful, need only look at works like Qutb's *Milestones*, which pre-date Bat Yeor's exposition by 20 years. Qutb openly talks about the inferior status of Dhimmis under Islam. See *Milestones*, p. 53, p. 55, p. 63. In an Islamic society, the theory is that Christians and Jews have Dhimmi status, *i.e.* they are 'protected' from death/slavery, because they pay 'protection money'. This is rather like the Mafia demanding 'protection money' from their 'clients'; if the clients do not pay, then they are subject to extreme violence, even death, as punishment for their insubordination. The payment of 'protection money' accords Jews and Christians a third class citizenship, because the payment is a continued admission that they recognise their inferior status *vis-à-vis* Muslims. Non-payment is seen as a rejection of this inferiority, an assertion that Jews and Christians are human beings like Muslims. Those of other religions are not offered even this third class status: they can convert to Islam, be enslaved or be killed. See *Reliance of the Traveller*, o9.8 and o9.9.

58 Sayyid Qutb, *Milestones*, p. 94.

is a totalitarian society, all other values are to subordinated to Islamic values. But if anyone in Britain dares to criticise Islam, they will be denounced and told they live in a multicultural society, and must accept these totalitarian values.

7.4 Stories from the Hadith

Whilst the Koran is believed by Muslims to be the literal words of their god, Allah, spoken through an angel, and surviving during the time of Mohammed via oral repetition, the Hadiths are stories about Mohammed told by his companions, and passed down via lineages of varying trustworthiness. The Hadiths are less compelling guidance than the Koran (particularly those Hadiths which are considered less reliable), but even those which are considered least reliable must still have shaped Islamic religion and culture. The Hadiths are a major component of sharia law.

As we saw with the Koran, the Hadiths also permit Muslims to rape women who are captured after a battle (whereupon they become the property of Muslims, that is, they become slaves). Mohammed told his men not to perform *coitus interruptus* when raping the women they have captured and enslaved (that is, the Muslim men should ejaculate inside the slave woman instead):

> "O Allah's Apostle! We get female captives as our share of booty, and we are interested in their prices, what is your opinion about coitus interruptus?" The Prophet said, "Do you really do that? It is better for you not to do it. No soul that which Allah has destined to exist, but will surely come into existence."[59]

It is not that Mohammed was allowing a lower moral standard for his soldiers, and had a higher moral standard for himself. Mohammed even took sex slaves off other Muslim men:

> I drove them along until I brought them to Abu Bakr who bestowed that girl upon me as a prize. So we arrived in Medina. I had not yet disrobed her when the Messenger of Al-

---

[59] Bukhari Hadith, Volume 3, Book 34, Number 432 http://www.usc.edu/org/cmje/religious-texts/hadith/bukhari/034-sbt.php. This question pertains to whether or not the slave will fetch a lower price at the slave market, if she has been raped.

lah (may peace be upon him) met me in the street and said: "Give me that girl."[60]

These two stories about the life of Mohammed, come from the Bukhari and the Sahih Muslim Hadiths. The Bukhari and the Sahih Muslim Hadiths are considered the most reliable of all the Hadiths. As we can see, they reinforce the idea that there is nothing immoral or illegal about Muslim men having slaves or raping their slaves.[61] This morality, which devout Muslims dare not question, would be totally alien to a devout Christian.

7.5 *The Life of Mohammed (Sira)*

The Sira (The Life of Mohammed) is a chronological story of Mohammed's life. His biography was written by Ibn Ishaq, a Muslim who lived about 100 years after Mohammed. It is of third level importance when considered as religious/legal instruction for Muslims. Some modern Muslims, appalled that non-Muslims are easily able to discover from this book how Mohammed has been viewed by Muslims throughout history, dispute the accuracy of parts of the *Sira*. However, as one Professor of Islamic Studies has said: 'No biographical sketches of Muhammad exist that do not depend on Ibn Ishaq. If an analysis of Ibn Ishaq's book establishes that for whatever reason it cannot be seen as an historical source, all knowledge we possess about Muhammad evaporates.'[62] If Muslims or their apologists wish to rule the *Sira* of Ibn Ishaq out of court, then they might as well admit that there is no evidence that Mohammed ever existed. If what is contained in *The Life of Muhammed* was considered blasphemous, or made Mohammed out to be anything other than a perfect example for Muslims to follow, Ibn Ishaq's biography would not be the basis of all modern biographies of Mohammed.

Even if modern day Muslims are prepared to reject the Mohammed as portrayed by Ibn Ishaq, the book has still been immensely powerful

---

60 Sahih Muslim Hadith, Book 19, Number 4345 http://www.usc.edu/org/cmje/religious-texts/hadith/muslim/019-smt.php

61 In case it needs to be spelled out: a man who forces his slave to have sex with him against her will is still raping her. See also the discussion among Muslims here: http://www.sunniforum.com/forum/showthread.php?36750-Sex-slaves-in-Islam

62 Prof. Johannes Jansen, Professor of Modern Islamic Thought at the University of Utrecht, quoted in Fjordman, 'Unmasking Muhammad's Dubious Existence', *Frontpage*, 2 May 2012, http://frontpagemag.com/2012/fjordman/unmasking-muhammads-dubious-existence/

in shaping the Islamic view of the world, since Muslims throughout the last millennium did not reject the image of Mohammed as portrayed by Ibn Ishaq: this is the Mohammed that Muslim cultures throughout the world have passed on by word of mouth to their children for generation after generation. Moreover, the current edition of this book was reissued in modern day Pakistan, a state whose full title is The Islamic Republic of Pakistan. This Islamic state condemns to death those convicted of defaming Mohammed.[63] Since 1967 Oxford University Press have been selling this Guillaume edition of *The Life of Muhammed*, which is printed in Pakistan. No-one from that company has been charged with 'defaming the Prophet Mohammed', so we can take take from this continued publication and the lack of prosecutions, that contemporary Pakistani Muslims do not consider this work blasphemous.[64] Thus, any contemporary Muslims who regard as defamatory the character of Mohammed as portrayed in the *Sira* of Ibn Ishaq are either duplicitous or are not typical of other Muslims. If this book was considered to portray Mohammed in a negative manner, we can be sure that Oxford University Press in Pakistan would have felt the wrath of Muslims there.

Modern liberals in the West will find Mohammed's behaviour in this book shocking, for he is not a religious leader like Jesus or Buddha. From *The Life of Muhammed* we learn that he sold women and children who had been captured and enslaved: 'Then the apostle sent Sayid... and Abdul... with some of the captive women... and he sold them for horses and weapons.'[65] We can see that Muslims are aware of these stories found in *The Life of Muhammed*, by looking at what Muslims were shouting in a protest outside the Danish embassy: Muslim men saying that they will take Danish wives as 'war booty' *i.e.* to be raped, to be sold as slaves, or

63 Rob Crilly and Aoun Sahi, 'Christian woman sentenced to death in Pakistan "for blasphemy"', *The Telegraph*, 9 Nov 2010, http://www.telegraph.co.uk/news/religion/8120142/Christian-woman-sentenced-to-death-in-Pakistan-for-blasphemy.html

64 In Pakistan it is not unknown for even the lawyer who defends someone on such a charge to be killed as an accessory to such defamation. 'Pakistan "blasphemy lawyer" shot dead in Multan office', *BBC News* website, 7 May 2014, http://www.bbc.co.uk/news/world-asia-27319433

65 Ibn Ishaq, *The Life of Muhammed*, 1955 (reissued Pakistan 1967), translated by A. Guillaume, Oxford University Press, p. 466. Those Muslims who reject Ibn Ishaq's account of Mohammed taking slaves, must also presumably reject the accounts in the Hadiths where Mohammed takes slaves. See http://quranexplorer.com/Hadith/English/Hadith/bukhari/005.059.362.html and http://www.quranexplorer.com/Hadith/English/Hadith/bukhari/001.008.367.html. The Bukhari Hadiths are considered the most trustworthy of all Hadiths. Muslims who claim they reject the Hadiths and only follow the Koran cannot even know when Ramadan occurs, as this is not specified in the Koran.

to be kept as sex slaves.[66] Mohammed married some of the women he took as slaves, but not all of them: after one battle Mohammed beheads the men and boys, and sends the women off to be sold as slaves, but he keeps the 15 year old Rayhanah as his sex slave. She never became his wife, never became a Muslim.[67] And when Mohammed has Kinana, a Jewish man, tortured to death for his gold, Mohammed takes the wife of Kinana as his own sex slave.[68]

We know from the fatwa on Salman Rushdie, that Muslims take insults to Mohammed very seriously. If the English translation of this book was in any way blasphemous, Alfred Guillaume, the editor and translator, would not have been made a Fellow of various Arabic professional societies (Arab Academy of Damascus and the Royal Academy of Baghdad), nor invited to be the first non-Muslim lecturer in Christian and Islamic theology at Istanbul University. Guillaume was also Professor of Arabic at the School of Oriental and African Studies (University of London).[69] Muslim approval shows Guillaume's work was highly regarded.

From this brief analysis of the core texts of Islam we have seen evidence for the Muslim attitudes towards slavery and towards sex with slaves. And again, these attitudes are entirely alien to the morality of those brought up in a Christian or humanist tradition.

7.6 Sharia Law: Child Marriage

Even those Muslims who are not considered extremists, have made it clear that they have no intention of subjugating sharia law and Muslim culture to the laws of Britain or British culture. As long ago as 1990, an organisation in Britain calling itself The Muslim Parliament produced a document where they made it plain that they put Islamic doctrine and Muslim culture before everything else.

> Muslims living under the protection of a non-Muslim State must obey the laws of that State, so long as such obedience does not conflict with their commitment to Islam and the Ummah. [...] There are laws on the British Statute Book that are in direct conflict with the laws of Allah; these relate to

---

66 http://www.youtube.com/embed/5o1FPkWWV2s
67 Ibn Ishaq, *The Life of Muhammed, op. cit.*, p. 466.
68 *Ibid.*, p. 511.
69 http://en.wikipedia.org/wiki/Alfred_Guillaume

such matters as usury, abortion, homosexuality, gambling, sale and consumption of alcohol, and the abolition of capital punishment; *Muslims can neither agree with nor condone any part of a legal and social agenda which so flagrantly violates the laws of nature as well as of God.* [..] Muslims make it clear to the State, and all sections of British society, that they do not expect to be and will not tolerate being insulted and abused on grounds of their religion, culture and traditions. Maxim: We are Muslims first and last.[70] (emphasis added)

That appeared in a section of the document entitled 'Relationship with the British Authorities'. In this context, it is of fundamental importance that we understand what allowances and prescriptions obtain in sharia law and the history of Islamic states.

All the previous Koranic injunctions and stories about Mohammed are brought together in a manual of sharia law called *The Reliance of the Traveller*. Even though the original Arabic version of this book dates from the 14th century, this book was translated into English in the 1990s, thus demonstrating its contemporary relevance for Muslims who are promoting the implementation of sharia law. If one reads Muslim forums to see what books on sharia law are recommended to English-speaking Muslims, this book is commonly recommended. From this book, we can see that the legal and moral values which are derived from the Koran, from the Sunnah (the behaviour of Mohammed) and from past judgements by Muslim jurists are very different from anything that a modern liberal democracy would recognise as valid.

The Reliance of the Traveller states that if a husband wishes to divorce his wife, he must wait 3 months before doing so, in case she has become pregnant during the marriage, even if she is pre-pubescent.[71] Here are the relevant sections from this manual of sharia law:

n9.1 There is no waiting period for a woman divorced before having had sexual intercourse with her husband.

n9.2 A waiting period is obligatory for a woman divorced after intercourse, whether the husband and wife are prepu-

---

70 'The Muslim Manifesto - a strategy for survival', http://www.muslimparliament.org.uk/MuslimManifesto.pdf

71 Ahmad Ibn Naqib Al-Misri, *Reliance of the Traveller: a Classic Manual of Islamic Sacred Law*, Keller translation, 1991.

bescent, have reached puberty, or one has and the other has not. Intercourse means copulation (def: n7.7). If the husband was alone with her but did not copulate with her, and then divorced her, there is no waiting period.

n9.3 When a waiting period is obligatory (O: [sic] upon a woman, cause of divorce or annulment of marriage), then if she is pregnant, the waiting period ends when she gives birth...

A Muslim cannot say that these sections of this manual of sharia law are no longer a part of Islam. The book was only translated into English in 1991, and it was then certified as authentic by Al Azhar University (Cairo), one of the world's foremost authorities on sharia law. Moreover, the Sheikh who translated this manual did *not* translate the section on the legality of slavery (section number K42), saying that these laws are no longer relevant.[72] If the section on sex with (and divorce from) prepubescent wives was no longer relevant, that section too would have remained untranslated.[73]

British Muslims and their allies might claim that such manuals of sharia law are relatively obscure. Throughout the 20th century Maulana Maududi (1903-1979) has been probably the most influential Muslim across the world and especially on Muslims in Britain (the single largest group of Muslims in Britain are those of 'Pakistani heritage'). In his book *The Meaning of the Qur'an*, Maududi says of the Koran:

72 See http://en.wikipedia.org/wiki/Reliance_of_the_Traveller. It is our belief that it is currently not politic for Muslim fundamentalists to admit that slavery is legal under sharia law, and so these sections on slavery have not been translated into English (note: the sections were not edited out of those editions of *The Reliance of the Traveller* which contain parallel English/Arabic text, which means those Muslims who are serious enough about their religion to learn Arabic can still read the sections on the legality of slavery). As the Muslim populations in the English-speaking world increase in size and political power, we fully expect to see this section of *The Reliance of the Traveller* be translated in future editions of the book. In the future, we expect to see more Muslims be consistent and admit, since they believe sharia law to be eternal and perfect and unchanging, that slavery is legal in Islam. As we will demonstrate below, in the last 60 years both a UN expert panel on slavery and Muslim jurists have have concurred that slavery is legal under Islamic law.

73 Because the regulations on slavery are missing from the English translation, we do not know what they would say about the legality of slavery. For that we must turn to a modern work by an Islamic jurist. See our discussion on Sultan Tabandeh's book below.

making mention of the waiting-period for the girls who have
not yet menstruated, clearly proves that it is not only permissible to give away the girl in marriage at this age but it is also
permissible for the husband to consummate marriage with
her.[74]

Maududi founded the Islamic political party Jamaat-e-Islami, whose
followers control many of the major Muslim organisations in Britain.[75]
Thus, his political, theological and cultural influence on Muslims in
Britain is enormous.[76] Those who claim that 'sex with children is un-Islamic' are ignorant of the conclusions of Maududi, or are attempting
to deceive non-Muslims. Multiculturalists demand we respect the heritage of Pakistani Muslims in Britain, but these multiculturalists refuse
to look at what that heritage might be.

We can see many examples of Muslims in Britain who are engag-
ing in sexual activities with under-age girls. We have already cited the
case in London, where imams were marrying-off 9-year-old girls, who
went to primary school in the day, but were providing the sexual functions of wives in the evening. We have seen evidence that the grooming
gangs are targeting primary schools, and that they have a liking for girls
younger than 14 years of age. In a trial of a Muslim man, showing many
of the key behaviours of the grooming gangs, he was convicted of keeping a brothel full of under-age girls. In his defence he said 'In my country it doesn't matter about age.'[77] When asked to cite the Islamic texts
that justify such beliefs, most Muslims would probably be unable to do
so. Nevertheless, there is reason to believe that these values are passed
down to many Muslims conversationally. Most Muslims could not cite

---

74 Maulana Sayyid Abul Ala Maududi, *The Meaning of the Qur'an*, footnote 13 on Section 64 on 'Divorce' in Islam, http://englishtafsir.com/Quran/65/index.html. Maududi
spent 30 years of his life on this book, starting in 1942.

75 Andrew Gilligan, 'Labour: London borough becomes "Islamic republic"', *The Telegraph*, 22 Oct 2010, http://blogs.telegraph.co.uk/news/andrewgilligan/100060304/la-
bour-london-borough-becomes-islamic-republic/; see also 'Maulana Maududi: Radical
Islam's Missing Link', http://www.pwhce.org/maududi.html

76 'Maududi has written over 120 books and pamphlets and made over 1000 speeches
and press statements of, which about 700 are available on record', *The Story of Pakistan*,
http://storyofpakistan.com/maulana-abu-ala-maududi/.

77 Paul Sims, 'Police missed chances to catch takeaway owner who groomed girls as
young as 12 for sex after victims' complaints went unheard', *The Daily Mail*, 15 May
2012, http://www.dailymail.co.uk/news/article-2144295/Police-missed-chances-bring-
paedophile-takeaway-own er-justice-complaints-girls-young-12-acted-upon.html

where the Koran mandates that they eat halal food, or that women should wear a hijab or burka, but most Muslims will still say these things are mandatory and are an essential part of Islam.

7.7 Sharia Law: Legality of Slavery

After the first edition of *Easy Meat* was published, the news media in the West were finally forced to acknowledge the reality of islamic justifications for taking women and girls as sexual slaves. By the end of 2014, even Amnesty International was denouncing these Islamically-justified slavers.[78] The BBC summarised the Islamic State's theological justification for taking girls as sex slaves thus: 'It is a depraved and depressing document, at odds with mainstream Islam, though well-researched with Koranic verses and hadiths, or reports of what the Prophet Muhammad said or approved.'[79] As we will show, the justification of slavery as legal under sharia law is not at odds with mainstream Islam: slave-taking pervades the history of Islam.

In the second decade of the 21st century, the actions of devout Islamic terrorist groups such as Boko Haram (Nigeria) and ISIS (Iraq, Syria) meant that this facet of Islam could no longer be denied. At the end of April 2014 the *BBC* began to talk about Boko Haram 'adhering to the ancient Islamic belief that women captured during war are slaves with whom their "masters" can have sex'.[80] For some years the western media have translated the phrase 'Boko Haram' as meaning 'western education is forbidden', but this is a euphemistic attempt to direct attention from the real philosophy of this group of devout Muslims.[81] In reality, western

78 'ESCAPE FROM HELL TORTURE AND SEXUAL SLAVERY IN ISLAMIC STATE CAPTIVITY IN IRAQ', Amnesty International, De-cember 2014, http://www.amnesty.org.uk/sites/default/files/escape_from_hell_-_torture_and_sexual_slavery_in_islamic_state_captivity_in_iraq_-_english_0.pdf. It appears that Amnesty published this document around December 23rd 2014. If Amnesty had wanted to bury this report they could hardly have chosen a better day on which to do this, with most of the news media shutting down for Christmas, and with the news media unlikely to want to put people off their Christmas jollity.

79 'Islamic State: Yazidi women tell of sex-slavery trauma', *BBC News* website, 22 Dec 2014, http://www.bbc.co.uk/news/world-middle-eas t-30573385

80 'Chibok abductions: Nigeria girls "taken abroad"', *BBC News* website, 29 April 2014, http://www.bbc.co.uk/news/world-africa-27206449

81 For example, as late as May 2014, it was still possible to find articles on the *BBC* website purporting to explain what the group dubbed Boko Haram stood for, without any mention that this was not the name the group gave itself, and no mention that the group's real name related to strictly following the behaviour of the founder of Islam.

education is not the concept around which this group names itself.[82] This group's true name, when translated from Arabic, is 'People Committed to the Propagation of the Prophet's Teachings and Jihad'.[83] Their guiding ideology is to follow, in the strictest fashion, the behaviour of the founder of Islam, as recorded in the core texts of Islam. Groups like Boko Haram and Islamic State would not be taking young non-Muslim girls as sex slaves if such behaviour was not found in core Islamic texts as being the behaviour of Mohammed, the founder of Islam.[84]

As the Islamic State's new Caliphate rose to prominence throughout 2014, the media had to recognise the phenomenon of sex-slavery there too: 'Islamic State jihadists have given detailed theological reasons justifying why they have taken thousands of women from the Iraqi Yazidi minority and sold them into sex slavery.'[85] And Nigeria's (so-called) 'Boko Haram' declared their support for the new Caliphate in Syria.[86] The abhorrent practice of taking young girls as sexual slaves (booty) was a behaviour which both groups followed because Islamic texts show that the founder of Islam did this. 'Once enslaved, they can be handed out

---

'Who, What, Why: Exactly what does the phrase Boko Haram mean?', *BBC News* website, 13 May 2014, http://www.bbc.co.uk/news/blogs-magazine-monitor-27390954

82 '"Boko Haram" doesn't really mean "Western education is a sin"', *Christian Science Monitor*, 6 May 2014, http://www.csmonitor.com/World/Security-Watch/Backchannels/2014/0506/Boko-Haram-doesn-t-really-mean-Western-education-is-a-sin

83 'Who are Nigeria's Boko Haram Islamists?', *BBC News*, 21 Jan 2015, http://www.bbc.co.uk/news/world-africa-13809501

84 Rukmini Callimachi, 'ISIS Enshrines a Theology of Rape', *New York Times*, http://www.nytimes.com/2015/08/14/world/middleeast/isis-enshrines-a-theology-of-rape.html:

> Claiming the Quran's support, the Islamic State codifies sex slavery in conquered regions of Iraq and Syria and uses the practice as a recruiting tool. [...] In the moments before he raped the 12-year-old girl, the Islamic State fighter took the time to explain that what he was about to do was not a sin. Because the preteen girl practiced a religion other than Islam, the Quran not only gave him the right to rape her — it condoned and encouraged it, he insisted.

85 'Thousands of Yazidi women sold as sex slaves "for theological reasons", says Isil', *The Telegraph*, 29 April 2014, http://www.telegraph.co.uk/news/worldnews/islamic-state/11158797/Thousands-of-Yazidi-women-sold-as-sex-slaves-for-theological-reasons-says-Isil.html. See also 'estimates put the number of girls still being held by extremist fighters at up to 4,000', '"Nine-year-old pregnant" after being raped by at least 10 Islamic State paedophiles', *Daily Express*, 10 April 2015, http://www.express.co.uk/news/world/569556/Islamic-State-Nine-year-old-pregnant-rape-torture

86 'Nigeria's Boko Haram pledges allegiance to Islamic State', *BBC News*, 7 Mar 2015, http://www.bbc.co.uk/news/world-africa-31784538

as a "share" of war booty, and then sold on.'[87] Some reports even stated that the devout Muslims of the new Caliphate were selling girls aged between one and nine years old as sex slaves.[88] Some newspapers reported that these islamic religious rulings stated the conditions 'when it is justified to rape prepubescent girls'.[89] If the devout jihadis in Syria, Iraq and Nigeria are expounding the legitimacy under sharia law of taking girls as sexual slaves, why should we think that other Muslims around the world have not also discussed the place such ideas have in their religion? During the prosecution of a large grooming gang of Somali origin in Bristol, it was reported that 'one of those convicted for abusing multiple victims told the court at his trial that sharing girls for sex "was part of Somali culture" and "a religious requirement"'.[90]

What we are seeing in Nigeria, Bristol and Syria are not really aberrant interpretations of Islam, expounded by uneducated people with nothing more than a Koran with missing pages as their guide. In the 1960s the Islamic jurist Sultan Tabandeh produced a Muslim 'response' to the UN Declaration of Human Rights.[91] The UN Declaration outlaws slavery, which as we would expect, would mean the UN Declaration is incompatible with sharia law.[92] In his response, Tabandeh confirms that under Islam, slavery is legal: 'slavery is a genuine legal condition.'[93]

---

87 Richard Spencer, 'Watch: Isil jihadists boast about buying Yazidi sex slaves', *The Telegraph*, 03 Nov 2014, http://www.telegraph.co.uk/news/worldnews/islamic-state/11205321/Watch-Isil-jihadists-in-new-video-joke-about-buying-Yazidi-sex-slaves.html

88 Johnlee Varghese, 'Shocking: ISIS Official "Slave" Price List Shows Yazidi, Christian Girls Aged "1 to 9" Being Sold for $172', *International Business Times*, 05 Nov 2014, http://www.ibtimes.co.in/shocking-isis-official-slave-price-list-shows-yazidi-christian-girls-aged-1-9-being-sold-613160

89 John Hall, 'ISIS's "Slavery for Dummies": Jihadists compile chilling checklist of how to treat thousands of kidnapped sex slaves', *The Daily Mail*, 10 Dec 2014, http://www.dailymail.co.uk/news/article-2867179/ISIS-s-Slavery-Dummies-Jihadists-compile-chilling-checklist-treat-thousands-kidnapped-sex-slaves.html

90 'Hotel rape exposed Bristol child sex abuse ring', *BBC News*, 27 Nov 2014, http://www.bbc.co.uk/news/uk-england-bristol-30095960

91 An English translation of this book was published in 1970.

92 We believe this is the reason why the Organisation of Islamic Conference adopted in 1990 The Cairo Declaration on Human Rights In Islam, which makes sharia law pre-eminent over any secular law, such as the UN Declaration. Thus the Islamic world implicitly rejected the UN Declaration of Human Rights. http://www1.umn.edu/humanrts/instree/cairodeclaration.html

93 Sultan Tabandeh, *A Muslim Commentary on the Universal Declaration of Human Rights*, translated by F.T. Goulding, London, 1970, p. 25.

If Muslims regard themselves as being at war with non-Muslims, they will believe they can take slaves and do as they want with them. Some Muslims will argue that slaves can only be taken in jihad, and jihad can only be authorised by the ruling Muslim (the Caliph). But individual Muslims who decide they are at war with us 'kafirs' may well believe they are acting Islamically in taking non-Muslim women as their sex-slaves, with or without the existence of a Caliph to initiate this jihad. And as we have seen,[94] there are a variety of Muslim organisations in Britain who are working for the return of the Caliphate, some organisations being able to get thousands of Muslims to attend their meetings in Britain. Some of these pro-Caliphate organisations in Britain have also been associated with campaigns attempting to get Muslim men to seduce non-Muslim girls.

There are other features of British society which indicate that Muslims do see themselves as being at war with secular liberal democracies and our values. Let us ignore the more than 300 Muslims who have been convicted of terrorist offences since 2001,[95] as they can be said to be atypical of the way most Muslims behave. Far more significantly, Muslims are 5% of the UK population, but only 0.4% of the armed forces. This significant under-representation is indicative that most Muslims view the UK as the enemy, their loyalty lying elsewhere. Al Qaeda states that Muslims are free to deceive non-Muslims in any way they like, but the limit to this is they must not join the army in a non-Muslim country.[96] If we consider how the Muslim population of Britain is disproportionately youthful, then this discrepancy between the number in the total population compared with the number in the armed forces is far greater.[97] In 2015 we were told that there were more British Muslims fighting for the Islamic State (Caliphate) than there were in the British army.[98]

---

94 See section 3.7 *2001 Derby and 'Real Caliphate'* and section 3.11 *2005 Luton and 'Real Caliphate'*.

95 https://www.mi5.gov.uk/home/the-threats/terrorism/international-terrorism/international-terrorist-plots/arrests-and-convictions.html

96 See Raymond Ibrahim, *The Al-Qaeda Reader*, 2007, p. 92.

97 For example, Muslims are 21% of those in 'young offender' institutions. 'Muslim youth custody numbers rise', *BBC News* website, 7 Dec 2012, http://www.bbc.co.uk/news/uk-20630628. We assume this is not a sign that Muslims are much more criminal than average, but rather a sign that a higher proportion of young people are Muslims. If the number of young Muslims is closer to 20% than to 5% we see how much more stark is the contrast that Muslims are only 0.4% of the armed forces. Statistically speaking, there are no Muslims in the armed forces.

98 Zeeshan Hashmi, 'Why more British Muslims are fighting for ISIL than the Army',

No doubt some will argue we are misunderstanding the idea that slavery is legal in Islam. However, in the 1950s, the United Nations expert panel on slavery also concluded that slavery is legal under Islamic law.[99] Muslims in Sudan and Arabia had no problem taking and buying slaves in the decades after 1924, when the Caliphate was abolished. If they had applied the rule that slavery was only permissible when there was a Caliph-approved jihad, then there would have been no need for the U.N. to press for Muslim countries to abolish slavery after World War II. The abolition of the Caliphate would have seen the abolition of slaves in Muslim countries. But slavery continued even after the Caliphate was abolished in 1924. Even though the very Islamic Gulf states finally outlawed slavery in the 1960s and 1970s, slavery is still going on in Muslim countries like Mauritania and Sudan.[100] It is clear from this,

---

The Telegraph, 28 Feb 2015, http://www.telegraph.co.uk/news/worldnews/islamic-state/11439401/Why-more-British-Muslims-are-fighting-for-ISIL-than-the-Army.html. There is no indication that such 'British Muslims' are revolted by reports that the Islamic State are taking non-Muslim girls and women as sex-slaves.

99 United Nations, Ad Hoc Committee of Experts on Slavery - Draft Report, 1951, p. 77. This document is also known by the title Draft preliminary report of the Ad Hoc Committee of Experts on Slavery of the United Nations. The document is exceedingly difficult to locate, and it is even claimed that distribution of the report was to be restricted. Some university libraries have copies of this little-known report. It appears that the report was prepared by C.W.W. Greenidge, Secretary of the Anti-Slavery Society, London, and a member of the Ad Hoc Committee of Experts on Slavery. According to a website which aggregates bibliographic information from universities across the world, the report was classified as 'Restricted', which could explain why so few people are aware of what the United Nations has to say about the legality of slavery under Islam. See http://www.worldcat.org/title/draft-preliminary-report-of-the-ad-hoc-committee-of-experts-on-slavery-of-the-united-nations/oclc/841410856

100 http://csi-usa.org/slave_liberation.html
Slavery in Sudan was revived in 1983, when the Arab Muslim government of Sudan began using slave raids as a weapon in its war to put down Southern rebellion against the government's imposition of Islamic law. The government armed Arab Muslim militia groups, and encouraged them to raid Southern villages, steal their property, and take their women and children as slaves. Tens of thousands of people were captured and enslaved. A peace treaty in 2005 put an end to the slave raids, and paved the way for the south to become an independent country in 2011. However, the treaty provided no way home for those already enslaved – as many as 35,000 people. Today, CSI continues working to bring these people home.

Normally the Left are obsessed with the issue of slavery, but it transpires their interest is really only an interest in slavery where white people are the masters and black people are the slaves. When it comes to Islamic slavery they essentially ignore it, and will do all they can to even avoid mentioning Islam in this context. Thus, even when a Left-wing publication like *The Guardian* does make a rare reference to the on-go-that the Muslim attitudes to slavery have persisted, despite the absence of a Caliph, and despite the UN Declaration of Human Rights saying that slavery is to be illegal.

The 1951 UN report estimated that there were 750,000 slaves living in Arabia.[101] Even during World War II, whenever the Royal Navy was preoccupied elsewhere, ships carrying slaves would arrive for the slave markets in Arabia. There is thus plenty of evidence that the Islamic penchant for slavery existed long after the end of the Caliphate. Some black historians have pointed out that Muslims took more black people as slaves than Europe and America ever did: 'even more vast millions of slaves were taken from Africa to the Islamic countries of the Middle East and North Africa over the centuries than to the Western Hemisphere.'[102] For Muslims, race is not the issue. Muslim supremacism is about contempt and hostility for those who are not Muslims, whatever the colour of their skin. So, Muslims took white people, black people and Asians as their slaves. Over a 300 year period, Muslims took more than 1 million white Europeans as slaves.[103] And as we have seen with the Muslim grooming gangs: race is not (primarily) the issue: they groomed and prostituted Asian (Sikh) girls as well as white non-Muslim girls.

Whilst the Atlantic slave trade was principally about using black slaves as labourers, in the Islamic slave trade, slaves were also used as soldiers and for sexual pleasure. Some 10th century Muslim rulers would have harems consisting of 12,000 sex slaves, but even lowly tradesmen might have a couple of sex-slaves.[104] Muslims invaded Spain and occupied that land for 700 years:

---

ing enslavement of black people by Muslim Arabs in Mauritania, the Left refer to the slavers as 'Moors', with no mention of Islam or sharia law. Monica Mark, 'Slavery still shackles Mauritania, 31 years after its abolition', *The Guardian*, 14 Aug 2012, http://www.theguardian.com/world/2012/aug/14/slavery-still-shack les-mauritania

101 See United Nations, Ad Hoc Committee of Experts on Slavery - Draft Report, 1951, p. 84.

102 Thomas Sowell, *Race and Culture*, 1994, pp. 208-209.

103 For a very readable account of this, see Giles Milton, *White Gold: The Extraordinary Story of Thomas Pellow and North Africa's One Million European Slaves*, London, 2005. Milton expresses his own shock at being able to find the original document by Pellow in archives in Britain.

104 Ronald Segal, *Islam's Black Slaves*, 2001, p.39. Similar stories have emerged about the deposed Libyan leader Colonel Gaddafi. Becky Evans, 'Inside Gaddafi's harem: Shocking book reveals depraved dictator's sexual abuse of schoolgirls he kept locked in basement below fortress', *Daily Mail*, 25 Aug 2013, http://www.dailymail.co.uk/news/article-2401702/Gaddafis-harem-Shocking-book-reveals-dictators-sexu-al-abuse-schoolgirls.html

Islamic Spain became the hub of a vast new slave-trade. Hundreds of thousands of European slaves, both from Christian territories and from the lands of the pagan Slavs, were imported into the Caliphate, there to be used (if female) as concubines or to be castrated (if male) and made into harem guards or the personal body-guards of the Caliph.[105]

This carried on in north Africa, where many British sailors were captured and enslaved. Prof. Davis has calculated that, between 1500 and 1800, more than 1 million white Christians were enslaved by Muslim slaving ships in the Mediterranean and off the coast of North Africa.[106] Slave-taking raids were not unknown on land, and in such land raids about 40% of those captured were females of reproductive age.[107] Prof. Davis observes that a minority of those enslaved at sea or on land would be sold back to their country of origin. However, this was not the case for women and girls who were enslaved, as 'many of them ended up as concubine slaves', *i.e.* sex-slaves.[108] One 18th century sailor who escaped wrote a memoir, and noted that 'the Sultan had more than 4,000 concubines...The Sultan's harem contained European slave girls who had been captured at sea.'[109] In the 115 years leading up to 1681, one writer calculates that more than 3 million Hungarians were enslaved by Muslims and shipped to the Ottoman empire, the Caliphate.[110]

Western historians are not the only people to have examined the various facets of 1300 years of Islamic slave-taking. The Indian historian K.S. Lai produced a book called *The Muslim Slave System in Medieval India*, where he noted:

> From the day India became a target of Muslim invaders its people began to be enslaved in droves to be sold in foreign lands or employed in various capacities on menial and

105 Emmet Scott, *Mohammed and Charlemagne Revisited*, New English Review Press, Nashville, 2012, p. 189.

106 Robert C. Davis, *Christian Slaves, Muslim Masters: White Slavery in the Mediterranean, the Barbary Coast, Italy, 1500-1800*, Palgrave MacMillan, 2004, p. 23.

107 *Ibid.*, p. 36.

108 *Ibid.*, p. 172.

109 See Giles Milton, *White Gold: The Extraordinary Story of Thomas Pellow and North Africa's One Million European Slaves*, Hodder & Stoughton, London, 2005, pp. 120-121.

110 Paul Fregosi, *Jihad in the West: Muslim Conquests from the 7th to the 21st Centuries*, Prometheus Books, New York, 1998, pg. 329.

not-so-menial jobs within the country. To understand this phenomenon it is necessary to go into the origins and de-velopment of the Islamic system of slavery. For, wherever the Muslims went, mostly as conquerors but also as traders, there developed a system of slavery peculiar to the clime, ter-rain and populace of the place.[111]

Slavery thus pre-existed British rule in India, and was abolished there in 1843, when the East India Company became part of the British Em-pire.[112] K.S. Lai notes that from the original armed invasion of India by Muslims, down to the time that Muslims in India began to lose power to European imperial interventions there, Muslims were taking women as sex slaves: 'from the day the Muslim invaders marched into India to the time when their political power declined, women were systemati-cally captured and enslaved throughout the length and breadth of the country.'[113] Obviously, since most of the Muslims in Britain trace their recent ancestry back to the area within the geographic bounds of the countries now known as Pakistan, Bangladesh and India, they have an ancestral history of 1000 years where women and girls were taken as sex-slaves. As K.S. Lai says, the 'interest of Muslims in sex slavery was universal and widespread.'[114] Thus we see that throughout the history of Islam, slave-taking was endemic and persistent. Moreover, slaves were drawn from every corner of the Islamic empire: white slaves, black slaves, Asian slaves. Thus many experts recognise that slave-taking has been a fundamental feature of Islam from the 7th century to the 20th century. Multiculturalists will find this difficult to accept, because they only pay lip-service to 'diversity', and will avoid contemplating what it really means for people to have fundamentally different values: deep down multiculturalists think that everyone in the world is a liberal who wants equality for all.

In the early 19th century it was exceptional for any family in Mecca

---

111 K.S.Lai, *The Muslim Slave System in Medieval India*, Aditya Prakasha, New Delhi, 1994.

112 http://en.wikipedia.org/wiki/Abolition_of_slavery_timeline

113 K.S. Lai, *The Muslim Slave System in Medieval India, op. cit.*, http://voiceofdharma. org/books/mssmi/ch12.htm. He cites one battle in 1761, when the Muslims behead-ed all the men and took 22,000 women and children as slaves, clearly emulating the behaviour of Mohammed. See Ibn Ishaq, *The Life of Muhammed*, p. 464.

114 *Ibid.*

not to have black slaves.[115] Throughout the 19th century, it was Britain who was determined to destroy the slave trade, and it was only under duress in the decades after World War II that many Islamic states begrudgingly 'outlawed' slavery. One could argue that the working conditions of many modern day immigrant workers in those countries is little better than the working conditions of slaves. The Saudis replaced the 450,000 slaves of the 1950s with 8.4 million guest workers. These workers are often treated like slaves, but they are not property and are therefore even more disposable than the slaves were. Exact numbers are hard to come by, but Nepal alone reported 265 worker deaths in Saudi Arabia in a single year.[116]

In 2011, British newspapers carried a story of a female political activist and celebrity in Kuwait, who advocated a return to the legalisation of sex-slaves, and suggested that female prisoners could be forced to become such sex-slaves. 'There was no shame in it and it is not haram (forbidden) under Islamic Sharia law.'[117] She doesn't suggest that Muslim women should be sex-slaves; the sex-slaves were to be drawn from non-Muslim women. It was reported that she had visited Mecca, and asked Saudi muftis if such sex-slavery was permitted, and they told her it was. In reports from Arabian media, she is quoted saying that the religious experts told her 'the only solution for a decent man who has the means, who is overpowered by desire and who does not want to commit fornication, is to acquire *jawari*' [sex-slaves].'[118] In fact, one can find discussions of slavery on 21st century English-language websites, with devout Muslims expressing how much better their life would be if they had sex-slaves.[119] Another Pakistani forum has a post from 2000, which

---

115 Ronald Segal, *Islam's Black Slaves*, 2001, p. 50.

116 Daniel Greenfield, 'Saudi Arabia: The Middle East's Real Apartheid State', *Frontpage*, 24 Feb 2014, http://www.frontpagemag.com/2014/dgreenfield/saudi-arabia-the-middle-easts-real-apartheid-state/. See also Jamie Glazov, 'The Exploitation of Immigrant Workers in the Middle East', *Frontpage*, 10 Jul 2012, http://frontpagemag.com/2012/jamie-glazov/the-exploitation-of-immigrant-workers-in-the-middle-east/ and Human Rights Watch, 'Bad Dreams: Exploitation and Abuse of Migrant Workers in Saudi Arabia', 14 Jul 2004, http://www.refworld.org/docid/412ef32a4.html.

117 'Men should be allowed sex slaves and female prisoners could do the job - and all this from a WOMAN politician from Kuwait', *Daily Mail*, 7 Jun 2011, http://www.dailymail.co.uk/news/article-2000292/Men-allowed-sex-slaves-female-prisoners-job--WOMAN-politician-Kuwait.html

118 *Ibid.*

119 The following discussion even pre-dates the Kuwaiti woman's advocacy, thus it was not occurring because she had caused a stir. http://www.ummah.com/forum/showthread.php?288555-Sex-with-slaves-Global-misunderstanding-or-permissible-!.

says: 'It is permissible to have sex even with a prostitute (free of cost) once you take control of her by force and declare her a kafir.'[120] We find it very hard to imagine devout Christians expressing such sentiment. But then, we are prepared to admit that not all cultures have the same values.

Given all this history, how can anyone dismiss an Islamic basis to the grooming gang phenomenon? We are not saying that all the Muslims involved in these grooming gangs have set about these activities with a systematic theological plan to take non-Muslim girls as sex-slaves as some form of *jihad* (although, if the stories of Muslim fundamentalist organisations encouraging Muslims to use alcohol to seduce non-Muslims are true, then that may well be a reasonable interpretation). What we are doing is looking at Islam to see how it is that Islamic theology and the life of Mohammed could make Muslims consider this abuse reasonable: other Muslims have known about these gangs for decades, but done nothing to stop them, and have even attempted to pervert the course of justice to protect their Muslim 'brothers' who were raping non-Muslim schoolgirls. And we think that even this short analysis can show that sex-slavery is something that many Muslims are aware of as a perk of Islam, even if they cannot cite surah and verses which permit it and under what circumstances. Since references are found in the Koran, the Hadiths and the Sira to taking slaves, selling slaves, raping slaves, prostituting slaves how could Muslims be entirely unaware of this part of Islamic doctrine? Just as children in the West grow up hearing stories of Jesus' birth and death, of chivalrous knights, of Robin Hood and Richard the Lionheart, so too Muslim children must be told stories of Mohammed's battles, of the Jews of Khaybar whom he killed, of the powerful Muslim dynasties, of their slave armies, of their harems and concubines. Just because the media and schools in Britain have robbed the population of the popular knowledge of the millions of Europeans taken into the white slave trade, it does not mean that in the Muslim communities in Britain Muslims have not been keeping this history of slave-taking alive.

A history of legitimising slavery pervades the history of Islam,[121]

Here is another discussion of this topic, which also occurred before Salwa al Mutairi acquired some global notoriety with her suggestions. http://www.islamicboard.com/importance-etiquettes-seeking-knowledge/134304880-why-islam-alow-have-sex-slave-without-marry.html

120 http://www.paklinks.com/gs/religion-and-scripture/39527-is-it-ok-to-have-sex-with-female-slaves-in-islam.html

121 A recent article in *The Economist* described the actions of jihadists like Boko Haram and ISIS as a 'revival of slavery' under Islam, but pointed out that there has

with core Islamic texts showing that the founder of Islam authorised the rape of slaves. In addition to accepting that slavery is both moral and legal under Sharia, and that raping slaves is acceptable, Islam also has a history of contempt for non-Muslims, with a legal system which regards non-Muslims as third-class citizens. Islam regards Muslim women as second-rate, and accordingly that women who do not dress appropriately deserve whatever abuse they get. Moreover, in sharia law there is a different attitude to childhood and sex than there is in English law: Mohammed had sex with Aisha, his favourite wife, at the age of 9, and this serves as exemplary behaviour in many Muslim countries to this day. These are aspects of Islam that seem to offer a good explanation for how these gangs in Britain (principally Pakistani Muslims) and in Holland (principally Turkish and Moroccan Muslims) could justify to themselves this systematic and criminal exploitation aimed at young girls. Most of what we have outlined above could have been mooted by journalists in Britain during the past three decades in order to explain the grooming gang phenomenon. Even if many or most of the Muslims in the grooming gangs could not cite texts, this does not stop the values from being passed down through their culture. None of this should be taken to mean that all Muslims are walking round abusing schoolgirls, and hating non-Muslims. Many Muslims are good people and do not follow all the strictures of Islam. We are not condemning all those people who were brought up as Muslims. However, it behoves us all to consider in what ways the very different values of Islam are going to cause conflict with the Christian, liberal and secular values of our society.[122]

---

been a 'persistence' of this throughout history, and that there is pervasive slavery found in Islamic countries not dominated by Boko Haram or ISIS: 'Islam and slavery: The persistence of history', *The Economist*, Aug 22 2015, http://www.economist.com/news/international/21661812-islamic-states-revival-slavery-extreme-though-it-finds-disquieting-echoes-across

122 In the last year, at least two cases have occurred (Bradford, Manchester) where Muslims kept young girls or young women as sex slaves.

A police investigation revealed that she had been brought into the UK by Imrich Bodor and kept in the Bradford area by him and Petra Dzudzova before being sold to Abdul Shinwary. Shinwary then sold the victim to Azam Khan, who is the nephew of Nusrat Khan. She was then married to Azam Khan in a Nikah ceremony at a Burnley Mosque on October 13, 2012 at a time when he was due to be deported to Pakistan, after being refused leave to remain in the UK. 'Trafficking gang jailed for more than 30 years', *Telegraph & Argus* 10 Oct 2013, http://www.thetelegraphandargus.co.uk/news/10731235.Trafficking_gang_jailed_for_more_than_30_years/

Note that the mosque took part in performing a fake Islamic marriage. This was ap-

7.8 Sermon against Localised Grooming

Mohammed Shafiq insists that the prostituting of sex-slaves 'is a crime Islam forbids',[123] but we have not seen him provide any reference to the Koran or to texts of sharia law to show that Islam does indeed forbid it. We have shown that slavery has been a part of the history of Islam from the beginnings of the religion until after after World War II and beyond; there are very good reasons for Muslims to think that the prostituting of sex slaves is permitted by Islam. As many Muslims in 21st century Britain are still insisting on wearing a burka or niqab (a kind of clothing that might make sense in 7th century Arabia), why should we believe that they have forsaken cultural practices which were permitted to Muslims throughout the past 1300 years? In 2011, Mohammed Shafiq was saying 'I would like to see imams and mosques addressing these crimes in their Friday sermons, explaining the Islamic ruling on such evil acts and stressing that an attack on a white girl is as forbid-

---

parently to enable a Muslim illegal immigrant to remain in the UK. A whole string of Muslims were involved in the rape and enslavement of this woman. We are left to wonder if the enslavement and fraudulent marriage were made known to the imam too.

In the second case, a Pakistani husband and wife in Manchester were convicted. A 10 year old deaf girl was trafficked into the UK, where she lived in a cellar as a domestic slave, being raped by the elderly husband.

"Throughout these proceedings not one of you have shown any remorse. You are deeply unpleasant, highly manipulative and dishonest people." At an earlier hearing, the jury at Manchester Crown Court heard that the girl, who is from Pakistan, and is profoundly deaf and cannot speak, was beaten and slapped as well as being forced to work for Ashar and his family and friends in virtual slavery as a domestic servant. [...] Ashar used his victim to satisfy his sexual desires as well as enlisting his wife to use the girl's details to steal more than £30,000 in benefits and set up several bank accounts in her name. Two female jurors wept as the guilty verdicts were delivered, and the judge said he was excusing the jurors of further jury service for a decade after hearing traumatic evidence. Adam Withnall and Cahal Milmo, 'Pensioner Ilyas Ashar sentenced to 13 years in jail for raping deaf and mute girl trafficked to UK from Pakistan', *The Independent*, 23 Oct 2013, http://www.independent.co.uk/news/uk/crime/pensioner-ilyas-ashar-sentenced-to-13-years-in-jail-for-raping-deaf-and-mute-girl-trafficked-to-uk-from-pakistan-8884843.html.

Note that Ilyas Ashar has the beard of a devout Muslim, and that members of his family and his friends were all making use of this enslaved deaf girl. Clearly many people in the community around this family knew what was going on, but did not see that there was anything immoral or illegal here. It is not clear if the deaf girl was a Muslim, a Christian or a Hindu at the time when she was trafficked into Britain.

123 http://www.mohammedshafiq.net/the-times-article---grooming.php See also http://www.mohammedshafiq.net/grooming---june-2011.php

den as an attack on our own daughters and sisters.'[124] Yet it wasn't until 2013 that mosques in Britain did what Mohammed Shafiq wanted, and this only seemed to occur because Parliament agreed that the evidence showed the grooming gangs were almost entirely made up of Muslim men.[125] However, what the media did not dwell on, was the fact that only a minority of mosques read out this sermon. If, despite decades of cover-up, the evidence finally showed that Muslims were overwhelmingly the members of the grooming gangs, why would most mosques not read this sermon? Perhaps because most Imams did not agree that this 'is a crime Islam forbids'?

We will not attempt to set ourselves up as greater religious authorities than the Sheikhs, but we will briefly examine this sermon. The sermon does at least contain the recognition of the prevalence of Muslim men amongst the grooming gangs, and condemns their actions, and welcomes the convictions.[126] Moreover, it instructs Muslims who see something suspicious to report it to the police.[127] However, if we pay attention to this last point, we will see that it corroborates our argument: Muslims believe they owe allegiance to other Muslims, not to non-Muslims. And this allegiance applies, no matter what. In the sermon it says:

> if you see something that is suspicious or you suspect that sexual grooming is taking place, report it to the authorities (social services or the police). *If you need any motivation* other than it is the right and Islamic thing do to just consider this – what if it was your daughter and someone you knew had not taken that step? (emphasis added)

Notice that devout Muslims are having to be explicitly given 'motivation' to co-operate with the police to prevent their 'brothers' from luring non-Muslim children into prostitution. Can you imagine a congrega-

---

124 http://www.mohammedshafiq.net/the-times-article---grooming.php

125 This powerlessness of Mohammed Shafiq once more raises the question: in what sense is Mohammed Shafiq any kind of leader, if no-one does what he recommends?

126 'Khutba - Tackling Street Grooming in the UK', 2013, http://www.mcb.org.uk/uploads/Khutbah%20-%20Street%20Grooming%20final%20version.pdf

127 These are both good first steps. However, we should note, that as late as 2009, the Muslim Council of Britain was still insisting that the claim that Muslims were overwhelmingly found among the perpetrators of grooming gangs was a 'racist myth': 'The BNP spread racist myths about Asian men "grooming" white girls in Keighley; that year, they gained four seats on Bradford Council.' http://www.mcb.org.uk/vote2009/stopfarright.html

tion of Jews or Christians having to be given 'motivation' to report a serious crime like child-rape to the police?

When it comes to Islamic doctrine, the two principle sections of the Koran on which this sermon relies, are 24:30 and 17:32.

> Tell the believing men to lower their gaze (from looking at forbidden things), and protect their private parts (from illegal sexual acts, etc.). That is purer for them. Verily, Allâh is All-Aware of what they do [Qur'an 24:30]

> And come not near to unlawful sexual intercourse. Verily, it is a Fahishah [*i.e.* anything that transgresses its limits (a great sin)], and an evil way [Qur'an 17:32]

At first sight, these verses seem to say that Muslims are not to look at forbidden things, nor to indulge in illegal sexual intercourse. However, we need to bear in mind, that 'legal' in this context means 'legal under sharia law'. And we would contend that many Muslim men do not regard non-Muslim women (and even unveiled Muslim women) as being 'forbidden'.[128] There is also the problem with abrogation (where later

---

128 It is well-known that any woman who travels without the protection of a man in a Muslim country will be sexually-assaulted, many times a day, even in public and in broad daylight. Clearly the Muslim men in Muslim countries do not consider such women to be 'forbidden'. "'Please God, make it stop!" British female journalist, 21, describes horrific sexual assault in Egypt's Tahrir Square after election result', *Daily Mail*, 28 June 2012, http://www.dailymail.co.uk/news/article-2165445/British-journalist-Natasha-Smith-22-recalls-horrific-sexual-assault-Egypts-Tahrir-Square.html. There are many other instances of such assaults, including Muslim girls from Britain on charitable missions to Libya, raped by jihadis there. Esam Mohamed, 'Libyan official: 3 Pakistani activists raped', 29 Mar 2013, *Yahoo News*, http://news.yahoo.com/libyan-official-3-pakistani-activists-raped-130540911.html. There are many other instances of such assaults, including Muslim girls from Britain on charitable missions to Libya, raped by jihadis there. Esam Mohamed, 'Libyan official: 3 Pakistani activists raped', 29 Mar 2013, *Yahoo News*, http://news.yahoo.com/libyan-official-3-pakistani-activis ts-raped-130540911.html. This point was vividly brought home at the end of 2015, when 1000 to 2000 men (described as mostly Arabic or North African) engaged in hours of violent and sexual attacks on over 500 non-Muslim Germans, mostly women. 'Cologne sex assaults: North Africans and Arabs "almost exclusively responsible" for New Year's attacks, says minister', *The Independent*, 11 Jan 2016, http://www.independent.co.uk/news/world/europe/cologne-sex-assaults-north-africans-and-arab-migrants-almost-exclusively-responsible-for-new-years-a6806286.html. The politically-correct media in Germany did not initially report the attacks for days. The politically-correct German politicians initially claimed there was no evidence that the attackers were immigrants.

verses in the Koran countermand earlier verses, should they contradict each other). Thus, the latest verse cited by this sermon is 24:30. However, as we have seen above, there is a later verse (24:33) which states: 'do not compel your slave girls to prostitution, when they desire to keep chaste, in order to seek the frail good of this world's life; and whoever compels them, then surely after their compulsion Allah is Forgiving, Merciful'.[129] It may well be that the majority of mosques do not accept this sermon, because they know that this sermon does not deal with the verses which permit Muslims to rape their slaves, and to prostitute their slaves.[130] Let us remember the Kuwaiti advocate of sex-slavery who we mentioned above: she was advocating these sex-slaves as a way of Muslim men avoiding 'fornication' (the word used by *Reliance of the Traveller*, when it refers to Koran 17:32).[131] Thus, as far as some Muslims are concerned, the sex which occurs between an owner and his sex-slaves is not fornication, and Koran 17:32 (the scriptural basis for this sermon) does not apply to such acts.

We contend that the failure of the majority of mosques to read this sermon suggests that most Muslims do not believe that it is their place to condemn Muslims who systematically groom non-Muslim schoolgirls, luring them into a life of prostitution. So the next time someone tells you 'prostituting sex-slaves is a crime which Islam forbids', demand that they tell you where this prohibition is to be found.[132] The case of the Oxford grooming gang in 2013 brought out probably the worst details so far in all the prosecutions of the previous 16 years. Despite that, and despite the anti-grooming sermon initiative coming after that Oxford trial, some of the mosques in Oxford actively refused to read the sermon.[133] We have to ask again: if this crime is forbidden in Islam, why

---

129 The Koran, surah 24, verse 33 http://corpus.quran.com/translation.jsp?chapter=24&verse=33

130 A Jordanian Sheikh has issued a fatwa, where he instructs Muslim men that they can rape the women who fall into their control during war. Khaled Abu Toameh, 'Raping Women in the Name of Islam', http://www.gatestoneinstitute.org/3655/islam-raping-women. As we have argued above, there are indicators to suggest that far more Muslims in Britain consider themselves to be at war with our country, besides those 300 Muslims who have been convicted of terrorism offences since 2001.

131 See *Reliance of the Traveller*, section P.12.0.

132 We think it highly significant that the 1991 translation of *Reliance of the Traveller*, a manual of sharia law, explicitly refuses to translate the Islamic laws pertaining to taking slaves and how slaves can be treated - legally and morally - in Islam. http://en.wikipedia.org/wiki/Reliance_of_the_Traveller#Keller_translation.

133 Ben Wilkinson, 'National sermon on child grooming shunned as a stunt by

would mosques in the city with one of the worst cases refuse to read the sermon? What will it take to get such Muslims to condemn these crimes? Is it even possible for them to do this without rejecting parts of Islamic doctrine (something which would make them apostates, and thus candidates for assassination by other Muslims)?

Even if all the mosques in Britain did read out this sermon, we do not believe, following decades of lucrative business, and almost no likelihood of being punished for these crimes, that such a sermon would persuade a group of criminal men to stop an activity from which they benefit sexually and financially, the victims of which activity are always drawn from a community which Islamic doctrine and Muslim culture holds in contempt. There is evidence to show that even the most liberal, most educated, most high-profile Muslims in Britain will, behind closed doors, happily cite Islamic doctrines and texts which refer to non-Muslims in contemptuous and derogatory terms. Mehdi Hasan, the former politics editor of the Left-wing *New Statesman*, and now political editor of the Left-wing *Huffington Post*, was accidentally exposed referring to non-Muslims as unthinking animals and using the derogatory term 'kafir', with no condemnation of such derogatory terms from him or his Muslim audience.[134] Hasan was not sacked when his speech was exposed, and he is still invited to appear on high-profile *BBC TV* programmes: if he had been a non-Muslim (white or Asian), and had referred to Muslims as 'animals' it is unlikely that he would have escaped criminal investigation (and probably he would have received a criminal conviction). Even if such legal action did not follow, he would almost certainly have been sacked and would no longer be broadcast by the *BBC* into the living rooms of millions of those about whom he used such offensive language. If an Anglicised, public school and Oxford-educated writer such as Mehdi Hasan will use such derogatory language behind closed doors, we can only begin to imagine the hatred and abuse towards non-Muslims with which many non-Anglicised Muslims have been indoctrinated, both in Britain and abroad. At the end of 2010, the

many Muslims in Oxford', *Oxford Mail*, 29 Jun 2013, http://www.oxfordmail.co.uk/news/10516465.National_sermon_on_child_grooming_shunned_as_a_stunt_by_many_Muslims_in_Oxford/

134 See Douglas Murray, 'Mehdi Hasan and the EDL', *The Spectator*, 30 Jul 2013, http://blogs.spectator.co.uk/douglas-murray/2013/07/mehdi-hasan-and-the-edl/, and 'So, Mehdi Hasan, can I call you an extremist (or at least a cab)?', *The Commentator*, 11 Jun 2011, http://www.thecommentator.com/article/223/so_mehdi_hasan_can_i_call_you_an_extremist_or_at_least_a_cab. See also http://www.youtube.com/watch?v=APA-PqT3QdFU

BBC broadcast a documentary which exposed Islamic schools and clubs in Britain teaching Jew-hatred and homophobia:

> It claims to have found 5,000 Muslim schoolchildren being taught that some Jews are transformed into pigs and apes and that the penalty for gay sex is execution. Some textbooks are said to teach the correct way to chop off the hands and feet of thieves. A spokesman for the programme said the pupils, aged six to 18, attend a network of more than 40 weekend schools across the country which teach the Saudi national curriculum to Muslim children.[135]

It goes without saying, that if Islamic schools in Britain are teaching Muslim children that gay people are to be killed, and that Jews are animals, then we can take it for granted that within such schools and mosques, non-Muslims will be routinely referred to in derogatory terms. In the light of such casual and endemic 'kuffarphobia', it would be no surprise if even the least religious Muslims in Britain should hold non-Muslims in low esteem.

The doctrine of multiculturalism has no basis on which to condemn such practices. Multiculturalism asserts that all cultures are equal, and that we are not to judge those whose culture differs from our own. As Prof. Barrett pointed out, when faced with the grooming gang phenomenon our society has been prepared to abandon the strictures of The Children's Act (1989), even where the advice given is that the rights of the child must come before those of an adult. Our society has done this on the political expedient of maintaining the incoherent doctrine of multiculturalism. The elites whose lives and families are furthest removed from such cultural conflicts have shown a preparedness to sacrifice our laws, our culture and our children, rather than face up to what it means to have an alien culture such as Islam growing in our country.

It is one thing to profess ignorance about whether or not Islam could be a factor. To insist that it could not have been a factor (when even non-experts can find much contradictory evidence), means the elite have spent many years misdirecting those who want to stop these gangs. The advocates of multiculturalism are the very people who should be willing and able to openly examine the differences between

---

135 Haroon Siddique, 'BBC's *Panorama* claims Islamic schools teach antisemitism and homophobia', *The Guardian*, 22 Nov 2010, http://www.theguardian.com/media/2010/nov/22/bbc-panorama-Islamic-schools-antisemitism

British culture and Islamic culture, differences which could lead to Muslim men being so disproportionately represented among the perpetrators in these grooming gangs. Instead, we have had decades where those who champion difference and diversity have refused to countenance the possibility that those from other cultures and ethnicities which form a new, minority group within our society might have some significantly different values from the mainstream. And what is society to do when these differences lead to terrible consequences, such as the organised grooming and prostituting of schoolgirls? The answer from multiculturalists appears to be: pretend it is not happening.

Does Islam cause the grooming gangs? Unless one is in the controlled conditions of a chemistry lab, events often have more than one causal component. This is almost certainly the case in complex social phenomena with history to them. Islam is very probably a necessary condition for the grooming gangs in western Europe (since this kind of criminality is new here),[136] but in an environment where Muslims are not a majority, that alone is not sufficient for these gangs to succeed. In a tolerant, liberal society, where women and girls have far more freedom than in other societies, many factors had to come into play. The following are all probable contributing factors:

  · teachers, police officers and social workers deciding that it wasn't worth the trouble to perform some of their duties, and so turning a blind eye
  · schools and social workers being unable to warn the children in their care, for fear of being thought 'racist'
  · parents being unable to warn their children because they simply did not know that the problem existed or didn't know the full extent of the problem
  · Muslims refusing to inform on their 'brothers' to the police, putting their allegiance to child-rapists above their allegiance to decent people and to children
  · Muslims, political activists and academics insisting that it is racist to point out the religious homogeneity of the perpetrators, and how the religious background of the perpetrators differs from that of the victims
  · local media ignoring the events happening in front of

---

136 We will see in the following chapter that the activity of luring girls into prostitution is not entirely new in Britain. However, what is entirely new is how nowadays Britain has an army of child-care professionals who turned a blind eye to such activities.

their eyes
· national media ignoring the common features between events in different areas
· sociologists preferring a safe, non-contentious life, rather than using their academic freedom to say what cannot be otherwise said
· Muslims, theologians, academics and journalists refusing to actually look into the history of Islam to see if there could be any parallels between the grooming gangs and that history
· feminists not caring what happens to these girls, because they think that race comes higher than gender on some hierarchy of victimhood
· the advocacy of multiculturalism and political correctness demanding that people do not judge other cultures, demanding that certain things never be said; such advocacy leading Muslims to believe that their cultural values can be transported to the host culture
· politicians preferring to brush the problem under the carpet, hoping that it won't appear again before they are next elected

No doubt all these things contributed to the grooming gangs evolving, learning what worked, learning what they could get away with. At one point in *Edge of the City*, one of the women who spoke to Anna Hall heard a Muslim man outside her home, saying to the woman's daughter: 'We Muslims are going to have to be careful what we do with you girls, as the police are starting to come down on us'. That was 2003. But it wasn't until 2013 that mass arrests for grooming happened in that area. There is no indication yet if the people who have been arrested now were active in 2003. If not, then that means many more Muslims have got away with this grooming since 2003 and earlier. And we are sure that the grooming gangs are already evolving, in response to the upsurge in prosecutions since 2009.

EIGHT
Victims of Multiculturalism

[T]hough we are living in the 21st century, some people have retained medieval attitudes towards young girls. The barbaric treatment in this case was depraved, almost beyond imagination and must never be allowed to happen again.
– NSPCC, The Independent, 2013

A S WE have seen from our brief examination of Islamic doctrine and history, sexual slavery was developed as a religious weapon, a way of furthering domination by Islam, and was employed throughout the history of Islam (slavery only being outlawed in Saudi Arabia in 1962). Slavery and concubinage have served the power interests of Islam, helping it advance, from the domination of the Arabian Peninsula to the conquest of the lands from Portugal to Afghanistan, and the lands from Central Africa to Central Europe. That slavery is still envisaged as part of the future of Islam, can be found from a clarification given by a Sheikh (a Muslim Bishop) to an Arabic TV channel, as late as 2011:

> Spoils, slaves, and prisoners are only to be taken in war between Muslims and infidels. Muslims in the past conquered, invaded, and took over countries. This is agreed to by all scholars—there is no disagreement on this from any of them, from the smallest to the largest, on the issue of taking spoils and prisoners. The prisoners and spoils are distributed

among the fighters, which includes men, women, children, wealth, and so on.

When a slave market is erected, which is a market in which are sold slaves and sex-slaves, which are called in the Qur'an by the name *milk al-yamin*, "that which your right hands possess" [Qur'an 4:24]. This is a verse from the Qur'an which is still in force, and has not been abrogated. The *milk al-yamin* are the sex-slaves. You go to the market, look at the sex-slave, and buy her. She becomes like your wife, (but) she doesn't need a (marriage) contract or a divorce like a free woman, nor does she need a *wali*. All scholars agree on this point–there is no disagreement from any of them.[1]

For all their blather about 'diversity', multiculturalists do not like to face the consequences which follow from other cultures having different histories and different values from those which obtain in modern Western Europe. The slave-trade was but a small part of the history of Christian Europe (beginning in Iberia in the 15th century, in all likelihood an institution acquired anew, following 700 years of enforced Islamisation endured by the Portuguese and Spanish, before the Reconquista by Christians).[2] Within 300 years of the start of the Atlantic slave trade, Christians in Europe started to bring the slave trade to an end. And it was devout Christians who set about ending this 400 year return of slav-

---

1 'Video: Shaykh al-Huwayni: "When I want a sex slave, I just go to the market and choose the woman I like and purchase her"' http://www.translatingjihad.com/2011/06/video-shaykh-al-huwayni-when-i-want-sex.html

2 A glance at the commonly accepted timeline for the beginning of the Atlantic slave trade shows it began with the Portuguese in the mid-15th century. Much of the Iberian peninsula had been occupied by the armies of Islam for 700 years, and the Christians of Spain would have witnessed first-hand how Islamic society exploited slavery to its advantage. The first slaves the Portuguese took they got from Mauritania and sub-Saharan Africa, an area where Muslims to this day have hundreds of thousands of slaves. See 'The Story of Africa: slavery timeline', *BBC* website, http://www.bbc.co.uk/worldservice/africa/features/storyofafrica/9generic3.shtml. Note how the *BBC* is only interested in slavery by European Christians: the *BBC*'s "slavery timeline" ignores Islamic slave-taking in Africa, which pre-dates Christian involvement in slave-taking by many hundreds of years. The *BBC*'s slavery timeline ends in 1936, when many Muslim countries were still taking slaves for decades after that (many of the Arabian states did not outlaw slavery until the 1960s and 1970s). Even today, slavery is still an enormous problem in Mauritania, but ignored by the *BBC*'s timeline. For more details of the enormous, but unacknowledged, impact of Islam on Europe see Emmet Scott, *The Impact of Islam*, New English Review Press, 2014.

ery to Christian Europe. In the 1300 years of slave-taking in Islam, there was never an indigenous Islamic anti-slavery movement: it was Britain, Christianity and enlightenment values which eventually brought the Islamic slave trade to some kind of end. Yet the multiculturalists want to pretend that they glory in diversity, whilst secretly believing that there is no such thing as genuinely diverse values—the unspoken assumption of multiculturalists is that all people, all over the world, and throughout all of history, have held the same beliefs as western European liberals of the last 50 years. Those who honestly subscribe to the moral relativism of multiculturalism should simply state: slavery is wrong in the context of Western culture, but not in the context of Islamic culture. They should admit they have abandoned any belief in universal human values, and that those who encounter Muslims in Britain should simply be prepared to adopt a position of subjugation as mandated by Islam.

Modern multiculturalism has been a short-sighted and cowardly doctrine, designed to suppress the conflicts between value systems of different cultures. It has meant that for 20 to 50 years, there has been mounting pressure (driven by a metropolitan elite[3] who mostly live in middle-class, monocultural, Anglophone enclaves) to suppress any signs of the cultural conflict between the host culture and some antagonistic minority cultures. In the context of the suppression of information and inaction on the grooming gangs, thousands of innocent schoolgirls have had their lives ruined, ruined in ways that most British people thought ended in the distant past. These schoolgirls were sacrificed so that the middle-class, monocultural elite did not have to entertain the disturbing idea that some cultures think that slavery is legitimate, or that a 50 year

---

3 Some people object to the concept that there is 'an elite' in modern democracies, groupings of people with disproportionate influence on politics and society, whose interests diverge wildly from the interests of the majority of citizens. Let us simply point out the wide number of books on this topic over the last century or so (frequently from a Left-wing viewpoint). Robert Michels, *Political Parties: A Sociological Study of the Oligarchical Tendencies of Modern Democracy* [1915], New York, 1952; James Burnham, *The Managerial Revolution*, New York, 1941; C. Wright Mills, *The Power Elite*, New York, 1956; Christopher Lasch, *The Revolt of the Elites and the Betrayal of Democracy*, New York, 1995; Richard L. Zweigenhaft & G. William Domhoff, *Diversity in the Power Elite*, Lanham, 2006; Peter Oborne, *The Political Class*, London, 2007. Burnham's book of 1941 was to serve as the inspiration for Orwell's dystopian *1984*. The idea of an elite who make democracies more like oligarchies is an idea so little-discussed these days that when Oborne's book came out in 2007, it was as if what he was saying was entirely new. Sowell's book on the Anointed is also germane to the discussion of the modern elites. The idea that the elite is simply made up of 'Right-wing Jewish bankers' is useless in understanding how society works.

old man having sex with a 9 year old girl is an act of piety.

In October 2010, Angela Merkel, the German Prime Minister announced that multiculturalism was dead.[4] Within 4 months, the British Prime Minister and the French President had joined her in announcing that in their countries too, it was now recognised that multiculturalism was a failed doctrine.[5] What was the British Prime Minister promoting as the core set of values, which all groups in Britain were expected to support?

> Do they believe in universal human rights – including for women and people of other faiths? Do they believe in equality of all before the law? Do they believe in democracy and the right of people to elect their own government? Do they encourage integration or separatism?[6]

Essentially, Cameron was claiming that there were Islamic groups in Britain who opposed the values enshrined in the UN Declaration of Human Rights,[7] and that these groups must no longer receive state aid nor must the organs of the state accord them any status as representatives of the beliefs of Muslims. Does Cameron not know that the Cairo Declaration of Human Rights in Islam, puts sharia law above everything?[8] We sincerely doubt that any government agency is going to go through

---

4 Kate Connelly, 'Angela Merkel declares death of German multiculturalism', *The Guardian*, 17 Oct 2010, http://www.theguardian.com/world/2010/oct/17/angela-merkel-germany-multiculturalism-failures

5 'Nicolas Sarkozy joins David Cameron and Angela Merkel view that multiculturalism has failed', *Daily Mail*, 11 Feb 2011, http://www.dailymail.co.uk/news/article-1355961/Nicolas-Sarkozy-joins-David-Cameron-Angela-Merkel-view-multiculturalism-failed.html

6 Prime Minister David Cameron's speech to the Munich Security Conference, 5 Feb. 2011, http://webarchive.nationalarchives.gov.uk/20130109092234/http://number10.gov.uk/news/pms-speech-at-munich-security-conference/

7 http://www.un.org/en/documents/udhr/

8 The Cairo Declartion consists of 25 articles http://www1.umn.edu/humanrts/instree/cairodeclaration.html. The last 2 articles put sharia law above everything, including the preceding 23 articles.

    ARTICLE 24: All the rights and freedoms stipulated in this Declaration are subject to the Islamic Shari'ah.

    ARTICLE 25: The Islamic Shari'ah is the only source of reference for the explanation or clarification of any of the articles of this Declaration.

Thus, for most Muslim organisations, there are no human rights except what is found in sharia law (including the legality of slavery).

each item of the UN Declaration of Human Rights and ask each Muslim organisation to avow support for each Article before giving them state largesse. And if they did do this, the government would probably find that only a small minority of Islamic organisations would be eligible for government subsidies. One survey found that about one quarter of British Muslims would admit that those Muslims who choose another religion should be killed.[9]

Cameron made a distinction between Islam and 'Islamist Extremism'. It seems he believes there are moderate Islamists, 'people who may reject violence, but who accept various parts of the extremist worldview.'[10] Despite these distinctions, in Britain Left-wing politicians and Muslim organisations took the Prime Minister's announcement as an attack on Islam and on Muslim enclaves within non-Muslim countries.[11] As proof of his belief in the compatibility of Islam with liberal democracy, Cameron told his audience to look at what was happening in Tunisia and Egypt. When Cameron made this speech, these upheavals across the Middle East were being called 'the Arab Spring' by journalists, politicians and experts (they were thus implying, day after day, that the events were analogous to the Praque Spring, where gradual liberalisation was crushed by the Soviet Union). In the subsequent years, with the pro-Caliphate, Nazi-inspired[12] Muslim Brotherhood coming to power in Egypt, these same journalists and experts have quietly dropped any mention of 'the Arab Spring', in the realisation that their optimism was built on nothing, but with no acknowledgement concerning the rash naïveté with which they mis-characterised those events. We wonder if Cameron still believes that the bloodshed and subsequent coup in Egypt demonstrate the compatibility of Islam and liberal democracy.

Cameron appeared to believe that multiculturalism had itself given birth to 'Islamist extremism':

> Under the doctrine of state multiculturalism, we have en-

---

9 'British Muslims poll: Key points', *BBC News*, 29 Jan 2007, http://news.bbc.co.uk/1/hi/6309983.stm

10 Prime Minister David Cameron's speech to the Munich Security Conference, *op. cit.*

11 See 'State multiculturalism has failed, says David Cameron', *BBC News* website, 5 Feb 2011, http://www.bbc.co.uk/news/uk-politics-12371994. It seems that they do not accept his view that a distinction can be drawn between Islam and Islamism.

12 See Ishak Musa Husaini, *The Moslem Brethren - the Greatest of Islamic Movements*, Beirut, 1956, p. 33, p. 91. See also Brigette Marachal, *The Muslim Brothers in Europe - Roots and Discourse*, Leiden, 2008, p. 24.

couraged different cultures to live separate lives, apart from each other and apart from the mainstream. We've failed to provide a vision of society to which they feel they want to belong. We've even tolerated these segregated communities behaving in ways that run completely counter to our values... this all leaves some young Muslims feeling rootless. And the search for something to belong to and something to believe in can lead them to this extremist ideology.[13]

However, since violent 'Islamist' organisations like the Muslim Brotherhood (which seeks to restore the Caliphate) have been in existence in Egypt since 1928, it seems unlikely that this anti-democratic, theocratic totalitarianism[14] can be laid at the door of weak-minded western liberals. There was no mention of 'multiculturalism' in Britain until the 1980s at the earliest.[15] By the end of that decade we had the Rushdie Affair, with Muslims marching around, threatening to kill those who criticised Islam. Muslims and Sikhs were reproducing the 'communal violence' seen in India at the start of the 20th century. It was in response to these un-British forms of behaviour that the metropolitan elite set about propounding the doctrine of multiculturalism. The outlawing of female genital mutilation in 1985 shows that there was no conception of multiculturalism at that time, as there was still some naïve hope that Muslims would respect the law of the land (it is thought there are now over 100,000 females in the UK who have endured FGM, without one single conviction of the parents). Multiculturalism did not produce Islamic extremism, but once Islamic extremism manifested itself in Britain in the 1980s and beyond, then multiculturalism was extended to protect Islam.

In his speech, it appears that Cameron is not opposed to Islam or Islamism *per se*, only to Islamist extremism *i.e.* those Islamists who seek to use violence to destroy democracy and human rights. But later, he says that 'as evidence emerges about the backgrounds of those convicted of terrorist offences, it is clear that many of them were initially influenced

13 Prime Minister David Cameron's speech to the Munich Security Conference, *op. cit.*

14 Ishak Musa Husaini, *The Moslem Brethren - the Greatest of Islamic Movements*, Beirut, 1956, pp. 41, 44, 63, 95.

15 From the contents of The British Library catalogue, books with the word 'multiculturalism' in the title did not start to appear until the 1970s, and the first 30 such books published all related to Canada. A search of a database archive of articles from *The Times*, dating back to 1985, did not find the occurrence of the word 'multiculturalism' until 1987.

by what some have called "non-violent extremists", and they then took those radical beliefs to the next level by embracing violence.'[16] Cameron made no attempt to quantify the proportion of Muslims in Britain who can be considered to be 'Islamists.' Of course, not all immigrants and not all Muslim immigrants have sought to destroy the western democracies which had given them citizenship, but significant numbers of Muslim immigrants wanted to subvert the secular state, with around 40% of Muslims admitting to wanting sharia law.[17] In 2003, the European Court of Human Rights ruled that sharia law is 'incompatible with the fundamental principles of democracy.'[18] We can thus conclude that at least 40% of British Muslims are Islamists: sharia law contains instructions on how to pray, how to conduct divorce, that anyone who leaves Islam must be killed,[19] and how to run a country in a discriminatory and non-democratic way.[20]

In announcing the death of 'state multiculturalism', the British Prime Minister was really just proposing that government organisations stop providing money to the Muslim groups who advocate the destruction of democracy and human rights: 'fail these tests and the presumption should be not to engage with organisations – so, no public money, no sharing of platforms with ministers at home.'[21] He was not proposing any positive project that would undo the damage of 30 years of islami-

---

16 Prime Minister David Cameron's speech to the Munich Security Conference, *op. cit.*

17 See 'The latest WikiLeaks revelation: 1 in 3 British Muslim students back killing for Islam and 40% want Sharia law', *Daily Mail*, 22 Dec 2010, http://www.dailymail.co.uk/news/article-1340599/WikiLeaks-1-3-British-Muslim-students-killing-Islam-40-want-Sharia-law.html and 'British Muslims poll: Key points', *BBC News* website, 29 Jan 2007 http://news.bbc.co.uk/1/hi/6309983.stm If rather than asking British Muslims if they want sharia law, the question was broken down into individual policies such as 'do you want to see homosexuality criminalised', the proportion of Muslims who want to enact such instances of sharia law rises to 61% to 71%. The full survey, on which that BBC summary is based, contains some shocking details.

18 See p.21 of Annual Report 2003, European Court of Human Rights, http://www.echr.coe.int/Documents/Annual_report_2003_ENG.pdf

19 See section f1.3 of *Reliance of the Traveller*.

20 Section o25.3 of *Reliance of the Traveller* states that in an Islamic state a non-Muslim cannot be the ruler. The vast majority of people in Britain would denounce any political party that said 'only a white man can be the Prime Minister', yet mostly the media in Britain are silent about the sheer number of Muslim organisations agitating for sharia law.

21 Prime Minister David Cameron's speech to the Munich Security Conference, *op. cit.* Incredibly, Cameron seems to be leaving the door ajar for the funding of a Muslim group who fails these tests, but can argue a case for receiving public money.

sation, the damage of 30 years of multiculturalism. To Cameron, the failure of multiculturalism is to be remedied by cutting off the funding to 'Islamist' organisations who seek to subvert democracy, and beyond that, he has no vision: 'instead of encouraging people to live apart, we need a clear sense of shared national identity that is open to everyone.'[22] In the following years there has been no sign that his government had any positive project in mind. In giving examples of this 'shared national identity', he suggested that it was important for immigrants to be able to speak English (yet almost all of the more than 300 Muslims convicted of terrorist offences in Britain since 2001[23] spoke English, and as if to prove to Cameron that this wasn't the problem, a few months after his speech, a Muslim student who was predicted to achieve a first class degree in English from a top University, attempted to assassinate a British MP in his own office).[24]

In Britain, multiculturalism was never announced as an official policy. There was never any national debate about what this doctrine meant, what problems it was intended to solve, or what would constitute criteria for assessing the success or failure of the project. No political party put it forward as an electoral pledge, it was never something that the people voted for, or on which we were even asked our opinion. Instead, it was often simply announced that 'we live in a multicultural society', with the implication being that we had better just get on with muddling through whatever problems arose from this. Political leaders across Europe have still not put forward any plan to rectify the consequences of this failed, undemocratic experiment. The state might not be going to fund and advocate multiculturalism, but the conflicts and damage caused by the clash of values between an unchanging, totalitarian 7th century desert religion and a modern liberal democracy are not going to just disappear, they are just going to intensify.

History will no doubt look back on turn-of-the-century Europe with incredulity: that the politicians of liberal democracies had spent 30 years facilitating 'Islamist' groups, encouraging groups of first, second and third generation immigrants to propound an ideology that sought to destroy the very countries which had given them the privilege of cit-

---

22 *Ibid.*

23 https://www.mi5.gov.uk/home/the-threats/terrorism/international-terrorism/international-terrorist-plots/arrests-and-convictions.html

24 Vikram Dodd, 'Stephen Timms attacker faces sentencing for attempted murder', *The Guardian*, 3 Nov 2010, http://www.theguardian.com/uk/2010/nov/03/stephen-timms-attack-sentencing

izenship, countries which had accorded equal rights (and sometimes given preferential treatment) to these immigrants. We do not see any sign that the media, academics, politicians or religious leaders have any inkling of the scale of the problem, nor do they show any determination to remedy their lack of understanding, never mind resolve the incoherence of multiculturalism. The stupidity, incoherence and short-termism of multiculturalism is laid bare by several decades in which the lives of thousands of schoolgirls have been ruined, vulnerable and innocent children left in ignorance of the dangers posed by the grooming gangs. Rather than risk offending the community who shielded the grooming gangs, schools did not even show the educational film specifically made to enable the schoolgirls to protect themselves. These schoolgirls' lives were sacrificed in order to pretend that multiculturalism can work.

Unless schools can train schoolgirls how to avoid being lured into the control of the grooming gangs, the supply of victims will continue. That *My Dangerous Loverboy* has not been distributed since it was commissioned in 2008 gives us little hope that educationalists or government agencies will do anything to bring about a reduction in the supply of victims for the gangs. At the end of 2013, following the conviction of three Muslim men in the north-east of England (and five years after *My Dangerous Loverboy* was left on the shelves), a *Barnardo's* official said:

> "This is not one-off sexual abuse of a child within a family, we're talking about groups of men who abuse young teenage girls." Ms Shepherd said one of the "great problems" is that victims do not realise what is happening to them until it is too late. "They don't see the grooming," she said. "They don't see the huge con to get them to have sex with many people at the will of the man that has become their boyfriend. They really want to believe in the goodness that actually he wouldn't really treat me that way, he wouldn't want to harm me."[25]

The only way that information about the grooming gangs and their techniques is getting out to potential victims is in an unstructured way via the media and popular opinion. A report from Bolton shows the deviousness of Muslim taxi-drivers in making contact with schoolgirls: the taxi driver asked his 13 year old passenger to phone his mobile phone so that he could check his phone was working. After doing this she thought

25 Andrew Glover, 'Middlesbrough grooming case: How big is the iceberg', *BBC News*, 5 Dec 2013 http://www.bbc.co.uk/news/uk-england-tees-25119285

his behaviour strange and got out of the taxi at the earliest opportunity, and contacted the police. She is now fearful of ever taking a taxi in her area, where the vast majority of taxi drivers are Muslims.[26] This is the kind of scenario an educational film would use to even up the skills of victims to match those of the grooming gangs. Devious adults are sharing techniques and working in teams to groom schoolgirls, and our society is doing nothing to help the potential victims become aware of what might be used to entrap them. But instead of training and fore-warning the victims, it is the gangs who have been left undisturbed for decades, honing their techniques and ruining lives.

For a few years after 2010, the police seemed to be having a crack-down on the grooming gang's criminal activities, but we have no idea what proportion of the gangs are caught up in this crackdown. Perhaps when agencies like CEOP and The Children's Commissioner start to ful-fil the job of national agencies protecting children, we will have a better indication of the scale of the problem, and can then ascertain whether or not the current spate of prosecutions is anything more than a drop in the ocean. That The Children's Commissioner's final report on gangs who abuse children came out at the end of 2013, yet contains almost nothing about the Muslim grooming gangs, suggests that the central agencies already think that the outrage over these grooming gangs is dying down.[27] If this is true, then we can expect to see the number of prosecutions fall in coming years. However, seeing how the national media repudiated the attempt to single out Rotherham as a unique case, there is some hope that pressure on national agencies and politicians can be maintained. We can be sure that Muslim organisations and their Left-wing allies are doing all they can to return to the days when people were too afraid of transgressing political correctness to speak about the grooming gangs. We have no Dr. Barnardo, no W.T. Stead.

It is clear from the Parliamentary report, that the politicians have

26 'Taxi driver who "tricked 13-year-old girl into giving him her phone number" loses licence appeal', *The Bolton News*, 30 Oct 2013, http://www.theboltonnews. co.uk/news/10772703.Taxi_driver_who tricked_13_year_old_girl_into_giving_ him_her_phone_number loses_licence_appeal/. It is disgraceful that national police agencies leave these young victims to work out for themselves what pleasantry might lead to a live of misery.

27 In The Children's Commissioner 'interim report' of 2012, by far the largest number of victims were victims of localised grooming. See "'I thought I was the only one. The only one in the world": The Office of The Children's Commissioner's Inquiry into Child Sexual Exploitation In Gangs and Groups', Nov 2012, http://www.childrenscommis-sioner.gov.uk/info/cseggl p. 57, p. 86, p. 92 and p. 96 .

no real idea of the size of the problem, and that they have tried to do little more than scapegoat the councils of Rotherham and Rochdale (until a case at the end of 2013 received publicity, who knew that police were investigating a case in Newcastle, with more than 100 victims and more than 20 men charged?) Perhaps the only significant step to come out of the Parliamentary report, was the initiative to read a sermon in mosques denouncing this crime (but as we have seen, this initiative was mostly a failure). The Muslim population will probably continue to double in size every decade, and the grooming gang phenomenon is just as likely to continue doubling in size every decade. Announcing that government will no longer fund Muslim organisations which seek to use violence to destroy our country is just re-arranging deckchairs on a sinking ship. It beggars belief that a government would ever have thought that funding those groups was a good thing to do.

By the end of 2014, the MP for the northern English town of Rochdale blamed the importation of Pakistani politics for the decades of cover-up of the grooming scandal:

> [A] culture of intimidation and closing of ranks within parts of the Asian community had mired politics in towns and cities across northern England for years. He said Asian councillors were under constant pressure from the community to "conform" and other politicians acquiesced for fear of being accused of racism, failing to face up to evidence of abuse as a result. [...] He described it as "a looking after your own" within the Asian community which other politicians had accepted.[28]

Once again we see one of the leaders of this country refuse to address the real problem. The issue is not to do with Pakistan or Asia. The grooming

28 John Bingham, 'Rotherham: politics "imported from Pakistan" fuelled sex abuse cover-up – MP', *The Telegraph*, 31 Aug 2014 http://www.tel egraph.co.uk/news/politics/11066646/Rotherham-politics-imported-from-Pakistan-fuelled-sex-abuse-cover-up-MP.html. Bearing these observations in mind, we must draw attention to a strange anomaly: in those parts of England where the greatest population density of Muslims and Muslim politicians are to be found, we have seen the fewest number of convictions for grooming crimes (for example the areas of Bradford, Birmingham, Leicester, east London have seen very few trials and convictions compared to towns with proportionately far fewer Muslim *e.g.* towns like Oxford, Bristol and Rotherham). Are the police, politicians and local media in these areas complicit in concealing and suppressing prosecutions, where Muslims hold far more power than in towns like Rotherham, Oxford and Bristol?

gangs do not consist of Pakistani Christians or Pakistani Hindus, but of Muslims from many countries and from many races. No explanation is given why 'politics from Pakistan' should be any different than politics by immigrants from Ireland or the Caribbean or from India. The elephant in the room is the Islamic cultural background of these politicians, not the country from which they hail. Many Muslims, whilst not members of the grooming gangs, were refusing to do anything to stop these gangs because the gangs were drawn from their own community. If the indigenous British people attempted to even speak about the grooming gangs, they were easily silenced by accusations of 'racism' and the threat of criminal prosecution. For many of us, being labelled as 'racist' is worse than any other kind of stigmatisation. Yet the majority of the political class, who were drawn from the indigenous community, simply did not care about the lives of the working-class schoolgirls on whom these Muslim gangs preyed. Thousands and thousands of schoolgirls were sacrificed so that the elite in Britain could make obeisance to their religion of multiculturalism.

There is no reason to expect that the majority of the public in Britain between 1950 and 2010 would have known anything about Islam, or of the religiously-justified slave trade operated by Muslims since the creation of Islam. By the 1970s, TV comedy shows were joking about 'The White Slave Trade', as if it was something that only existed in the hysterical fantasies of sexually-repressed Victorian ladies. Indeed, when the author of a 21st century book on the white slave trade first heard stories of this trade whilst visiting a Muslim country, he assumed (wrongly) that there would be no trace of this history in official historical documents in the UK. Yet the history of art shows us that across Europe in the 19th century, there were many painters who were depicting this trade in white slaves, particularly with white women as the sex slaves of Muslims. These paintings are now often characterised as being of the 'Orientalist' genre (an implication these days that they were racist fantasies, falsely imposed on the Muslim world).[29] Examples of such paintings dating from 1838 to 1925 can be found, and the nationalities of the artists included British, French, Swiss, Austrian, Polish, Greek, Russian, Italian, Czech. For 100 years there were artists across the continent of Europe who were memorialising the Islamic slave trade, particularly the trade in White European women for sexual slavery.

---

29 From the way the sex slaves are depicted in these paintings, one might rather be led to conclude that the artists grossly romanticised the conditions in which these sex slaves were held by their Muslim captors.

Artist	Period	Painting Title
J.A.D Ingres	1780-1867	Odalisque With Slave
Sir William Allan	1782-1850	Slave Market, Constantinople
David Roberts	1796-1864	A Slave Market in Cairo
W.J. Müller	1812-1845	The Cairo Slave Market
J.L. Gérôme	1824-1904	Slave Market
Jaroslav Čermák	1831-1878	Abduction of Herz. Woman
Luigi Crosio	1835-1915	The Beautiful Slave
Nikolaos Gyzis	1842-1901	The Slave Market
Vasily Vereshchagin	1842-1904	The Slave Market
J.W. Waterhouse	1849-1917	The Slave
Ettore Cercone	1850-1896	Inspecting The Slaves
Maurycy Gottlieb	1856-1879	Cairo Slave Market
Giulio Rosati	1857-1917	Inspection of New Arrivals
" "	"	Picking the Favourite
Ernest Normand	1859-1923	Bitter Draught of Slavery
E. Anson-Hoffman	1862-1955	White Slaves in the Desert
" "	"	The Slave Market
Otto Pilny	1866-1932	Slave Market

Most of the artists listed above were still alive in the 20th century. Eugene Anson-Hoffman was a particularly prolific artist in this genre. He did not die until 1955, when slavery was still legal in the Gulf states, and when Muslims were beginning to migrate to the UK. It is no surprise to see that artists from Poland, Russia, Greece and Italy are represented in this genre, since their regions in particular were plundered by Muslims for the capture of slaves. In addition to such paintings, one can also find books from the 19th century which discuss sexual slavery in Muslim countries with minimal (if any) horror.[30]

30 See for example John Auldjo, *Journal of a Visit to Constantinople and Some of the Greek Islands in the Spring and Summer of 1833*, Longman & Co., London, 1835.
  Nowadays a white slave is seldom found in the market, the Russians protecting the Circassian and the Georgian, and the French and English the Greek. When they do appear, they are generally disposed of at a high price. GEORGIAN SLAVE. This beautiful captive, who proved to be a Georgian, was neither bashful nor timid. She saluted us with smiles, severing her raven locks, and trying to captivate the spectators, by making her beauty appear to the greatest advantage. However, it did not seem to possess any power over the Turks; and as to the Christians, they are not allowed to purchase slaves publicly, though sometimes it is done indirectly, and by the assistance of some friendly Osmanli. I saw but three or four men-slaves, with a few boys, all Nubians, and, like their female companions, in a dirty, miserable condition. They were chained together, two

Further evidence that the political and intellectual elite in Britain in the 19th and 20th centuries must have been aware of the centuries-old connection between Islam and slavery can be found in the story of General Gordon, who died in the Sudanese capital of Khartoum. Towards the end of the 19th century *The Spectator*, a Right-wing political magazine despised by the Left, reported approvingly of Gordon's attempts to outlaw slavery in Sudan.

> General Gordon, during his rule in the Soudan [sic], had discovered that slavery itself was so entwined with the social and religions [sic] ideas of the people, that it was impossible to suppress it without governing the country, that all regulations against the transfer of slaves were evaded, with immense suffering to the victims, who died from forced marches, concealment in close confinement, and want of food ; and that the true slave-trade, the kidnapping and the sale to foreigners, must be stopped by force in the kidnapping regions —the object of his mission to the Congo — and suppressed in the seats of demand, Egypt and Arabia. With the supply cut off from the South, and the foreign market closed, slavery in the Soudan will be mitigated into a kind of serfage, which is bad enough in all conscience, but which is less bad than the system as it exists under the half-hearted Egyptian efforts to suppress it. All English-men will regret the necessity

---

and two, by the ankles. Having now satisfied my curiosity in regard to this much talked-of but loathsome spot, I was most glad to hear the proposition that we should adjourn to Mustapha's. From him we learned that the Georgian beauty had been exposed to sale for several days; but that no one had offered to purchase her, the sum demanded being exorbitant. Her proprietor was a rich man, and could afford to wait until some one consented to put down the 2500 piastres at which he valued her. http://www.gutenberg.org/files/27484/27484-h/27484-h.htm#Page_106
Another example of a 19th century English book which documented the White Slave Trade is Charles Sumner, *White Slavery In The Barbary States*, Low and Company, London, 1853. http://www.gutenberg.org/files/35222/35222-h/35222-h.htm. There were also fictional treatments of Muslim's enslaving white women, for example Raymond Raife, *The Sheik's White Slave*, Sampson Low & Co., London, 1895. Following several conferences, a (League of Nations/United Nations) treaty was agreed between 1904 and 1910 for the suppression of the White Slave Trade. Almost no Muslim countries are listed as signatories to this treaty. https://treaties.un.org/pages/ViewDetails.aspx?src=TREATY&mtdsg_no=VII-6&chapter=7&lang=en. Yet even in the 1960s, authors were documenting the continued existence of the slave trade in Muslim countries; see Sean O'Callaghan, *The White Slave Trade*, Robert Hale, London, 1965.

for such a decree, which will be quoted incessantly in Turkey and Egypt as an argument for allowing the slave-market to be reopened; but it does not add to human suffering, it only recognises a result which follows of necessity on the evacuation of the Soudan, and it is judged by a deadly enemy of the slave-trade, himself the only man competent to form an opinion on all the circumstances, indispensable to the pacification which he was sent out to secure.[31]

In 1884 General Gordon, with little support from the British government, was dispatched to Sudan to put down the jihadist uprising by Muhammad Ahmad, a Muslim cleric who had declared himself to be The Mahdi, a messianic Islamic leader.[32] The heroic actions of General Gordon were memorialised in statuary in London (in Trafalgar Square, St. Paul's Cathedral, and Westminster Abbey), Chatham, Gravesend, and Southampton.[33] Thus from famous military campaigns, from travel journals and from the pictorial arts, the educated elite in Britain by the start of the 20th century could not have been unaware of the Muslim trade in slaves (White European and Black African), with captive women being traded as sex slaves in markets as far afield as Algeria, Egypt, Arabia, Turkey and Sudan.

We can assume that throughout the 20th century, the educated elite in the UK were aware of the White Slave Trade, and there are examples of modern academics betraying this awarenes, discussing that when one painting depicting the White Slave Trade went on sale in London in 1875, it fetched a record price.[34] With further investigation we

---

31 http://archive.spectator.co.uk/article/23rd-february-1884/6/general-gordon-in-khartoum

32 Gordon had previously attempted to eradicate slavery in the Sudan in the 1870s. http://en.wikipedia.org/wiki/Charles_George_Gordon#Governor-General_of_the_Sudan

33 http://en.wikipedia.org/wiki/Charles_George_Gordon#Memorials

34 Rana Kabbani, *Europe's Myths of the Orient*, London, 1986, pg. 78. It is quite significant that in Kabbani's book, supposedly concerned with distinguishing fact from myth, there is no mention of the reality of over 1000 years of Islamic slave-trading. By the mid-1980s in Britain fact and provable doctrine had become myth: within a century, something that was well-known enough to bring record prices in the sale of a painting, had become 'a myth', the reality of which was contested by no-one. As early as 1974, elderly scholars of Islam in the West were pointing out that 'the anti-colonialist left... often goes so far as to sanctify Islam... to number among the conceptions permeated with imperialism, any criticism of the Prophet's moral attitudes... Understanding has given way to apologetics pure and simple.' Maxime Rodinson, "The Western Image and

could uncover more evidnce of the educated elite in different subjects betraying their awareness of these alien values. There are other examples from the 17th century onwards of European artists using pictorial media other than painting (*e.g.* engraving, line drawing) which we have not even attempted to list. And whilst most of our focus here is on white female slaves, other pictorial representations can be found of black slaves, and of white male slaves. Instead of considering what this long history of Islamic slave-taking might mean, when from the 1970s onwards the Muslim population of the UK grew apace, this form of sexual slavery was turned into a joke, or even dismissed by the Left as some kind of 'racist' Orientalist lie.[35]

By the end of the 20th century, the educated elite in universities, politics and the media of Britain were pushing the doctrines of multiculturalism and political correctness. It is no surprise that this should be accompanied by a deliberate 'forgetting' of what Europeans had known about Islam in the previous 1000 years and even as recently as the first half of the 20th century. Indeed, military heroes of the 19th century such as General Gordon needed to be marginalised, the existence of 1000 years of Islamic slave-taking had to be ignored, the concept of Europeans being taken as slaves by Muslims had to be turned into a joke. Because of several centuries of involvement in the Atlantic Slave Trade, the history of the nations of Britain and America had to be repeatedly denigrated in the media, in schools and in museums. No mention was to be made of the 1300-year culture of slave-taking found across the Muslim world and founded in the core texts of Islam. Through these techniques, the elite could maintain that Islam was 'The Religion of Peace' and could make incredible the rare reports in the British media concerning the sex-slavery by organised groups of Muslims. Thus does multiculturalism simultaneously praise diversity whilst working to conceal that such diversity exists.

Western Studies of Islam", in Joseph Schacht (ed.) *The Legacy of Islam*, Oxford, 1974.
35 Articles can be found dated 2013 on far-Left websites stating that the White Slave Trade was a myth, *e.g.* 'The late 19th century saw scares about a "white slave trade" in Western women' in 'The myth of the predatory black male and white woman slave', *Socialist Worker*, 21 May 2013, https://socialistworker.co.uk/art/33391/ The+myth+of+the+predatory+black+male+and+white+woman+slave As late as 2010, the Left-wing organisation Unite Against Fascism and the Muslim Council of Britain were united in claiming that the Muslim grooming gangs were 'racist myths'. See the election leaflet distributed by them in the months before the 2010 general election in Britain. http://uaf.org.uk/wp-content/uploads/2010/04/070407uafandmcb.pdf A page from this leaflet is reproduced in *Appendix 12*.

NINE

Victorian Values

*The age of consent is designed to protect young people from
exploitation by people who are older, worldlier and stronger
than them.*

– Margaret McDonagh, *The Spectator*, 2015

S OMETIMES we hear apologists for the grooming phenomenon
claim that child prostitution in Victorian England was just as
bad. However, when we give some consideration to the events around
1885, we have to conclude that the Victorians reacted swiftly to the problem which presented itself then. Moreover, the scale of that problem
appears to have been considerably smaller than the phenomenon which
has swept England in the past 25 years. There is nothing to indicate that
the Victorian equivalent of the grooming phenomenon was occurring
on an 'industrial scale'. Sadly, our modern army[1] of police officers, social
workers, teachers, civil servants, etc. did not attempt to eradicate the
modern-day industrial prostitution of schoolgirls. Rather, they turned

---

1 The combined force of police officers, teachers and social workers in the UK is
approximately 500,000 full-time staff. At 100,000 staff, the contemporary British army
is significantly smaller. 'British Army could be cut to just 50,000 over next four years,
report warns', *The Telegraph*, 09 Mar 2015, http://www.telegraph.co.uk/news/uknews/
defence/11449136/British-Army-could-be-cut-to-just-50000-over-next-four-years-re-
port-warns.html

their backs on the victims, and helped enforce political correctness, ensuring that the phenomenon could not even be openly discussed.

In 1885, W.T. Stead, the father of modern journalism,[2] exposed a child prostitution racket, and was imprisoned for doing so.

> Stead entered upon a crusade against child prostitution by publishing a series of four articles entitled *The Maiden Tribute of Modern Babylon*. In order to demonstrate the truth of his revelations, he arranged the "purchase" of Eliza Armstrong, the 13-year-old daughter of a chimney sweep. [...] Though his action is thought to have furthered the passing of the Criminal Law Amendment Act 1885, his successful demonstration of the trade's existence led to his conviction for abduction and a three-month term of imprisonment. [...] He was convicted on technical grounds that he had failed to first secure permission for the "purchase" from the girl's father.[3]

Let us consider Stead's campaign in the mid 1880s, and compare the child prostitution he uncovered in London with the grooming gang phenomenon in England over the last 25 years. Stead was astounded to discover that 'little girls were bought and sold for vicious purposes, and this unnatural combination of slave trade, rape, and unnatural crime seemed to justify further inquiry.'[4]

Stead's articles on child prostitution are still readily available.[5] Stead claimed that it wasn't the individual criminals whom he particularly wanted to expose, but 'but to lay bare the working of a great organization of crime.'[6] Stead saw a network that existed to lure unwitting virgins into a life of prostitution (Stead was not opposed to prostitution per se, but was opposed to the systematic corruption of innocent girls who were not making some kind of informed decision).

According to Stead, naïve girls from the provinces were lured into London by credible offers of marriage or of employment by agents of the brothels. The parallels with how contemporary grooming gangs operate

---

2 Raymond L. Schults, *Crusader in Babylon: W.T. Stead and the Pall Mall Gazette*, Lincoln, 1972, pp. 29-31.

3 https://en.wikipedia.org/wiki/William_Thomas_Stead

4 http://www.attackingthedevil.co.uk/pmg/tribute/mt1.php

5 *Ibid.*

6 *Ibid.*

are clear. What follows is an account of the activities by one of the agents working for the pimps:

> The getting of fresh girls takes time, but it is simple and easy enough when, once you are in it. I have gone and courted girls in the country under all kinds of disguises, occasionally assuming the dress of a parson, and made them believe that I intended to marry them, and so got them in my power to please a good customer. How is it done? Why, after courting my girl for a time, I propose to bring her to London to see the sights. I bring her up, take her here and there, giving her plenty to eat and drink – especially drink. I take her to the theatre, and then I contrive it so that she loses her last train. By this time she is very tired, a little dazed with the drink and excitement, and very frightened at being left in town with no friends. I offer her nice lodgings for the night: she goes to bed in my house, and then the affair is managed. My client gets his maid [virgin], I get my £10 or £20 commission, and in the morning the girl, who has lost her character, and dare not go home, in all probability will do as the others do, and become one of my "marks" - that is, she will make her living in the streets...[7]

As with the contemporary grooming industry, the girls were often drugged. Once such a girl had been raped, Stead claimed she was no longer considered a credible witness and would not be believed should she attempt to have her rapist prosecuted. It is amazing to think that with all the advances in feminism and womens' rights this past century, that this excuse was still being used by police and state prosecutors in recent years. Many of those in the neighbourhood of a brothel knew what was going on, but were indifferent to the plight of the girls. The parallels with today's phenomenon are evident. Not only were the poor girls drugged, but those who would tempt them away from their family would even loiter around schools: 'against their wiles the law offers the child over thirteen next to no protection.'[8] We have seen that in the past 3 decades, the law in England still seemed to afford the schoolgirls no protection.

One major difference between the grooming behaviour of 1885

---

7 *Ibid.*

8 *Ibid.*

and of 1995, is that back in Victorian England there was an attempt by the agents to keep within the law.

> The victims of the rapes [...] are almost always very young children between thirteen and fifteen. The reason for that is very simple [...] The moment a child is thirteen she is a woman in the eye of the law, with absolute right to dispose of her person...[9]

Modern grooming gangs show no fear of the law. They blithely corrupt schoolgirls from the ages of 11 to 16; the Victorian groomers would target girls above the age of 13, as that was the age of consent. We cannot over-emphasize how important is this distinction. The adult men who had sex with the groomed girls in Victorian London were not breaking any law regarding the age of consent: but contemporary grooming gangs have no concern for the laws regarding the age of consent in Britain. Girls aged 13 in Victorian England had almost always left school by that age: contemporary grooming gangs are targeting schoolgirls. Unlike Victorian London, modern Britain has a veritable army of teachers, social workers and police officers who should have been implementing the laws passed in the last 100 years, laws which were designed to protect these children.

Even though the Victorian grooming industry was providing virgins who were above the age of consent, Stead was cognizant that these victims could not really understand what it meant for them to lose their virginity in this way: even if it was not illegal for a 13 year old girl in Victorian England to have sex, and even if such girls were

> willing to be seduced, [they] are absolutely and totally ignorant of the nature of the act to which they assent. I do not mean merely its remoter consequences and the extent to which their consent will prejudice the whole of their future life, but even the mere physical nature of the act to which they are legally competent to consent is unknown to them...[10]

It seemed that this Victorian journalist had a far greater understanding of what this rape would mean for a 13 year old girl than do our contemporary army of social workers, police officers and journalists.

---

10 http://www.attackingthedevil.co.uk/pmg/tribute/mt2.php

The report from W.T. Stead not only has points of similarity and contrast with the contemporary grooming phenomenon, but has a direct historical connection. Whether or not Stead's journalism and prison sentence led to changes in the law may be a moot point. However, Stead does specifically address the problem which reformers such as he were facing in getting laws passed to protect the victims. As with the grooming threat faced by girls in England these past three decades, people like Stead were met with denial that the problem existed or if it did, with the claim that people were helpless to stop it.[11] Stead claimed that even imprisonment did not deter those who would deceive young virgins in order to turn them into prostitutes. For reformers like Stead the solution was that the age of consent be raised, so that by the time the men would dare to seduce these girls, the girls would be old enough and wise enough to resist the deception. The Criminal Law Amendment Act was finally passed in 1885. It raised the age of consent from 13 to 16, and made it a criminal offence to procure girls for prostitution by administering drugs, intimidation or fraud.[12] Just over 100 years after reformers like Stead suffered imprisonment to end 'child prostitution', we have witnessed three decades when the child-care professionals and the legal system stood by whilst gangs of Muslims across England lured schoolgirls into 'child prostitution'. It is as if the age of consent in England was never raised to sixteen. Remember: in 2013 when the Parliamentary committee reported on the grooming gangs, the committee felt it necessary to remind our army of child-care professionals that a girl under 16 cannot legally consent to sexual activity (and if prostitution is involved, then a girl must even be 18 years of age to consent).

As we can see from the the grooming phenomenon, seducing schoolgirls as much as 5 years below the age of consent is no barrier to the contemporary organized criminal gangs. Moreover, we can be assured that the conditions in prisons in the 21st century are far more agreeable to those convicted than were conditions in the 19th century: those Muslims convicted of grooming offences in contemporary Britain will be provided in prison with halal food and copies of the Koran. The implications of this should be clear: the situation in Britain over recent decades is of a far more serious nature than the child prostitution of Victorian England. There is no indication that the Victorian public (beyond the vicinity of a brothel) had any idea of what was going on until Stead's courageous journalism revealed it to them. Following Stead's crusading

11 http://www.attackingthedevil.co.uk/pmg/tribute/mt3.php
12 http://en.wikipedia.org/wiki/Criminal_Law_Amendment_Act_1885

journalism he organised a protest in London which was attended by somewhere between 40,000 and 100,000 people.[13] The establishment attempted to cover up what Stead had revealed, by punishing him as if he was one of the perpetrators. Would any of our heroic investigative journalists have taken the risks of Stead these past three decades? Evidently not. But their lack of outrage is mirrored across the population of the UK: when these crimes were revealed to the British public in 2004, was anyone able to organise a protest of even 10,000 people? Of course not. The establishment's efforts to cover up the modern 'child prostitution', such efforts facilitated almost entirely by Muslim groups, 'anti-racist' groups, and Left-wing groups, were extraordinary. For three decades the abuse was concealed, even when the implications of this abuse were far worse than those of the abuse in Victorian London. Victorian England did not have an enormous public sector, employing an army of police officers, teachers and social workers. The number of public employees now whose job it is to look after children dwarfs the number employed in Victorian England. But the Victorians did not have to fight a 30-year battle against the establishment in order to get this child prostitution stamped out. The Victorians acted swiftly, following the heroic journalism of W.T. Stead, whilst the British people of the last 30 years have been deceived and undermined whenever they have attempted to face up to the problem of the grooming gangs.

The public in Victorian England had a sense of shared values, and their Parliament reacted swiftly when it was revealed that these values were being abused. No-one has been prepared to risk imprisonment, the way Stead was, in order to draw attention to the thousands of schoolgirl victims of the grooming gangs. Stead suffered a torrent of vilification and abuse from the rest of the media and from politicians in the House of Commons. Even the actions of a journalist like Julie Bindel or Anna Hall pale into insignificance compared to the persistence and dedication of Stead. Throughout the history of this grooming phenomenon in recent decades, almost no leadership has been shown by middle-class professionals in the UK. With very few exceptions, the desperation of professionals to conform to political correctness ensured their silence. The abuse of the narrative of racism protected thousands of men who could systematically abuse schoolgirls. Within 6 months of Stead being asked to help prostituted girls in 1885, his efforts ensured that the Victorian Parliament took measures to protect them, measures which even Parliament in the 21st century was invoking as the fundamental protec-

---

13 Schults, *op.cit.*, pg. 174. Stead claimed 250,000 attended the protest.

tion available to contemporary victims of grooming gangs. Stead risked his magazine, his social standing and even endured imprisonment for this cause. But for decades, modern journalists just looked the other way and allowed perhaps as many as 100,000 schoolgirls to be abused and raped. The damage done to our society by political correctness is impossible to grasp.

Conclusion

Of course the majority of sex abusers are white because the majority of the population is white.
                        – Yasmin Alibhai-Brown, *Daily Mail*, 2012

I N 2013 the British Parliament finally acknowledged not only that 'localised grooming' exists, but that the available evidence shows that Muslims are hugely disproportionately represented among the perpetrators of this crime. We have seen that in 2011 and 2012, national governmental agencies scrambled to produce hurried reports, based on data which was admitted to be inadequate. The data was not available because government departments and the national agencies had been almost entirely passive since the grooming phenomenon was first encountered by the authorities (with the creation of *Barnardo's Streets and Lanes* project in Bradford in 1995). The story about what was going on in Bradford, which burst onto the national agenda in 2003, was basically buried for a decade. Thousands of girls lost their childhood, thousands of families suffered, and the grooming gangs probably made hundreds of millions of pounds in profits.

Whilst the Parliamentary report simplistically singled out the councils of Rotherham and Rochdale for criticism, it is clear that this is a national problem, and one which, having received no opposition and almost no publicity, has not only endured but has thrived. The gangs can be expected to be operating in almost every major town in England. If a

town is not already listed among those where a gang has been successfully convicted in the courts, mention of that town will still probably
be found in official reports, such as the report which West Midlands
Police (WMP) was forced to publish in 2015: the report identified ten
or more towns in that region where the grooming phenomenon was
identified, whilst the report simultaneously bemoaned the lack of data
and emphasized that 'there are significant numbers of CSE [Child Sexual Exploitation] victims that are not identified by Local Authorities'.[1]
Despite WMP identifying the problem in ten different towns in that region, our table of convictions (*Appendix 1: Grooming Gang Convictions*)
only lists a single case in Birmingham where two men were convicted of
grooming offences. This case is the only conviction for grooming offences in the West Midlands which we can find, and this despite the West
Midlands being the first place where the grooming phenomenon was
publicly identified back in the 1980s (see the section 3.1 on 1988 Sikh/
Muslim violence in chapter 3 Chronology: Cover-up to Collapse).

Given the preponderance of Muslim men among the perpetra-
tors, and given the spread of the incidents across the country, it is likely
that the only towns where the gangs will not be operating, will be those
towns without a mosque (but even there, with the national network
which the grooming gangs have established, they may be shipping girls
into those towns on demand). When it comes to police forces and social services looking for the activities of the grooming gangs, then given
the huge over-representation of Muslim men among those convicted for
these crimes, it makes sense for agencies to concentrate their resources
gathering intelligence in towns with mosques.

We have shown that there has been systemic failure from the local level (schools, councils, police) to the national level (CPS, courts,
the SOCA agencies, The Children's Commissioner, Parliament and
even children's charities like *Barnardo's*). The failure can be attributed
to political correctness, used to protect the incoherent doctrine of multiculturalism, which meant that individuals and organisations felt they
would be persecuted by allegations of 'racism' if they treated Muslim
(Asian) offenders the same way they would treat offenders who were
Caucasian. Even academics, who supposedly have the freedom to say
what is otherwise taboo in society, have shown that they were reluctant
to investigate and write about these grooming gangs. And when the evidence of their research supported the view that Muslim men were vastly

---

1 Child Sexual Exploitation Problem Profile, Oct 2014, http://foi.west-midlands.police.
uk/wp-content/uploads/2015/04/724_ATTACHMENT_011.pdf, p. 8.

over-represented amongst those involved, the ideological blinkers of academics meant they had to reject the evidence.

For a decade or more, the actions of Muslim organisations and Left-wing activists ensured that this problem could not be spoken about, let alone tackled in any extensive way. The silence of journalists (with a few honourable exceptions), ensured that the gangs continued to operate unhindered. We think it likely that *Barnardo's* were instrumental in SOCA commissioning the educational video *My Dangerous Loverboy* in 2008, but political correctness ensured that this video could not serve the intended function of warning schoolgirls about the insidious techniques of the grooming gangs, a danger which lurked outside the school gates, at takeaway restaurants, in shopping malls, bus stations and taxi ranks.

From the earliest reports in 1988 until the creation of the English Defence League in 2009, nothing seemed to motivate police forces to tackle the grooming gangs. In the 11 years to 2009 there were less than 20 convictions for what can be classified as 'localised grooming', but in the 5 years starting in 2009, there were around 140 convictions for 'localised grooming'. The rate has increased from an average of 1 conviction every 6 months, to an average of 30 convictions every 6 months. Some of the largest grooming cases so far are currently pending trial: more than 50 different gangs have been identified and are facing prosecution, which would typically mean another 150 perpetrators could be imprisoned in the next few years. In 2010 highly regarded Muslim organisations were still able to dismiss the grooming phenomenon as 'a racist myth'. Such claims went unchallenged by the news media, academics, child-care professionals, children's charities, government departments and even those individual MPs in whose constituencies the gangs were wrecking lives.

We cannot say with any certainty what brought about this change: was it the formation of the EDL in 2009 and the scores of protests they undertook in the subsequent years, or was it the 2008 *Panorama* documentary? It is hard to find any other significant events between 2004 and 2010 which could have brought about this change. As we have pointed out, the *Panorama* documentary was largely allusive when it came to identifying Muslims ('Asians') as being connected to this form of criminality, and after the programme was broadcast it merited no more than a tangential remark in the House of Lords. Whilst Andrew Norfolk's 2011 analysis is credited by the Parliamentary inquiry as being pivotal, that analysis was written after he had reported on an EDL demonstration in the summer of 2010 and after the rate of prosecutions had already started to increase.[2] We have no doubt that the number of prosecutions and the rate of conviction will continue to increase in the coming years. But if the issue falls off the national agenda, then these prosecutions will probably tail off. It will be in the interests of Muslim groups and multiculturalists to return to claiming that the grooming gangs are a racist myth.

What we believe is required is a full-scale Public Inquiry. The country needs to know the true scale of the problem. Just a few years ago, CROP were estimating that there were 10,000 victims. When the first edition of *Easy Meat* was published, people greeted this estimate with disbelief. But by 2014 the Association of Chief Police Officers were stating that, each year alone, there were considerably more than this number of victims. The Member of Parliament for Rotherham, the borough apparently being scapegoated, has suggested that there might be as many as 1 million victims nationally. Assuming that what occurred in Rotherham was not much different from what was occurring in Rochdale, Bradford, Oxford, Birmingham, etc. then even simple arithmetic would lead one to conclude that 100,000 victims was easily within the bounds of possibility. How could a child-care scandal so large have been concealed across so many towns and so many agencies for so many decades? A Public Inquiry was held into journalists hacking into the mobile phone voicemails of celebrities and politicians: isn't it more of a scandal that, for decades, an army of state-funded employees ignored the systematic rape of schoolgirls, with barely a whimper from journalists? After all the research we have undertaken into this phenomenon, even we find the scale of this scandal to be mind-boggling in its potential implications.

This Public Inquiry must look into the failures of national agencies, child-care charities, and academics to study this problem. The Inquiry must look into what police forces knew and when they knew these things. Is it true that Lancashire Police knew about grooming gang activities in the 1970s? How much information did they have, and how credible was it? Why has the problem of the grooming of Sikh girls by these gangs been kept off the national agenda from 1988 to 2013? Did Islamic fundamentalist organisations encourage Muslim men to go out and deceive and groom non-Muslim women? Who is responsible for the educational film *My Dangerous Loverboy* never being shown to its intended audience? Did some teachers' unions play a part in preventing

2 See *Appendix 2: Grooming Gang Chronology*.

schoolgirls from being taught about this threat, or was it local authorities who ruled that the schoolgirls must not be warned? Why would only a fraction of mosques read the sermon condemning grooming gangs? Which government departments knew about the grooming gangs but failed to do anything about this problem? We know that the Home Office was party to many secret studies of girls being groomed. The Inquiry must consider the role that multiculturalism and political correctness have played in this, 'the biggest child protection scandal of our time'. Were Muslims being misled into believing that they could practise the morality of the Dark Ages enshrined in the Koran and books of sharia law, on the assumption that they would never be punished for such values coming into conflict with our legal system? The Inquiry needs to investigate how the guidance of The Children's Act (1989) has been ignored. It needs to consider how it could be that the majority of Local Safeguarding Children Boards were not implementing statutory provisions, and nobody noticed this until the grooming gang phenomenon finally became impossible to ignore after 2009. Moreover, it needs to investigate why trial procedures recommended in the 1990s have still not been implemented.

People might want to criticise this book for only focussing on the Muslim grooming gangs. We have no fear of such criticism. National agencies like the Serious Organised Crime Agency, the Child Exploitation and Online Protection Centre, and the UK Human Trafficking Centre should have been focussing on this criminality, instead of just focussing on the forms of child-sexual exploitation that were not controversial. We have felt the need to write this book because of their failings in this area. We have no doubt that experts in this field were better suited to write this book than we are, but we will offset any failings of ours against their failure to even approach the subject.

The evidence that the gangs were predominantly Muslim can be traced back to the work of CROP, to the *Edge of the City* documentary (2004), to the *Streets and Lanes* project (1995), and even to the first recorded news story, where Sikhs in the West Midlands were provoked by police inactivity to take up violence to try and stop the Muslim gangs (1988). In other situations, governments and the media have had no problem identifying a minority group with whom a problem was associated: with the appearance of AIDS in the early 1980s, governments banned all homosexual men from donating blood, regardless of whether or not the man had AIDS, was HIV negative, or was even celibate.[3] If

---

3 Mike Darling, 'Banned for life: Why gay men still can't donate blood', *NBC News*, 14

governments had refused to note any association between AIDS and homosexual men in the 1980s, then the blood ban would never have taken place. By the 1990s all donated blood was being screened for the presence of HIV[4] and the ban could have been lifted, but the ban remained in place for another 20 years.[5] Most homosexual men were not and are not HIV positive, but that ban was kept in place for decades:[6] most Muslim men are not members of the grooming gangs, but all the evidence shows that they are the demographic group most closely associated with this problem, yet we have had decades of governments taking no action to protect schoolgirls, and decades of national agencies and the media not even acknowledging the prevalence of Muslim men among grooming gangs. In all that time when steps were taken to protect the blood supply by banning all homosexual men from donating blood, there have been no steps taken to protect schoolgirls, for fear of offending Muslims by publicly discussing (or even privately investigating) the prevalence of Muslim men in the grooming gangs. If the Association of Chief Police Officers is right, and each year there are 'tens of thousands' of schoolgirls who fall victim to these grooming gangs,[7] then there must surely be a case for negligence against these government agencies.[8] A 'belt and braces' procedure was put in place to protect the blood supply: those associated with AIDS were banned from donating blood, and all donated blood was tested. The steps which are needed to protect the schoolgirls would be far less drastic than testing all donated blood, banning people

---

Jul 2013, http://www.nbcnews.com/health/mens-health/banned-life-why-gay-men-still-cant-donate-blood-f6C10622947

4 'Tests on your blood - A guide for donors', http://www.blood.co.uk/resources/leaflets/tests-on-your-blood/

5 Perhaps this ban has only been lifted now because of the high number of heterosexual Africans in Britain who are HIV positive. Either the same ban would need to be put in place stopping all Africans from donating blood, or it would have to have been lifted for homosexual men.

6 James Gallagher, 'Gay men blood donor ban to be lifted', *BBC News*, 8 Sep 2011, http://www.bbc.co.uk/news/health-14824310. Even when the ban 'has been lifted', gay men are only allowed to donate blood if they have not had sex for 12 months. No such restriction applies to black people in Britain, who also have a higher than average incidence of HIV infection. Thus we see that government agencies and the media have no problem with discriminatory practices addressed to some minority populations.

7 'Police chief warns of more Rotherham-style abuse cases', *BBC News*, 16 Oct 2014, http://www.bbc.co.uk/news/uk-29639374

8 In a report on *Russia Today*, Andrew Norfolk also states that there was official neglect. https://www.youtube.com/watch?v=RZCQ9ZWfCuQ#t= 249

from giving blood and banning them from travelling.[9] But even allowing schoolgirls to see the one film specifically made to warn and educate them was too much: the film did not even identify the perpetrator as a Muslim, but as vaguely 'Asian', yet still it was not shown.[10] If in the last 30 years the gay community had the same power as the Muslim community and their allies, then there would never have been a ban on donating blood, there would be no travel restrictions in place, and the media would have refused to even discuss whether or not there was any association between the behaviour of homosexuals and the occurrence of AIDS, for fear of offending the gay community. In the 1980s and 1990s, AIDS was being widely associated with homosexual men, drug addicts, and prostitutes, and there was great fear that the disease would spread throughout the rest of the population, which is why the ban against blood donation was seen as uncontroversial. However, the authorities and the media seemed to have no concerns about a generation of schoolgirls being turned into prostitutes and drug addicts, with all the risks of them acquiring AIDS.

The British public may not silently tolerate the actions of the grooming gangs in the coming years, the way they passively accepted them before the authorities stepped up the prosecutions from 2009. We do not want to see communities feeling they have to resort to violence, the way Sikhs have on a number of occasions. Anna Hall reported that it was 1996 when staff at *Barnardo's*, working on the front-line of this grooming phenomenon in Bradford, suggested making a film to warn teenagers and educate parents '...the girls were white and living in multi-cultural Bradford and the perpetrators were Asian... everybody wanted to pretend it wasn't happening. All anyone seemed concerned about was the risk of a race riot if we mentioned it.'[11] This fear of 'race riots' was used over and over again by police officers and social workers in the subsequent decades. If there were genuine fears that the indigenous population would riot because of the grooming gangs, then that's all the

---

9 For 20 years the United States banned those who tested HIV+ from entering the country. 'U.S. Ban on HIV-Positive Visitors, Immigrants Expires', *ABC News*, 05 Jan 2010, http://abcnews.go.com/Politics/united-states-ends-22-year-hiv-travel-ban/story?id=9482817

10 Indeed, the film is so vague in its warning, that the Sikh Awareness Society felt the need to add sub-titles to it to make the danger and techniques clearer: http://www.youtube.com/watch?v=Kjwvo8HlqyM. No satisfactory explanation has ever been given about why this film has never been shown in schools.

11 Anna Hall, 'Hunt For Britain's Sex Gangs, C4' *Broadcast* 2 May 2013, http://www.broadcastnow.co.uk/in-depth/hunt-for-britains-sex-gangs-c4/5054504.article

more reason for decisive action to be taken to destroy this grooming phenomenon. Our society cannot brush a problem of this magnitude under the carpet. It is astounding that it was kept hidden for so long.

Almost 20 years since the idea of educating and warning the victims in Bradford was first mooted by front-line child-care professionals, this film sits gathering dust. In 2015, the local newspaper in Bradford issued an editorial, saying that schoolgirls need to be educated and warned about how the grooming gangs operate.[12] This moral outrage by the local newspaper comes 20 years after *Barnardo's* charity was given almost £700,000 for a project which was clearly related to the operation of the grooming gangs in Bradford (a project which was reported in the very same local newspaper at the time). In the Eternal Now of political correctness, there is no history: facts must be suppressed, those who draw public attention to those facts must be vilified and destroyed. The police agencies and government departments could pretend they had known nothing of the grooming phenomenon, when it is clear that what they were claiming was news to them from 2009 onwards had been known and publicly discussed by the relevant charities more than a decade before. There was evidence of Muslim grooming gangs operating in England from 1989 onwards, yet until 2011 there was barely any concerted national reporting on this phenomenon. Then from 2012 until 2014, there was a deluge of reportage on the subject; but by 2015, the media had once again consigned the scandal to the memory hole. Extensive grooming trials of Africans (Muslims), in parts of England far from the Asians (Muslims) of Rotherham, were all but ignored by the national media; such trials demonstrated that the problem was not confined to just one area nor just one ethnicity. It appeared that the tacit policy was that prosecutions would roll on around the country, but with these prosecutions only being reported in the local media. The national news media would do their best to ignore these prosecutions and convictions, focusing all their attention on blaming the institutional failure of local government and policing in one town: Rotherham. The problem had been 'contained': the problem being that the grooming gangs had become a subject of national debate, not that thousands of schoolgirls were being preyed upon sexually in a systematic way, with the local and national agencies as clueless about how to tackle this problem now as

---

12 'Making our children aware of dangers', *Telegraph & Argus*, 9 Sep 2015, http://www.thetelegraphandargus.co.uk/opinion/featuresourview/13656419.Making_our_children_aware_of_dangers/

they were during the previous 20 years.[13]

An entire generation of non-Muslim schoolgirls across England has been sacrificed to multiculturalism.[14] Every year, in scores of towns in England, a new crop of schoolgirls find some alluring young Muslim man pursuing them with money and flattery, little knowing what his organisation's true plans for them are. It is within the power of the gov-

---

13 At the end of 2015 one researcher reported on her attempts to query police and local government agencies for the latest aggregated statistics concerning ethnicity and organised child-sexual exploitation. After months of making Freedom of Information requests, she finally concluded from the responses of these agencies, that the aggregated relevant data is still not being recorded in any way that would easily permit these agencies to provide statistics required to analyse the scale of this phenomenon, a complaint made by CEOP in 2011 and by The Childrens' Commissioner a year later

> [I]n investigating the matter myself, I found widespread and continuing (despite the Jay Report) lack of any coherent recording of or response to organised gang-rape. What stands out particularly is the lack of data held by local authorities, who in almost all cases, kept no numeric data on children under their care who have reported sexual assault or rape. In almost all cases, I was informed that this information could not be provided as it would take authority staff outside of the 18 hour working time they are obliged to perform on freedom of information requests. The reason it would take longer than 18 hours to provide the data, is that it would entail reading separately through the individual files of all children in their care. In other words, even post-Rotherham, most councils are not attempting to separately record sexual assaults on children under their care, or to paint a broader picture of the problem. Police records present the same problems. Recording of ethnicity or nationality is widely inconsistent; in many cases the ethnicity of the alleged offender is not recorded, and it is not recorded for victims at all. It is impossible therefore to know just how often this happens, or how many times it has happened.

See http://www.annemariewaters.org/rotherham-the-perfect-storm-an-investigation-in-to-muslim-grooming-gangs/

If the lamentations in the reports by CEOP and The Childrens' Commissioner had made any difference, one might expect that these local agencies would by now be keeping, acquiring and aggregating this information so that it could be fed back to government, national agencies and child-care charities. Perhaps these local agencies are confident that the town of Rotherham has successfully performed the role of scapegoat.

14 News reports tell us that in England grooming is now so common, that it is regarded as normal. 'Such was the scale of the grooming in the South Yorkshire town at the time, Sarah said "lots of girls were being groomed like I was. To us, grooming was normal."' in 'Raped in a playground at 11, abused by seven men a night aged 12', *Daily Mail*, 8 Jul 2015, http://www.dailymail.co.uk/femail/article-3151387/Raped-playground-11-abused-seven-men-night-aged-12-Victim-Rotherham-Asian-sex-gang-scandal-tells-truly-horrifying-story.html. See also 'Child Grooming "Normal" In Parts Of Greater Manchester, Report Says In Wake Of Rotherham Scandal', *Huffington Post*, 30 Oct 2014 ,http://www.huffingtonpost.co.uk/2014/10/30/child-grooming_n_6073014.html

ernment to change this immediately, but they refuse to follow through on advice given to them 20 years ago by experts in the field. Instead, the media, feminists and politicians simply turn a blind-eye to 'the biggest child protection scandal of our time'.[15]

---

15 Andrew Norfolk, 'Police Files Reveal Vast Child Protection Scandal', *The Times*, 24 Sep 2012 http://www.thetimes.co.uk/tto/news/uk/crime/article3547661.ece

Appendix 1: Grooming Gang Convictions

This table is based on the technique used by Andrew Norfolk, in the analysis which demonstrated there was an obvious pattern of exploitation by Muslim gangs, based on the names of the men convicted in 'grooming trials'. A grooming conviction (not yet a legally-defined entity) is one where a series of men who know each other are convicted for their systematic actions in luring a child (a schoolgirl) into sexual activities, often leading to a life of rape and prostitution. Where it is clear that a perpetrator is not a Muslim, this has been indicated by putting his name in bold text, showing how exceptional it is for a member of a grooming gang to be a non-Muslim.

Table A.1: Grooming Gang Convictions (1997-2015)

	date	town	first name	surname	age
1	11/1997	Leeds	Mohammed	Rashid	21
2	11/1997	Leeds	Abid	Sadique	21
3	02/2005	Keighley	Shabir	Ahmed	32
4	02/2005	Keighley	Munwar	Khan	30
5	04/2006	Blackpool	Puppy	Parmar	31
6	04/2006	Blackpool	Sandeep	Chauhan	28
7	06/2007	Oldham	Shahzad	Masood	33
8	06/2007	Oldham	Mohammed	Suleman	39
9	08/2007	Blackburn	Zulfqar	Hussain	46
10	08/2007	Blackburn	Qaiser	Naveed	32
11	11/2007	Sheffield	Ayad	Mahmood	35
12	11/2007	Sheffield	Aziz	Hamed	24
13	08/2008	Oldham	Shofiqul	Islam	21
14	08/2008	Oldham	Shamim	Ahmed	21
15	11/2008	Manchester	Mirza	Baig	35
16	11/2008	Manchester	Mohammed	Ditta	39
17	11/2008	Blackburn	**Ian**	**Hindle**	32
18	11/2008	Blackburn	**Andrew**	**Wells**	49
19	04/2009	Blackburn	Imran	Pervez	27
20	04/2009	Blackburn	Zaheer	Khan	24
21	07/2009	Skipton	Mohammed	Zackriya	21

22	07/2009	Skipton	Mohammed	Taj	37
23	07/2009	Skipton	Mohammed	Shabir	36
24	07/2009	Skipton	Shafaq	Hussain	21
25	02/2010	Rochdale	Ajmal	Afridi	19
26	02/2010	Rochdale	Imtiaz	Syed	20
27	02/2010	Rochdale	Tayub	Hussain	19
28	02/2010	Rochdale	Mustafa	Arshad	17
29	02/2010	Rochdale	Mohammed	Raja	20
30	06/2010	Nelson	Azeem	Shah	23
31	06/2010	Nelson	Tabassum	Shah	24
32	08/2010	Rochdale	Asad	Hassan	28
33	08/2010	Rochdale	Mohammed	Basharat	28
34	08/2010	Rochdale	Mohammed	Atif	29
35	08/2010	Rochdale	Aftab	Khan	31
36	08/2010	Rochdale	Abid	Khaliq	30
37	08/2010	Rochdale	Mohammed	Safi	31
38	08/2010	Rochdale	Ahmed	Noorzai	29
39	08/2010	Rochdale	Mohammed	Khan	26
40	08/2010	Rochdale	Najibullah	Safi	32
41	09/2010	Preston	Mohammed	Moosa	24
42	09/2010	Preston	Faisal	Ghani	25
43	11/2010	Rotherham	Razwan	Razaq	30
44	11/2010	Rotherham	Umar	Razaq	24
45	11/2010	Rotherham	Zafran	Ramzan	21
46	11/2010	Rotherham	Mohsin	Khan	21
47	11/2010	Rotherham	Adil	Hussain	20
48	11/2010	Derby	Abid	Siddique	27
49	11/2010	Derby	Mohammed	Liaqat	28
50	11/2010	Derby	Mohamed	Rehman	26
51	11/2010	Derby	Faisal	Mehmood	24
52	11/2010	Derby	Akshay	Kumar	38
53	11/2010	Derby	Naweed	Liaqat	33
54	11/2010	Derby	Farooq	Ahmed	28
55	11/2010	Derby	**Graham**	**Blackham**	26
56	11/2010	Derby	Ziafat	Yasin	31
57	08/2011	Accrington	Amjad	Hussain	38
58	08/2011	Accrington	Shahid	Hussain	34
59	08/2011	Accrington	Tanveer	Butt	39
60	03/2012	Telford	Shamrez	Rashid	20
61	03/2012	Telford	Amar	Hussain	21

62	03/2012	Telford	Jahbar	Rafiq	28
63	03/2012	Telford	Adil	Saleem	20
64	03/2012	Telford	Amer	Choudhrey	20
65	05/2012	Rochdale	Kabeer	Hassan	25
66	05/2012	Rochdale	Abdul	Aziz	41
67	05/2012	Rochdale	Abdul	Rauf	43
68	05/2012	Rochdale	Mohammed	Sajid	35
69	05/2012	Rochdale	Adil	Khan	42
70	05/2012	Rochdale	Abdul	Qayyum	43
71	05/2012	Rochdale	Mohammed	Amin	45
72	05/2012	Rochdale	Hamid	Safi	22
73	05/2012	Rochdale	Shabir	Ahmed	59
74	05/2012	Bradford	Shabir	Ahmed	39
75	05/2012	Bradford	Munwar	Khan	42
76	02/2013	Ipswich	Surin	Uddin	31
77	02/2013	Ipswich	Mohammed	Sheikh	31
78	02/2013	Ipswich	Hamza	Ali	38
79	03/2013	Birmingham	Raja	Khan	23
80	03/2013	Birmingham	Adeeb	Sultan	27
81	03/2013	Keighley	Shazad	Rehman	30
82	03/2013	Keighley	Bilal	Hussain	23
83	05/2013	Oxford	Kamar	Jamil	27
84	05/2013	Oxford	Akhtar	Dogar	32
85	05/2013	Oxford	Anjum	Dogar	31
86	05/2013	Oxford	Assad	Hussain	32
87	05/2013	Oxford	Mohammed	Karrar	38
88	05/2013	Oxford	Bassam	Karrar	34
89	05/2013	Oxford	Zeeshan	Ahmed	28
90	07/2013	Barking	Naeem	Ahmed	25
91	07/2013	Barking	Nabeel	Ahmed	24
92	07/2013	Barking	Hassan	Raza	24
93	07/2013	Manchester	Shamin	Uddin	26
94	07/2013	Manchester	Giash	Uddin	27
95	07/2013	Manchester	**Robert**	**Jackson**	23
96	08/2013	Leicester	Aabidali	Ali	39
97	08/2013	Leicester	Rakib	Iacub	20
98	08/2013	Leicester	Wajid	Usman	21
99	08/2013	Leicester	Hamza	Imtiaz Ali	28
100	08/2013	Leicester	Bharat	Modhwadia	25
101	08/2013	Leicester	Chandresh	Mistry	37

102	10/2013	London	Mohammad	Shabbir	34
103	10/2013	London	Muhammad	Shabbir	25
104	11/2013	Rochdale	Mohammed	Abubaker	32
105	11/2013	Rochdale	**Freddie**	**Kendakumana**	27
106	11/2013	Rochdale	Roheez	Khan	27
107	11/2013	Rochdale	**Chola**	**Chansa**	33
108	11/2013	Rochdale	Abdul	Huk	37
109	12/2013	Middlesbro.	Ateeq	Latif	17
110	12/2013	Middlesbro.	Shakil	Munir	32
111	12/2013	Middlesbro.	Sakib	Ahmed	19
112	01/2014	Peterborough	Hassan	Abdulla	33
113	01/2014	Peterborough	**Zdeno**	**Mirga**	18
114	01/2014	Peterborough	**Jan**	**Kandrac**	17
115	01/2014	Peterborough	**Renato**	**Balog**	18
116	01/2014	Peterborough	anon	?	14
117	01/2014	Leeds	Mohammed	Hussain	28
118	01/2014	Leeds	Shah	Miah	28
119	01/2014	Leeds	Harris	Uddin	30
120	04/2014	Chesham	Nazakat	Mahmood	28
121	04/2014	Chesham	Ghulfaraz	Nawaz	27
122	04/2014	Chesham	Haroon	Rauf	30
123	04/2014	Chesham	Omar	Sharif	25
124	05/2014	Blackburn	Imran	Khan	36
125	05/2014	Blackburn	Zhaid	Mohmmed	44
126	05/2014	Peterborough	Yasir	Ali	28
127	05/2014	Peterborough	Daaim	Ashraf	19
128	06/2014	Burton	Umber	Farrouq	21
129	06/2014	Burton	Anees	Hanif	19
130	06/2014	Burton	Matab	Ali	21
131	06/2014	Burton	Junaid	Ali	20
132	07/2014	Bristol	Mustapha	Farah	21
133	07/2014	Bristol	Liban	Abdi	22
134	07/2014	Bristol	Arafat	Osman	20
135	07/2014	Bristol	Abdulahi	Aden	20
136	07/2014	Bristol	Mustafa	Deria	22
137	07/2014	Bristol	Idleh	Osman	22
138	10/2014	Sheffield	Shakeal	Rehman	26
139	10/2014	Sheffield	Mohammed	Shapal	22
140	10/2014	Sheffield	Usman	Ali	21
141	10/2014	Sheffield	Bekir	Rasheed	37

142	10/2014	Sheffield	Yaseen	Amini	37
143	10/2014	Chesham	**Lee**	**Wakelin**	32
144	10/2014	Chesham	Arslan	Khan	21
145	11/2014	Bristol	Sakariah	Sheik	21
146	11/2014	Bristol	Abdirashid	Abdulahi	21
147	11/2014	Bristol	Jusu	Abdirizak	20
148	11/2014	Bristol	Mohamed	Dahir	22
149	11/2014	Bristol	Omar	Jumale	20
150	11/2014	Bristol	Said	Zakaria	22
151	11/2014	Bristol	Mohamed	Jumale	24
152	02/2015	Slough	Esmatullah	Haidaree	46
153	02/2015	Slough	Azim	Ahmed	23
154	03/2015	Banbury	Ahmed	Hassan-Sule	21
155	03/2015	Banbury	Mohammed	Saleh	21
156	03/2015	Banbury	**Kagiso**	**Manasae**	26
157	03/2015	Banbury	Said	Saleh	20
158	03/2015	Banbury	**Takudzwa**	**Hova**	21
159	03/2015	Banbury	**Zsolt**	**Szalontai**	18
160	06/2015	Leeds	Zafar	Iqbal	41
161	06/2015	Leeds	Tariq	Islam	31
162	06/2015	Leeds	Amir	Zaman	25
163	06/2015	Leeds	Nasir	Sultan	24
164	06/2015	Leeds	Junaid	Rashid	22
165	06/2015	Oldham	Hasan	Ali	20
166	06/2015	Oldham	Bilal	Ahmed	27
167	06/2015	Oldham	Dilon	Rasul	23
168	06/2015	Leeds	Farahk	Younis	24
169	06/2015	Leeds	Arshid	Younis	32
170	06/2015	Leeds	Abid	Younis	35
171	06/2015	Leeds	Shazabe	Hussain	20
172	07/2015	Aylesbury	**Vikram**	**Singh**	46
173	07/2015	Aylesbury	Asif	Hussain	33
174	07/2015	Aylesbury	Arshad	Jani	33
175	07/2015	Aylesbury	Mohammed	Imran	38
176	07/2015	Aylesbury	Taimoor	Khan	28
177	07/2015	Aylesbury	Akbari	Khan	36

Appendix 2: Grooming Gang Chronology

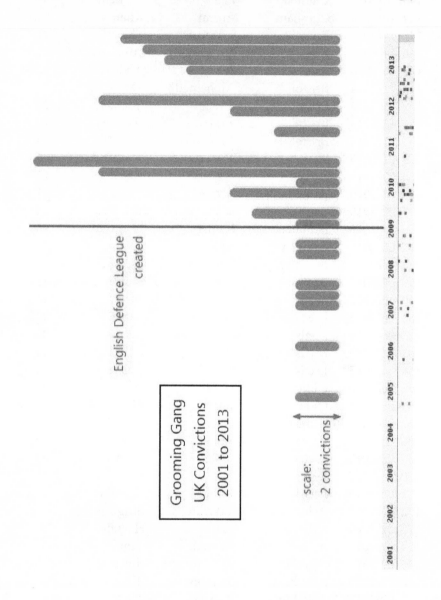

Grooming Gang
UK Convictions
2001 to 2013

English Defence League
created

scale:
2 convictions

2001 2002 2003 2004 2005 2006 2007 2008 2009 2010 2011 2012 2013

Appendix 3: Name Distribution of Convicts (to 2013)

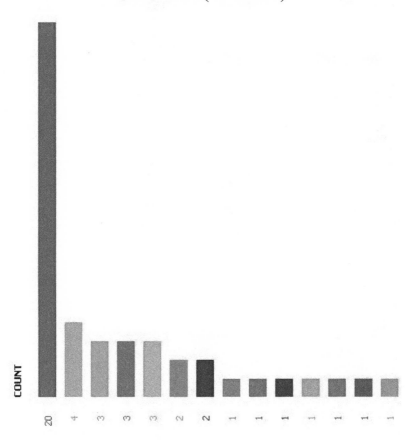

COUNT

NAME1

Mohammed — 20
Abdul — 4
Shabir — 3
Adil — 3
Abid — 3
Munwar — 2
Faisal — 2
Tanveer — 1
Assad — 1
Akhtar — 1
Shakil — 1
Kamar — 1
Aftab — 1
Raja — 1

Appendix 4: Leeds School Warning

Broadgate Primary School
North Broadgate Lane, Horsforth
LEEDS LS18 5AY

JUNE NEWSLETTER

Dear Parent/Carers,

Welcome back to our final half term of the year. Let's hope that the weather improves as we have plans for lots of summery events over the next seven weeks or so!

Please be vigilant

I have received notification that last weekend a girl from the high school was approached by 2 Asian men (approx 30 years and 17 years) in a silver peugeot and offered sweets and cigarettes. The same car was seen three times on Broadgate Lane, Low Road and Butcher Hill. The police have been informed of this incident, but please could I ask that you all remain vigilant and if you see anything that causes you concern please inform the police straight away. We shall be talking to the children about staying safe but if you could also reinforce this message and ensure that your children, particularly if they walk to or from school on their own, are aware of keeping themselves safe. Many thanks.

Dates

10th/Tues 11th June – Y6 residential to London

12th June – Y3, 4 & 5 Countryside day

12th June – Meetings for parents of new reception children for Sept 2013

13th June – Friends of Broadgate meeting 9.00am

June – Training day – school closed for pupils

24th – Fri 28th June – Curriculum theme week – Pirates and Healthy Living Week

– Reception visit to Temple Newsam

for July will be confirmed in the July newsletter

Summer Barbecue

We are hoping to hold this event on Friday 5th July, 5.30 until 8.30pm. More information will follow and we will keep crossing our fingers for good weather. Linked to this the Friends of Broadgate will be meeting on Thursday at 9.00 to discuss plans for the day. They will be in the school staff room, so please come along after

Figure 1: Warning to Parents of Children Under 11
(Leeds, June 2013)

Appendix 5: Sheffield School Warning

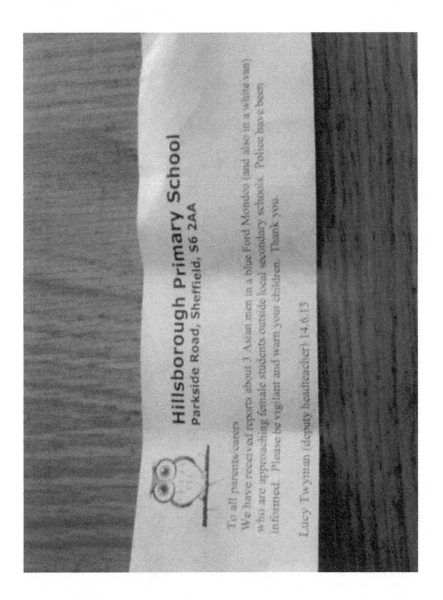

Figure 1: Warning to Parents of Children Under 11
(Sheffield, June 2013)

Appendix 6: Real Khilafah
Letter to Moslem Youth

A MESSAGE TO MOSLEM YOUTH

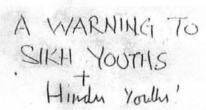

Real Khilafa – A Political Reality
From Dr. K M Farukh.

For Private Circulation .

We are each and every weekend having stalls where we give out literature about Islam . We have these stalls in many areas especially in areas where there are a lot of kafirs [Sikh Hindu jews AND OTHER NONBELIEVERS] We would like to extend our activities further.

We are in many ways surprised that so many Moslems have come to buy our books and provide funds for relieving the distressed Moslems of the world especially in places such as Kossovo and Kashmir .The government and local authority is not interested in our cause as they would rather fund Gurdawaras and Gays and Homos.

We have many interesting books about Islam showing why Islam is the only human way of life and other so called religions are animalistic . The teaching of the great Prophet Mohammed must be passed on until the whole world is Islam . The world will only thus be saved.

We call upon our fellow youth to come and join us in our mission -universal and global islam.

The job is big but nothing is impossible.

If the Kafir non believer does not accept by gentle persuasion or reasoning then other methods which are allowed for in the holy Quran must be used such as- going to war with the kafir or converting them by manipulation . We need to send out our boys to bring the sikh girls into the umma or community of Islam.

This task is getting easier by the day as the sikh and Hindu girls are not taught [as is done in islam] much about their religion at all . They have a more westernized upbringing and the school college and university campus is the ideal place for our youth to carry out their duties easily in this way.

It is easy to take the sikh girls out on a date as they generally like a good drink and from there gradually they can be brought into Islam . This is not a hard job at all as the Kafir women they like Moslems. Hardly surprising as we are attractive and intelligent compared with Kafirs . This is common sense and everybody knows . Otherwise why would Indian films have so many Moslem actors .There is not a single Hindu or Sikh actor in Pakistani films . We need more funds desperately to carry on our job and we need volunteers from amongst the youth specially . Come and join us this weekend and every weekend as we will be in an area near you.

We need your help at this crucial time when our moslem brothers and sisters are being killed in countries all over the world.

THE REAL KHILAFAH MOVEMENT - THE EYES THE EARS THE VOICE OF ISLAM

WATCH THIS SPACE.

Figure 1: Letter Attributed to Muslim Fundamentalists (2001)

Transcription of Real Khilafa Letter

A Message to Moslem Youth
Real Khilafa - A Political Reality From Dr. K M Farukh. For Private Circulation

We are each and every weekend having stalls where we give out literature about Islam. We have these stalls in may [sic] areas especially in areas where there are a lot of kafirs (Sikh Hindu Jews AND OTHER NONBELIEVERS) We would like to extend our activities further.

We are in many ways surprised that so many Moslems have come to buy our books and provide funds for relieving the distressed Moslems of the world especially in places such as Kossovo and Kashmir. The government and local authority is not interested in our cause as they would rather fund Gurdawaras and Gays and Homos.

We have many interesting books about Islam showing why Islam is the only human way of life and other so called religions are animalistic. The teaching of the great Prophet Mohammed must be passed on until the whole world is Islam. The world will only thus be saved.

We call upon our fellow youth to come and join us in our mission - universal and global Islam. The job is big but nothing is impossible.

If the Kafir non believer does not accept by gentle persuasion or reasoning then other methods which are allowed for in the holy Quran must be used such as - going to war with the kafir or converting them by manipulation. We need to send out our boys to bring the Sikh girls into the umma or community of Islam.

This task is getting easier by the day as the Sikh and hindu [?] girls are not taught (as is done in Islam) much about their religion at all. They have a westernized upbringing and the school college and university campus is the ideal place for our youth to carry out their duties easily in this way.

It is easy to take the Sikh girls out on a date as they generally like a good drink and from these gradually they can be brought into Islam.

This is not a hard job at all as the Kafir women they like Moslems. Hardly surprising as we are attractive and intelligent compared with Kafirs. This is common sense and everybody knows. Otherwise why would Indian films have so many Moslem actors. There is not a single Hindu or Sikh actor in Pakistani films. We need more funds desperately to carry on our job and we need volunteers from amongst the youth specially. Come and join us this weekend and every weekend - we will be in an area near you.

We need your help at this crucial time when our moslem brothers and sisters are being killed in countries all over the world.

THE REAL KHILAFAH MOVEMENT - THE EYES THE EARS THE VOICE OF ISLAM

WATCH THIS SPACE

Appendix 7: Luton Article on Real Khilafah

Newsdesk 01582 707707

CALL TO MUSLIMS TO SEDUCE SIKH GIRLS INTO ISLAM

Exclusive by Clive Gresswell

A RACIALLY explosive leaflet urging Muslim men to – quite literally – seduce Sikh girls into the faith, is being hawked on the streets of Luton.

Although the extremist literature, which suggests the best way to do it would be to get the women drunk, has been condemned by local Asian leaders it, could lead to tension in the town.

The leaflets have been given out to Muslim men at different locations in the town, including Luton railway station.

One which we obtained says: 'It is easy to take the Sikh girls out on a date as they generally like a good drink and from there they can be gradually brought into Islam.

'We need to send our boys out to bring the Sikh girls into the arms of Islam. The teachings of the great prophet Mohammed must be passed on until the whole world is Islam. The world will only thus be saved.'

Under the heading 'For Private Circulation' the leaflet advocates

■ Condemned leaflet: Mohammed Sulaiman of Bury Park mosque

'converting them by manipulation' as something the Qur'an advocates.

It adds: 'We call upon our fellow youth to come and join us in our mission for universal and global Islam. The job is big but not impossible.

The task is getting easier by the day as the Sikh and Hindu girls are not taught much about their religion at all. They have a more western-ised upbringing.

'The school, college and university campus are ideal places for our youth to carry out their duties easily in this way.'

Describing other faiths as 'animalistic', it even adds that Muslims are more attractive and intelligent than other people which should be helpful in the seduction process.

Issued by a group calling themselves The Real Khilafah Movement: The Eyes, the Ears, the Voice of Islam, it ends with an appeal for money and a chilling warning: 'watch this space'.

The Muslim man who handed us the leaflet and did not want to be named said: "Nowhere in the Qur'an does it say that either God or the great prophet Mohammed

Figure 1: Report that Muslims Encouraged to Seduce Sikh Girls (Luton 2005)

Appendix 8: Children's Commissioner Charts

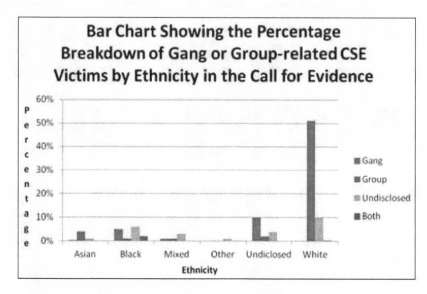

Figure 1: Interim Report (2012): Victims

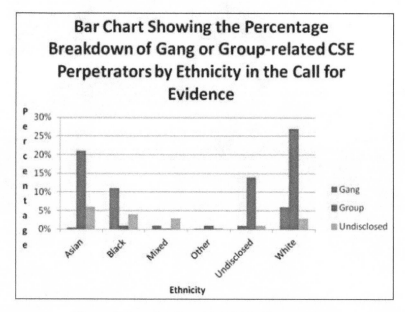

Figure 2: Interim Report (2012): Perpetrators

Appendix 9: Victims to Perpetrators

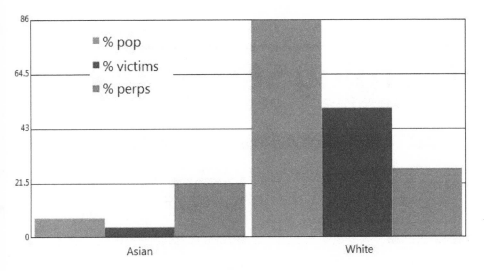

Figure 1: Children's Commissioner Data 2012: meaningful comparison

For those who would deny that there is any significant disparity between the ethnicity of the perpetrators and the ethnicity of the victims, this chart is a visualisation of the best evidence they have for their denial. This chart consolidates the relevant data from The Children's Commissioner (2012) interim report. We have excluded data concerning other races than white and Asian, and excluded data concerning street gangs. We have included the percentage of the UK population who are Asian or white, so that meaningful comparisons can be made concerning the proportion of victims or perpetrators who are Asian or white.

Appendix 10: Police Report on EDL

Get in to

Morning Star
online.co.uk

Join the camp
Take a share

| Britain | World | Editorial | Features | Culture | Sp |

Loading

Britain

'EDL not far-right,' says police extremism chief

Tuesday 23 November 2010 by John Millington   ✉ Email 🖶 Printable

The new head of police domestic extremist units was condemned today after denying that the English Defence League was a right-wing extremist group.

Detective Chief Superintendent Adrian Tudway, who took over the role of national co-ordinator for domestic extremism last week, claimed police had to walk a "tightrope" when targeting small groups which they believe are bent on violence.

Senior officers have gone on the offensive following the student protests and the resulting occupation of 30 Millbank two weeks ago, saying that more resources are being invested in identifying potential "flashpoints of disorder."

Mr Tudway said his officers were focusing on the "fringe" where protest "spills over" into violence and disorder.

His comments came on the eve of tomorrow's wave of protests against rising university fees.

The National Public Order Intelligence Unit, National Domestic Extremism team and National Extremism Tactical Co-ordination Unit employ about 100 people with a budget of £8.1 million.

Figure 1: Police Extremism Experts: "EDL not far-right"

320

Appendix 11: Map of Grooming Gang Convictions

Key

L London
Ay Aylesbury
Ba Banbury
Bi Birmingham
Bn Blackburn
Bl Blackpool
Bd Bradford
Br Bristol
Bu Burton
Ch Chesham
De Derby
Ip Ipswich
K Keighley
Le Leeds
Lr Leicester
Ma Manchester
Mi Middlesbrough
Ol Oldham
Ox Oxford
Pe Peterborough
Pr Preston
Ro Rochdale
Rm Rotherham
Sh Sheffield
S Skipton
Sl Slough
Te Telford

Figure 1: Map Image from Wikimedia Commons
https://commons.wikimedia.org/wiki/File:England_location_map.svg

Appendix 12: Excerpt from Election Pamphlet (2010)

2001: the BNP stoked racist hostilities which provoked disturbances in Oldham — spreading racist lies about 'no go areas for whites' and racist attacks by Asian people on white people.

By challenging its racist lies and increasing voter turnout, a united campaign against the BNP means Oldham Council is BNP free.

2004: the BNP spread racist myths about Asian men 'grooming' white girls in Keighley; they gained four seats on Bradford Council.

2006: the BNP declared their election campaign a 'referendum on Islam'. Its recruitment leaflet uses images from the appalling London bombings — attacking mainstream Islam as a 'threat …to our British culture, heritage and ways of life'. The BNP more than doubled its council seats, bringing the total to 49 councillors across England.

This year, the BNP is whipping up Islamophobia on the back of plans to build mosques in Dudley and Stratford in East London.

The BNP can grab seats where the majority of people don't vote. We must all stand united against these peddlers of hate.

The Muslim Council of Britain and Unite Against Fascism are asking Muslims to vote with fellow Britons on 3 May. Whoever you vote for, vote for local matters that concern you and stop the BNP.

Participating in local elections is your civic duty and is in the best traditions of Islam.

USE YOUR VOTE TO STOP THE FASCIST BRITISH NATIONAL PARTY

Printed and published by Unite Against Fascism, PO Box 36871, London WC1X 9XT

unite
against fascism
www.uaf.org.uk

MCB
www.mcb.org.uk

Figure 1. This pamphlet issued by Left-wing group Unite Against Fascism for the 2010 general electoin purports to be issued jointly with the Muslim Council of Britain. Note the claim (under the heading '2004') that the grooming gangs are a 'racist myth'.

Appendix 13: Key Organisations

Barnardo's - a British charity dating from 1866, with a current turnover of around £200 million per year. The organisation is primarily concerned with caring for children and with campaigning for their well-being. The *Barnardo's Streets and Lanes* project (1995) was one of the earliest projects to receive statutory funding. Records show that by 2000 *Barnardo's* staff were describing the grooming gangs. Those who worked for *Barnardo's* were reportedly key informants, leading to the ground-breaking television documentary *Edge of the City* (2004).

BNP - British National Party: (1982 to 2016) a party associated with racism throughout its existence. Until 2010, when forced by legal measures, the party's constitution restricted membership to the indigenous British population. The BNP took up the issue of the grooming gangs in 2004, when it was reported that *Channel 4* was under pressure from organisations like UAF not to show a documentary about grooming gangs.

CEOP - Child Exploitation and Online Protection: a subsidiary organisation of SOCA, created in 2006. Now part of NCA. Produced the 2011 'rapid assessment' on 'localised grooming' in the UK. Despite its name, this organisation seems to have principally focused on 'online protection' rather than exploitation.

CPS - Crown Prosecution Service: The Crown Prosecution Service it is the public prosecutor for criminal prosecutions in England and Wales. It is headed by the Director of Public Prosecutions and supervised by the Attorney General, who is answerable to Parliament. The CPS provides legal advice to the police during the course of criminal investigations, decides whether a suspect should face criminal charges, and if so, conducts the prosecution in court. The CPS is to provide information, assistance and support to victims and prosecution witnesses. The CPS was established in 1986.

CROP - Coalition for the Removal of Pimping: a charity formed in Leeds in 1996, bringing together the parents of children who were groomed and advocating for policy change.

EDL - English Defence League: a street protest movement formed in 2009 which campaigned for the defense of English values and against Islamic extremism. Characterised by the media as 'far right', despite the founders (white men and black men) appearing on national TV news burning a swastika flag and denouncing racism. It appears that the protests of EDL were pivotal in breaking decades of silence on the grooming phenomenon.

LSCB - Local Safeguarding Children Boards: An LSCB must be established for every local authority area to improve the wellbeing of children in the local area. These Boards must be established in every local authority area under the requirements of the Children Act 2004. The Board has a range of roles and statutory functions, including developing local safeguarding policy and procedures and scrutinising local arrangements. They include representatives from the local authority, and others who have a strategic role in child welfare within their organisation. Those statutory members represent organisations who will carry out the functions of the Board.

MCB - Muslim Council of Britain: established in 1997, an umbrella organisation which has been said to represent as many as 500 Muslim groups in Britain. Their website currently lists 95 affiliated Muslim organisations, some of which also claim to represent a group of Muslim organisations. For example, one of its affiliates is Bolton Council of Mosques, which currently claims to represent '25 established mosques in Bolton'. If any organisation in Britain can be said to speak for Muslims it is the MCB. Documents from 2010 say the grooming gangs were a 'racist myth' according to the MCB (similar documents from 2009 on the MCB website have since been removed). In 2013 the Sheikh from the MCB testified before a Parliamentary committee investigating the grooming gang scandal. Some months later, many mosques affiliated with the MCB read a sermon condemning the grooming gangs.

NASUWT - National Association of Schoolmasters Union of Women Teachers: a major supporter of UAF.

NCA - National Crime Agency: a non-ministerial government department; created in 2013 to replace SOCA.

NSPCC - National Society for the Prevention of Cruelty to Children: a charity concerned with the welfare of children.

NUT - National Union of Teachers: trade union for school-teachers: a major supporter of UAF.

PACE - Parents Against Child Sexual Exploitation: from 2013, the new name for CROP.

PCS - Public and Commercial Services Union; a trades union for civil servants and the employees of other public organisations. A major supporter of UAF.

SAS - Sikh Awareness Society: organisation created in 1998 providing a discreet service of counselling and support to Sikhs in the West Midlands, whose daughters had been groomed. In 2006, SAS became a national organisation.

SOCA - Serious Organised Crime Agency. A national law enforcement agency, created in 2006 and became NCA in 2013. It was formed from the merger of the National Crime Squad and the National Criminal Intelligence Service. When created, SOCA was described by the media as 'the British FBI'. It focused primarily on England and Wales. It incorporated both CEOP and UKHTC.

UAF - Unite Against Fascism: a Left-wing self-proclaimed 'anti-fascist' group; jointly campaigned with Muslim Council of Britain to claim that grooming gangs were a 'racist myth' (2010). From 2009 when EDL was created, UAF was the principal opponent of EDL and its campaigns. UAF was cited as playing a key role in the suppression of the first television documentary (2004) on the grooming gangs.

UKHTC - United Kingdom Human Trafficking Centre: a subsidiary organisation of SOCA. Now part of NCA. A combined police research and intelligence unit, created with the aim to increase knowledge and understanding of human trafficking amongst police and partner agency staff and to solicit information from the public. Commissioned (2008) an educational film about how the grooming gangs lure schoolgirls into their clutches and what the consequences are for those trapped in this way. The anodyne film was never seen by its intended audience.

CPSIA information can be obtained
at www.ICGtesting.com
Printed in the USA
LVHW100953311022
731982LV00002B/18